DEVELOPMENT AND DECEPTION

DEVELOPMENT AND DECEPTION

Experiences from Eastern and North-Eastern India

(In Two Volumes)

(Vol. 1)

Kalipada Deb

KALPAZ PUBLICATIONS

DELHI-110052

Development and Deception

ISBN: 81-7835-449-7 (Set)
ISBN : 81-7835-505-1 (Vol. 1)

Published in 2006 in India by
Kalpaz Publications,
C-30, Satyawati Nagar, Delhi-110052
E-mail : kalpaz@hotmail.com

Laser Typesetting at : Master Computers, Delhi
Printed at : Salasar Imaging System, Delhi

Contents

Preface

India became Independent in 1947 and the Constitution that came into existence in 1950 aimed to establish an ideal socialistic society in the country. The preamble to the Constitution promised to the people : "Justice, social, economic and political; Liberty of thought, expression, belief, faith and worship; Equality of status and of opportunity; and to promote among them all Fraternity assuring the dignity of the individual and the unity of the nation ....". The Directive Principles of State Policy contain a variety of assurances in these directions. For example, Section 43 states:

"The state shall endeavour to secure, by suitable legislation or economic organisation or in any other way, to all workers, agricultural, industrial or otherwise, work, a living wage, conditions of work ensuring a decent standard of life and full enjoyment of leisure and social and cultural opportunities ....".

Similarly, Section 46 states :

"The state shall promote with special care the educational and economic interests of the weaker sections of the people, and, in particular, of the Scheduled Castes and Scheduled Tribes, and shall protect them from social injustice and all forms of exploitation".

Such pronouncements were there in the Plan and other documents also. The First Five-Year Plan underscored the need for changing the socio-economic framework in order to "accommodate progressively the fundamental urges which expressed themselves in the demands for the right to work, the right to adequate income, the right to education and to a measure of insurance against old age, sickness and other disabilities". (p. 8). The Second Five-Year Plan was also no less progressive; it expressly incorporated the objective of bringing a socialist pattern of society in the country.

What has happened to these objectives over the five decades of planned development efforts? Did the government try its utmost to provide food and other basic necessities to the semi-starved billions? Was there adequate effort to reduce the regional imbalance in development? Did the government exert itself fully to mobilize all possible resources? How far the resources were directed towards the rural areas? The objective of this study is to look into the experiences of the Eastern Region, the most backward at the time of Independence.

The Eastern Region presently comprises of four large states, viz., Bihar, West Bengal, Orissa and Assam, and seven very small-states—Tripura, Manipur, Meghalaya, Nagaland, Arunachal, Mizoram and Sikkim. Assam and the small-states were put in a separate region, the North-East, officially. Excepting Nagaland, all the small-states came into existence in the seventies and after. At the time of Independence, there were four large states and 30 small princely states, 24 of which were in and around Orissa. A large part of the present North-East was in an independent or semi-independent condition.

There were wide variations in the resource endowment and the level of development to begin with. After the re-organisation of the states in 1956, in terms of area, the largest state was Assam (222,204 sq km), followed by Bihar (174,038 sq km), Orissa (155,782 sq km) and West Bengal (87,694 sq km). Assam's size was greatly reduced within a decade, and presently it is the smallest among the four. In terms of population, the largest was Bihar, followed by West Bengal, Orissa and Assam. In 1951, the density of population per sq mile was as much as 778 in West Bengal, more than four times that in Assam.

The seven small-states—existing in different forms then-are also of greatly varying sizes. In area, Arunachal is the largest—larger than Assam and eight times that of Tripura. The population in 1961 was only 3.37 lakh, less than a third of that in Tripura; and the density per sq km came to only four as against 109 in the latter. All the other small-states also had much less density than Tripura's. For Mizoram it was 13, Nagaland 22, Sikkim 23, Meghalaya 34 and Manipur 35. The topography of these states vary but all are hilly and mountainous.

The level of development reached at the time of Independence was extremely uneven. West Bengal was the most developed not only among the eastern states, in certain respects even among all the states in the country. Its per capita income in 1949-50 was the highest, and so also the value of industrial output. The proportion of urban population in 1951 was 25 per cent, the second highest, and the literacy rate, at 24 per cent, also in the same position. The development was, however, concentrated in and around Calcutta. The other eastern states were far behind in all the indicators of development. Industrially, Assam was the most backward; and Orissa and Bihar were also not much better. The per capita income was below the national average for each of the three. The present small-states were in a far worse position, with Arunachal in the worst. All the states were almost exclusively dependent on agriculture. There was no transportation system for most part of these states; and were largely self-dependent economies of the primitive type.

The partition of the country was a big blow to West Bengal and also to the North-Eastern states as a whole. For the latter, there was a complete dislocation of the transportation system with the rest of the country. And then, there was a heavy influx of people both to West Bengal and Assam from the erstwhile East Pakistan. The population became a burden rather than a resource; and ultimately gave rise to the insurgency problem in the North-East.

The study is divided into seven parts, comprising 28 chapters. The first part is introductory and has two chapters: the first dealing with the situation at Independence; and the second giving a brief idea about the nature of development that took place in each of the states since then. The following four parts are on the larger eastern states—Bihar, West Bengal, Orissa and Assam–each dealing with one; and the fifth on the seven small-states as a whole.

Each of the five parts has as many chapters. The first one deals with the pattern of resource mobilisation and deployment, and has two parts : the government's budgetary resources, and the banking resource. The focus is on whether there was scope for larger collection and better deployment. The second chapter is on the measures for human resource development, and is divided into two parts: education, and health and family planning. The following two chapters are on the productive sectors of agriculture and industry. The first one is divided into two parts : agriculture proper, that is, crop farming; and allied activities covering animal husbandry, fishery and forestry. The final chapter is on the poverty alleviation measures, discussing the direct measures like wage-employment and self-employment programmes and the public distribution system. The analysis in every chapter is largely on comparative basis—comparison inter-state, and intra-state among the districts.

Some of the salient points that have emerged from the study may be noted here. The Eastern Region as a whole continues to be the most backward in the country. The per capita income is much below the national average, and the proportion of BPL population higher. The state of social and economic infrastructure is deplorable. The schooling facility is very poor and the schools utterly ill-equipped. The health facilities are also extremely poor. The quality of human resource available in the region continues to be in general very poor, with virtually no effort at improving it.

Among the states, there is great variation in economic performance. West Bengal continues to be in the best position among the four, despite a downhill journey in most areas. The per capita income is now significantly below the national average, and the relative share in all-India industrial output less than a quarter of the earlier level. The unemployment rate is very high, and the proportion of BPL population higher than the national average. In the social sector, education and health facilities both are in shambles The rural-urban and inter-district disparity in development are extremely high. Everything here is concentrated in and around Kolkata. The nature of development here is a matter of shame for all Left-minded people. The Marxists have deceived the poor in a calculated way; they are totally pro-rich and anti-poor.

The worst position is of the largest state, Bihar. Its per capita income is the lowest among all the states, and less than half the national average. The proportion of BPL population has been generally the second highest. The infrastructural situation is extremely poor. Per capita power consumption here is less than half the national average. The literacy rate is the lowest in the country, and for females it is shamefully low. The birth rate is very high and so too the death rate. The health facilities are extremely poor. The state's future also appears grim with the separation of the Jharkhand region.

Orissa's darkest spot is its level of absolute poverty. The proportion of BPL population has been generally the highest here, and presently it is 21 percentage points higher than the national average. The IMR is highest and the life expectancy very low. The infrastructural situation is extremely poor. The drinking water facility covers a small proportion of the households. Intra-state disparity in development continues to be very high. The tribals inhabited districts remain utterly neglected.

Assam had a sharp deterioration in economic position. The per capita income, which was higher than the national average earlier, has now become lower. Similar is the position of BPL population—becoming higher from lower earlier. The performance in the industrial sector is very poor. In the all-India total output of the factory sector its share stood at only 0.87 per cent in 1999-00, around a third of the level in 1960. The infrastructural situation is the worst here. Per capita power consumption is less than a third of the national average.

On resource mobilisation, none of the states performed well. The per capita total receipts was lower than the all-states average for each of them. The worst position was of Bihar. During 2000-03, it was only 29.5 per cent of the all-states average. The own-revenue collection was very low for each of them. The reliance on the Centre was very high for Assam—a special category state. The deployment of fund left much to be desired. The per capita development expenditure was always below the all-states average for each of the states; the most depressing was the situation of Bihar. Salaries, pension and other fixed expenses are eating away almost the entire revenue in each of the states. Incredible is the situation of West Bengal; it has reached 111.5 per cent of the revenue.

The small-states as a whole continued to be in a very poor state. The proportion of BPL population is higher than the national average for all but Mizoram. Agriculture continues to be largely of the traditional type, with irrigated area constituting an extremely small proportion, except for Manipur. The industrial sector is very small, with the infrastructure in a dismal situation. Among the states, Meghalaya's performance is the worst in most respects.

The resource mobilisation by the small-states was extremely low; and relied overwhelmingly on the Central transfer, with the exception of Sikkim. In recent years, the Centre financed more than 80 per cent of total expenditure in four of the states. The own collection varied greatly from state to state. The per capita OTR in Sikkim during 1996-99 was five-and-half times that in Arunachal and Mizoram. On the ONTR, the variation was much wider. The level of expenditure also varied greatly. The lowest was in Tripura and the highest in Sikkim.

In the way of development, the most challenging problem is the management of human resource—their development and proper location. No socialist pattern of society can be built by people with feudal mentality, but there was virtually no attempt to bring the right orientation. The quality of leadership itself is abominably poor. There is a strong aversion to taking any unpleasant action, which is critically necessary for bringing the right type of development. Corruption and inefficiency are rampant almost everywhere, and this greatly reduced the real value of expenditure. And this was despite a very high level of salary and pension enjoyed by the employees.

Finally, seeing the pattern of development in the last half a century, one is compelled to conclude that the Directive Principles of State Policy and the development plans are meant for deceiving the poor majority. If the poor are really to be benefited, the expenditure in the rural areas, and targeted primarily towards them, must be raised many times over. There has to be a reverse flow of resources from the urban concentrations to the rural areas. The expenditure on education and health and on the rural infrastructure have to be greatly increased. This will be possible, only if strict austerity measures are imposed by the ruling class on themselves, including all the organised sections of the employees. An integral part of this process has to be a total rooting out of corruption and misappropriation of funds by the government departments.

In the completion of this work my debt is indeed very extensive. I have collected data from different government departments, research institutes and Universities, and in the process many people came to my help. Among the government departments, particularly helpful were the library of the Planning Commission, New Delhi, and the Directorate of Economics and Statistics and Planning Department of the relevant state governments. Among the institutes, particularly important were the A N Sinha Institute of Social Studies, Patna, NKC Centre for Development Studies, Bhubaneswar, Centre of Studies in Social Sciences, Kolkata, and the Tripura State Tribal Cultural Research Institute, Agartala.

Due to lack of space it is not possible to acknowledge my debt individually to all the people who helped me in different ways. The range is very wide, from railway stations to guest houses and a variety of persons in libraries and government offices. I express my deep sense of gratitude to everybody. To name a few persons here : At New Delhi, Mrs. Prabha Krishnan and Mrs. C. K. Arora of the Planning Commission, and D. C. Nandwani of the Reserve Bank of India; at Patna, S. F. Rab and Ram Beli Singh of the A N Sinha Institute, and Bijoy Pratap Singh and Durga Prasad Nagvansi of the Directorate of Economics and Statistics; at Kolkata, Amarendra Nath Das of the Development & Planning Department, and P. Chatterjee of the Centre for Studies in Social Sciences; at Bhubaneswar, G. C. Kar of the NKC Centre for Development Studies, and Kishore Chandra Sahu and J. N. Rout of the Directorate of Economics & Statistics; at Guwahati, N. C. Dhekial Phukan and M. N. Deka of the Directorate of Economics & Statistics, S. Chakrabarty of the Department of Planning and Hem Barua of Gauhati University; at Agartala, P. K. Halder of Tripura University, and Amarendra Deb Barman of the Tribal Research Institute.

It is needless to add that the environment in my work place, the North Bengal University, was a great contributor to the completion of the work in the short time that I did, although it is derived from a negative aspect of the University. From the angle of my work, therefore, I express a deep sense of gratitude to the people in the University. The library staff here deserve a special mention because of the excellent service I received from them. Finally, no word is adequate to express the debt to my wife, Kalpana, without whose cooperation the work would not have been possible.

Kalipada Deb

PART–I
INTRODUCTION

1

Eastern India at Independence

The pace of progress in any development effort is greatly determined by the status of the base from where it is launched, particularly the level development already reached and the quality of resources available. Therefore, in this chapter we look into the position of the eastern states on the eve of the economic planning that began in 1951. First, certain major changes that came with the Independence have been considered, and then the level of development the different states had to begin with.

Major Changes

The most significant change that came with independence and had a far-reaching consequence on the entire eastern region was the partition of Bengal. The geographical area that came under West Bengal was only around 40 per cent of that for the undivided Bengal. Not only this, the most fertile part of the Gangetic delta went to the other side, the then East Pakistan. Assam also lost some land; almost the entire Sylhet district, which was a part of Assam, went there.

The more troublesome problem that came from the partition was, however, the immigration from East Pakistan, and this affected almost the entire region. Between 1947 and 1950, a total of 19, 97,694 persons had entered West Bengal, and another 4, 77,186 came during 1951 and 1952 (BCCI 1971: 22-23). The decennial growth of population rose to 32.80 per cent in 1951-61 as against 13.22 per cent in the preceding decade. The immigration into Assam, which was going on for many decades, accentuated further after the partition. The 1951 census gave the number of refugees in Assam as 2, 74,455; by December 1957 it reached 4, 87,000 (GOI 1959). The influx continued in the following years also and ultimately gave rise to the problem of ousting the illegal migrants. Probably, the most severely affected were the tribals of Tripura. Tribals constituted 53.16 per cent of the total population in 1941 but by 1951 they were reduced to 37.23 per cent and further to 31.50 per cent in 1961.

The North-Eastern states were affected by the partition in another way also. It brought almost a complete dislocation of the transportation system existing earlier. The water way linking Calcutta port with the Assam hinterland was disrupted as the route passed through East Pakistan. The rail and road communications were also affected. By December 1949, all routes via Pakistan from Assam and Tripura to the rest of India were completely closed.

The second major change affecting the region was the integration of the princely states to the Indian union. In and around Orissa, there were 24 states and all of them were completely merged with the state in August 1949. In Bihar also, in May 1948, the states of Saraikela and Kharsawan became a part of Singhbhum district and thus of Bihar. Tripura, Manipur and Cooch Behar also similarly merged with the Indian Union. While the first two subsequently, in 1957, became Union Territories (UT), Cooch Behar became a part of West Bengal at the time of merger itself, in 1950. Seeing the later developments, it is difficult to say whether the mergers were good for the respective areas or for the Indian Union.

The manner of reorganization of the state's geographical area in 1956 also created problems. The area under Bihar decreased from 1, 11,581 sq km to 1, 08,118 sq km whereas for West Bengal it increased from 76,343 to 87,694. In addition to Cooch Behar and Chandernagore—formerly a French settlement-some parts of Bihar came under West Bengal. In the country's total area, Bihar's share became 5.29 per cent and of West Bengal 2.67 per cent. The area under Orissa became 1, 55,782 sq km and of Assam 2, 22,204 sq km, constituting respectively 4.74 per cent and 6.76 per cent of all-India total. In case of Assam, however, the state government did not have complete jurisdiction over the entire area, and within a decade the state's size was reduced to 78,523 sq km—constituting 2.39 per cent of India's total—with the creation of the new state of Nagaland.

The constitution of India came in January 1950 and it laid down the rights and obligations of the states. Articles 12 to 35 granted the citizens certain fundamental rights like right to equality before law, right to freedom of speech and expression, right against exploitation, and cultural and educational rights. Then, in the Directive Principles of State Policy many tall promises were made to the people. The objectives of government policy were laid down as assuring citizens adequate means of livelihood, improved public health, free and compulsory education for children, etc. Almost everything good in this Earth was assured under it but at the same time made unenforceable by law. The Constitution became largely a propaganda material. In the following years, a lot of controversies arose on the provisions of the Constitution, and it had to be amended many times. In fact, within a decade there were nine amendments and by 1995 a total of 78.

For achieving the objectives of the Directive Principles, economic planning was made an imperative necessity and the Government of India introduced five-year plans throughout the country from 1951. But the nature of the Government, and its ability, showed from the beginning itself that the planning was a mockery on the vast masses of poverty-stricken people. Mobilization of resources was far behind what was required, and the plans were not implemented in the manner needed. The Government's control over the economy was far from what the situation demanded. The size of public sector remained small. The inefficiencies of different ministries soon became transparent. The government functionaries' lack of time sense became evident when the document of First Five-year Plan could be readied only one-and-half year after the implementation had started (for details, Deb 1997, 2001). Below we give a brief look into the status of development in each of the states around the time of launching the plan.

Level of Development

West Bengal

Among the eastern states, or in some respects even in the country as a whole, West Bengal was the most developed at the time of Independence. The per capita income of the state in 1949-50 stood at Rs 353.10 at current prices, which was the highest among all the states. The monthly consumer expenditure (MPCE) in rural areas was Rs. 28.10 per capita in 1952 as against the all-India average of Rs. 27.81. The share of expenditure on food in it was 59.2 per cent, lower than in most other states. Naturally, the people were able to spend more on non-food items (Table 1.1).

Economic diversification was relatively high. In 1951, of the total working population, only 53.4 per cent were engaged in the primary sector as against 69.8 per cent at the national level. The secondary occupations accounted for 15.3 per cent, the second highest among the states. The total value of output from manufacturing industries stood at Rs 338.30 crore in 1955 and constituted 24.0 per cent of all-India total. The productivity of the employees was, however, low; per employee the output came to Rs 6,936 as against the national average of Rs 7,892. In the agricultural sector, however, the productivity of workers was high. The gross value of output per worker came to Rs. 1,022.60 in 1952-53, which was double the national average.

On the availability of infrastructure, the state's position was relatively good. Road mileage per Lakh population stood at 75.5 miles in 1956, which was exceeded by only three of the states (Prasad 1967: 140). In power, the position was still better. The installed capacity in 1951 stood at 546 thousand kW, constituting 29.75 per cent of all-India total. Per capita consumption of electricity came to 41.68 Kwh, next only to Bombay (NCAER 1962).

As regards the social sector, on the literacy rate, the state's position was good. At 24.0 per cent in 1951, it was next only to Kerala. The educational facility was better here than in most other states. There were 14,795 primary and pre-primary schools in 1950-51, 1,261 middle schools and 1,107 High schools. In the all-India total, these constituted respectively, 7.0, 9.2 and 17.5 per cent (GO I 1972). The health situation of the people was also relatively good, to the extent it can be inferred from the death rate. During 1941-50, the death rate per thousand population in West Bengal stood at 27.0 as against the national average of 28.5; among the 13 major states, it was lower than in seven (NCAER 1962). The infant death rate was 120 during 1951-61 as against the all-India average of 139 (GO I 1965). The medical facility was relatively good. Number of Doctors per Lakh population came to 81.8 in 1956, nearly four times the national average (Table 1.1).

A serious aspect of west Bengal's development is, however, that it is highly concentrated in and around Calcutta. Percentage of urban population was less than 10 in as many as nine districts—with Malda having only 3.7-in 1951 as against the state average of 25.0. In the total number of registered working factories at 2,625 in 1952, 24-Parganas alone accounted for 38.4 per cent and Howrah and Calcutta together 35.7 per cent (Chaudhuri 1971: 84).

The higher level of development in West Bengal was largely due to the political position of Bengal. Calcutta was the capital of British India until 1912 and afterwards also it was the headquarters of Eastern Region. The prominence of Bengalis in the bureaucracy also played an important part in it. Bengal was not endowed with a very high level of natural resources. Its share in the all-India total of land area in 1951 was only 2.4 per cent. Among minerals, only coal was important. In the early fifties, coal accounted for 99 per cent of the state's total value of mineral output (ibid.)

Bihar

Bihar is the largest state in eastern region, both in area and population, but in terms of development it was nowhere near West Bengal. The per capita income in 1949-50 stood at only Rs. 199.80, around half the level in West Bengal and much below the national average. The MPCE in rural areas came to only Rs. 24.03 in 1952, and 67 per cent of it went to meet the food needs. In the expenditure on food, grains alone took up 71 per cent, Rs. 11.42 out of Rs. 16.10.

Sectoral diversification of economic activities was very limited. In 1950-51, the primary sector accounted for 63.54 per cent of the state's income as against the secondary sector's only 10.98 (GOB 1928: 24). Of the total working population, 81.0 per cent were engaged in the primary sector. And then, they had a very low productivity. Gross value of output per worker came to only Rs 371.17 in 1952-53 as against the all-India average of Rs. 512.53. In the secondary sector, the contribution of manufacturing industries was low. In 1955, the total value of output came to Rs. 121.75 crore, constituting 8.64 per cent of all-India total. The productivity of workers was, however, not bad. At Rs. 10,454 per person, it was much higher than the national average (Table 1.1).

On the availability of infrastructure, the state's position was distressingly poor. Road mileage per lakh population stood at only 40.0 miles in 1956 as against the all-India average of 67.8. On power, the installed capacity in 1951 stood at only 47 thousand kW, constituting 2.56 per cent of all-India total. The per capita power consumption came to only 2.95 kwh compared with 13.25 kwh at the national level.

In the social sector, the literacy situation was extremely poor. Bihar had only 12.2 per cent literate in 1951, with females at 3.8. The latter was less than half the national average. Not only this, 85 per cent of the literates here were below middle standard. The schooling facility apparently was not bad. Bihar accounted for 11.3 per cent of the primary and pre-primary schools in the country in 1950-51, 15.9 per cent of middle schools and 10.2 per cent of high schools. In enrolment, however, the position was very poor, being respectively, 7.9, 6.4, and 7.4 per cent of all-India total (GOI 1972); Bihar's share in India's total population was 10.74 per cent. As regards health facilities, presumably the situation was very poor. The death rate per thousand population came to 29.8 during 1941-50, which was higher than the national average. The infant death rate stood at 145 during 1951-61 compared with 139 at the national level. The availability of doctors was very low here. In 1956,there were 14.3 doctors per lakh population as against the all-India average of 21.3 (Table 1.1).

This was the situation of Bihar's development, despite being quite rich in natural resources. In mineral resources, it led other states in the output of coal, mica, iron ore, copper, china clay, fireclay, kyanite, asbestos, felspar and quartz. Bihar accounted for more than 75 per cent of India's mineral wealth (Ahmad 1965). In Iron ore, the state's share was 47 per cent in 1950 (GOI 1958). The usable land area of the state was also not low; at 143.67 lakh hectares, it was 7.04 per cent of all-India total (GO I 1959).

Orissa

Orissa's position was probably the worst at the time of Independence. The per capita income in 1949-50 stood at only Rs. 188, lower than in all but Rajasthan. The MPCE was also in a similar position. At Rs 15.02 in 1952, it was only 54.0 per cent of all-India average. After meeting the expenditure on food–being 67.3 per cent of total—very little was left for other items. In the expenditure on food again as much as 71 per cent was taken away by grains alone (Table 1.1).

Table 1.1: The Relative position of Eastern States on Selected Indicators of Development

States	*Per capita Income (Rs.) 1949-50*	*Gross output per worker in agriculture (Rs.) 1952-53*	*Total value of output from manufacturing (Rs.) 1955*	*MPCE in rural areas (Rs.) 1952*	*Literacy rate 1951*	*Death rate per '000 pop. 1941-50*	*No. of docts. per lakh Pop.* 1956*	*Percent of urban pop. 1951*	*Density of pop. per Sq mile 1951*
Assam	237.00[a]	917.11	949 (0.67)	24.24	18.3 (7.9)[d]	34.9	26.6	5.0	188
Bihar	199.80	371.17	12175 (8.64)	24.03	12.2 (3.8)	29.8	14.3	6.8	577
Orissa	188.10	754.32	1181 (0.84)	15.02	15.8 (4.5)	33.3	8.8	6.9	243
W.Bengal	353.10	1022.60	33830 (24.01)	28.10	24.0 (12.2)	27.0	81.8	25.0	778
Andhra P.	228.80	526.93	4523 (3.21)	—	13.2 (6.5)	25.1	3.4	17.3	293
Kerala	234.10	1106.08	1752 (1.24)[b]	18.64[c]	40.7 (31.5)	19.9	5.4	13.5	903
Madhya P.	255.40	391.14	3357 (2.38)	16.40	9.8 (3.2)	37.2	9.0	13.5	151
Madras	229.00	758.07	11756 (8.34)	18.28	20.8 (10.0)	22.7	36.0	24.4	598
Bombay	272.60	399.11	44041 (31.25)	19.32	20.9 (9.8)	25.8	55.1	31.0	270
Punjab	333.70	645.12	2680 (1.90)	31.96	15.2 (8.5)	28.2	28.6	19.0	342
Rajasthan	172.60	341.28	1312 (0.93)	—	8.9 (3.0)	32.6	—	17.0	121
U.Pradesh	262.00	426.92	13699 (9.72)	23.45	10.8 (3.6)	30.1	10.7	13.7	556
All India	246.30[a]	512.53	140921 (100.0)	27.81	16.6 (7.9)[c]	28.5	21.3	17.3	312

*Notes: a: relate to 1950-51, at 1948-49 prices; b: relates to Travancore-Cochin; c: refers to Travancore only; d: on females; e: excluding Jammu & Kashmir.; * : based on 1951 population figures.*

Sources: Prasad 1987; BCCI 1971; NCAER 1962; GOI 1961, 1964, 1959; GOA 1957: 78.

The sectoral diversification of activities was slightly better here. In 1950-51, in the total state income at Rs 286.59 million (at 1956-57 prices), the share of agriculture was Rs 165.40 million-that is 57.7 per cent. Within agriculture, cultivation provided 48.8 per cent and animal husbandry 6.4 per cent. The share of mining, manufacturing, etc was 10.6 per cent, of which 7.0 per cent came from non-factory enterprises. Mining provided only Rs. 4.52 million, 1.6 per cent of the total (NCAER 1962).

As for the distribution of workers, in 1951, 72.9 per cent were engaged in the primary sector and 8.6 per cent in the secondary sector; at the national level, while the former was lower by 3.1 points, the latter higher by 1.9. Number of factory workers per thousand population came to only 1.4 here as against 7.4 at the national level. The productivity of workers was also low. In 1955, per person it came to Rs 7,262, lower than the national average. The productivity of agricultural workers was, however, relatively better, as evident from table 1.1.

The infrastructural situation of the state was very poor. Road mileage per square mile of area in 1956 came to only 0.195 as against the all-India average of 0.226. As regards power, the installed capacity at the end of 1951 stood at 5000 kW, constituting a negligible 0.27 per cent of all-India total. The per capita power consumption this year was a measly 0.35 kWh, one-thirty-eighth of all-India. In relation to Bihar-not to speak of West Bengal-it was less than one-eight.

In the social sector also the position was similar. The percentage of literate came to only 15.8 in 1951, with females at 4.5. Both were significantly below the national average. The quality of this literacy was also extremely poor. As much as 89.7 per cent of the literates were below middle standard, 5 points below the national average. The schooling facility was very poor. Number of primary and pre-primary schools in 1950-51 stood at 9,801 and middle schools only 502, constituting respectively 4.7 per cent and 3.7 per cent of all-India total; number of high schools in the state was only 172, 2.7 per cent of national total. In the area of health also the situation was not good. The death rate in Orissa stood at 33.3 during 1941-50, higher than in all but two of the states. The infant death rate was also very high, being 159 per thousand during 1951-61, much above the national average. The incidence of certain diseases was very high. Number of deaths from fever came to 11.4 per thousand population in 1957, more than double that at the national level; on dysentery and diarrhea and smallpox also it was in a similar position (NCAER 1962). The availability of doctors was extremely low in Orissa. Per lakh population, in 1956, there were only 8.8 doctors as against 21.3 at the national level.

This poor state of development in every area is not warranted by the resource availability in the state. In a number of minerals, the state accounted for a large share of all-India output. The most important was, however, iron ore.

With a total output of 1,527 thousand tons in 1950, the state's share in all-India total came to 50.6 per cent. Among other minerals, in limestone it was 31.1 per cent, in dolomite 90.8 per cent, in manganese 17.1 per cent and in chromites 13.5 per cent (Ibid). With regard to land also the states position was good. The density of population per square mile was only 243 in 1951, noticeably below the national average. The topographically usable area was 103 lakh ha, 5.0 per cent of all-India total. The forest area of the state in 1955-56 was 35.61 lakh ha, 7.0 per cent of national total (GOI 1959).

Assam

Assam's position at the time of Independence was relatively good. The per capita income in 1950-51 stood at Rs. 237 (at 1948-49 prices), which was higher than in at least three of the states. In terms of consumer expenditure, the situation was much better. The MPCE in rural areas stood at Rs. 24.24 in 1952 which was higher than in most of the states, including the three eastern states. However, the expenditure on food took away a large part of it, as much as 65.3 per cent as against the all-India average of 59.9 per cent. In the expenditure on food again, the share of grains was 65.9 per cent compared with 57.8 per cent at the national level. Naturally, not much was available for other items.

The diversification of economic activities was relatively good. Of the total workers, 73.2 per cent were engaged in the primary sector in 1951 and 14.8 per cent in the secondary sector. Both were significantly higher than the national average. The productivity of workers in the primary sector was better than in many other states. The gross value of output per agricultural worker stood at Rs. 917 in 1952-53; nearly double that at the national level. In the secondary sector, the contribution from manufacturing industries was very low. The total value of output stood at only Rs. 948.60 lakh in 1955 and contributed 0.67 per cent to the national total. The state's share in value added by manufacturing was still lower; at Rs. 155.23 lakh, it was merely 0.35 per cent. The productivity of workers was, however, relatively high. The output per person came to Rs. 11,470 this year as against the all-India average of Rs. 7,892 (Table 1.1).

The infrastructural situation was extremely poor in Assam. Road mileage per sq mile of area in 1956 stood at only 0.115 mile. The position of railway was also very poor. The dislocation caused by the partition has been noted earlier. As regards power, the installed capacity in 1951 stood at only 3,000 kW, lowest among all the states. Power sold to ultimate consumers totalled 15.867 million kWh and constituted 0.17 per cent of all-India total (GOI 1959).

In the social sector, the situation was not so bad. The percentage of literate in 1951 stood at 18.3, with females at 7.9; both were higher than in many of the states. The schooling facility was relatively good. The state accounted for 5.1 per cent of primary and pre-primary schools in the country, 6.7 per cent of middle schools and 4.3 per cent of high schools in 1950-51 (GOI 1972). As regards health facilities, from the position of death rates, the situation does not appear good. The death rate per thousand population came to 34.9 in 1941-50, which was much above the national average. The infant death rate was also high—as much as 184 during 1951-61 (GOI 1965).

This situation of Assam was totally incongruous with its resource endowment. The geographical area under the state, as noted earlier, was high. The topographically usable area was also not bad, being 91.6 lakh hectares, constituting 4.5 per cent of all-India total. The net sown area in 1955-56 was, however, only 20.64 lakh ha. The state had a rich forest area—constituting 9.6 per cent of all-India total—with valuable timbers and other products. There was a huge reserve of coal, and for petroleum Assam was the only source in the country till early fifties. The hydro-power potential of the state was very high. It was estimated at 4 million kW in 1948, constituting 27.89 per cent of all-India total (Goswami 1988: 6-8).

This is the background in which the planned development efforts began in the eastern states in 1951. The following chapter gives a brief look into what could be achieved over the last five decades.

2

Five Decades of Development: An Overview

Economic planning was formally introduced in the country in 1951 to achieve the objectives laid down in the Directive principles of the Constitution. By the end of 2004, 53 years had passed, and the country was going through the tenth five-year plan; it could not be eleventh because of interruptions in the planning process. Here, in this chapter, we take a brief look into what could be achieved over the years in each of the eastern states. First we deal with the four major states, viz., Bihar, West Bengal, Orissa and Assam, and then with the seven tiny states of Tripura, Manipur, Meghalaya, Nagaland, Arunachal, Mizoram and Sikkim. The focus is on the growth of income, diversification of activities, trend in absolute poverty, progress in the social sector, the infrastructural situation, and the extent of intra-state disparities in development.

Bihar

Bihar is the second largest state in the country in terms of population, and, therefore, the pace of progress here has a great bearing on the overall picture for the country. With a population of around 100 million, prior to the division of the state in November 2000, it accounted for one-tenth of the country's total; there are only ten countries in the world with a population larger than Bihar's. Presently Bihar has a population of 82.9 million, with the area at 94,164 sq km. Jharkhand's population stands at 26.9 million and the area at 79,714 sq km. The state is not only better in terms of land-population ratio, it is also rich in other natural resources. Below we look into the situation, primarily of the undivided Bihar.

Income and Employment

The net state domestic product (NSDP) of Bihar had a very low growth over the years. Between 1980-81 and 1996-97, it multiplied around seven times, from Rs. 6,349 crore to Rs. 41,188 crore, as against nearly ten times for the net national product. Bihar's relative share in the latter declined from 5.74 per cent to 3.78 per cent (GOI 2000a). It may be noted that in the Eighth plan the NSDP had grown at an annual rate of only 2.2 per cent as against 6.7 per cent at the national level; and in the Ninth plan at 4.0 and 5.4 per cent, respectively (GOI 2002a: 41). The growth in per capita income was very low. Over the long period of nearly four decades, 1960-63 to 1994-97, it had risen by only 361 per cent, less than half the rate at the national level (Table 2.1).

After the division of the state, in 2000-01 Bihar's GDP came to Rs. 46,259 crore (at current prices), and constituted 2.41 per cent of all-India total. The per capita income this year was only Rs.5,650, constituting a mere 30.0 per cent of all-India average, the latter being Rs. 18,820. Jharkhand's position is much better. Its per capita income this year came to Rs. 10,772, that is, nearly double that of Bihar's. The GDP stood at Rs. 30,511 crore and constituted 1.51 per cent of the national total (CMIE 2004).

The sectoral diversification of income was insignificant, and did not move consistently. The primary sector's share decreased to 53.37 per cent in 1965-66 and then rose again to 59.86 per cent in 1973-74. The contribution of secondary sector increased from 14.58 to 18.62 per cent in this period. The share of manufacturing industries in it, however, declined, from 13.67 per cent in 1965-66 to 10.21 per cent in 1975-76 (GOB 1978: 24). Bihar's relative postion among the states continued to be very poor. During 1994-97, the proportion of SDP from agriculture came to 33.77 per cent compared with 26.93 per cent at the national level. For manufacturing industries, these were respectively 14.67 and 21.27 per cent (RBI 1997, 1998).

The position of new Bihar is much more depressing as industries were heavily concentrated in the Jharkhand region. In 2000-01, the share of manufacturing in GDP came to only 5.04 per cent and for industry as a whole at 11.3 per cent, whereas for agriculture etc it rose to 38.6 per cent. The tertiary sector has gained significantly in recent years. It accounted for 50.1 per cent in the latest year, rising from 41.3 per cent in 1993-94. In this sector, the community and personal services have become the most important now, accounting for as much as 42.8 per cent in 2000-01, followed by trade, hotel etc at 31.8 per cent. In Jharkhand, the economic activities are much more diversified. This year, the share of agriculture etc was only 16.6 per cent whereas industry accounted for 49.1 per cent. The tertiary sector's contribution increased from 28.2 per cent to 34.3 per cent over the eight-year period. The proportions at the national level for the three sectors were respectively 25.0, 25.9 and 49.2 per cent in 2000-01.

As regards the inter-sectoral distribution of workers, the primary sector continued to account for an overwhelming proportion. In the total of main workers, it declined from 85.7 per cent in 1961 to 82.4 in 1991; the proportion at the national level in the latest year was only 67.4 per cent. The share of the secondary sector also declined, and stood at only 4.64 per cent in 1991, around a third of that at the national level (Table 2.2). As regards the latest position, in

1999-00, only 7.33 per cent of total workers (on the basis of usual principal and subsidiary status) were engaged in manufacturing as against 10.89 per cent at the national level; in 1993-94, it was respectively 4.93 and 10.66 per cent (NSSO 2000a, 1997c).

The work participation rate, although declined in every state, had a sharper fall here, and stood at only 32.2 in 1991 as against 37.46 at the national level. The labour force participation rate in 1999-00 came to only 31.1 per cent, which was not only below the national average but also the lowest among the eastern states. The growth in workforce (main workers) during 1991-2001 was only 0.72 per cent here as against 0.81 at the national level (Table 2.1; NSSO 2002; 2002a: I).

Trend in Absolute Poverty

In this situation, naturally poverty could not be anything but overwhelming. The MPCE of the rural population in Bihar stood at only Rs. 155 in 1996, much below the national average. In the expenditure again, food items took away a large portion. In the rural areas it was to the extent of 71 per cent compared with the all-India average of 63.2 per cent (Table 2.1). Naturally, very little was left for non-food items. Fractile group-wise, the situation was alarming. For the bottom 40 per cent in rural areas, the MPCE in 1995-96 stood at only Rs. 211.50. Earlier, in 1987-88, percentage of rural households with less than Rs. 125 was as much as 56.9 as against the all-India average of only 46.4 (Table 2.3).

The proportion of population below the poverty-line[1] continued to be far above the national average. In 1973-74, Bihar had 61.9 per cent of the total population at BPL level as against 54.9 per cent for all-India. After one decade, in 1983, it rose to 62.2 per cent whereas the national average declined to 44.48 per cent. In the following years also the relative position did not improve; in 1999-00, while the all-India average was 26.1 per cent, for Bihar it was as much as 42.6 per cent. This was the situation despite rural households' asset-holding being relatively good. In 1992, the proportion with asset value of less than Rs. 20,000 was only 27.8 per cent, lowest among the eastern states (Table 2.3).

The Social Sector

In the social sector, Bihar's performance in the most critical area of education—greatly determining the performance in most other areas—was extremely poor. Even in bare literacy, the situation was very depressing. Virtually nothing was done in the first three decades of development efforts. In 1981, the state had only 26.2 per cent of the total population literate, with females at 13.6 per cent; in 1961, it was respectively 18.4 and 6.9 per cent. In the following years also the improvement was not any thing remarkable. The disparity with the national average rose to 17.9 percentage-points in 2001, from only 5.6 in 1961. Bihar's position was the worst among the states. In terms of level of education, in 1995-96 the state had only 23.0 per cent of the population, aged

15 years and above, with middle school and above as against 32.0 per cent at the national level. In rural areas, only 8.7 per cent of the females had it (Table 2.4).

As regards the health situation of the people, we may look at the level of death rate and life expectancy. The state's position on the former deteriorated greatly over the years. From being below the national average in 1957, by mid-eighties it became higher, and stood at respectively 10.0 and 8.9 in 1997. On infant mortality rate, the situation was relatively good. From 145 per thousand during 1951-61 it was down to 67 in 2001; the latest is much below the national average. The life expectancy at birth was particularly low for females. In 2001, at 65 years, it was below the all-India average. The birth rate, which has an impact on the health situation of a family, was very high in Bihar. In 1997, it stood at 31.7 per thousand as against 27.2 at the national Level. Probably because of this, the proportion of severely malnourished children was found to be as much as 26.2 per cent here in 1998 as against 12.3 per cent at the national level (Table 2.4 and GOI 2003).

Two facilities that have a significant bearing on the health situation are availability of drinking water and sanitary facility. But Bihar's position on both of them was extremely poor. Percentage of households with safe drinking water facility stood at only 58.8 in 1991, much below the national average. In 1998 only 8.1 per cent of the households in the state had tap water as against 36.3 per cent at the national level; for rural areas, it was respectively 3.0 per cent and 23.2 per cent. The position of sanitary facility was still worse (Table 2.3).

The growth in urbanization was very low in Bihar. In 1991, only 13.1 per cent of the state's population was living in urban areas, around half the national average. The infrastructural situation of the state continued to be very poor. An index prepared by using 13 variables gave Bihar only 81.1 in 1992-94, taking all-India at 100. The per capita consumption of electricity stood at only 141 kWh in 1999-00, which was less than half the national average (CMIE 1997; Table 2.4). In this situation, it is no surprise that the state has the lowest value on the human development index. In 2001, it stood at 0.367 as against 0.472 for all-India (Table 2.3).

Inter-District Disparity

Inter-district, there was wide variation in the level of progress. We are presenting the situation in only five of the indicators. On the most important one, proportion of BPL population, the variation was between the highest of 88.34 in Godda and the lowest at 15.83 in Patna in 1993-94. There were six districts—Sahibganj, Gumla, Palamau, Dumka and Lohardaga, apart from Godda—with the proportion at above 65 per cent (Parikh and Radhakrishna 2002 : 269).

On the work participation rate also the variation was high. In 1991, the highest was 46.7 per cent in Ranchi and the lowest at 23.9 in Gopalganj, with

Table 2.1: Trend in income, consumption and work participation rate : Relative position of the States

States	*Per capita 1960-63 (a.a.)*	*Net State 1 980-83 (a.a.)*	*Domestic Product 1994-97 (a.a.)*	*% increase**	*MPCE (Rs.) 1996*	
					Rural	*Urban*
Bihar	223 (65.8)	933. (50.9)	1028 (31.4)	361.0	154.99 (71.0)[c]	222.07 (62.9)[c]
W. Bengal	399 (117.7)	1227 (94.3)	2724 (83.2)	582.7	186.30 (66.8)	265.19 (55.3)
Orissa	240 (70.8)	1265 ((69.1)	1561 (47.7)	550.4	149.58 (68.1)	232.60 (57.8)
Assam	352 (103.8)	1374 (75.0)	1628 (49.7)	362.5	186.49 (72.3)	273.67 (59.7)
Madhya P.	279 (82.3)	1369 (74.7)	1861 (56.8)	567.0	154.24 (61.2)	215.68 (52.8)
Uttar P.	252 (74.3)	1299 (70.9)	1681 (51.3)	567.1	168.28 (61.5)	217.77 (56.0)
Andhra P.	331 (97.6)	1492 (81.4)	2293 (70.0)	592.7	172.05 (59.6)	219.95 (60.8)
Kerala	292 (86.1)	1487 (81.2)	2231 (68.1)	664.0	236.03 (60.5)	266.27 (53.9)
Maharashtra	418 (123.3)	2452 (133.8)	4600 (140.5)	1000.5	162.17 (59.5)	280.91 (39.4)
All-India	339 (100.0)	1832 (100.0)	3274 (100.0)[b]	865.8	177.77 (63.17)	250.32 (-)

Work participation rate[d]		Daily status unemployment rate (%)		
1961	*1991*	*1977-78*	*1993-94*	*1999-00 (rural)*
41.40	32.16	8.01	6.25	7.00
33.17	32.19	10.15	9.87	17.00
43.65	37.53	8.13	7.26	7.10
43.26	36.09	1.81	7.96	7.40
52.30	42.82	3.09	3.42	3.80
39.12	32.20	4.12	3.45	3.60
51.87	45.05	10.67	6.67	8.10
33.31	31.43	25.69	15.50	21.70
47.90	42.97	7.99	4.97	6.50
43.00	37.46	8.18	6.03	7.20

*Notes: a: at current prices for 1960-63 and for other years at constant 1980-81 prices; b: based on 1993-94 prices deflated by the rise in index number of wholesale prices between 1980-81 and 1993-94; c: figures in brackets here are percentage of expenditure on food items; d: total workers as percentage to total population; *: between 1960-63 and 1994-97. a. a.: annual average.*

Sources: GOI 2000, 2000a. 2002a: I, 1981, 1963; BCCI 1971.

Table 2.2: Trend in sectoral Distribution of Main Workers: Relative Position of the States

States	*1961*			*1981*[a]			*1991*		
	Primary	*Secondary*	*Tertiary*	*Primary*	*Secondary*	*Tertiary*	*Primary*	*Secondary*	*Tertiary*
Bihar	85.75	2.66	11.59	81.51	7.18	11.31	82.36	4.64	13.00
West Bengal	63.25	12.65	24.10	59.13	18.03	22.84	56.49	17.82	25.69
Orissa	82.38	1.60	16.02	77.93	8.04	14.03	75.83	7.51	16.66
Assam	84.06	2.77	13.16	-----	——	——	73.99	5.56	20.45
M.Pradesh	87.19	2.87	9.94	78.98	9.43	11.59	77.54	8.37	14.09
U.Pradesh	82.10	3.58	14.32	75.11	10.04	14.85	73.01	8.98	18.01
A. Pradesh	81.50	3.66	14.85	72.47	11.49	16.04	71.25	10.48	18.27
Kerala	55.86	10.51	33.63	51.65	18.86	29.49	48.02	18.17	33.81
Maharastra	76.41	8.14	15.45	64.03	16.07	19.90	61.51	15.80	22.69
All-India	78.60	5.35	16.05	69.41	12.96	17.63	67.37	12.13	20.50

Note: a: all-India figures exclude Assam and Jammu & Kashmir for this year.

Source: GOI 1965a, 1993.

the state average at 33.0 per cent. There were five districts with the WPR at above 40 per cent while 14 had below 30. Diversification of economic activities was extremely low in many districts. The proportion of main workers engaged in the primary sector was at the highest of 92.7 per cent in Madhepura and the lowest at 51.8 in Purbi Singhbhum. Earlier, number of districts was much less and, as in some cases backward areas were attached to more developed ones, the variation was relatively low. In 1961, at the highest it was 87.0 per cent in Palamau and the lowest at 68.6 in Patna (Table 2.5).

In the social sector, on literacy rate a high level of disparity existed even in 1991. The highest was 59.0 per cent in Purbi Singhbhum and the lowest at 22.2 in Kishenganj. There were ten districts with less than 30 per cent literate. At the beginning of planning, in 1951, the variation was between 22 per cent in Patna and 7.8 per cent in Palamau. The disparity in female Literacy was much higher, as may be seen from Table 2.5. The variation in infant mortality rate was also very high. In 1991, while Dhanbad had only 40 per thousand, at the highest it was 136 in Kishenganj. Earlier the disparity was higher; in 1956, the highest was 4.6 times the lowest. The probability of dying before reaching age 5 also varied noticeably among the districts.

The Quality of Government

A basic reason behind this distressing situation is the virtual nonexistence of a government in the state for many years. The non-development and wide disparity spatially and inter-caste had brought extreme of lawlessness in the state by mid-seventies. And presently Bihar is probably the most violent state in the country. Murders, both political and non-political nature, are common in the state. Number of violent incidents during elections increased from some 260 in 1977 to 617 in 1984. Nearly 100 people were killed in the 1985 election, including four candidates running for office (Times 1986). In recent years, the situation aggravated further. During the first eight years of Laloo Yadav's rule, 51,528 people were murdered, excluding the victims of caste and political conflicts. There were 24,000 dacoities, 24,699 incidents of loot and 7,290 cases of rape (Thakur 2000: 23).

A recent report on Bihar, prepared by the Institute of Human Development, stated thus: "Law and order problem has assumed alarming proportion primarily due to interplay between criminalization of politics and politicization of crime coupled with unholy nexus between politicians, bureaucrats and contractors. This ensures minimal private sector investment..........Casteism has widely percolated from politics to bureaucracy, educational institutions and even social levels. In significant number of cases, caste is the sole determinant behind appointments and postings, which severely affects the efficiency of the entire system." *(Bihar Development Report*, quoted in: The Statesman: 2003).

Political instability contributed greatly to this situation. The 1967 elections reduced the congress Party's majority in many parts of India, and Bihar was no

Table 2.3: Trend in selected Poverty Indicators of the states

States	*% of households with MPCE of less than Rs 125 (Rural) 1987-88*	*MPCE in rural areas (1995-96) for bottom*		*Percentage of population below poverty-Line*							
				1973-74		*1983-84*		*1993-94*		*1999-2000*	
		20%	*40%*	*Total*	*Rural*	*Total*	*Rural*	*Total*	*Rural*	*Total*	*Rural*
Bihar	56.9	176.00	211.50	61.91	62.99	62.22	64.37	54.96	58.21	42.60	44.30
W. Bengal	45.3	202.14	246.00	63.43	73.16	54.85	63.05	35.66	40.80	27.02	31.85
Orissa	60.5	184.16	227.40	66.18	67.28	65.29	67.53	48.56	49.72	47.15	48.01
Assam	37.3	213.00	262.80	51.21	52.67	40.47	42.60	40.86	45.01	36.09	40.04
Madhya P.	56.6	199.75	242.28	61.78	62.66	49.76	48.90	42.52	40.64	37.43	37.06
Uttar p.	45.1	196.40	238.20	57.07	56.53	47.07	46.45	40.85	42.26	31.15	31.22
Andhra P.	47.2	204.83	246.50	48.86	48.41	28.91	26.53	22.19	15.92	15.77	11.05
Kerala	25.4	284.60	355.40	59.79	59.19	40.42	39.03	25.43	25.76	12.72	9.38
Maharashtra	48.1	217.84	275.60	53.24	57.71	43.44	45.23	36.86	37.93	25.02	23.72
All-India	46.4	204.66	253.83	54.88	56.44	44.48	45.65	35.97	37.27	26.10	27.09

% of rural hhs. with asset holding of less than Rs 20,000	*% of hhs. with*		*Human development index@*	
	safe drinking water: 1991	*Latrine facility 1992-93*	*1981*	*2001*
27.8	58.8 (8.1)b	16.5 (16.4)c	0.237	0.367
35.7	82.0 (20.5)	40.4 (41.6)	0.305	0.472
40.4	39.1 (9.8)	12.2 (11.0)	0.267	0.404
29.7	45.9 (10.0)	49.6 (81.2)	0.272	0.386
28.2	53.4 (25.5)	21.3 (19.2)	0.245	0.394
14.8	62.2 (16.3)	22.9 (22.0)	0.255	0.388
44.5	55.1 (47.4)	24.4 (25.4)	0.298	0.416
12.1	18.9 (17.9)	70.9 (77.4)	0.500	0.638
29.5	68.5 (64.5)	40.8 (37.5)	0.363	0.523
27.0	62.3 (36.3)	30.3 (31.6)	0.302	0.472

Note: @: HDI takes values between 0 and 1; b: percentage of households with tap water in 1998; c: the position in 1998.

Source: GOI 1999, 2000, 2001 2002b; NSSO 1998a, 1998b, 2000; IIPS 1995.

Table 2.4: Trend in Selected Socio-economic Indicators: Relative Position of the States

States	*Education (Percentages) Literacy*				*Health and Hygiene Indicators*			
					With Middle School and above (1995-96)[c]		*Life expectancy at birth (2001-06)*	
	1961	*1981*[a]	*1991*[b]	*2001*	*Total*	*Rural*	*M*	*F*
Bihar	18.4 (6.9)[d]	26.2 (13.6)[d]	38.5 (22.9)[d]	47.5 (33.6)[d]	23.0	18.9 (8.7)[d]	65.7	64.8
W.Bengal	29.3 (17.0)	40.9 (30.2)	57.7 (46.6)	69.2 (60.2)	28.7	19.6 (12.6)	66.1	69.3
Orissa	21.7 (8.6)	34.2 (21.1)	49.1 (34.7)	63.6 (51.0)	26.6	22.3 (14.4)	60.0	59.7
Assam	27.4 (16.0)	– –	52.9 (43.0)	64.3 (56.0)	36.0	32.8 (26.7)	59.0	60.9
M. Pradesh	17.1 (6.7)	27.9 (39.5)	44.2 (28.8)	64.1 (50.3)	23.9	15.8 (7.4)	59.2	58.0
U. Pradesh	17.6 (7.0)	27.2 (14.0)	41.6 (25.3)	57.4 (43.0)	28.1	23.4 (9.9)	63.5	64.1
A. Pradesh	24.0 (13.0)	29.9 (20.4)	44.1 (32.7)	61.1 (51.2)	25.4	16.3 (9.6)	62.8	65.0
Kerala	46.8 (38.9)	70.4 (65.7)	89.8 (86.2)	90.9 (87.9)	57.5	54.9 (52.0)	71.7	75.0
Maharashtra	31.4 (18.2)	47.2 (34.8)	64.9 (52.3)	77.3 (67.5)	44.8	32.0 (20.9)	66.7	69.8
All-India	24.0 (13.0)	36.2 (24.8)	52.2 (39.3)	65.4 (54.2)	32.0	23.7 (14.6)	63.9	66.9

(Table 2.4 Contd.)

Death Rate			I.M.R.		Birth Rate			Per Capita Consumption of Electricity (kWh)		% of Urban Pop.	Index of soc. & econ. Infra.	
1957	*1985*	*1997*	*1951-61*	*2001*	*1970*	*1985*	*1997*	*1974-75*	*1999-00*	*1961*	*1991*	*1999*
7.8	15.0	10.0	145	67	32.0	37.8	31.7	48.0	140.8	8.4	13.1	81.3
10.0	9.6	7.7	120	53	27.8	29.4	22.4	106.1	204.4	24.4	27.5	111.2
19.0	14.0	10.9	159	98	38.1	30.7	26.5	69.2	354.6	6.3	13.4	81.0
4.7	13.2	9.9	184	78	38.8	34.3	28.2	24.0	95.5	7.7	11.1	77.7
—	14.2	11.0	175	97	39.3	39.4	31.9	61.3	351.7	14.3	23.2	76.8
8.5	15.8	10.3	186	85	45.4	37.6	33.5	50.0	175.8	12.8	19.8	101.2
15.7	10.3	8.3	111	66	35.4	29.9	22.5	55.4	391.0	17.4	26.9	103.3
9.6	6.5	6.2	120	16	31.6	23.3	17.9	79.4	261.8	15.1	26.4	178.7
15.0	8.4	7.3	109	49	31.5	29.0	23.1	126.4	484.1	28.2	38.7	112.8
11.0.	11.8	8.9e	139	71	36.8	32.9	27.2	174.9	354.7	17.6	25.7	100.0

Notes: a : the all-India figures exclude Assam; b: all-India figures exclude Jammu & Kashmir; c: Persons of age 15 years and above, NSSO-52nd Round: d: for females; e: excluding Mizoram, Nagaland and Jammu & Kashmir.

Sources: GOI 1959, 1999a, 200b, 2002a: III, 1976, 1965, 2004; NSSO 1998b; IIPS 1995; CMIE 1997, 1985.

Table 2.5: District-Wise Disparity in Development of Bihar

District	Work participation rate[a]	% of main workers in primary sector		literacy rate (person)		I. M. R.		% of urban Population	
	1991	1961	1991	1951	1991[c]	1956	1991[e]	1961	1991
Patna	32.2	68.6	62.4	22.0	56.3 (41.4)[d]	87.3	709 (56)[f]	20.1	38.0
Nalanda	27.5	—	83.4	—	46.9 (30.0)	—	93 (71)	—	14.8
Bhojpur	32.8	—	80.8	—	47.2 (27.1)	—	76 (57)	—	11.3
Rohtas	26.6	—	83.8	—	45.4 (27.0)	—	90 (68)	—	10.1
Aurangabad	29.5	—	84.4	—	45.1 (26.7)		91 (68)	—	7.7
						12.61g			
Jahanabad	29.5	—	87.1	15.9	45.8 (26.8)		90 (70)	—	6.3
Gaya	30.4	82.2	82.4	14.3	40.5 (24.2)	100.0	100 (75)	7.3	13.4
Nawada	32.8	—	87.3	—	39.0 (21.8)	—	96 (73)	—	7.0
Saran	31.7	82.5	82.0	12.2	41.8 (22.7)	52.7	100 (75)	4.2	9.1
Siwan	24.2	—	84.1	—	39.1 (21.3)	—	82 (64)	—	5.3
Gopalganj	23.9	—	89.0	—	35.0 (17.7)	—	69 (48)	—	5.7
Paschim Champaran	26.6		89.4		28.0 (14.4)		101 (73)		10.0
		86.9		8.4		64.8		4.6	
Purba Champaran	34.9		90.4		27.6 (13.7)		79 (66)		5.7
Sitamarhi	30.9	—	88.0	—	28.1 (15.3)	—	125 (95)	—	5.6
Muzaffarpur	29.9	81.2	82.6	8.0	36.1 (22.3)	56.7	100 (72)	4.5	9.3
Vaishali	28.9	—	83.8	—	40.6 (24.1)	—	71 (51)	—	6.7
Begusarai	25.5	—	81.1	—	36.9 (23.5)	—	96 (73)	—	9.8
Samastipur	28.2	—	83.3	—	36.4 (21.2)	—	103 (69)	—	5.0
Darbhanga	28.1	78.6	84.1	11.2	34.9 (20.1)	52.2	96 (74)	4.3	8.7
Madhubani	29.5	—	88.8	—	33.2 (16.7)	—	94 (72)	—	3.6
Saharsa	32.5	86.2	91.0	8.4	29.0 (14.7)	32.2	102 (77)	3.9	6.9
Madhepura	37.5	—	92.7	—	27.7 (14.4)	—	110 (82)	—	6.5

(Table 2.5 Contd.)

Purnea	37.7	79.2	90.0	9.6	28.5 (16.8)	55.0	109 (77)	6.0	8.4
Katihar	36.4	—	86.6	—	28.7 (16.9)	—	124 (89)	—	9.4
Khagaria	33.7	—	88.3	—	32.3 (19.8)	—	91 (62)	—	6.0
Munger	32.7	74.5	81.7	13.1	41.6 (25.3)	59.5	94 (69)	11.1	16.6
Bhagalpur	33.0	74.3	83.8	13.7	38.9 (24.4)	69.8	87 (70)	10.9	12.1
Godda	32.8	—	88.8	—	34.0 (18.0)	—	84 (65)	—	2.7
Sahebganj	39.6	—	82.8	—	27.0 (16.3)	—	118 (87)	—	7.3
Deoghar	45.2	—	77.3	—	37.9 (19.7)	—	128 (91)	—	13.4
Dumka	40.3	—	85.9	—	34.0 (17.9)	—	82 (65)	—	6.1
Dhanbad	34.9	74.2	54.8	16.5	55.5 (37.9)	27.6	40 (28)	25.1	51.3
Giridih	27.6	—	78.7	—	36.0 (17.7)	—	96 (74)	—	15.5
Hazaribagh	33.8	85.1	78.3	8.3	38.0 (21.2)	64.1	73 (58)	8.4	18.1
Palamau	33.3	87.0	86.8	7.8	31.1 (16.2)	68.9	118 (91)	4.7	5.4
Lohardaga	35.3	—	85.9		40.8 (26.1)		103 (77)	—	11.0
				9.3[b]		29.4[b]			
Gumla	41.0	—	89.9		39.7 (27.5)		128 (89)	—	4.5
Ranchi	46.7	86.3	68.5	11.8	51.5 (36.6)	77.9	70 (56)	9.5	33.0
Purbi Singhbhum	39.3		51.8		59.0 (45.5)		44 (38)	21.7	52.7
		74.1		15.6		31.8			
Paschim Singhbhum	34.3		79.6		38.9 (22.4)		79 (66)	21.7	15.8
Araria	44.3	—	91.4	—	26.2 (14.0)	—	85 (67)	—	6.3
Kishenganj	35.1	—	90.2	—	22.2 (10.4)	—	136 (95)	—	10.1
Bihar	33.0	80.2	82.4	12.1	38.5 (22.9)	67.8	94 (70)	8.4	13.1

Notes: a: main plus marginal Workers; b: refer to Santhal Parganas; c: for age seven years and above; d: female literacy rate; e: probability of a new born dying before age 5; f : probability of dying before age 1; g: such figures in-between two districts refer to the undivided district.

Sources: GOI 1963a, 1996; GOB 1959; Rajan and Mohanachandran 1998.

exception. Congress became a minority party, and several opposition parties that claimed to represent the backward castes gained in significance. None of those parties was in a position to form a government by itself; only a coalition government was possible. Bihar thus entered a period of governmental instability. Presidential rule was imposed three times. There were 13 changes in governments in Bihar between 1967 and 1972. The longest that any government lasted was around 300 days (Prasad 1978: 62-63). Factional strife within the ruling party was also often prominent. Between 1988 and 1989, Bihar had four new chief ministers. Throughout the 1980s, the Congress government was unable to Act with even a modest degree of cohesiveness.

In the 1990s, Laloo Prasad Yadav came to power, and after some good work, in order to retain his hold on state power, he perverted rules of politics and administration. All the rungs of Officialdom were encouraged to treat the state as their private property. Corruption reached unprecedented levels within a short period. Hundreds of government departments and undertakings went without audit for years. Central funds for various schemes vanished into the select hands of Laloo's men. The comptroller and auditor general of India (CAG) pulled up Laloo Yadav for spending more than Rs. 630 crore to service his "business and political interests" (The Sunday Statesman 2000)

The future of Bihar appears quite dim. Apart from the anarchy in governance, the creation of new Jharkhand state has deprived the state of a major portion of its resources. Bihar used to draw 67 per cent of its revenue from the mineral rich 18 districts of the new state. It has lost revenue from the mines and forests and has suffered a heavy loss of commercial taxes from the major industries there. The special assistance from the Centre will not compensate the state for all its losses. There might be a major power crisis also, for the state has lost its main source of energy, the patratu, Sikidiri and Tenughat power projects. There may, however, be some improvement in the system of governance and the law and order situation in Bihar, as the election in November 2005 has brought an end to the Lalu Prasad's uninterrupted rule for 15 years.

West Bengal

In terms of population, West Bengal is the fourth largest state in the country, after Uttar Pradesh, Maharashtra and Bihar. In 2001, with a population of 80.22 million, its share in all-India total came to 7.81 per cent. The state's geographical area is, however, only 2.70 per cent of all-India's. The density of population increased noticeably over the years, rising from 394 per sq km in 1961 to 767 on 1991; presently, West Bengal's is the highest density among the states. The state had started with a superior economic position after Independence, as noted in the preceding chapter. We give a brief look below on how the state progressed in the last half a century.

Income and Employment

Within a few years after Independence, West Bengal started its downhill journey. From the highest level of per capita income among the states in 1949-

50, by 1960-63 it became the second and slipped further in the following years. The state's per capita income was 117.7 per cent of all-India's during 1960-63 but by 1994-97 it was down to 83.2 per cent (Table 2.1). The total NSDP of the state had risen by only 645.9 per cent between 1980-81 and 1996-97 as against 884.4 per cent at the national level, and the relative share declined from 8.67 per cent to 6.57 per cent. In more recent years, there has been slight improvement in the position. The per capita income during 1998–01 averaged Rs. 16,147 (at current prices) and constituted 92.0 per cent of all-India average. The state's GDP came to Rs. 139969 crore in 2000-01, and the relative share rose to 7.3 per cent (CMIE 2004).

On diversification of economic activities, the state's performance deteriorated noticeably in the last two decades. In the aggregate of SDP, the secondary sector's share rose to 29.7 per cent in 1980-81, from 21.1 in 1951-52, but in the following years it declined and stood at only 19.6 per cent in 1995-96. The value of output of the sector had multiplied 16.8 times between 1951-52 and 1980-81 but in the following 16 years it was only 4.7 times. Within the sector, manufacturing performed very badly. Its contribution to the SDP declined to 13.8 per cent in 1995-96 from 24.6 in 1980-81 (BCCI 1971; GOW 1995, 1999). In relation to the all-India average, the picture is very depressing. During 1994-97, the average contribution here came to 16.9 per cent as against 21.27 per cent at the national level (RBI 1997, 1998). In more recent years also the situation has remained more or less the same. In 2000-01, the contribution of manufacturing came to 13.1 per cent and for industry as a whole at 20.7 per cent; at the national level, these were respectively 15.7 and 26.6 per cent.

The share of primary sector in the SDP showed some decline till 1990-91 but in the following years it increased and stood at 37.8 per cent in 1995-96. In the primary sector, agriculture contributed 33.0 per cent of the SDP in 1995-96, rising from 28.4 per cent in 1990-91; in 1951-52, it was 35.1 per cent. The growth in agricultural output was high since early eighties. Between 1980-81 and 1995-96 it had increased 8.3 times compared with 9.7 times in the preceding three decades. In recent years, the contribution of agriculture etc has shown a noticeable fall, being at 29.7 per cent in 2000-01and the average for 1998–01 at 31.8 per cent. Even this is, however, higher than the national average, being at 26.3 per cent in the latest period.

The contribution of tertiary sector showed a decline in the eighties but in recent years it increased noticeably. In 1995-96 it stood at 42.6 per cent of the SDP, rising from 36.6 in 1980-81; in 1951-52 it was 38.3 per cent. In the tertiary sector, banking and insurance had the highest growth, followed by trade, hotels and restaurants. The share of the former in SDP rose to 7.8 per cent in the latest year, from 4.6 in 1980-81and 1.1 in 1951-52. The latter's share rose to 14.1 per cent in 1995-96 from 10.9 in 1980-81 (BCCI 1971; GOW 1995, 1999). In recent years, the tertiary sector improved its position further; the contribution rising to 49.6 per cent in 2000-01. In its composition, finance, insurance etc became the most important, with a share of 18.8 per cent in GDP, followed by community and personal services at 13.6 per cent (CMIE 2004).

As regards the sectoral distribution of workers, the reliance on agriculture was relatively less here. The proportion engaged in primary sector declined to 56.5 per cent in 1991 from 63.2 in 1961. The proportion in the secondary sector increased but the margin of advantage with the national average decreased. As regards the latest position, according to the NSSO survey, the proportion of total workers engaged in manufacturing stood at 18.11 per cent in 1999-00, with rural areas at 15.01 per cent; at the national level, it was respectively 10.89 and 7.40 per cent. Earlier, however, the situation was still better; in 1993-94, for all areas it was respectively 20.00 and 10.66 per cent (NSSO 2000a, 1997c).

A distressing feature of West Bengal's economy is that the work participation rate has been always low. In 1991, West Bengal had 32.19 per cent as against 37.46 per cent at the national level. In recent years also the situation has not improved. In 1999-00, it stood at 32.3 per cent as against 37.0 per cent in the latter. The rate of unemployment continued to be much higher than the national average. In 1999-00, the rural unemployment rate was 17 per cent, more than double that at the national level (Table 2.1; NSSO 2002).

Trend in Absolute Poverty

On poverty alleviation, the state's performance was very poor until recently, as evident from Table 2.3. In 1973-74, 73 per cent of the state's rural population was living below the poverty line as against the national average of 56 per cent. No other state had such a high proportion. After another decade, in 1983, also there was not much improvement. Only in the nineties, a noticeable reduction came, being at 31.8 per cent in 1999-00; even this was 4.76 percentage-points higher than the all-India average. Further, the rural-urban disparity is very high in West Bengal. Even in the latest year, it was by 16.99 points compared with only 3.47 points at the national level. Thus, the government's attention was largely concentrated in urban areas. This level of performance is utterly shameful for a state with quarter century of communist rule; West Bengals communists' concern for the poor is only crocodile tears.

The depth of poverty here becomes transparent if we look at the level of consumer expenditure. In 1987-88, percentage of households with MPCE of less than Rs 125 was as much as 45.3 in rural Bengal, which was higher than in many other states. In 1995-96, the bottom 40 per cent of the rural population had an MPCE of only Rs. 246.00 as against the national average of Rs. 253.83. Even the average situation here was quite gloomy. In 1999, the MPCE of rural households was found to be Rs 450 and in urban areas at Rs 829, both were much below the national average (NSSO 2000). In the MPCE again, the food items took away a large proportion. The rural households' asset-holding was very low in West Bengal. Percentage of households with assets worth less than Rs. 20,000 was as much as 35.7 in 1992 as against the all-India average of 27.0.

The Social Sector

In the social sector, the educational scenario has been quite depressing. On the literacy rate, the relative position of the state worsened noticeably over the years. In 1951, the literacy rate here was 7.4 percentage-points higher than the national average—being respectively 24.0 and 16.6 per cent—but this lead was drastically reduced in the following years; and in 1981, it was 4.7 points higher. After another two decades, in 2001, although the literacy rate rose to 69.2 per cent from 40.9 in 1981, in relation to the national average it was only 3.8 points higher. The relative position among the states is now after five of the major states as against lower than in two only in 1961 and the second highest in 1951. The position of female literacy may be seen from Table 2.4.

The quality of this literacy was also very poor. Those with middle school and above constituted only 28.7 per cent in 1995-96 compared with the national average of 32.0 per cent. At the beginning of economic planning, in 1951, the relative position was much better. The proportion with middle school and above was more than double the national average, being respectively 32.0 per cent and 15.3 per cent (GOI 1959).

As regards the people's health condition, West Bengal's relative position was not bad. The death rate has been always below the national average, and declined from 10.0 per thousand in 1957 to 7.7 in 1997. The IMR was also similarly placed, declining from 120 in 1951-61 to 53 in 2001; at the national level, it was respectively 139 and 71. However, the proportion of malnourished children is high here. It was found to be 49.6 per cent in 2002 compared with 47.7 per cent at the national level. The situation of life expectancy at birth was not bad. In 2001, for males it was 66.1 years and for females 69.3; both were higher than the national average (Table 2.4 and GOI 2003).

The urban areas are in general with better facilities, but the growth of urbanization in West Bengal was very slow. Percentage of total population living in urban areas increased by only 3.1 points between 1961 and 1991, from 24.4 per cent to 27.5 per cent; at the national level the rise was by 8.1 points (Table 2.4). Furthermore, the urban population here is heavily concentrated in a few cities. The proportion living in class I cities (100,000 plus) increased from 72.14 per cent in 1961 to 81.71 per cent in 1991, while all other categories recorded declines. For class III (20,000-49,999), it was down to 7.66 per cent from 11.12 per cent, and for class IV from 5.52 per cent to 2.59 per cent. The infrastructural situation in the state also continued to be poor. To look at the position of electricity only, in 1999-00 the per capita consumption came to only 204 kWh, 57 per cent of that at the national level; earlier the position was better (Table 2.4).

Inter-District Disparity

A striking aspect of the development in West Bengal is that it is heavily concentrated in a few districts. Table 2.6 below presents the pattern of inter-district disparity on some selected variables. On the extent of economic diversification, there was wide variation from district to district. In 1991, percentage of main workers engaged in the secondary sector was less than 10 in seven of the districts, with the lowest at 6.6 in West Dinajpur, as against more than 20 in five districts and the highest at 39.3 in Howrah. The share of Primary sector was more than 70 per cent in six districts, against the state average of 56.5 per cent. Percentage of BPL population in 1993-94, varied between the highest of 79.83 in Cooch-Behar and the lowest at 8.18 in Calcutta. Even South 24-Parganas, by the side of Calcutta, had 55.08 per cent (Parikh and Radha Krishna 2002: 273).

The level of banking activities—reflecting both the economic condition of the people and the extent of economic activities–also differed greatly. The per capita deposit in 1999, excluding Calcutta, was at the lowest Rs 1,175 in W.Dinajpur and at the highest Rs. 5,440 in North 24-Parganas, that is, the latter 4.6 times the former. In per capita advances, the disparity was much wider. For seven districts, it was less than Rs. 500; on the other hand, Calcutta had Rs. 31,368, 90 times the lowest—Rs. 347 in W.Dinajpur. Even the second highest was only Rs. 1,574, in Darjeeling. The credit-deposit ratio was as much as 61.6 per cent for Calcutta as against only 12.8 per cent in North 24-Parganas and the state average at 41.9 (Table 2.6). There was virtually no effort at dispersal of activities by the government or the banks.

In the social sector, the variation in literacy rate has decreased considerably over the years. In 1961, the highest was around four times the lowest, being respectively 59.3 per cent in Calcutta and 13.8 per cent in Malda. After three decades, in 1991, the highest was 77.6 per cent and the lowest at 35.6 in the same districts. The female literacy in the latest year was less than 30 per cent in four districts against the state average of 46.6 per cent. The variation in IMR continued to be very wide. In 1991, the highest was 98 in Malda and the lowest at 25 in Calcutta against the state average of 67. Earlier, in 1955-57, the highest was 135 in Calcutta and the lowest at 29.1 in Purulia. While most of the districts have shown a fall in the IMR over the years, six districts showed notable increases.

The growth in urbanisation also varied widely among the districts. Even in 1991, six districts had less than 10 per cent of the population living in urban areas, while another six had more than 30 per cent. Three decades earlier, in 1961, with the state average at 24.4 per cent, nine districts had less than 10 per cent. The districts with very low growth in urbanisation were Cooch Behar, Malda, Midnapore, Bankura, Purulia, Birbhum and Murshidabad (Table 2.6).

A human development index calculated by using literacy rate above 7 years of age, infant survival rate, and per capita real domestic product gave the value of only 0.0524 to West Dinajpur, 0.1034 to Cooch Behar, 0.1852 to Murshidabad and 0.1980 to Malda against the highest of 1.0000 to Calcutta and the state average of 0.4866. (Bhattacharya 1998: Table 4).

It is rare to find another state in this country with such wide intra-state disparities in development. Almost every development effort here was concentrated in and around Calcutta. And this has happened in a state with long period of communist rule! It is no surprise that terrorist groups are now raising their heads in this state also. There are the Kamtapuri Liberation Organisation, the Gorkha Liberation Organisation and Naxalites in Midnapore and Purulila. The West Bengal communists' objective appears to be to promote inequities and disorder. We give a brief look below on the nature of the government the state had in the last half a century.

The Nature of Government

In West Bengal the Congress party was in power till 1967, as was the case with most other states and the Centre. The following decade, 1967 to 1977, was a period of political chaos. There were three coalition governments in the state between 1967 and 1971. The first two were mostly of the Left and the last one with Congress as the leading force. There were Presidential rule three times in a short period of five years. In the 1972 election the Congress Party again came back with a massive victory. But it could not last long as the national emergency was imposed in 1975. In the election held in 1977, the Communist Party of India-Marxist (CPM) emerged as the ruling party. The Congress which had bagged 216 seats in the 1972 Assembly election now got only 20 seats. In the following two-and-half decades the Left Front, with CPM as the leading force, ruled the state, and it is still continuing.

Before we look into the nature of CPM party, let us have an idea about the extent of chaos West Bengal went through until 1977. In the fall of Congress—which was a personalistic party—the death of B.C.Roy in 1962 was an important factor. From then on factionalism in the Congress became obvious, and often it took an ugly form. Naturally the administration suffered. The years since 1967 were marked by extreme of chaos. *Gheraos*, forced distribution of land, internecine fighting among political parties, riots and political murders became the order of the day. The Left forces had ordered the police in 1967 not to interfere in class struggles. This deliberate thwarting of state power led to complete chaos. Number of *gheraos* averaged less than 100 per year before 1967 but this year alone it reached 811 (GOW 1970). Between 1969 and 1971, there were 415 political disturbances, 199 deaths by police firing, 139 deaths of political cadres in inter-party clashes, 331 attacks on schools and colleges, 1,771 political murders, and the arrest of 7,462 people without trial (Basu 1982: 92). Conflicts within the Congress party also became more and more severe, and clashes between different factions led to 102 murders between

1972 and 1975. The state machinery was completely within the grip of the gangsters and armed action squads of political parties (Ibid. 159, 161).

This is the background in which the CPM came to power. However, the Party's emergence as the ruling party since 1977 is largely due to the change in its ideology. Immediately after coming to power, the CPM set to itself the task of limiting the expectations of the economically disadvantaged. The chief minister Jyoti Basu stated:

"The aim of our program is to alleviate the sufferings of the rural and urban people and to improve their conditions to a certain extent. We do not claim anything more, as we are aware that without structural changes in the socio-economic order it is hardly possible to bring about any basic change in the conditions of people." (GOW 1985: i-ii).

The ideological fall of the CPM has a number of reasons behind it. Most of the leaders had become aged and wanted to have some taste of power before leaving this world. This is again rooted in their family background and nature of upbringing. Most of the party leaders were from affluent landed families, or at least of bourgeoisie origin. The CPM's cadres continued to come mostly from what the party would describe as petite bourgeoisie. The party has been more of a middle-class character, rather than lower class. A sample survey of 100 village *panchayats* in 1979 found that 50.7 per cent of *panchayat* members were owner cultivator and 14.0 per cent teachers; landless labourers constituted only 4.8 per cent and sharecroppers 1.8 per cent (GOW 1980: 42). It is now well-known that the panchayats in West Bengal are dominated by the same old class of rural vested interests, including money lenders.

Given this character of the party, after some good work in the initial years, it lapsed into almost the same lawlessness and serving of vested interests as prevailed in the Congress period (Roy Chowdhury 1980). The Left Front continued in power primarily because there was no credible alternative, Congress being severely affected by factionalism. After mid-eighties, the CPM was no better than any other party. Its only concern became somehow to remain in power, and in this pursuit started protecting and promoting all sorts of unproductive and criminalised elements. Corruption and nepotism reached unimaginable levels, and gradually the police and administration became totally ineffective. I cite below a few instances of the nature of corruption and lawlessness in the state:

(i) Central funds were diverted to personal ledger accounts by violating official norms, and the money was used for helping the CPM leaders and cadres. The CAG report for the year 1999-00 pointed out such transfers by five district magistrates to the extent of Rs. 6.15 Crore (Statesman 2002). Manash ghosh wrote recently: "Corruption is so thoroughly institutionalised that it pervades all walks of rural life. In Nanoor, the going "black market rate" for getting electric

Table 2.6: District-wise Trend in Selected Indicators of Development in West Bengal

Districts	*% of main Workers in (1991)*		*Per capita Bank*[a]		*Literacy rate (%)*			*I MR*		*% of Urban Population*	
	P	*S*	*Deposit (Rs.)*	*Advcs. (Rs.)*	*1961*	*1991 P*	*F*	*1955-57 (av.)*	*1991*	*1961*	*1991*
Cooch-Behar	75.5	7.9	1320	422 (32.0)[b]	21.0	45.8	33.3	80.7	92	7.01	7.8
Jalpaiguri	68.7	8.9	2441	462 (18.9)	19.2	45.1	33.2	70.5	76	9.11	16.4
Darjeeling	57.1	9.6	6758	1574 (23.3)	28.6	57.9	47.8	68.5	56	23.16	30.5
W. Dinajpur	79.4	6.6	1175	347 (29.5)	17.1	39.3	27.9	80.4	78	7.48	13.3
Malda	72.4	13.2	1545	403 (26.1)	13.8	35.6	24.9	69.0	98	4.16	7.1
Murshidabad	62.7	21.5	1507	411 (27.3)	16.0	38.3	29.6	71.0	74	8.54	10.4
Nadia	58.5	18.5	2352	515 (21.9)	27.3	52.5	44.4	60.5	71	18.41	22.6
N. 24 Parganas	35.8	27.8	5440	694 (12.8)			58.0		68		51.2
					32.5*	55.1*		71.7*		31.81*	
S. 24 Parganas	59.7	17.1	2518	421 (16.7)			40.6		80		13.3
Calcutta	1.1	29.9	50894	31368 (61.6)	59.3	77.6	72.1	135.2	25	100.0	100.0
Howrah	26.6	39.3	5361	875 (16.3)	36.9	67.6	57.8	127.6	43	40.48	49.6
Hooghly	48.8	24.6	4233	715 (16.9)	34.6	66.8	56.9	62.7	36	25.96	31.2
Midnapore	69.4	11.6	2487	513 (20.6)	27.3	69.3	56.6	69.5	65	7.70	9.9
Bankura	76.1	9.4	2199	543 (24.7)	23.1	52.0	36.5	75.7	55	7.34	8.3
Purulia	77.1	8.7	2114	425 (20.1)	17.8	43.3	23.2	29.1[C]	59	6.80	9.4
Bardhaman	60.6	15.6	5097	1052 (20.6)	29.6	61.9	51.5	77.2	54	18.20	35.1
Birbhum	74.2	9.2	2434	651 (26.7)	22.1	48.6	37.2	83.3	76	6.97	9.0
West Bengal	56.5	17.8	6469	2713 (41.9)	29.3	57.7	46.6	80.7	67	24.45	27.5

*Notes: a : as at June-end 1999; b: in brackets are percentages in relation to deposit; C: average for 1957-59; *: refer to the undivided district of 24-Parganas.*

Sources : GOI 1964a, 1996; GOW 1966, 2000.

connection for submersible pumps is Rs. 6000. Contractors share this money with local leaders". (Ghosh 2000).

(ii) In the management of bureaucracy, while favoured officers were left undisturbed in plum posts, those who did not conform were banished from the secretariat. Recently, an efficient and upright bureaucrat was transferred four times in 30 months. Another instance is appointment of health secretary, Ashok Chakravarty, by superseding at least 10 senior officers, five of whom were eminently suited to the job but were not considered. Consequent on such policies, frustration has forced a few bureaucrats to take premature retirement (Statesman 2000a). At lower levels also politicisation has taken an ugly form (The Telegraph 2004b: 1).

(iii) People have lost their faith in police and have started taking law into their own hands. Number of lynching increased noticeably in recent years. During 1996 to 1999, there were 129 lynching in South 24-Parganas, 66 in North 24-Parganas, 62 in Hooghly, 58 in Jalpaiguri, 57 in Burdwan, 52 each in Howrah, Nadia and Murshidabad, 38 in South Dinajpur, 36 in Malda and 32 in Midnapore (Statesman 2000b). It may also be noted that the minimum qualification required for constables in West Bengal is standard VIII pass as against a school-final pass certificate in the rest of the country (The Statesman 2000a).

(iv) Political killings have increased enormously in recent times. On July 27, 2000, the CPM supporters massacred 11 agricultural workers at Suchpur because of their allegiance to the Trinamul Congress. On January 4, 2001, 18 Trinamul workers were massacred in Gorbeta's Chhota Anguria (The Statesman 2001). The elections have become a farce in West Bengal now. In the one held in May 2001, the CPM unleashed political terror and violence on the Trinamul-BJP with full government backing (Statesman 2001 e). It also subsequently came out that there were 6.9 million bogus voters on the electoral rolls prior to the poll (Statesman 2002 e, 2002f: 4). The Lok Sabha poll in 2004 was also no better (Ghosh 2005).

(v) The lawlessness in West Bengal has to be seen to be believed. Any party can call a *bandh* any day. Even the government of West Bengal sponsors *bandhs*. Then there are blockades of roads on any flimsy ground at any time, apart from Puja pandals in the midst of streets. A legendary failure of government is of course the unauthorised occupation of footpaths by hawkers. A number of times the government attempted to free the footpaths in Calcutta but could not. In fact, the government encourages lawlessness, directly or indirectly. Recently, even the High Court order banning *bandh* was violated and the government looked the other way (The Telegraph 2004).

(vi) The work culture in West Bengal had always been poor, but the CPM has made it scandalous. In the Secretariat, although the working hours are from 10.30 a.m. to 5.30 P.M., it has been found that more than half of the workers come after 10.45. Many do not attend office before 12 noon. It is reported that generally an employee works for one-and-half to two hours daily. Number of holidays are also too many in West Bengal. The state government employees can avail of at least 171 days of leave in a single year, if he avails all the paid leaves. Otherwise also it is 104 days, including the weekend (Statesman 2001a, 2001b).

We may conclude the section on West Bengal by giving some idea about the personality of the preceding chief minister Jyoti Basu, the CPM's topmost leader for 23 years. Even after remaining chief minister for so many years and becoming an octogenarian, he found it difficult to leave the post. In the last three years, he expressed his desire to resign many times but could take the decision finally only on 27 October, 2000 (Statesman 2000c). And after resigning also he continued to enjoy most of the privileges he used to get as chief minister. And what was his achievement all these years? The constituency which returned him every time since 1977, Satgachhia in South 24-Parganas—less than 25 km from Calcutta—is yet to have electricity for many of its villages. (Statesman 2000d). Basu also indulged in corrupt practices. Recently, the Supreme Court, in a scathing judgment, cancelled the allotment of a plot by him to Justice B P Banerjee in 1987 (The Telegraph 2004a).

If this is the model of a top communist leader in West Bengal, it is too much to expect any noticeable improvement in the living condition of the poor. If they had the slightest desire to improve the situation, much could be done despite the existence of a bourgeoisie party at the Centre. In fact, non-communist parties have performed much better in a number of states.

Orissa

Orissa is a relatively resource-rich state. It comprises of 4.74 per cent of India's landmass but has a population share of only 3.57 per cent, as per the 2001 census. The density of population per sq km came to 236 this year as against the national average of 312. Orissa has good mineral resources and there is also an abundance of water resource. The economic development of the state was, however, very poor, as will be evident from the analysis below.

Trend in Income and Employment

Orissa's growth in income was very poor. Over a long period of nearly four decades, between 1958-59 and 1995-96, the per capita income had risen only 7.6 times, from Rs. 216 to Rs. 1,634; and the NSDP 15.6 times, from Rs. 359 crore to Rs. 5,623 crore. In the last 16 years, beginning from 1980-81, the growth (at constant prices) in the former was a mere 24.4 per cent and in the latter 63.4

per cent (GOR 1971, 1985, 1997, 2000). The relative position of Orissa among the states was very gloomy, as may be seen from Table2.1. In 1994-97, its per capita income came to only 47.7 per cent of the national average. In the all-India total of NSDP, Orissa's share had declined from 3.11 per cent in1980-81 to 2.29 per cent in 1995-96[2]. In recent years, there has been some improvement. During 1998-01, the per capita income averaged Rs. 10,438 and constituted 59.4 per cent of the national average (CMIE 2004).

The sectoral diversification of income was substantial over the years. The contribution of primary sector to the NSDP, which was around 70 per cent till mid-seventies, showed a significant fall since early eighties and stood at 44.9 per cent during 1993-96. The share of secondary sector was nearly trebled over the period, rising from 7.1 per cent during 1958-61 to 14.4 during 1980-83 and 19.3 per cent in 1993-96. In the secondary sector, however, the contribution of manufacturing industries declined greatly, from as much as 92.2 per cent in 1958–61 to 65.4 per cent in 1989-92 (GOR 1971, 1985, 1997, 2000).The trend is similar in recent years also. In 2000-01, the contribution of agriculture etc declined to 31.3 per cent and for industry it rose to 28.8 per cent; In the latter, however, the share of manufacturing stood at only 44.5 per cent. The tertiary sector also raised its share somewhat, rising from 37.4 per cent in 1993-96 to 38.3 in 1998-01. In the tertiary sector, the most important contributor in recent years was community services etc, followed by trade, hotel etc. In 2000-01, they provided respectively 38.3 and 22.8 per cent. At the national level, the contribution by both agriculture and industry was lower, being respectively 24.9 and 26.6 per cent in 2000-01, but for the tertiary sector it was much higher, at 48.5 per cent (CMIE 2004).

In the provision of employment, agriculture continued to have the overwhelming proportion. In 1991, the primary sector contributed 75.8 per cent of total, a mere 6.5 point fall over 1961. The share of secondary sector increased greatly between 1961 and 1981 but in 1991 it declined and stood at only 7.5 per cent; at the national level, industry's share was much higher in the latest year (Table 2.2). In recent years, the situation appears to have improved somewhat. In 1999-00, 9.50 per cent of total workers were engaged in manufacturing, with that for rural areas at 8.31; at the national level, it was respectively 10.89 and 7.40 per cent (NSSO 2000a).

The work participation rate in Orissa declined noticeably over the years. It stood at only 37.53 per cent in 1991 as against 43.65 in 1961. The rate of unemployment continued to be quite high. In 1993-94, the daily status unemployment rate stood at 7.26 per cent, significantly higher than the national average. In recent years, the situation has improved somewhat, as may be seen from Table 2.1. However, it needs to be noted that the growth in workforce of main workers was (-)0.81per cent during 1991-01 as against positive 0.81 at the national level (2002a: I).

Extent of Poverty

With this level of growth in income and employment, naturally the absolute poverty remained high. The percentage of BPL population increased from 66.2 in 1973-74 to 70.1 per cent in 1977-78; both were the highest among the states. In the following years it declined but the relative position generally remained the same. In 1999-2000, the proportion in Orissa stood at 47.1 per cent as against the all-India average of 26.1 per cent (Table 2.3).

This is not a surprising situation. In 1995-96, 40 per cent of rural population in Orissa had an MPCE of less than Rs. 227.40, which was lower than in all but Bihar. Earlier, in 1987-88, 60.5 per cent of rural households had an MPCE of less than Rs 125. Even the average situation was very gloomy here. Rural Orissa had only Rs. 149.58 in 1996, which was the lowest among the states. The proportion going for food items was as much as 68.1 per cent, and thus very little was left for other items. The rural households' asset-holding was very poor. Percentage of households with asset value of less than Rs. 20,000 was as much as 40.4 in 1992 (Table 2.3).

The Social Sector

In the social sector Orissa's performance was very poor. In the area of education, the literacy rate was always below the national average, although it increased from 21.7 per cent in 1961 to 63.6 in 2001. For females, the rise was from 8.6 per cent to 51.0 per cent; the latter was higher than in only two of the states. At higher levels, the relative position was somewhat better. Those with middle school and above constituted 26.6 per cent in 1995-96, higher than in three of the states. In rural areas, the situation was much better, the proportion being higher than in four of the states and the difference with the national average much less (Table 2.4).

The health situation of the state was very poor, as may be inferred from the death rates and the life expectancy. The death rate was always significantly higher than the national average. In 1957 it stood at 19 per thousand in Orissa as against the national average of 11. After four decades, in 1997, these were respectively 10.9 and 8.9. On the IMR, the relative position worsened over the years. In 2001, it stood at 98 per thousand, which was not only much above the national average, among the selected states it was the highest; earlier, it was below three of the states. The proportion of malnourished children in Orissa was found to be as much as 54.4 per cent in 2002 as against 47.7 per cent at the national level. In this situation, the life expectancy remained very depressing; being much below the national average in 2001.

On two of the very basic facilities, availability of safe drinking water and sanitary facility, Orissa's position was extremely poor. In 1991, only 39 per cent of the households had drinking water facility, rising from 14.6 per cent a decade earlier. The tap water was available to only 9.8 per cent of households in

1998.The position of latrine facility is still worse. In 1998, only 11.0 per cent of the households had it, with the rural areas at 2.9 per cent.

The level of urbanisation in Orissa was very low. In 1991, only 13.4 per cent of the population was living in urban areas, rising from 6.3 in 1961; the latest was around half the national average. The infrastructural situation continued to be very poor. An index of social and economic infrastructure gave the state a value of only 81.0 in 1999, taking all-India at 100 (Table 2.4).

Inter District Disparity

The spatial distribution of development in Orissa was very uneven. On sectoral diversification of economic activities, some of the districts had even slipped backward. The dependence on primary sector rose to as much as 85 per cent of the main workers in Phulbani in 1991 from 78.7 in 1961. Similar increases were recorded by Kalahandi, Koraput, Ganjam, Bolangir and Dhenkanal. The share of secondary sector varied between 16.4 per cent in Sundargarh and the minimum at 4.1 in Koraput. There were four districts with less than 5 per cent of main workers engaged in this sector. The extent of disparity was lower in 1961. The work participation rate also varied greatly from district to district (Table 2.7). The variation in proportion of BPL population was, however, low here. In 1993-94, at the highest it was 45.24 per cent in Mayurbhanj and at the lowest 13.14 in Ganjam (Parikh Radha-Krishna 2002: 271).

In the social sector, the variation in literacy rate continued to be high. In 1991, it was between 63.8 per cent in Puri and the lowest at 22.7 in Koraput. For females, the variation was between 13.1 per cent in the same Koraput and 50.4 in Cuttack. There were five districts with female literacy at less than 25 per cent. As regards the IMR, although the data presented in the Table are not comparable over time, it is apparent that the disparity has considerably narrowed down. In 1991, the variation was between 81 in Mayurbhanj and 151 in Balasore-that is, the former 53.6 per cent of the latter. Two-and-half decades earlier, in 1965, it was between 26.2 in Sambalpur and 134.8 in Mayurbhanj—that is, the former 19.4 per cent of the latter.

On urbanisation, the extent of disparity has narrowed down considerably. In 1961, the proportion of population living in urban areas was at the highest 17.9 per cent in Sundargarh and the lowest at 1.2 per cent in Phulbani, that is, the former around 15 times the latter. After thee decades, in 1991,the highest was 33.4 per cent and the lowest at 5.9, in the same districts. Some of the districts like Bolangir, Ganjam and Balasore had recorded a very low growth in urbanization (Table 2.7). Despite this, probably the extent of disparity on urbanization in Orissa is much less than in many other states.

In an important area like village electrification–essential for industrial progress–the inter-district variation was very high. Till March 1999, percentage of villages electrified stood at only 33.95 in Deogarh and less than 50 in five districts as against more than 90 in eight districts.

Behind this depressing situation of development in Orissa, no doubt governmental inefficiency and corruption were primarily responsible. But certain natural disadvantages also played an important part. Natural calamities have become synonymous with the state. Cyclones and droughts are almost an annual phenomenon; if it is not cyclone, it is drought. Between 1972 and 1981, a total of 15.18 million people were involved in different types of natural disasters. In six of these years, the number affected crossed a million, with the highest at 6.32 million in 1979. Value of property lost and damaged in the decade totalled Rs. 144.52 crore, with the amount exceeding Rs. 30 crore in each of 1979 and 1980 (GOR 1985 : 502). In recent times, the super-cyclone of October 29, 1999 damaged as many as 1.961 million houses; over 8,000 families were rendered homeless. The official death toll for Jagatsinghpur alone was 6,905 (Statesman 2000e, 2000f). Drought is an annual scourge in the districts of Kalahandi, Koraput and Bolangir. In 1998, 3,000 lives were lost in the heat wave (Statesman 2000g).

On the level of efficiency of the government, we give just one example here. Six months after the super cyclone, it was found that many families were yet to receive the ex-gratia payment of Rs. 75,000 to each victim's next of kin. In Jagatsinghpur district, only 405 families had received compensation till April 2000. The power supply could be restored to the extent of only 15 per cent in this period, and none of the lift-irrigation could be made functional (Statesman 2000e). Inefficiency and corruption in the government are probably not something unexpected. The present Orissa assembly has a number of members with criminal cases pending against them in the courts.

Assam

In the North-eastern part of the country—which is covered by mountains and plateaus to the extent of 70 per cent—Assam is the largest state in terms of population. In 2001, with a population of 26.64 million, it accounted for 69 per cent of the region's total and 2.59 per cent of the country's. The area under the state has been greatly reduced over the years, and presently it is only 78,438 sq km, constituting 2.39 per cent of all-India total and 32.8 per cent of the region's. The economic growth of the state was hampered by a variety of factors, and its relative position worsened greatly over the years, as will be evident from the analysis below.

Trend in Income and Employment

The growth in Assam's NSDP was very low. Over a period of nearly four decades, between 1960-61 and 1996-97, It had risen only 42.7 times (at current prices), from Rs. 409 crore to Rs. 17,480 crore; at the national level, it was 84.1 times (BCCI 1971; GOI 2000a). Assam's share in the latter consequently declined form 3.16 per cent to 1.60 per cent. In recent years also there has not been any improvement. During the Eighth and Ninth plan, the state's domestic product had risen at an annual rate of only 2.8 and 2.1 per cent respectively, as against 6.7 and 5.4 per cent for all-India (2002a: 41).

The per capita income of the state had increased by only 362 per cent over the period of 37 years; at the national level it was 866 per cent. Assam's per capita came to only 49.7 per cent of all-India's in 1994-97, declining from 103.8 per cent in 1960-63 (Table 2.1). In recent years, there has been some improvement; with a rise to Rs. 10,936 during 1998–01, it became 62.3 per cent of the latter's (CMIE 2004).

The sectoral diversification of economic activities was very low in Assam. Nearly two-and-half decades after economic planning began, during 1972-75 (at 1948-49 prices), the primary sector contributed as much as 50.6 per cent, with the share of agriculture at 46.3 per cent; the secondary sector accounted for 19.3 per cent, and the balance came from the tertiary sector. In the secondary sector, the share of manufacturing was 12.6 per cent; and in the tertiary sector, transport etc provided 13.0 per cent and government services 10.8 per cent (GOA 1979). After another nearly three decades also the diversification was not appreciable. During 1998–01, the share of agriculture etc declined to 38.0 per cent, and for industry and services it increased to 22.2 per cent and 39.7 per cent, respectively; at the national level, for the first two it was 26.3 per cent each and for services at 47.4 per cent in the same period. In the secondary sector, the contribution of manufacturing was 15.1 per cent, similar to that at the national level. In the services sector, community and personal services provided 17.0 per cent, followed by trade, hotel etc at 12.1 per cent; at the national level, the former was lower and the latter higher (CMIE 2004).

In terms of employment also the diversification was far from satisfactory. In the total of main workers, the share of primary sector stood at as much as 74 per cent in 1991, nearly 7 points higher than the national average; three decades earlier, in 1961, the disparity was lower. The share of secondary sector stood at only 5.56 per cent in the latest year, less than half that at the national level (Table 2.2). In recent years also the situation continued to be depressing. In 1999-00, only 4.55 per cent of total workers were engaged in manufacturing here as against the all-India average of 10.89 per cent (NSSO 2000a).

The employment situation in Assam deteriorated sharply over the years. The daily status unemployment rate increased from 1.8 per cent in 1977-78 to 7.96 per cent in 1993-94 and presently also it is higher than the national average. Particularly worrisome is the urban unemployment rate. The CDS rate in 1999-00 was as much as 11.90 per cent as against 7.70 at the national level. No other state had recorded such a sharp rise. The trend in work participation rate was also disappointing. In 1999-00, it was 31.9 per cent as against 37.0 at the national level (Table 2.1 and NSSO 2002).

Trend in Poverty

As the economic situation deteriorated, Assam's position on absolute poverty also worsened. Till 1987-88, the proportion of BPL population was less than the national average, but the following two surveys found it to be significantly higher. In 1999-00, it stood at 36.1 per cent, declining from 40.86 in

Table 2.7: District-wise Disparity in Orissa's Development

Districts	*Percentage of main Workers in Primary Sector*		*Secondary Sector*		*Work participation rate*	*Literacy*		*IMR*[c]		*% of urban Population*	
	1961	*1991*	*1961*	*1991*	*1991*	*1961a*	*1991b*	*1965*	*1991*	*1961*	*1991*
Sambalpur	73.8	74.8	11.1	10.6	43.4	22.9 (8.6)*	494 (33.6)*	26.2	109	7.6	17.2
Sundargarh	67.9	61.6	12.7	16.4	39.4	19.7 (8.0)	530 (39.6)	35.1	87	17.9	33.4
Keonjhar	83.1	80.8	7.8	5.9	38.8	17.7 (5.9)	44.7 (30.0)	47.9	104	4.3	12.5
Mayurbhanj	84.7	81.7	7.7	7.3	45.8	14.2 (4.5)	37.9 (23.7)	134.8	81	2.4	6.2
Balasore	80.6	78.3	5.3	4.6	28.4	29.5 (12.7)	58.8 (44.6)	29.5	151	6.5	9.4
Cuttak	65.7	66.4	12.5	8.8	27.5	29.8 (14.0)	63.3 (50.4)	83.0	114	6.8	12.3
Dhenkanal	73.8	75.2	10.9	9.4	35.6	23.5 (7.9)	53.2 (37.3)	94.2	106	4.6	9.9
Phulbani	78.7	85.0	6.0	4.4	47.3	17.7 (4.3)	38.6 (20.3)	48.8	131	1.2	5.9
Bolangir	78.4	81.9	8.5	6.7	41.7	14.6 (4.2)	39.7 (21.9)	106.1	104	4.6	9.6
Kalahandi	80.4	85.6	6.2	4.5	45.2	11.1 (2.7)	30.0 (14.6)	105.4	112	2.8	6.5
Koraput	80.4	85.0	4.4	4.1	49.0	8.3 (3.0)	22.7 (13.1)	89.4	108	5.1	11.2
Ganjam	70.7	77.5	8.7	6.3	41.4	21.3 (8.2)	44.3 (28.1)	79.5	104	8.3	14.9
Puri	71.8	65.0	10.1	8.6	30.2	29.5 (13.3)	63.8 (49.9)	67.0	106	7.1	19.7
Orissa	75.1	75.8	8.9	7.5	37.5	21.7 (8.6)	49.1 (34.7)	71.9	108	6.3	13.4

*Notes: a: based on total population; b: based on population aged 7 years and above; c: the data for 1965 are based on actual death per thousand live births, and those of 1991 are probability of a new born child dying before age one; *: in brackets are female literacy rate.*

Source: GOR 1971; GOI 1996, 1965a; Rajan et al 1998.

1993-94; at the national level, it was respectively 26.1 and 36.0 per cent. The rural-urban disparity increased over the years as the rural proportion had a very small decline. Between 1983 and 1999-00, the latter had declined by only 2.56 points as against by 4.4 points for the total BPL population. In the latest year, rural Assam had 40.0 per cent as against 27.1 for rural India (Table 2.3).

The level of consumption expenditure in Assam was, however, relatively high. In 1999-00, the proportion of rural population in the MPCE range of Rs. 255–775 stood at 85.4 per cent as against 79.8 per cent at the national level (NSSO 2001). Earlier the situation was still better. In 1987-88, percentage of rural households with MPCE of less than Rs. 125 was only 37.3 here as against 46.4 at the national level (Table 2.3). This higher level of MPCE is, however, mainly due to higher prices of consumer goods in Assam. The proportion of expenditure on food items was very high. In 1996 it stood at 72.3 per cent in rural Assam as against 63.2 per cent at the national level.

The extent of poverty is reflected also in the quantum of asset-holding by households. In 1992, percentage of rural households with asset value of less than Rs. 20,000 was 29.7 here, higher than the national average (ibid.).

The Social Sector

In the social sector also Assam's performance was not good. In the area of education, on literacy rate, the state's position worsened considerably over the years. In 1961, it was higher than the national average by 3.4 percentage-points but by 2001 it was lower by 1.1 points. On female literacy, however, Assam's position was considerably better. It continued to be higher than the national average (Table 2.4). At higher levels, the situation was considerably better. In 1995-96, those with middle school and above constituted 36.0 per cent here as against 32.0 at the national level. For rural areas, the difference was still higher, being respectively 32.8 and 23.7 per cent. The improvement, however, came only in recent years. In 1987-88, only 17.1 per cent of rural men were having this level of education and for women at 11.6 per cent (GOI 2000).

On the health situation, Assam presents a very gloomy picture. The death rate which was less than half the national average in 1957, being at 4.7 and 11.0 respectively, rose to 9.9 and 8.9 in 1997. The IMR also continued to be much higher than the national average. The life expectancy at birth was very low. In 2001, for males it was 59.0 and for females 60.9 years; both were much below the national average and lowest among the eastern states. The birth rate which has an important bearing on the health situation, continued to be relatively high–always higher than the national average (Table 2.4).

The availability of drinking water facility was extremely low here. In 1991, only 45.9 per cent of the households had it as against the national average of 62.3. The tap water facility was there with only 10.0 per cent of the households in 1998 compared with 36.3 per cent for all-India. The living condition was also very poor. Only 2.2 per cent of the households had *pucca* house in 1992-93 compared with 23.7 at the national level; among the eastern states, it was the lowest. The latrine facility was, however, very good here. The consumption of electricity was extremely low in Assam. The per capita level came to only 95.5 kWh in 1999-00, less than a third of the national average (Table 2.4).

On urbanisation, the progress was extremely low in Assam. In 1991, only 11.1 per cent of the population was living in urban areas, which was less than half the national level and lowest among the eastern states. Over a period of three decades, the increase was by a mere 3.4 points here compared with 8.1 at the national level (Table 2.4). The infrastructural situation of the state was very poor. An index of social and economic infrastructure gave Assam only 81 in 1999, taking all-India at 100. Assam's level was the lowest among the eastern states (ibid.).

In this situation, it is no surprise that Assam presently has the second lowest human development index among the states, next to Bihar. In 2001, it got 0.386 as against 0.472 for all-India, and the rank at 14th; two decades earlier, in 1981, its rank was tenth (Table 2.3).

Inter-District Disparity

The district-wise variation in development was also not small in Assam. In the area of economic diversification, the proportion of main workers engaged in the secondary sector in 1991 varied between the highest of 11.9 per cent in Kamrup and the lowest at 2.2 in Dhemaji, that is, the former a little more than five times the latter (Table 2.8). Two decades earlier, in 1971, the proportions in these two districts were respectively 9.97 per cent and 2.11 per cent. The primary sector's share in Dhemaji had a nominal fall over the years—from 86.7 per cent to 85.7.

The variation in proportion of BPL population was very high here. In 1993-94, at the highest it was 85.29 per cent in Nalbari as against the lowest of 11.45 in Tinsukia. There were five districts—Dibrugarh, Sibsagar, Jorhat and Kamrup, apart from Tinsukia–with BPL population at below 25 per cent whereas three—Morigaon, Kokrajhar, in addition to Nalbari—had above 75 per cent (Parikh and Radha Krishna 2002 : 269).

In the social sector, on literacy rate, the disparity was not high. In 1991, it varied between the highest of 65.5 per cent in Jorhat and the lowest at 38.3 in Dhubri. In 1971, it was between 19.2 per cent in Karbi-Anglong and 39.1 in Sibsagar. The male-female disparity was, however, very wide in some of the districts (Table 2.8). On the health situation, the variation was much wider. The probability of a child dying before reaching age 5 was as much as 160 per thousand in Dhubri in 1991 as against only 71 in Jorhat. On infant mortality—that is, the probability of dying before age one–the highest was 112 in Dhubri and the lowest 46 in Jorhat against the state average of 85 in this year. The rural-urban disparity was very wide in some of the districts.

On urbanisation, the disparity appears to have increased over the years. In 1971, the proportion living in urban areas varied between the highest of 21.2 per cent in Kamrup and the lowest at 2.3 in Nalbari; there were four districts with less than 5 per cent. After two decades, in 1991, the highest was 32.8 per cent in the same Kamrup and the lowest at 1.9 in Dhemaji—that is, the former 17 times the later, as against only 9 times earlier. There are five districts that showed a fall in the proportion (Table 2.8). This level of disparity can be explained only partly by the change in boundaries of the districts.

Behind the low level of performance in Assam many factors have operated. Although basically it is the quality of human resource available that is to be blamed, certain objective factors also played an important role. Remoteness from the heartland of the country and consequent high transportation cost was an important factor. The demographic pressure following from the inflow of immigrants from East Pakistan/Bangladesh was another big problem. The density of population had risen fast in some of the districts. As against the state's growth of 53.8 per cent between 1971 and 1991, N.C.Hills had 93.7 per cent, Lakhimpur 93.0 per cent and Darrang 88.4 per cent (ibid.).

The heavy influx from Bangladesh ultimately gave birth to the united Liberation Front of Assam and created a disturbed situation in the state. The demand for detection and expulsion of illegal migrants led to the passing of the Illegal Migrants Determination by Tribunal Act of 1983, but it could not solve the problem. The Act made it more difficult to expel the immigrants, and this raised the level of terrorist activities in the state (Statesman 2000f; Lama 2002). The dissatisfaction of the Bodo people with their situation also created problems—the demand for Bodoland, and creation of the National Democratic Front of Bodoland and the Bodoland Liberation Tigers. The Bodo Accord of 1993—under which the Bodoland Autonomous Council was created—could not solve the problem. The BLT is now waging an armed struggle for a separate state for the Bodos.[3]

The Small-states

The seven small-states of the eastern region have a total population of 12.397 million as per the 2001 census, constituting 1.21 per cent of the country's total. They together do not have even half of Assam's population. The total of area under them is, however, as much as 183,741 sq km, which is 5.59 per cent of all-India total; in relation to Assam, the area is nearly two-and-half times.

The largest among the small-states in terms of population is Tripura, followed by Manipur, Meghalaya, Nagaland, Arunachal Pradesh, Mizoram and Sikkim, in this order. In terms of area, however, the largest is Arunachal—alone accounting for 46 per cent of the total. At a great distance, and of nearly equal size, are Meghalaya, Manipur and Mizoram. Below we give a brief look into the performance of each of these states over the years.

Tripura

Tripura has a population of 3191 million as per the 2001 census, with the area at 10,486 sq km–lower than in all but Sikkim. It is a predominantly hilly area with the major portion of land under forest. Even the plain land is broken by many low hills and *tillas* of 30 to 60 metres in elevation. The density of population in Tripura was 304 in 2001, which is many times higher than in any of the small-states. It became a state only in 1972.

A peculiar feature of Tripura is that, due to heavy influx of people from the erstwhile East Bengal the indigenous people have become minority in their own land. The scheduled tribes constituted only 30.9 per cent of total population in 1991. As the immigration put a severe strain on the living condition of the local people, gradually ethnic violence and insurgency problems took a menacing form and hampered development activities.

Trend in Income and Poverty

Tripura had a very low growth in income. Over a period of nearly two decades, the net SDP had risen only 6.4 times in current prices, from Rs 264 crore in 1980-81 to Rs 1.703 crore in 1996-97. This was the lowest growth among the small-states. Tripura's share in all-India total declined from 0.24 per cent to 0.16 per cent over the period. The per capita income had a still lower growth, only 4.2 times—from Rs. 1,307 in 1980-81 to Rs. 5,432 in 1996-97. At constant prices, it was merely a 59.7 per cent rise, from the annual average of Rs. 1,298 in 1980-83 to Rs 2,073 in 1994-97. In relation to the national average, Tripura's per capita declined from 70.9 per cent to 63.3 per cent over the period, as the former had registered a 78.7 per cent rise (Table 2.9). In the last few years, the relative position appears to have improved considerably. In 2000-01, the gross SDP of the state stood at Rs. 5,270 crore and constituted 0.27 per cent of all-India total. The per capita income this year came to Rs. 16,510, which is 87.7 per cent of the latter's (CMIE 2004).

The diversification of economic activities was, however, better here. The share of real output from agriculture to SDP averaged 25.9 per cent during 1994-97 compared with 26.6 per cent in all-India. The proportion for manufacturing, however, stood at only 4.5 per cent, around a fifth of that at the national level. This was the position despite a compound annual growth of 8.0 per cent during 1991-92 to 1996-97; the base of manufacturing was extremely low here (RBI 1997, 1998).

In the last few years, some notable changes have come in diversification of activities. During 1998–01, the share of agriculture in the GDP rose to 30.0 per cent, higher than at the national level. The secondary sector provided 17.8 per cent but the contribution of manufacturing in it was only 2.96 per cent of the SDP; the lion's share came from construction, at 12.3 per cent. The services sector gained noticeably, providing an average of 52.3 percent–much higher than at the national level. In this sector, community services etc contributed as much as 27.5 per cent and trade, hotel etc 15.4 per cent (CMIE 2004).

With regard to sector-wise employment, recent years' data are not available. In 1991, the percentage of main workers engaged in the primary sector stood at 64.1 declining from 70.2 in 1981. The proportion in the secondary sector also showed a decline, from 7.4 per cent to 6.4; at the national level, it was much higher in both the years (Table 2.9).

The work participation rate in Tripura was the lowest among the small-states, and also much below the national average. In 1991, Tripura had only 31.1 per cent as against more than 40 in each of the small-states (Table 2.9). The level of unemployment was high here. In 1993-94, the daily status unemployment rate stood at 5.43 per cent, highest among the small-states. Earlier also the situation was similar (Table 2.10). In recent years also the situation has not shown any improvement. In 1999-00, the labour force participation rate on daily status basis was only 30.0 per cent here, which was not only below the national average, among the small-states it was the lowest (NSS 2002).

The poverty situation of the state worsened noticeably in recent years. Till 1987-88, it was substantially below the national average, but from early nineties became much higher. In 1999-00, the percentage of BPL population stood at 34.44 here compared with 26.10 at the national level; in 1987-88, these were respectively 35.23 per cent and 38.86 per cent. Among the small-states, Tripura's latest proportion is higher than in all but one. The level of MPCE is, however, relatively high here, and this is mainly due to high prices of all consumer goods (Table 2.10). It may be noted that, in the North-east, the prices of essential commodities are invariably 35-40 per cent higher than in the rest of the country. (Lama 2002b).

The average earning strength of rural labour households in Tripura was always very low. In 1993-94 it stood at 1.48, lowest among the small-states. In terms of asset-holding also the state's position was very poor. The average value of asset per rural household came to only Rs 53,306 in 1992; at the national level, it was double this figure. The proportion with assets of less than Rs. 20,000 was as much as 37.9 per cent, highest among the small-states, and 11 points more than the national average (Table 2.10).

The Social Sector

In the social sector, the educational scenario was relatively good. The literacy rate was always higher than the national average, and among the small-states it became the second highest in 2001. The female literacy was also in a similar position. At higher levels, however, the situation was not good. In 1995-96, those with middle school and above constituted 34.3 per cent, which was lower than in three of the states; and on the secondary and above, it was only 13.8 per cent, much below the national average (Table 2.11).

Table 2.8: District-Wise Disparity in Selected Indicators of Development in Assam

Districts	% of Main Workers in (1991)		Literacy Rate (%)		Child Mortality		% of Urban Population		Density per Sq Km		
	Primary Sector	Secondary Sector	1971	1991[a]	Total	Rural	1971	1991	1971	1991	%rise
Dhubri	75.9	5.9	20.0 (11.3)[b]	38.3 (28.7)[b]	160	166	11.0	12.2	310	470	51.6
Kokrajhar	84.0	2.9	21.3 (12.0)	40.6 (30.9)	97	92	3.5	6.3	150	256	70.7
Bongaigaon	75.0	4.6	—	49.1 (38.7)	153	147	—	9.1	—	322	—
Goalpara	75.2	4.9	25.3 (16.4)	46.8 (37.6)	129	133	8.1	7.8	233	366	57.1
Barpeta	76.3	5.3	23.3 (14.3)	43.2 (33.2)	137	140	7.1	7.0	294	427	45.2
Nalbari	71.7	6.4	27.5 (16.2)	56.0 (44.2)	114	117	2.3	2.3	346	450	30.1
Kamrup	45.6	11.9	34.1 (22.7)	65.0 (55.0)	94	113	21.2	32.8	256	460	79.7
Darrang	84.0	3.1	22.8 (14.3)	42.0 (32.5)	141	145	3.9	4.9	198	373	88.4
Sonitpur	77.8	4.0	25.3 (17.1)	48.1 (38.6)	103	105	7.9	7.3	172	268	55.8
Lakhimpur	80.5	3.3	29.6 (19.1)	59.0 (48.8)	135	136	6.4	6.5	171	330	93.0
Dhemaji	85.7	2.2	28.1 (15.4)	53.8 (41.1)	151	152	—	1.9	94	148	57.4
Marigaon	82.2	4.7		48.0 (39.2)	150	153	—	5.2	270	410	51.9
			28.9 (20.0*)								
Nagaon	74.4	5.6		54.7 (46.3)	116	121	9.5	10.9	315	476	51.1
Golaghat	81.1	3.9	33.2 (25.3)	58.5 (49.8)	89	92	5.3	5.9	152	236	55.3
Jorhat	69.5	6.3	37.0 (27.8)	65.5 (56.9)	71	71	13.3	15.3	226	306	35.4
Sibsagar	78.8	3.5	39.1 (30.2)	64.5 (56.1)	84	91	6.2	7.2	251	340	35.5
Dibrugarh	70.7	6.3		58.3 (48.9)	73	82	14.2	17.6	220	308	40.0
			30.5 (21.6)*								

(Table 2.8 Contd.)

Tinsukia	73.8	7.9		50.3 (40.0)	80	87	18.7	16.5	180	254	41.1
Karbi Anglang	85.0	3.5	19.2 (10.3)	45.6 (34.3)	106	106	2.7	106	37	64	73.0
N.C.Hills	64.3	6.3	27.2 (17.5)	57.8 (47.3)	88	102	6.8	22.9	16	31	93.7
Karimganj	69.0	7.5	29.8 (20.0)	54.7 (44.8)	143	145	10.0	7.3	316	457	44.6
Hailakandi	77.3	5.1	27.1 (15.9)	53.1 (41.0)	136	140	7.2	7.6	232	338	45.7
Cachar	69.4	5.9	32.4 (21.2)	59.2 (48.8)	119	124	6.7	9.8	218	321	47.2
Assam	74.0	5.6	28.1 (18.6)	52.9 (43.0)	117	115	8.8	11.1	186	286	53.8

*Notes: a: for population aged seven years and above; b: in brackets are female literacy rates; c: probability of a child dying before age 5; *: refer to the combined district.*

Sources: GOI 1996; GOA 1979; EPW 1998.

As regards the health condition of the people, from the data on death rates it does not appear good. Both the death rate and the IMR were the second highest among the small-states. In reducing birth rate, however, the state's performance was quite good. In 1997 it stood at only 18.3 per thousand population, declining from 27.3 in 1985. The latest is the second lowest among the small-states. The natural increase in population was also similarly placed. However, the growth in population was not low. In the last four decades (1951-91), the decennial growth was always much above the national average. Consequently, the density of population per sq km increased from 109 in 1961 to 263 in 1991 (Table 2.11).

On the provision of certain basic facilities Tripura's situation is very depressing. Particularly poor is the position of drinking water facility. The coverage of rural households stood at only 30.6 per cent in 1991, rising from 22.2 in 1981. The latest is only around half the national average. The coverage with tap water was, however, higher than at the national level. The provision of electricity was very low. In 1992-93, only 45.1 per cent of the households had electricity, which was the second lowest among the small-states. The per capita consumption of electricity stood at only 110 kwh in 1998-99, less than a third of all-India average. The living condition was so poor in Tripura that in 1992-93 only 3.1 per cent of the households had *pucca* house. The latrine facility was there with only 11.2 per cent of the households in 1998. The infrastructural situation as a whole was extremely poor. An index of social and economic infrastructure gave Tripura only 74.87 in 1999, taking India at 100. Proportion of population living in urban areas was extremely low; at 15.3 per cent in 1991, it was worse than in all but two of the states.

Although Tripura is a very small state, intra-state variation in development is not small. Out of the three districts in Tripura, the south district, which has the highest proportion of ST population, is the most backward. Here, in 1991, 76.4 per cent of the main workers were engaged in the primary sectors as against 55.1 in West Tripura; the secondary sector's share in South Tripura was only 3.6 per cent. The WPR here was 39.7 per cent compared with 55.2 in the west. The proportion of urban population in the two districts was respectively 5.9 per cent and 24.4 per cent (GOI 1996.).

With this pattern and pace of growth, it is probably not surprising that the extremists have raised their heads, and formed organisations like the Indigenous people's Front of Tripura, Tripura National Volunteers and the National Liberation Front of Tripura. Attacks by the NLFT ultras have become almost a day-to-day affair now (Statesman 2002 c), and it is affecting the state's development.

Manipur

Manipur has an area of 22,327 sq km, with the population in 2001 at 2.39 million. Physiographically the state is divided into three divisions: the Manipur

Hills, the Manipur Valley and the Barak basin. The hills cover an area of 20.513 sq km—that is 92 per cent of total. Manipur is the home of at least 30 ethnic groups, with Meitei constituting more than half. The state is endowed with a number of mineral resources like limestone, lignite, chromite, nickel and copper. There are also possibilities of getting petroleum and natural gas. The location of the state, however, stands in the way of easy utilisation of the resources. Manipur became a state in 1972.

Trend in Income and Poverty

Manipur's economic growth has been very poor in relation to the resources available. The NSDP here had increased only 7.8 times in current prices over the last 17 years, 1980-81 to 1996-97, from Rs. 200 crore to Rs. 1,571 crore. In the all-India total, its share declined from 0.18 per cent to 0.14 per cent. On per capita Income, the position was still worse. It stood at the annual average of only Rs. 2,018 during 1994-97, which was the second lowest among the small-states, and in relation to the national average, only 61.6 per cent. In early eighties, the relative position was significantly better, as may be seen from Table 2.9. In recent years, there has been some improvement. During 1998–01 the per capita income averaged Rs. 13,489, and constituted 76.8 per cent of all-India's (CMIE 2004).

Diversification of economic activities has been very low. In 1994-96, the contribution of real output from agriculture to SDP averaged 29.8 per cent compared with the all-India average of 27.5 per cent; from manufacturing, it was respectively 2.8 per cent and 21.0 per cent. In the last few years, the manufacturing activities made some significant improvement. During 1998–01, it constituted 8.5 per cent of the GDP, with the amount averaging Rs 258 crore. This proportion was, however, still only around half the national average. The share of agriculture remained more or less the same, while services gained. The latter contributed 46.6 per cent of the GDP in this period, with the share of community services etc rising to 29.4 per cent.

On the sectoral pattern of employment, recent years' data are not available. But in 1991, in the total of main workers the share of primary sector stood at as much as 70.0 per cent, higher than in four of the small-states. The proportion in secondary sector was 9.7 per cent, declining from 13.3 in 1981. However, among the small-states, it was still the second highest (Table 2.9).

A good feature about Manipur is that the WPR showed a noticeable growth over the years. It rose to 42.2 per cent in 1991 from 34.6 in 1971; the latest is, however, lower than in all but two of the small-states. In recent years, the situation appears to have worsened considerably. The daily status labour force participation rate (LFP) stood at only 33.2 per cent in 1999-00, which is below the national average and the second lowest among the small-states (NSSO 2002).

Table 2.9: Trend in Income, Consumption and the WPR in the Small-states

States	Per capita N S D P (Rs)[a]			% of main workers engaged in				M PC E (Rural) (Rs)		Work participation rate (%)	
	1980-83 (a.a.)	1994-97 (a.a.)	% increase	Primary sect. 1981	Primary sect. 1991	Secondary sect. 1981	Secondary sect. 1991	1987-88	1996	1971	1991
Tripura	1298 (70.9)	2073 (63.3)	59.7	70.2	64.1	7.4	6.4	186.98	223.03 (64.8)[e]	27.8	31.14
Manipur	1443 (78.5)	2018 (61.6)	39.8	69.6	70.0	13.3	9.7	182.54	202.14 (67.5)	34.6	42.18
Meghalaya	1367 (74.6)	1773 (54.2)	29.7	79.8	74.8	4.2	3.7	169.99	217.16 (—)	44.2	42.67
Nagaland	1553 (84.8)	2138[c] (—)	37.7	73.6	75.3	3.5	3.5	—	286.89 (65.0)	50.8	42.68
Arunachal	1692 (92.4)	3459 (105.7)	104.4	75.3	67.4	8.9	8.7	199.00	195.26 (---)	57.7	46.24
Mizoram	1381[b] (—)	10224[b] (—)	640.3	73.9	66.0	4.9	5.1	241.17	238.56 (61.2)	45.4	48.91
Sikkim	1644 (89.7)	—	—	65.1	68.4	12.2	11.1	156.81	196.11 (65.6)	—	41.51
All-India	1832 (100.0)	3274[d] (100.0)	865.8	69.4	67.4	13.0	12.1	157.66	177.77 (63.2)	32. 9	37.46

Notes: a: at constant 1980-81 prices; b: on current prices; c: average of 1991-94; d: based on 1993-94 prices; e: percentage of expenditure on food items.

Sources: GOI 2000, 2000a, 1993, 1963, 1981; NSSO 1993.

That the economic situation of the state is relatively good is evident from the proportion of BPL population. In 1999-00, it stood at only 28.54 per cent, which is lower than in all but Mizoram although higher than the national average. Earlier the relative position was still better, being below the national average also. The level of MPCE is relatively high in all the N-E states, being higher than the national average. For Manipur, in 1999, the proportion of rural households with less than Rs. 330 came to only 11.7 per cent, which is less than half the national average, and among the small-states lower than in three (Table 2.10).

The Social Sector

In the social sector, Manipur's performance was one of the best. The literacy rate here was always higher than the national average, although the relative position worsened over the years. In 1971, at 32.9 per cent, it was the second highest, next only to Mizoram. But by 1991 it went below three of the states, and presently also in this position. At higher levels, the situation is much better. Those with middle school and above constituted 43.4 per cent in 1995-96, lower than in Nagaland only; and for those with secondary and above it was 25.4 per cent, highest among the states.

The health situation also appears to be good. The IMR stood at only 30 in 1997, less than half the national average. The probability of dying before reaching age 5 was only 42 here in 1991, lowest among the small-states. The death rate was also low, as may be seen from Table 2.11. A serious problem in Manipur is, however, the spread of drug addiction and HIV infection. Between September 1986 and November 2001, 12,817 HIV positive cases were detected. Already 193 deaths because of AIDS have been officially reported (The Statesman 2002d).

The birth rate was relatively low and showed a noticeable fall over the years. In 1997 it stood at 19.7 per thousand—7.5 points below the national average and among the small-states higher than in two only. The natural increase in population was down to 13.8 in 1997 from 20.8 in 1985. The growth rate of population was, however, not low. In every decade since 1951 it was higher than the national average. The density per sq km had increased by 70.8 per cent between 1961 and 1991—more than two-and-half times the rate at the national level, although among the small-states it is the second lowest.

On the provision of certain basic facilities Manipur's position was not good. Particularly depressing was the situation of safe drinking water. In the rural areas, percentage of households covered by 1991 stood at only 33.7, far below the national average. The tap water facility was there with only 12.5 per cent of the households, the second lowest among the states. The housing facility was also poor. In 1992-93, only 4.9 per cent of the households had *pucca* house compared with nearly 5 times as much at the national level. The

Table 2.10: Trend in Selected Indicators of Poverty in the Small-states

States	*% of population below the the Poverty-line*					*% of rural hhs. with MPCE of less than Rs 140*	*Rs 330*	*MPCE for bottom 40% in rural areas*	*Daily status unemploy-ment (%)*		*% of hhs. with asset holding less than Rs. 20,000 (rural)*
	1973-4	*1983*	*1987-8*	*1993-4*	*1999-00*	*(1987-88)*	*(1999)*	*1995-96*	*1977-78*	*1993-94*	*1992*
Tripura	51.0	40.0	35.2	39.0	34.4	32.1	13.4	310.00	5.04	5.43	7.9 (53)[a]
Manipur	50.0	37.0	31.3	33.8	28.5	24.5	11.7	302.25	2.00	2.50	108 (91)
Meghalaya	50.2	38.8	33.9	37.9	33.9	41.7	2.8	377.80	0.41	0.62	22.7 (48)
Nagaland	50.9	39.2	34.4	37.9	32.7	nil	nil	453.00	1.03	2.93	3.9 (74)
Arunachal	51.9	40.5	36.2	39.3	33.5	40.8	14.2	279.00	0.35	1.39	21.0 (62)
Mizoram	50.3	36.0	27.5	25.7	19.5	6.3	0.5	363.85	—	0.74	—
Sikkim	50.9	39.7	36.1	41.4	36.5	43.5	18.6	274.50	—	0.96	12.7 (139)
All-India	54.9	44.5	38.9	36.0	26.1	56.2	27.9	253.83	8.18	6.03	27.0 (107)

Note: a: average value of asset per household in Rs thousand.

Source: GOI 2000, 2001; NSSO 1998a.

latrine facility was there with only 9.7 per cent of the households in 1998. As regards electricity, the per capita consumption came to 75 kwh in 1998-99, lowest among the states and around a fifth of the national average.

The overall infrastructural situation of the state was also not good. An index of social and economic infrastructure gave Manipur 75.4 in 1999, taking all-India as 100. However, the proportion of households with electricity was relatively good. On Urbanisation also the state made a good progress. Percentage of population living in urban areas increased from 13.2 in 1971 to 27.5 in 1991. The latest was the second highest among the states (Table 2.11).

Inter-District Disparity

Although inter-state Manipur's performance was quite good, intra-state there was wide disparity in development among the districts. Progress was largely concentrated in the Manipur valley area. Out of the eight districts, three—Imphal, Bishenpur and Thoubal—generally received better attention. To look into the situation on some of the parameters : The sectoral diversification of activities was very low in some of the districts. In 1991, in the total of main workers, the share of primary sector varied between the highest of 85.6 per cent in Senapati and the lowest at 45.5 in Imphal. The secondary sector accounted for less than 2 per cent of workers in four districts as against 19.3 in Imphal.

In the social sector, the literacy rate varied between the highest of 70.7 per cent in Imphal and the lowest at 46 in Senapati in 1991. The female literacy also similarly varied. In the health area, the IMR was 28 per thousand at the lowest in two districts and the highest at 46 in Senapati. As regards urbanisation, the urban population was heavily concentrated in three valley districts. Among the hill districts, three—Senapati, Tamenglong and Ukhrul—had virtually no urbanisation. The distribution of population among the districts was also very uneven. Imphal alone actuated for 38.7 per cent of the state's total in 1991. The density per sq km was less than 25 in three districts—Tamenglong, Chandel and Ukhrul—as against 579 in Imphal (GOI 1996).

The extreme variation on population density is to a large extent due to the lack of dispersed development, although the terrain condition was also an important factor. Recently, the Naga leaders complained of the exploitation of hill people by the Meiteis. It was stated that funds meant for Naga-inhabited districts were diverted to Imphal valley. There are also allegations of partiality on appointments, transfer and postings (Statesman 2001d: 2).

Manipur has also been affected by insurgency problems in recent years. Apart from the demand for inclusion of Naga inhabited areas into Nagaland, there is the People's Liberation Army seeking separation from India. In fact, the Indo-Myanmar border is the home to almost all militant organisations fighting secessionist wars in the north-east. The mountains in the bordering areas are virtually controlled by the different militant groups. The area is not small; the border runs for 358 km (Statesman 2002d).

Table 2.11: Trend in Selected Socio-Economic Indicators of Development in the Small-states

States		*Education Literacy Rate*		*Education Middle School & above*	*IMR*		*Death Rate*	
	1971	*1991*	*2001*	*1995-96*	*19 97*	*1985*	*1990*	*1997*
Tripura	31.0	60.4 (49.6)[a]	73.7 (65.4)[a]	34.3 (13.8)[b]	51 (101)[c]	9.9	7.1	6.8
Manipur	32.9	59.9 (47.6)	68.9 (59.7)	43.4 (25.4)	30 (42)	7.7	5.9	5.9
Meghalaya	29.5	49.1 (44.9)	63.3 (60.4)	29.0 (12.9)	54 (98)	12.7	7.8	8.8
Nagaland	27.4	61.6 (54.7)	67.1 (61.9)	45.4 (20.5)	16 (67)	6.3	4.1	4.8[d]
Arunachal	11.3	41.6 (29.7)	54.7 (44.2)	21.1 (12.0)	47 (139)	14.3	13.2	5.8
Mizoram	53.8	82.3 (78.6)	88.5 (86.1)	38.7 (10.9)	19 (70)	—	—	4.8
Sikkim	17.7	56.9 (46.7)	69.7 (61.5)	25.4 (12.1)	51 (84)	10.7	7.3	6.5
All-India	29.5	52.2 (39.3)	65.4 (54.2)	32.0 (17.6)	71 (96)	11.8	9.7	8.9

Birth Rate			*Natural Increase in population*		*decadal growth in pop. (%)*				
1985	*1990*	*1997*	*1985*	*1997*	*1951-61*	*1961-71*	*1971-81*	*1981-91*	*1991-01*
27.3	24.9	18.3	17.4	11.5	78.7	36.3	31.9	34.3	15.6
28.5	21.1	19.7	20.8	13.8	35.0	37.5	32.5	29.3	29.9
39.1	31.8	30.2	26.4	21.4	27.0	31.5	32.0	32.9	30.3
25.3	16.2	20.4[d]	19.0	15.6[d]	14.1	39.9	50.0	56.1	64.5
35.5	30.1	21.4	21.2	15.6	—	38.9	35.1	36.8	26.7
—	—	15.0	—	10.2	35.6	24.9	48.5	39.7	29.1
33.1	26.3	19.8	22.4	13.3	17.8	29.4	50.8	28.5	31.7
32.9	30.2	27.2	21.1	18.3	21.5	25.8	25.0	24.7	21.4

(Table 2.11 Contd.)

Density per Sq km		Drinking water facility (rural areas) % of households		% of households with (1992-93)		% of urban population		Index of social and economic infrastructure
1961	1991	1981	1991	electricity	pucca house	1971	1991	1999
109	263 (76.5)[e]	12.91	30.60 (32.4)*	45.1 (110)f	3.1 (88.8)#	10.4	15.3	74.87
35	82 (70.8)	22.17	33.72 (12.5)	62.1 (75)	4.9 (80.3)	13.2	27.5	75.39
34	79 (75.6)	14.26	26.82 (41.3)	42.6 (150)	3.9 (64.5	14.6	18.6	75.49
22	73 (135.5)	43.43	55.60 (67.4)	76.9 (81)	8.4 (93.3)	9.9	17.2	76.14
4	10 (66.7)	40.16	66.87 (60.2)	63.1 (87)	2.2 (74.2)	3.7	12.8	69.71
13	33 (120.0)	3.57	12.89 (2.4)	76.0 (114)	6.0 (97.1)	11.4	46.1	82.13
23	57 (96.6)	21.70	70.98 (84.1)	—(185)	—(91.5)	9.4	9.1	108.99
142	274 (27.4)	26.50	55.54 (23.2)	50.9 (360)	23.7 (31.6)	19.9	25.7	100.00

*Notes: a: refer to female literacy; b: those with secondary and above; c: probability of dying before reaching age 5, relate to 1991; d: relate to 1994;e: percentage increase over the period; f: per capita consumption of electricity in 1998-99 (in kwh); *: percentage of households with tap water in 1998; #: percentage of households having latrine facility in 1998.*

Sources: GOI 1993, 2000, 1999, 1999a, 2000b: 218, 2002; NSSO 1998b, 2000; IIPS 1995; Rajan et al 1998.

While the problems are formidable, the quality of political leadership available is abominable. To give just one example: Recently, in the Assembly election held in February 2002, of the 59 sitting candidates in contention, 46 were fighting under different banners. Some of them had switched sides as many as four times (Statesman 2002h). Administrative instability is also no less serious. Ninety per cent of Manipur's all-India service officers are on deputation and manipulate their return to Delhi (Harakia 2002).

The present situtation of Manipur is totally anarchic. Any organisation be it underground or civil can dictate to the state government. The state witnessed at least 100 *bandhs* in 2000 and it cost about Rs. 4.4 crore daily. (Sandham 2005). Recently, in June-August 2005, there was a 54-day of Manipur due to the blockade of NH-39 by the All Naga Students Association (Manipur). Extortion by militant outfits has also taken a serious form and many business units have threatened to close down (The statesman 2005a).[4]

Meghalaya

Meghalaya is almost equal in size to Manipur both in area and population. It was a part of Assam until 1972. The state is completely mountainous with an average elevation of 1,496 metres. It has a high hydroelectric and thermal power potential. Location-wise, among the North-Eastern states, it is in the best position, if Sikkim is excluded. The state is also relatively peaceful. The scheduled tribes constituted 85.5 per cent of the total population in 1991. We give a brief look into how the state progressed.

Trend in Income and Poverty

On the growth of SDP, Meghalaya's performance was the worst. Over a period of 17 years, the per capita income had risen only 29.7 per cent, and stood at Rs. 1,773 during 1994-97 (at constant prices). The latest is the lowest among the small-states, and in relation to all-India average only 54 per cent, declining from 75 per cent in 1980-83 (Table 2.9). In recent years, the situation appears to have improved considerably. During 1998–01, the state's per capita averaged Rs. 14,917 at current prices and constituted 84.9 per cent of the national average (CMIE 2004).

The diversification of economic activities was considerable in recent years. The contribution of agriculture to SDP declined from 39.5 per cent in 1980-83 to 29.6 in 1992-95 and 24.6 in 1998–01. But the share of manufacturing also declined, from 16.2 per cent to 4.6 and then to only 2.1 per cent over the period. The gainer was the tertiary sector, and its share rose to as much as 53.9 per cent during 1998–01. In the tertiary sector, community services etc provided 23.8 per cent of the SDP (RBI 1995, 1997, 1983; CMIE 2004). The distribution of workers also showed a similar pattern, as evident from Table 2.9.

The work participation rate was quite high here. In 1991 it stood at 42.67 per cent, declining from 44.2 in 1971. Both were much above the national average. The extent of Unemployment increased over the years but still it was the lowest among the states (Table 2.10). In recent years also the relative position was very good. The LFP rate in 1999-00 stood at 44.2 per cent on daily status basis, highest among the small-states and also much above the national average (NSSO 2002).

The position of absolute poverty, however, worsened noticeably over the years. In 1999-00, the proportion of BPL population here stood at 33.87 per cent, which was not only much above the national average, among the small-states also it was higher than in all but two. Till 1987-88, the state's position was much better (Table 2.10). The level of MPCE is high. The proportion with less than Rs. 330 was only 2.8 per cent in 1999. This is largely due to high cost of living.

The Social Sector

In the social sector also the state's position was not good. The literacy rate here continued to be below the national average, as evident from Table 2.11. In 2001, it stood at 63.3 per cent, which was lower than in all but Arunachal Pradesh; in 1971, the relative position was much better. At higher levels also Meghalaya's situation was poor. Those with middle school and above constituted only 29 per cent in 1995-96, lower than in all but two of the states, and also below the national average.

As regards the health situation, on the IMR and death rate the state's position was not good. The former was lower than the national average but among the small-states it was the highest. For children the situation was particularly depressing. The death rate was also similarly placed. The birth rate, which influences the health condition of the people, was very high in Meghalaya. In each of the three time-points considered, it was the highest among the states. The natural increase in population was naturally the highest. The density of population per sq km increased noticably but it remained the lowest among the three comparable states.

On the provision of certain basic facilities, Meghalaya's position was very depressing. Percentage of households with drinking water facility in rural areas stood at only 26.8 in 1991, which was less than half the all-India average; and among the small-states, it was the second lowest. The coverage by tap water was, however, relatively good. The housing facility was very poor. The proportion of households with latrine facility was the lowest here. The provision of electricity was also very poor. The overall infrastructural situation itself was not good. (Table 2.11)

Inter-District Disparity

Although Meghalaya is a small state with only five districts, the inter-district disparity in development is enormous. Economic diversification was negligible in three of the districts. In 1991, East Garo Hills had 89 per cent of the main workers engaged in the primary sector, while the secondary sector had a negligible 1.1 per cent. On the other hand, East Khasi Hills had 57.1 per cent and 6.5 per cent respectively.

In the social sector, the literacy rate was only 35.3 per cent in Jaintia Hills in 1991 compared with the highest of 60.0 per cent in East Khasi Hills. On female literacy, West Garo hills had 31.3 per cent in contrast to 57.0 in East Khasi. On child mortality also the situation was similar. The two districts had, respectively, 125 and 80 per thousand. The level of urbanisation varied greatly in Meghalaya. Percentage of urban population was as much as 34.7 in East Khasi as against less than 11 in the remaining districts—with the lowest at 6.4 in East Garo Hills. The variation in density of population was, however, not much here. The lowest was in West Khasi Hills, at 42 per sq km, and the highest at 128 in East Khasi.

It is apparent that the development is heavily concentrated in East Khasi Hill. Meghalaya was separated from Assam on the ground of it being neglected by the Assam government; now the Garos are also demanding separation from Meghalaya. The Achik National Volunteer Council of the Garos is at the forefront of this demand. Neglect of backward areas continues in our system of governance unless there are agitations and insurgencies.

Nagaland

Nagaland has an area of 16,579 sq km with the population at 1.9886 million in 2001.[5] The state is a mountainous territory lying between the Brahmaputra Valley of Assam and Myanmar. The population of Nagaland is entirely tribal. There are many tribes and sub-tribes among the Nagas with their own languages and cultural features. Nagaland became a state in December 1963. The area was disturbed for many years due to secessionist movement. The Nagas had rejected the constitution of India in 1951, and demonstrated it through the boycotts of the first two Indian general elections in 1952 and 1957. A section of Nagas still do not consider Nagaland a part of India and want sovereignty (Statesman 2001c: 10). They are also creating problems for Manipur by demanding the inclusion of Naga inhabited areas to Nagaland. Below we give a brief look into the nature of progress in Nagaland over the years.

Trend in Income and Poverty

Nagaland's performance in the growth of per capita Income deteriorated considerably in recent years. Between 1993-94 and 1998-99, it had risen by only 35.1 per cent at current prices, from Rs. 10,033 to 13,552 as against 85.6 per cent at the national level. Over the long period of nearly two decades, between 1980-81 and 1998-99, however, it was 10.0 times—the per capita in 1980-81 being Rs. 1,361—and 8.5 times, respectively. In the last three years, 1996–99, the state's per capita averaged Rs. 13,558 and constituted 92.8 per cent of the national average (CMIE 2004). The relative position among the small-states may be seen from Table 2.9.

The growth in the state's NSDP was much faster than in all-India. Over the period of two decades, it was 20.8 times–rising from Rs. 105 crore in 1980-81 to Rs. 2,184 crore in 1998-99–as against 12 times in the latter; the relative share rose to 0.15 per cent from 0.09 (GOI 2003a). The lower growth in per capita income is due to the rapid rise in population.

On diversification of economic activities, there was virtually no improvement for a long period. The proportion of main workers engaged in the primary sector increased from 73.6 per cent in 1981 to 75.3 per cent in 1991. The share of secondary sector was static at 3.5 per cent, and it was the lowest among the small-states. In recent years, however, there has been considerable improvement. During 1996-99, the secondary sector's share in the SDP averaged 17.9 per cent and for services at 54.7 per cent. In the former, however, the major portion came from construction; the contribution of manufacturing being only 4.9 per cent. In the services, community services etc provided 23.5 per cent and transport etc 13.7 per cent (CMIE 2004).

On certain other indicators also the trend was similar. The WPR had a sharp fall between 1971 and 1991, although it remained above the national average. The level of unemployment increased greatly. The daily status unemployment rate was nearly trebled between 1977-78 and 1993-94, and became the second highest among the states (Table 2.10). In recent years, the situation appears to have improved considerably. The daily status LFP rate in 1999-00 stood at 43.2 per cent, higher than in all but two of the N-E states (NSSO 2002).

The situation of absolute poverty, however, greatly worsened over the years. The proportion of BPL population in 1999-00 stood at as much as 32.7 per cent, much higher than the national average; till the end of eighties, it was below the latter's. And this was the situation, despite there being no rural households with an MPCE of below Rs. 330 in 1999. The cost of living is very high in Nagaland. The average MPCE in rural areas stood at Rs. 287 in 1996, which was the highest among the states. The position of asset-holding was also good here. The proportion of rural households with asset value of less than Rs. 20,000 was only 3.9 per cent, lowest among the small-states (Tables 2.9 and 2.10).

The Social Sector

In the social sector, Nagaland's position on the whole was very good. On literacy, the state had a remarkable progress. It reached 61.6 per cent in 1991, the second highest among the small-states and 9.4 points higher than the all-India average; in 1971, it was below that in all but two of the states. In the following decade the progress was low; reaching 67.1 per cent in 2001, which was only 1.7 points higher than the national average. At higher levels, the relative position was much better. Those with middle school and above constituted as much as 45.4 per cent, highest among the states; the proportion with secondary and above was the second highest (Table 2.11).

The health situation also appears to be very good. The IMR was very low here; being only 16 per thousand in 1997, less than a quarter of that at the national level and lowest among the small-states. The death rate was also the lowest here. The birth rate was not high, being always much below the national average. But the growth in population was very high; and the density per sq km had the highest rise. However, the latter was still lower than in three of the states.

On the provision of certain basic facilities, Nagaland's position was very good. Percentage of households with drinking water facility in rural areas stood at 55.6 in 1991, which was higher than in all but two of the states. The facility of tap water covered 67.4 per cent of the rural households in 1998, highest among the N-E states (NSSO 2000). The housing condition was also relatively good; and the latrine facility covered 93 per cent of the households. On the provision of electricity the state's position was the best. In 1992-93, 77 per cent of the households had electricity. An index of the overall infrastructural situation, however, gave Nagaland only 76.14 in 1999, taking all-India at 100. Even this was, however, higher than in all but two of the states (Table 2.11).

Inter-District Disparity

Intra-state disparity in development is no less here than in the other states. There are seven districts in Nagaland, of which two—Mon and Tuensang—are very backward. In economic diversification, three districts—Kohima, Wokha and Mokokchung—are well ahead of others. Kohima had only 60.5 per cent of main workers engaged in the primary sector in 1991 as against 88.4 per cent in Mon. The share of secondary sector in them was respectively 5.7 per cent and 1.0 per cent.

On literacy rate also the variation was not low. The highest was 77.8 per cent in Mokokchung as against only 36 per cent in Mon in 1991. The female literacy rate was respectively 74.9 and 29.1 per cent. The health indicators also varied similarly. The IMR was 67 in Tuengsang in contrast to only 34 in Mokokchung. On child morality, it was still wider, being respectively 86 and 39. The level of urbanisation was very low in some of the districts. As against 30.3 per cent in Kohima, three districts had less than 10 per cent.

As regards the population growth, in some of the districts there was virtually no efforts at controlling it. The annual growth rate was as much as 5.30 per cent in Tuengsang as against the lowest of 2.83 in Zunheboto. The variation in population density was, however, quite low in Nagaland. At the highest it was 98 per sq km in Mokokchung and the lowest at 50 in Phek.

Arunachal Pradesh

Arunachal is the most sparsely populated state in the country. With an area of 83,743 sq km, it had a population of only 1.091 million in 2001. The state is entirely mountainous except for some thin strips of flat land. Dense forests cover more than two-thirds of the territory. Hydel potential of the state is very high. Arunachal is strategically important, being surrounded by international border on three sides: Bhutan on the West, China in the north and Myanmar in the east. The state was a union territory for 15 years, until February 1987. Below we give a brief look into the nature of progress over the years.

Trend in Income and Poverty

Arunachal's performance in the growth of income was quite good. The NSDP of the state had increased 14 times between 1980-81 and 1998-99, from Rs. 98 crore to Rs. 1,369 crore, as against 12 times at the national level. The per capita income grew by 8.4 times in this period, from Rs. 1,571 to Rs. 13,129. The latest is higher than in all but two of the states (GOI 2003a).

On diversification of economic activities, the state made appreciable progress. Percentage of main workers engaged in the primary sector declined from 75.3 in 1981 to 67.4 in 1991. None of the small-states could bring such a reduction. The proportion engaged in the secondary sector stood at 8.7 per cent in 1991, which was higher than in all but two of the states. As regards contribution to the SDP, in 1995-97, the average for agriculture came to 29.1 per cent and for manufacturing 6.6 per cent; the latter was the highest among the small-states.

The level of work participation rate had the sharpest fall here, declining from 57.7 in 1971 to 46.2 per cent in 1991. Even the latest was, however, the second highest and far above the national average. The rate of unemployment increased greatly over the years. The daily status unemployment rate rose to 1.39 in 1993-94 from 0.35 in 1977-78 (Table 2.10). The situation appears to have deteriorated further. The LFP rate on daily status basis was only 31.4 per cent in 1999-00, which was not only below the national average, among the small-states it was lower than in all but Tripura (NSSO 2002).

It is probably because of this, the progress in reducing the absolute poverty was very low in the last decade. The proportion of BPL population declined from 51.9 per cent in 1973-74 to 36.2 in 1987-88 but in the following years it increased. In 1999-00 it stood at 33.5 per cent, which was much above the national average. The level of MPCE in Arunachal was very low in recent years. It stood at only Rs. 279 in 1995-96 for the bottom 40 per cent in rural areas, which was the second lowest among the states. In 1996, the average for rural areas came to Rs. 195, lowest among the states (Tables 2.9 and 2.10).

The Social Sector

In the social sector, on the whole, Arunachal's position was not bad. But in the critical area of education it was very depressing. The literacy rate rose to only 54.17 per cent in 2001, far below that in any other small state. Three decades earlier, in 1971, it was 11.3 per cent—around a third of the national average. At higher levels, those with middle school and above constituted only 21.1 per cent in 1995-96, lowest among the small-states (Table 2.11).

As regards the health indicators, the position of IMR was not bad. At 47 per thousand in 1997, it was much below the national average, and among the small-states lower than in three. The child mortality rate was, however, very high' being the highest among the states. The death rate was again quite low. In 1997, it stood at 5.8 per thousand, lower than in all but two of the states. This is a noticeable performance; in 1985 it stood at 14.3, highest among the states. The birth rate in Arunachal was quite high. At 21.4 in 1997, it was the second highest among the states. The natural increase in population was relatively high; in fact, the second highest in 1997. The decadal growth in population declined noticeably only in the last decade. The density of population continued to be extremely low here (Table 2.11).

On the provision of certain basic facilities, Arunachal's position was quite good. Percentage of households with drinking water facility stood at as much as 66.9 in rural areas in 1991, the second highest among the states. The coverage with tap water was 60.2 per cent in 1998. The housing condition was, however, very poor. Only 2.2 per cent of the households had pucca house. The provision of electricity was relatively good. In 1992-93, 63 per cent of the households had it, much above the national average. The per capita consumption was, however, very low. The infrastructural situation as a whole was very poor here. The index of social and economic infrastructure stood at only 69.7 in 1999; Arunachal's was the lowest position.

Inter-District Disparity

Arunachal has 11 districts, and there is wide disparity in development. The share of secondary sector in the main workers varied between the highest of 14.0 per cent in West Kameng and the lowest at 2.8 in Tawang in 1991. The proportion in primary sector was at the highest 79.1 per cent in East Kameng and the lowest at 50.2 in West Kameng. The variation in literacy rate was also quite high, particularly on female. In 1991, female literacy stood at only 14.0 in East Kameng as against 36.2 per cent in Lohit. As regards the IMR, it varied between 158 at the highest in East Kameng and at the lowest 61 in East Siang, with the state average at 83 (GOI 1996).

The disparity was highest with regard to urbanisation. There were four districts—Tawang, East Kameng, Upper Subansiri and Changlang—with virtually no urbanisation. On the other hand, lower Subansiri had as much as 25.5 per cent of the population living in urban areas. No other state in the region had such a wide disparity.

The development was not always related to the density of population. The lowest density was in Dibang valley—only 3 per sq km—but all the indicators were in a better position here. The density in Tawang was more than four times higher but it remained backward. One important point of difference between the two districts is that the ST population constituted as much as 78.6 per cent in the latter whereas in the former it was only 45.4 per cent. Generally, the districts with high proportion of ST population had low level of development (ibid.).

The state was known as an oasis of peace until the mid-nineties but it is no longer so. The utter lack of development in some of the districts has led to the demand for separation. The backward districts of Changlang and Tirap are demanding the Union Territory status. The Khaplang faction of the NSCN is quite active here. Extortions and intimidation are frequent now (Statesman 2002 Z 13:4).

Mizoram

Mizoram is also quite sparsely populated. It has an area of 21,081 sq km, nearly equal to Manipur, but the population is less than a million. The state is bordering Myanmar on the east and south and Bangladesh in the west. It is a land of hills, with an average height of 900 metres. After prolonged agitation, Mizoram became a Union territory in 1972 and a full-fledged state in February 1987. We give a brief look into the nature of progress over the years.

Trend in Income and Poverty

Among the North-Eastern states, Mizoram's performance is probably the best. The total of NSDP here increased 18-fold between 1980-81and 1998-99, from Rs. 62 crore to Rs. 1,139 crore at current prices. No other state, big or small, had such a rapid growth. The per capita income also had the highest growth. Over the same period, it increased by 10.5 times, from Rs. 1,289 to Rs. 13,479; the latest is the highest among the small-states (GOI 2003a).

On diversification of economic activities, Mizoram's achievement was substantial. The proportion of main workers engaged in the primary sector declined from 73.9 per cent in 1981 to 66.0 in 1991. The latest is not only lower than the national average, among the small-states it is the second lowest. The share of the secondary sector, however, remained very low, rising nominally from 4.9 to 5.1 per cent over the period. There were as many as four states with higher contribution.

The level of WPR in Mizoram is very high. It stood at 48.91 per cent in 1991, highest among the small-states and 11 points higher than the national average. The level of unemployment was very low. In 1993-94, the daily status unemployment rate stood at only 0.74 per cent, the second lowest among the states and less than a sixth of the national average. In recent years also the position was good. In 1999-00, the daily status LFP rate stood at 43.9 per cent, next only to Meghalaya (NSSO 2002).

All these were reflected in a sharp reduction in the extent of absolute poverty. The proportion of BPL population here stood at only 19.47 per cent in

1999-00, declining from 50.32 in 1973-74. The latest is not only the lowest among the small-states, it is also below the national average-the only state to achieve this (Table 2.10). The level of MPCE is high here, being the second highest in 1996, and the proportion going for food items was relatively low (Table 2.9).

The Social Sector

In the social sector, Mizoram has a very good position. The literacy rate here was always the highest among the small-states; and in the latest year, 2001, stood at 88.5 per cent, 23.1 points higher than the national average. At higher levels, however, the situation was not good. In 1995-96, those with middle school and above constituted only 38.7 per cent of the population, and those with secondary education and above at 10.9 per cent; the former was lower than in two of the states, and the latter the lowest (Table 2.11).

On the health indicators also Mizoram's position was not bad. The IMR in 1997 stood at only 19 per thousand, around a quarter of that at the national level. The probability of a child dying before reaching age 5 was, however, very high. At 113 in 1991, it was the second highest among the states. The death rate, birth rate, and the rate of natural increase in population were the lowest here.

The growth in population was, however, not low. The decadal rates were much higher than the national average in four of the decades. The density of population had increased by 120 per cent between 1961 and 1991, the second highest among the states. The increases were primarily due to the influx of Chakmas from Bangladesh.

The level of urbanisation and the infrastructural situation were quite good in Mizoram. In 1991, 46 per cent of the total population were living in urban areas, which was far above that in any other small state. As regards the infrastructural situation, the index of social and economic infrastructure stood at 82.13 in 1999, which was the second highest among the states. The darkest spot in Mizoram is, however, the provision of drinking water in rural areas. In 1991, the coverage was only 12.9 per cent of the households, incomparably below that in any other state (Table 2.11). The coverage by tap water was a negligible 2.4 per cent in 1998 (NSSO 2000).

Although Mizoram is a very small state and having only three districts, inter-district disparity in development is not small. The share of secondary sector in the total of main workers was only 1.8 per cent in Chhimtuipui in 1991 as against 6.2 per cent in Aizwal. The literacy rate was 59.1 and 88.1 per cent respectively, and the IMR (probability) at 73 and 50 per thousand. The urban population is heavily concentrated in Aizwal. The district acounting for 69.3 per cent of the states population in 1991, had 54.3 per cent urban. The rural-urban disparity is very high even in Aizwal; the IMR in rural areas was as much as 76 as against 30 in urban areas.

Sikkim

Sikkim is the smallest of the small-states, both in area and population. It has an area of only 7,096 sq km and the population at 0.54 million in 2001. The state is entirely mountainous and about a third of the land is covered with dense forests. Sikkim has international boundary on three sides—Tibet on the North, Nepal on the West and Bhutan in the East. It became a state of the Indian Union in April 1975, from a kingdom until then. We give a brief look to the nature of progress since the state's merger.

Trend in Income and Poverty

Sikkim had an NSDP of only Rs 702 crore in 1998-99, rising from Rs 49 crore in 1980-81, that is, a growth of 14.3 times, at current prices. The increase in per capita income was eight times in this period, from Rs. 1,571 to Rs. 13,158; they were respectively 96.4 per cent and 91.4 per cent of the national average. Among the small-states, the latest was the second highest, next only to Mizoram (GOI 2003a).

On diversification of economic activities, Sikkim's position was relatively good. In 1991, 11.1 per cent of the main workers were engaged in the secondary sector, which was the highest among the small-states. The WPR was, however, relatively low here. At 41.5 per cent in 1991, it was the second lowest. The level of unemployment was, however, not high, at least until recent years. In 1993-94, the daily status unemployment rate stood at only 0.96 per cent, lower than in all but two of the states, and in relation to all-India average it was less than a sixth (Table 2.10). In the last few years, the situation has deteriorated greatly. The LFP rate on daily status basis came to only 35.5 per cent in 1999-00, which was below the national average and lower than in three of the small-states.

The poverty situation of the state deteriorated greatly in recent years. There has been virtually no reduction in the proportion of BPL population in the last two decades. Till late eighties, Sikkim's proportion was below the national average, but in the following years it became noticeably higher. In 1999-00, at 36.5 per cent, it was 10.4 points higher than the national average (Table 2.10). The level of consumption expenditure, even for the general population, was very low here; and for the bottom 40 per cent of rural population it was the lowest among the small-states in 1995-96. This was the situation despite having a good position on the households' asset-holding (Table 2.10).

The Social Sector

In the social sector, Sikkim's performance was good in some of the areas. On literacy rate the progress was appreciable. The proportion literate became higher than the national average by 1991 and reached 69.7 per cent in 2001, which was higher than in all but two of the states. At higher levels, however, the position was not good, as evident from Table 2.10.

On the health indicators, the relative position was not good. The IMR in 1997 was the second highest among the states, although much below the national average. The child mortality rate was as much as 84 in 1991, higher than in three of the states. The death rate was also higher than in most of the states. The birth rate declined noticeably over the years, and stood at 19.8 in 1997, which was below the level in three of the states and much lower than the national average.

The rate of natural increase in population declined noticeably, and the latest was much below the national average. The growth in population was, however, quite high. The decadal rate was significantly higher than the national average in each of the last four decades. This growth was primarily due to immigration from the neighbouring countries. The density of population increased noticeably over the years.

On the provision of certain basic facilities Sikkim's position was quite good. The drinking water facility was the best here. In 1991, 71 per cent of the rural households had it, and the coverage by tap water reached 84.1 per cent in 1998. The latrine facility was there with 91.5 per cent of the households (NSSO 2000).The overall infrastructural situation was the best here. In 1999, the index for social and economic infrastructure stood at 109, taking all-India at 100; no other N-E state could cross the national average. The level of urbanisation was however, extremely low. In 1991, only 9.1 per cent of the state's population was living in urban areas. There was absolutely no increase in the proportion over the last two decades.

Although Sikkim is the smallest state, with only four districts, inter-district disparity in development is very high. Most of the activities are concentrated in the East district, with a population share of 43.8 per cent in 1991, and the West and South districts were largely neglected. In the West in particular, there was very little development. The share of secondary sector in the total of main workers came to only 3.8 per cent here as against 17.1 per cent in the East. The literacy rate in the two districts was respectively 45.6 and 65.1 per cent in 1991. The child mortality rate in the rural areas of the west district was estimated at 123 as against 73 in the East district. The proportion of population living in urban areas was less than 3 per cent in three of the districts as against 17.9 per cent in East district. The density of population per sq km came to only 7 in the North compared with 187 in the East district.

From the above analysis of the pattern of growth in the eastern region's small-states, the following broad conclusions may be arrived at:

First, the growth of per capita income in most of them has been very low, and the relative position on poverty has worsened considerably for each one in recent years. The worst situation on per capita income is in Tripura, and on poverty Sikkim. The diversification of economic activities is extremely low in most of the states. There are limitations in the way of rapid progress in this direction due to the nature of terrain and resource base, but with concerted efforts much more could be done.

Second, in the area of literacy, good progress has been made by most of them, excepting Arunachal and Meghalaya. Particularly noteworthy are the achievements in Mizoram and Tripura. On higher levels of education, excepting Manipur and Nagaland, all others have performed very badly. The health situation appears to be relatively good in most of the states, to the extent it can be inferred from the IMR and the death rate. On an essential requirement like drinking water facility, however, the majority of states present a depressing picture. The overall infrastructural situation is also very poor, except for Sikkim.

Third, the population growth is a big problem for each of the small-states, and this was to a large extent due to influx from other countries. The birth rate has declined substantially in most of the states. There is need for a strict regulation of influx from other areas, and also a stricter control over the birth rate; the latter is particularly necessary for Meghalaya. The density of population has risen fast in each of the states, and it should be under a close watch. It is for the good of the country as a whole that we do not destroy our forests.

Notes

1. The poverty-line is based on the minimum diet of 2,400 calories. The MPCE related to it were estimated at Rs. 57.68 1773-74 for Bihar, Rs 54.49 for West Benga Rs 46.87 in Orissa, Rs 49.82 in Assam and Rs 49.63 for all-India. For 1993-94, these were respectively Rs. 212.16, Rs 220.74 Rs 194.03, Rs. 232.05 and Rs 205.84 (GOI 2000)
2. Based on current prices; Orissas NSDP stood at Rs 21,463 crore in 1995-96 and at the national level at Rs 936,548 crore (GOI 200a).
3. Even the creation of a separate state for the two hill districts is, however, unlikely to bring peace. The age-old bond of brotherhood between the Karbi and Dimasa tribes has been broken recently by an unprecedented spell of mayhem (Statesman 2005c).
4. The extortion of government officials by militant groups has been going (below) on for many years now. Every month when salaries are disbursed, a percentage is deducted and paid to them. When this is not possible, the militants queue up at their homes (Rammohan 2002).
5. It may be noted here that the question of how many people actually live in Nagaland is a major and sensitive issue. According to senior government officials and researchers, the actual population is not more than 14 lakh. Population figures are inflated to garner more central funds (Statesman 2005d).

PART–II
THE ECONOMY OF BIHAR

3

Resource Mobilisation and Deployment

Resource mobilisation and its proper deployment is the most difficult task in any development effort. It requires taking unpleasant actions, and therefore, a strong government is needed. This is not possible in the sort of democracy that is practised in India. A ruling political party, whose attention is focused on getting votes for coming to power again by hook or crook, cannot afford to take stern measures in the given socio-economic situation.

It is necessary to elaborate a little on why maximum resource mobilisation is not possible under a multi-party system of democracy. Resources are not scarce in a developing economy; the manpower itself is a big resource. But its mobilisation requires compelling people to hard work. There is also the need for a reverse flow of quality resources from urban concentrations to rural areas, and of taxing heavily the richer section of population. Full utilisation of capacity, both of labour and capital, is not possible by a weak government, consisting of people utterly self-seeking.

The scope of this chapter is, however, limited to only mobilisation and deployment of monetary resources through the government budget and the banking system.

BUDGETARY RESOURCES

The overall budgetary position of the Bihar government has been very gloomy. The gross fiscal deficit reached the annual average of Rs 2559 crore in 2000-03, from Rs 1315 crore in 1988-91, Rs 188.4 crore in 1975-78 and Rs 112.8 crore in 1965-68. On annual basis, in the last ten years, the highest was Rs 4884 crore in 2000-01 and the lowest at Rs 1364 crore in 1996-97. The relative position of Bihar among the states was very depressing. Fiscal deficit as percentage to GSDP averaged 4.23 during 1996-99 which was higher than the average for all low income states, being 3.40 (CMIE 2004a; GOI 2000b).

This situation was primarily due to mismanagement of the revenue account. The revenue account was continuously in heavy deficit in each of the years since 1990-91. It reached the annual average of Rs 6052 crore in 2000-03 from Rs 610 crore in 1996-99 and Rs 901 crore in the preceding three years. The revenue deficit as percentage to GSDP stood at 2.27 here during 1996-99 as against 2.00 for all low-income states.

Why the situation was so gloomy? We look below into the resource mobilisation efforts of the government, and also the pattern of expenditure over the years.

Resource Mobilisation

The growth of budgetary receipts in Bihar was very low. Between 1965-68 and 1996-99 the aggregate of receipts had increased by only 38.2 times compared with 67.0 times for all-states. Among the selected nine states, Bihar's was the lowest growth. The per capita receipt came to only Rs. 1,056 in 1996-99 and constituted 43.3 per cent of the all-states' average. In 1975-78, at Rs. 122, it was 62.8 per cent (Table 3.1). The down-hill journey continued in the more recent years also. During 2000-03, Bihar's per capita was only Rs 1140 as against Rs 3861 for all-states, that is the former less than a third of the latter.

In the aggregate of receipts, the share of revenue receipts rose noticeably to 86.2 per cent in 1996-99 from 69.3 in 1975-78 and 50.8 per cent in 1965-68. The growth in collection was, however, relatively low, and the per capita level remained much below the all-states average. In 2000-03, it stood at only Rs 826 as against Rs.2533 in the latter. The situation in the earlier years may be seen from Table 3.1. Below we look briefly into the trend in composition of revenue and capital receipts.

Revenue Receipts

In the revenue receipts, the share of tax revenue was relatively high here. In 2000-03, it stood at 89.0 per cent, rising from 75.7 in 1995-98 and 67.1 per cent in 1965-68; at the level of all-states, the proportion in the latest period was 70.8 per cent. The growth in tax revenue was, however, very low, as may be seen from Table3.2; and consequently, the relative share in all-states total declined to 4.45 per cent in 2000-03 from 5.69 in 1995-98 and 6.91 in 1965-68.

As the proportion of tax revenue increased, naturally that of non-tax revenue (NTR) declined. During 1995-98, the NTR had contributed only 24.3 per cent here as against the all-states average of 30.3 per cent. The growth in it was only 44.4 times over the entire period of more than three decades compared with 57.7 times for all-states. The relative share declined to 4.2 per cent from 5.5 per cent. In recent years, there was further deterioration in the situation. During 2000-03, with the collection averaging Rs 996 crore, the share in all-states was down to 1.33 per cent.

Table 3.1: Bihar among the States on Resource Mobilisation (Rs. Crore)

States	*Revenue Receipts*			*Capital Receipts*		
	1975-78 (a.a)	*1996-99 (a.a.)*	*growth*[b]	*1975-78 (a.a.)*	*1996-99 (a.a.)*	*growth*[b]
Bihar	533.0 (69.3)[a]	8667.5 (86.2)[a]	16.3	236.1 (30.7)[a]	1392.5 (13.8)[a]	5.9
West Bengal	627.6 (72.3)	8880.5 (60.7)	14.1	240.9 (27.7)	5756.0 (39.3)	23.9
Orissa	324.0 (74.8)	4491.1 (62.9)	13.9	109.0 (25.2)	2652.6 (37.1)	24.3
Assam	230.8 (78.2)	4229.3 (87.6)	18.3	64.5 (21.8)	600.1 (12.4)	9.3
Madhya Pradesh	604.8 (79.3)	10872.4 (75.1)	18.0	157.5 (20.7)	3605.9 (24.9)	22.9
Uttar Pradesh	1073.7 (71.9)	16992.8 (64.5)	15.8	420.2 (28.1)	9343.1 (35.5)	22.2
Andhra Pradesh	730.6 (79.3)	13098.0 (70.9)	17.9	190.6 (20.7)	5377.8 (29.1)	28.2
Kerala	394.3 (77.1)	6820.5 (73.8)	17.3	116.8 (22.9)	2426.6 (26.2)	20.8
Maharashtra	1181.5 (77.7)	20436.3 (73.1)	17.3	339.0 (22.3)	7511.1 (26.9)	22.2
All-states	8968.6 (75.6)	166528.3 (72.5)	18.6	2891.7 (24.4)	63073.7 (27.5)	21.8

Total Receipts			*Per Capita Receipts*					
1975-78 (a.a.)	*1996-99 (a.a.)*	*growth*[b]	*Total*		*Revenue*		*Capital*	
			1975-78	*1996-99*	*1975-78*	*1996-99*	*1975-78*	*1996-99*
769.1	10060.0	13.1	122.27	1056.28	84.74	910.07	37.53	146.20
868.5	14636.5	16.9	175.35	1922.31	126.71	1166.34	48.64	755.98
433.0	7143.7	16.5	177.53	2043.98	132.84	1285.01	44.69	758.97
295.3	4829.5	16.4	172.00	1910.40	134.42	1672.98	37.56	237.42
762.3	14478.3	19.0	161.47	1904.79	128.11	1430.39	33.36	474.40
1493.9	26335.9	17.6	151.05	1638.82	108.56	1057.42	42.49	581.47
921.2	18475.8	20.1	189.86	2511.66	150.58	1780.59	39.28	733.07
511.1	9247.1	18.1	216.02	2939.32	166.65	2167.99	49.37	771.33
1520.5	27947.4	18.4	267.22	3166.13	207.64	2315.20	59.58	850.92
11860.3	229602.0	19.4	194.85	2442.00	147.34	1771.16	47.51	671.55

Notes: a: as percentage to total receipts; b : in multiplies;c: per capita receipts for 1975-78 are based on the population estimate for 1976, and those for 1996-99 on 1997.

Source: RBIFA 1978, 1979; CMIE 1996, 2001.

Composition of Tax Revenue

Although the tax revenue constituted a very high proportion of the state's total revenue its own collection (OTR) was very poor. The proportion of OTR in the total decreased from 65.4 per cent in 1965-68 to 53.5 in 1975-78 and then to 36.2 in 1995-98; at the level of all-states, it was as much as 67.4 per cent in the latest period. Among the selected states also Bihar's was the lowest proportion. The OTR of Bihar increased only 37 times over the entire period compared with 76 times for all-states (Table 3.2). The per capita OTR collection in 2000-03 averaged only Rs 238 here compared with Rs 1281 for all-states The state thus relied too heavily on tax transfer from the centre. Bihar's share in the aggregate of tax transfer from the Centre increased from 8.9 per cent in 1965-68 to 10.4 per cent in 1975-78 and 11.0 per cent in 1996-99.

The scope for larger collection by the state was however not small, as can be inferred from Table 3.3.The collection concentrated heavily on sales tax. In the total of OTR, its contribution rose to as much as 69.9 per cent in 1988-91, from 54.7 per cent in 1975-78; during 1996-99 however, it was at a lower level-being 66.8 per cent. For all-states, the average came to 60.5 per cent in the latest period, rising from around 40 per cent in mid-seventies. Among other taxes, state excise, stamps and registration fees and taxes on vehicles were important. The contribution from the first one dropped substantially over the years. During 1996-99 it provided 9.4 per cent of total, declining from 12.3 per cent in 1975-78; at the level of all the states, it provided 13.9 per cent in the latest period.

There are a number of taxes contributing a very small amount in Bihar. The collection from land revenue provided only 1.0 per cent in 1996-99, declining from 10.9 per cent in 1975-78. The latest is below the all-states' average, being 1.32 per cent. During 2000-03, however, there was some improvement. With the collection averaging Rs 35.3 crore, it was 1.35 per cent of the OTR, higher than the all-states average. Even this amount was the lowest among the eastern states. The duties on electricity provided 2.5 per cent in 1996-99 as against around 4 per cent in mid-seventies. There has also been a sharp drop in the share of entertainment tax. In 1996-99, it provided only 0.8 per cent. Furthermore, in most of the taxes the collection fluctuated widely from year to year (Table 3.3).

The potential for raising the tax revenue thus remains largely unexploited. The per capita tax collection in Bihar was only 56 per cent of that at all-states' level during 1995-98; in 1975-78, it was 65 per cent. The tax-GSDP ration was also extremely low here-being only 3.83 per cent in 1994-97, lower than in all but Assam among the major states (GOI 2000b).

Composition of Non-Tax Revenue

In the Non-tax revenue also Bihar's own collection (ONTR) was very poor, as evident from Table 3.2. The relative share of ONTR declined from 44.2

per cent in 1975-78 to 40.4 per cent in 1995-98; both the proportions were much below the all-states' average. The growth in ONTR here was only 11.6 times in this period as against the all-states' average of 13.3 times. Over the longer period since 1965-68, it was respectively 40 times and 57 times. In 2000-03, the collection of ONTR here annually averaged only Rs 482 crore and constituted 1.45 per cent of the all-states'. Bihar, therefore, had to rely heavily on grants from the centre. The proportion of grants in NTR rose to 60 per cent in 1995-98 from 56 per cent in 1975-78; both the proportions were much higher than that for all-states.

The scope for larger collection from ONTR was not low. In a number of items the collection was very small, and fluctuated widely from year to year. The state public enterprises with huge investments in them have stopped making any contribution. With proper management and appropriate pricing policies, a substantial amount could be collected from them. At the level of all-states, this item contributed an average of 0.51 per cent during 1996-99.

The collection from general services was also extremely low. It provided only 9.8 per cent of the ONTR in 1996-99 as against 10.6 per cent in 1975-78. In relation to the all-states' average, Bihar's proportion is ridiculously low; in the former, it was 23.8 per cent in 1996-99. As regards social and community services, until recently it provided a very low share; rising from 3.0 per cent in 1988-91 to 7.5 per cent in 1996-99. The proportions are however, not of much importance. The per capita collection in 2000-03 came to only Rs 6.22 as against Rs 25.38 for all-states (Table3.4 and CMIE 2004a).

The state relied too heavily on collection from the economic services. In 1988-91, 93 per cent of the total under ONTR came from this source, rising from 73 per cent in 1975-78; during 1996-99, however, it was down to 70 per cent. At the level of all-states, the proportion was only 36.6 per cent in the latest period. Even here, however, there was much scope for larger collection. To look at the receipts from some of the items: The collection from forests averaged only Rs. 13.9 crore during 1996-99 as against Rs. 62.3 crore in 1988-91.No doubt, the forests needed to be protected, but such a sharp reduction would not have been necessary if proper regeneration measures were taken at the right time. The contribution from agriculture and irrigation also declined sharply. The annual average collection from agriculture during 1996-99 came to only Rs. 62 crore, a mere 7 per cent of that collected in 1988-91.The burden of collection fell heavily on industries, to the extent of as much as 60 per cent of the ONTR (Table3.4).

From the above analysis it is apparent that there was ample scope for raising both the tax and non-tax revenue, provided the government had the required motivation. But the nature of government in the state and also inappropriate policies from the Centre stood in the way. The system of central

Table 3.2: Trend in Tax and Non-Tax Revenue of Bihar Vis-à-Vis other States

(Rs. Crore)

States	*1965-68 (a.a.)*		*1975-78 (a.a.)*		*1995-98 (a.a.)*	
	Tax revenue	*Non-Tax revenue*	*Tax revenue*	*Non-tax revenue*	*Tax revenue*	*Non-tax revenue*
Bihar	89.8 (67.1)[a]	44.0	379.1 (71.7)[a]	153.9	6084.2 (75.7)[a]	1951.8
West Bengal	131.6 (73.4)	47.8	454.4 (72.2)	361.4	6791.9 (82.7)	1412.4
Orissa	36.4 (40.2)	54.2	143.0 (44.1)	181.0	2768.5 (64.8)	1501.3
Assam	33.2 (45.6)	39.6	111.2 (48.2)	119.6	1971.9 (51.2)	1880.5
Madhya P.	79.3 (58.0)	57.5	376.4 (62.2)	228.4	6780.8 (68.0)	3194.1
Uttar P.	158.1 (60.7)	102.4	712.3 (66.3)	361.4	12331.4 (75.8)	3940.3
Andhra P.	101.0 (64.8)	54.8	481.8 (65.9)	248.8	8342.6 (71.7)	3293.8
Maharashtra	201.2 (74.0)	70.6	829.8 (70.2)	351.7	14017.7 (74.9)	4692.6
Kerala	60.0 (58.4)	42.7	251.8 (63.9)	142.5	5111.2 (82.1)	1117.7
All-states	1298.7 (61.7)	804.6	5671.2 (63.2)	3297.4	106897.5 (69.7)	46416.0

Growth (1965-68-1995-98)		*State's Own Ta x Rev enue*			*Growth*
Tax Rev.	*Non-tax Rev.*	*1965-68 (a.a.)*	*1975-78 (a.a.)*	*1995-98*	*(1965-68-1995-98) (multiples)*
67.7	44.4	58.7 (65.4)[b]	202.9 (53.5)[b]	2204.8 (36.2)[b]	37.5
51.6	29.5	99.4 (75.5)	313.3 (68.9)	4302.9 (63.4)	43.3
76.1	27.7	21.6 (59.3)	77.7 (54.3)	1297.0 (46.8)	60.0
59.4	47.5	22.6 (68.1)	67.1 (60.3)	783.7 (39.7)	34.7
85.5	55.5	55.3 (69.7)	247.1 (65.6)	4062.0 (59.9)	73.5
78.0	38.5	107.0 (67.7)	438.4 (61.5)	6257.6 (50.7)	58.5
82.6	60.1	73.8 (73.1)	345.5 (71.7)	5371.9 (64.4)	72.8
69.7	66.5	155.7 (77.4)	659.6 (79.5)	12122.9 (86.5)	77.9
85.2	26.2	45.8 (76.3)	186.5 (74.1)	3927.4 (76.8)	85.8
82.3	57.7	948.3 (73.0)	3976.3 (70.1)	72065.4 (67.4)	76.0

(Table 3.2 Contd.)

Tax Efforts[c] (Rs.)			State's Own Tax Revenue			Growth
1975-78	*1995-98*	*Growth (multiples)*	*1965-68 (a.a.)*	*1975-78 (a.a.)*	*1995-98*	*(1965-68-1995-98) (multiplies)*
60.27	650.09	10.8	19.6 (44.5)[d]	68.1 (44.2)[d]	788.6 (40.4)[d]	40.2
91.74	905.71	9.9	26.8 (56.1)	75.9 (21.0)	398.1 (28.2)	14.9
58.63	800.84	13.7	19.3 (35.6)	72.5 (40.1)	550.3 (36.7)	28.5
64.76	792.88	12.2	6.4 (16.2)	30.2 (25.3)	346.3 (18.4)	54.1
79.73	779.22	9.8	34.0 (59.1)	164.0 (71.8)	1923.8 (60.2)	56.6
72.02	782.10	10.9	56.2 (54.8)	188.4 (52.1)	1669.9 (42.4)	29.7
99.30	1149.75	11.6	28.1 (51.3)	131.3 (52.8)	1672.8 (50.8)	59.5
145.83	1610.86	11.0	44.7 (63.3)	292.7 (83.2)	3390.4 (72.2)	75.8
106.42	1644.00	15.5	17.7 (41.5)	70.4 (49.4)	533.8 (47.8)	30.2
93.17	1155.44	12.4	411.3 (51.1)	1776.8 (53.9)	23625.0 (50.9)	57.4

Notes: a: figures in brackets here are percentage to total revenue; b: percentage to total tax revenue; c: average of total tax collection in the period divided by the population estimates for 1976 and 1996, respectively; d: percentage to total Non-tax revenue.

Source: RBIFA 1967, 1968, 1969, 1978, 1979; CMIE 2001

Table 3.3: Trend in Composition of Bihar's Own Tax Revenue (Rs. million)

Item	*1975-78 (a.a.)*	*1988-91 (a.a.)*	*1994-5*	*1995-6*	*1996-7*	*1997-8*	*1998-9*	*1996-99 (a.a.)*
Land revenue	221 (10.9)	178 (1.8)	258	288	249	236	247	244 (1.0)
Stamps & regist. fee	172 (8.5)	718 (7.4)	2642	2058	2274	2438	2698	2470 (10.1)
Sales tax	1110 (54.7)	6753 (69.9)	11220	13100	14964	15676	18218	16286 (66.8)
State excise	250 (12.3)	923 (9.6)	1634	1821	2187	2261	2395	2281 (9.4)
Taxes on vehicles	82 (4.1)	682 (7.1)	1770	1578	1608	1741	1650	1666 (6.8)
Taxes on goods & passgs.	55 (2.7)	22 (0.2)	150	61	289	869	598	585 (2.4)
Electricity duty	78 (3.8)	225 (2.3)	477	577	706	423	670	600 (2.5)
Entertainment tax	59 (2.9)	136 (1.4)	161	249	205	205	198	203 (0.8)
Total OTR	2029 (100.0)	9657 (100.0)	18360	19733	22508	23904	26716	24376 (100.0)

Source: RBIFA 1978, 1979, 1991, 1992; CMIE 1996, 2001.

transfers was managed in such a way that it was not conducive for compelling the states towards larger resource mobilisation. Below we give a brief look into the relative position of Bihar on central transfers.

Central Transfer

The aggregate of central transfer to Bihar had increased 96.7 times over a period of around three-and-half decades, from the annual average of Rs. 55.5 crore during 1965-68 to Rs. 5364.1 crore in 1996-99 as against 83.4 times for all-states. Bihar's share in the latter rose to 8.65 per cent from 7.46 per cent over the period. The per capita transfer, however, remained low. It was much below the all-States' average in each of the three periods considered (Table 3.5).

From the angle of backwardness of the state, Bihar did not receive the due attention. Its share of population in all-India total was always a little more than 10 per cent, but the transfer from the centre remained much lower. Among the eastern states, both Assam and Orissa received a relatively higher allocation although their per capita incomes were higher. However, in relation to the state's total revenue, the proportion increased at a faster rate here-from 41.5 per cent in 1965-68 to 61.9 in 1996-99; no other eastern state had this rate of rise.

In the transfer to Bihar, the proportion of grants-which were provided primarily for equalizing the standards of basic social services among the states-was relatively low. It declined to 21.7 per cent in 1996-99 from 43.9 per cent in 1965-68; at the all-states level, it was much higher. The amount of grants to Bihar had increased by only 47.9 times over the entire period as against 60.4 times for all-states; the share in the latter had declined from 6.2 per cent to 4.9 per cent.

There have been some significant changes in the composition of grants to Bihar. The share of both state plan schemes and central plan schemes had declined, the former from 42.1 per cent in 1975–78 to 40.6 per cent in 1996-99 and the latter to only 0.86 per cent from 12.7 per cent. At the level of all-states, the grants for SPS had a noticeable rise, from 33.7 per cent to 51.9 per cent, and for CPS the rate of fall was much less, being from 7.5 to 4.3 per cent. The proportion for centrally sponsored schemes was much less here than at the all-states level. Bihar had a rise from 9.4 per cent to 12.7 per cent over the same period as against from 14.3 per cent to 23.4 per cent for the latter. The trend in non-plan grants was also different here. Here it increased from 35.7 per cent in 1975-78 to 45.9 per cent in 1996-99 as against a sharp fall at the level of all-states, from 44.5 per cent to 19.9 per cent. This pattern of transfers is mainly due to the state's poor fund management and low priority to economic planning, as will be evident from the analysis later.

Changes in the criteria for allocation by the Finance Commission (FC) also did not favour Bihar. Since the Fourth Five-year plan, specific criteria, known as 'Gadgil formula', were laid down for the provision of Central Plan

Table 3.4: Trend in Collection from ONTR in Bihar (Rs. million)

Items	*1975-78 (a.a.)*	*1988-91 (a.a.)*	*1994-5*	*1995-6*	*1996-7*	*1997-8*	*1998-9*	*1996-99 (a.a.)*
Interest receipts	16.5 (2.4)	64.3 (0.7)	289.3	201.0	564.8	878.0	1360.0	934.3 (10.8)
Dividend & profit	0.1 (neg.)	0.3 (neg.)	3.1	—	—	—	—	—
General services	72.1 (10.6)	297.4 (3.5)	348.9	147.1	207.5	1316.9	1025.0	849.8 (9.8)
Social & Comm. services	—	257.2 (3.0)	340.8	293.2	242.5	922.5	784.0	649.7 (7.5)
Education etc.	—	—	52.7	29.9	32.4	566.0	223.0	273.8 (3.2)
Medical, etc.	—	—	125.7	91.7	81.1	114.7	148.0	114.6 (1.3)
Economic service	495.2 (72.7)	7991.0 (92.8)	8766.1	8504.0	9033.8	781.2	8291.0	6035.3 (69.7)
Forests	147.4 (21.6)	622.7 (7.2)	770.0	285.3	236.5	—	182.0	139.5 (1.6)
Agriculture	20.2 (3.0)	862.6 (10.0)	29.5	22.3	17.1	147.0	21.0	61.7 (0.7)
Irrigation, etc.	55.0 (8.1)	335.6 (3.9)	203.1	312.1	385.6	363.1	425.0	391.2 (4.5)
Industries	5.4 (0.8)	2727.2 (31.7)	7469.5	7697.4	8209.5	67.9	7419.0	5232.1 (60.4)
Total ONTR (100.0)	681.1 (100.0)	8610.1 (100.0)	9748.2	9145.3	10613.4	3898.6	11460.0	8657.3

Source: As in the preceding Table.

assistance. Some of the criteria laid down initially were : (i) 60 per cent of the available fund (after allocation to certain bordering states) to be provided on population basis; (ii) 10 per cent among the states with per capita income below the national average; (iii) 10 per cent on the basis of tax efforts; (iv) 10 per cent on the basis of spill-over into the Fourth Plan of major irrigation and power projects; and (v) 10 per cent for special problems of individual states. These criteria were modified subsequently.

As regards tax transfer, whose importance increased over the years, the Union excise duty provided the lion's share, followed by income-tax. During 1996-99, the former provided 57.6 per cent of the total in Bihar, declining from 62.0 per cent in 1975-78; the growth in receipts being 22.1 times. The transfer under income-tax had risen 27 times in this period.

The basis of tax transfer to states, and also the proportion available for distribution, changed from period to period. The criteria for transfers were generally the state's contribution, population, per capita income, specific indicators of backwardness, poverty criterion and tax-efforts, with varying weightage from time to time. In the sharing of income-tax, till the Seventh FC (1979-84) only two criteria were used, with population accounting fro 80 to 90 per cent and contribution the balance. From the Eighth FC, per capita income distance criterion became the most important, accounting for 45 per cent of the total, whereas for population it was reduced to only 22.5 per cent. In the Tenth FC (1995-2000), the former was raised to 60 per cent and the latter further down to 20 per cent. For the sharing of basic excise duties also the criteria and weightage were similar. Till the Sixth FC population accounted for 75 per cent or more, but was reduced to only 25 per cent in the Seventh FC and 16.84 in the Tenth.

The shares to states in the sharable taxes increased gradually under the different FCs. On income-tax, the proportion increased from 55 per cent in the First FC to 85 per cent in the Seventh and remained at this level till the Ninth FC (II) (1990-95). On basic excise duties, the proportion was 40 per cent in the First FC but limited to only three commodities. Gradually the commodity coverage was increased and in the Fourth FC all excisable commodities were included. The divisible proportion was reduced to 25 per cent in the Second FC, and in the Third through Sixth FC it stood at 20 per cent. In the Seventh FC it was raised to 40 per cent and then reached the maximum of 47.5 per cent in the Tenth FC (Guhan 1995).

Capital Receipts

The growth of capital receipts in Bihar was extremely low. Over the entire period of nearly three and half decades, it increased only 10.7 times, from the annual average of Rs. 129.7 crore in 1965-68 to Rs. 1392.5 crore in 1996-99. At the level of all-states, it was 49 times in the same period. In the last two and half decades, Bihar's capital receipts increased only 5.8 times compared with 21.8 times for all-states. Not only this, a large portion of the capital receipts here went to meet the revenue account deficit. During 1996-99, it was to the extent of 43.8 per cent; at the all state's level, it was 40.2 per cent (RBIFA 1967, 1968, 1969, 1978, 1979; CMIE 2001

As regards the sources of capital receipts, a very large portion came from the Union government in the from of loans and advances. In 1996–99, it was to the extent of 142 per cent, rising from 75.9 per cent in 1975–78. For all the states, on the other hand, the contribution from this source declined, from the average of 53.6 per cent to 50.2 per cent over the same period. Bihar's was the highest level of dependence on the Centre. However, in per capita term it was not very high. During 1996-99, it came to Rs. 207.90 as against the all-states' average of Rs 336.43.

In the loans from the centre, the state plan schemes accounted for the largest proportion-rising from 40.2 per cent in 1975-78 to 51.5 per cent in 1996-99. The non-plan receipts also had a rapid growth, the share rising from 33.9 per cent to 47.0 per cent in this period. Small savings accounted for the overwhelming proportion in this, particularly in recent years–rising from 59.2 per cent in 1975–78 to 99.8 per cent in 1996–99. In some of the years, there was a heavy reliance on ways and means advances; in 1995-96 the entire amount came from it.

Among other items, the growth in internal debt was quite high. Over the period of nearly two-and-half decades, 1975-78 to 1996-99, it had risen 32-fold, and the relative share rose to 48.8 per cent from only 9.0 per cent. The market loans in it accounted for the overwhelming proportion-as much as 95 per cent in the latest period. For all-states, the dependence on internal debt was much less; during 1996-99 it came to only 18.5 per cent. The contribution of small savings, PF etc was very low in Bihar, rising from 3.5 per cent to 5.0 per cent over the period. For all-states, it was 12.5 per cent in the latest period. On recovery of loans and advances, Bihar's performance was the worst. Its contribution to total capital receipts declined from 10.9 per cent in 1975-78 to 0.7 per cent in 1996-99.

Thus, in the mobilisation of capital resources also Bihar presented a very gloomy picture. And for this, the quality of economic management here is squarely to be blamed. Although the level of per capita loans from the Centre is very low, it cannot be expected to pour in funds unless there are proper plans for development and the state demonstrates its ability to utilise the fund properly.

It is also necessary to mention that although the growth in capital receipts was low, the state's debt burden became quite heavy over the years. Debt as

Table 3.5: Trend in Central Transfers to Bihar Vis-a-Vis other States

(Rs. Crore)

States	1965-68 (a.a.) Tax transfer	Grants	Total transfer	As % to total rev.	Per capita transfer[c]	1975-78 (a.a.) (contd.) Tax	Grants
Bihar (10.5)[a]	31.14	24.34 (43.9)[b]	55.5 (7.5)	41.5	10.57	176.1	85.8 (32.7)[b]
W.Bengal (8.1)	32.23	21.00 (39.5)	53.2 (7.2)	29.7	13.20	141.1	97.3 (40.8)
Orissa (4.0)	14.86	34.92 (70.1)	49.8 (6.7)	54.9	25.22	65.3	108.6 (62.4)
Assam (2.8)	10.61	33.20 (75.8)	43.8 (5.9)	60.2	31.61	44.1	89.4 (66.9)
Madhya P. (7.4)	23.97	23.53 (49.5)	47.5 (6.4)	34.7	12.86	129.3	64.4 (33.3)
Uttar P. (8.0)	51.06	46.18 (47.5)	97.2 (13.1)	37.3	11.72	273.8	1730.0 (38.7)
Andhra P. (16.6)	27.18	26.74 (49.6)	53.9 (7.2)	34.6	13.52	136.2	117.4 (46.3)
Kerala (3.9)	14.15	25.06 (63.9)	39.2 (5.3)	38.2	20.32	65.2	72.0 (52.5)
Maharashtra (9.1)	45.57	25.94 (36.3)	71.5 (9.6)	26.3	15.78	170.2	58.9 (25.7)
All-states (100.0)	350.48	393.31 (52.9)	743.8 (100.0)	35.4	15.24	1694.9	1520.6 (47.3)

(Table 3.5 Contd.)

	1975-78 (a.a.)				1996-99 (a.a.)		
Total transfer	As % to total reve.	Per capita transfer[c]	Tax transfer	Grants	Total transfer	As % to total rev. (Rs.)	Per capita transfer[c]
261.9 (8.1)	49.1	41.64	4197.9	1166.2 (21.7)[b]	5364.1 (8.6)	61.9	563.22
238.4 (7.4)	38.1	48.13	2720.0	1226.7 (31.1)	3946.7 (6.4)	44.4	518.35
173.9 (5.4)	53.7	71.30	1608.0	939.3 (36.9)	2547.3 (4.1)	56.7	728.84
133.5 (4.2)	57.9	77.76	1333.4	1633.7 (55.1)	2967.1 (4.8)	70.2	1173.69
193.7 (6.0)	32.0	41.03	2964.8	1390.3 (31.9)	4355.1 (7.0)	40.1	572.96
446.9 (13.9)	41.6	45.18	6319.5	2240.2 (26.2)	8559.7 (13.8)	50.4	532.65
253.7 (7.9)	34.7	52.28	3119.2	1573.2 (33.5)	4692.4 (7.6)	35.8	637.90
137.3 (4.3)	34.8	58.02	1298.9	630.7 (32.7)	1929.6 (3.1)	28.3	613.35
229.2 (7.1)	19.4	40.27	2961.4	1229.3 (29.3)	4190.7 (6.8)	20.5	474.76
3215.5 (100.0)	35.9	52.83	38290.0	23746.9 (38.3)	62036.9 (100.0)	37.3	659.18

Notes: a: percentage share of all-states' population; b: percentage to total transfer; c: based on population estimates for 1966, 1976 and 1997, respectively.

Source: As in Table 3.2.

percentage of GSDP stood at 33.1 here in 1998-99 compared with the all-states' average of 22.98. The per capita debt was however, relatively low, as may be seen from Table 3.6.

Expenditure

As the resource mobilisation was low, naturally the growth of expenditure could not be high. Over a period of nearly three-and-half decades, between 1965-68 and 1996-99, the total expenditure had multiplied only 41.2 times, from the annual average of Rs. 257 crore to Rs 10,598 crore as against 66.8 times for all-states. Bihar's relative share in the latter was down to 4.6 per cent from 7.4 per cent. In the more recent years, during 2000-03, there was a nominal rise in the proportion; with the annual average at Rs.18,509 crore, it became 4.86 per cent. The per capita total expenditure here was always much below the all-States' average, and the extent of disparity increased over the years. In 1965-68 it was 73 per cent of the latter's but in 1996-99 came to only 45 per cent. During 2000-03, Bihar's per capita stood at only Rs. 1686 as against Rs. 3768 for all-states (Table 3.7 and CMIE 2004a).

Revenue Expenditure

In the aggregate of expenditure, the share of revenue account had a rapid rise over the years. It reached as much as 87.5 per cent in 1996-99, from 58.1 in 1975-78 and 53.3 per cent in 1965-68. Among the states, Bihar's relative position worsened noticeably, as may be seen from Table 3.7. In the revenue expenditure again, the share of developmental declined, to 57.3 per cent in 1996-99 from 63.5 per cent in 1975-78. Bihar's proportion was always below the all-states average. Thus, the development activities got neglected while the non-developmental soared. The trend in composition of development expenditure is presented in Table 3.8.

In the development expenditure, social services always accounted for the lion's share. During 1996-99, it was 66.7 per cent, rising from 63.8 per cent in 1975-78; the all-states' average stood at 59.9 per cent in the latest period. Despite the high proportion, the per capita spending remained very small; being only Rs. 372.43 in the latest period as against the all-states average of Rs 746.85. In more recent years also the position is same; during 2000-03, it was respectively Rs. 532 and Rs. 1,062. In the expenditure on social services, education etc received the highest share-rising from 61.7 per cent in 1975-78 to 68.4 per cent in 1996-99. However, the per capita expenditure on education remained small; during 2000-03, it stood at only Rs. 360 as against the all-states average of Rs. 609.

The expenditure on economic services had a very low growth, and its relative share declined from 36.2 per cent to 33.2 over the period; at the level of all-states, it was 40.1 per cent in the latest period. The proportions are however,

Table 3.6: The Debt Position of Bihar Government Vis-à-vis other States

(Rs crore)

States	*Total March-end 1981*	*Debt March end 2000*	*% of central loans (2000)*	*Per capita debt (2000)[a] Rs*	*Debt as % of GSDP (1998-99)*
Bihar	1997 (8.2)	32055.8 (6.8)	50.0	3366	33.14
West Bengal	2111 (8.7)	43225.4 (9.1)	66.1	5677	26.19
Orissa	1176 (4.8)	19491.5 (4.1)	42.2	5577	37.79
Assam	733 (3.0)	8554.6 (1.8)	53.7	3384	23.23
Madhya Pradesh	1593 (6.6)	24987.8 (5.3)	44.0	3287	18.63
Uttar Pradesh	3477 (14.3)	71931.7 (15.2)	49.0	4477	27.97
Andhra Pradesh	1781 (7.3)	32479.3 (6.9)	49.4	4427	20.29
Kerala	1008 (4.2)	20191.7 (4.3)	32.5	6418	27.13
Rajasthan	1582 (6.5)	29558.7 (6.2)	41.3	5791	28.85
All-States	24254 (100.0)	473676.9 (100.0)	50.0	5038	22.98

Note : a: based on population estimate for 1997.
Source: RBI 1983; GOI 2000b.

not so important as the actual expenditure, and here Bihar's position was extremely poor. The per capita expenditure on economic services came to only Rs. 185.53 in 1996-99 as against the all-states average of Rs. 500.37. The disparity continues to rise; during 2000-03, it was respectively Rs. 227 and Rs.652–that is, the former 34.8 per cent of the latter as against 37.1 per cent in the preceding period (Table 3.8 and CMIE 2004a).

In economic services, the important items in recent years were rural development, agriculture and allied services, irrigation and flood control and transport and communication. Rural development-which covers mainly certain employment schemes-became important only towards the end of eighties, and during 1996-99 it received as much as 47.5 per cent. However, during 2000-03 it was down to 38.9 per cent, with the expenditure annually averaging Rs. 968.3 crore.

With the growth in rural development, agriculture lost its importance, the share declining from as much as 61.0 per cent in 1975-78 to only 19.2 per cent in 1996-99; at the level of all-states, it received 25.4 per cent in the latest period. The per capita expenditure on agriculture and allied services came to only Rs. 54.28 in 2000-03, rising from Rs. 35.68 in the preceding period; for all-states, it was three times as much. With this level of expenditure, naturally some of the important items under it got neglected. The expenditure on irrigation and flood control had a sharp fall in the nineties, receiving only 14.4 per cent in 1996-99 as against 30.0 per cent in 1988-91. However, in the last few years there was a noticeable recovery–the expenditure rising to an annual average of Rs. 749 crore in 2000-03, nearly three times the level in 1996-99.Transport and communication was largely neglected; with a growth in expenditure of only 11 times over the period, the relative share declined to 8.0 per cent from 12.5 per cent. The position of industry and minerals was still worse; the proportion going to it declined from 6.2 per cent to 4.8 per cent. This is mainly a product of the new industrial policy; at the level of all-states also it was only 4.5 per cent in 1996-99.

As regards non-development expenditure, its relative share rose to 40.7 per cent in 1996-99 from 38.2 per cent in 1975-78; at the level of all-states, it was from 32.0 per cent to 37.4 per cent. The most important item here is interest payment, registering a 27-fold rise over the period. The relative share in N-D expenditure rose to 40.7 per cent from 38.2. Interest payments took away 23.39 per cent of the revenue receipts during 1995-99 compared with 19.85 per cent for 15 non-special category states (GOI 2000b). However, during 2000-03, at the annual average of Rs. 2019 crore, it declined to 22.3 per cent (CMIE 2004a).

The next important item is administrative services, with a share of 29.0 per cent of the total in 1996-99, declining from 39.8 per cent in 1975-78. Bihar's proportion is, however, still higher than the all-states average, being 24.0 per cent. In the administrative services, the expenditure on police had a sharp rise and the relative share rose to 66.0 per cent in 1996-99; at the level of all-states, it was 60.1 per cent in this period. However, the per capita expenditure on police was not high; being Rs 115 in 2000-03 as against Rs 160 for all-states. The highest growth in expenditure was, however, in pension payment. It had multiplied 102 times between 1975-78 and 1996-99, and the relative share rose to 20.9 per cent from only 5.2. In recent years it has risen further. In 2000-03, pension payments averaged Rs 2713 crore, that is, a 228 per cent rise over 1996-99; in the total revenue expenditure, the share rose to 17.9 per cent from 8.9. At the level of all-states, it was 9.1 per cent in 2000-03.

As regards compensation and assignments to local bodies and panchayat raj institutions (PRIs), the third category, Bihar presented a very gloomy picture. The expenditure on it declined from the annual average of Rs. 2.34 crore during 1975-78 to Rs 2.03 crore in 1996-99. Such negligible transfers continued despite the PRIs not collecting any revenue on their own. The total revenue of Bihar's PRIs from all sources averaged only Rs. 397.31 crore during 1995-98 and constituted 2.43 per cent of all-states total (GOI 2001). It may be noted here that the elections for PRIs in Bihar was held only in April 2001, after a gap of 23 years. Thus, the government takes no interest in the development of the panchayat system, envisaged to be a key instrument for rural development.

Capital Expenditure

The capital disbursements in Bihar had a very low growth. Over the entire period of nearly three-and-half decades, it had grown by only 11 times—from the annual average of Rs. 120.3 crore during 1965-68 to Rs. 1320.3 crore in 1996-99. The relative share in the aggregate of expenditure dropped to only 12.5 per cent from 46.7 per cent; at the level of all-states, the proportion in the latest period was 17.4 per cent. In the last few years, there has been some improvement. During 2000-03, with an annual average at Rs. 3383 crore, the proportion rose to 18.3 per cent which is almost equal to the all-states average (RBIFA 1967, 1968, 1969; CMIE 2001, 2004a).

In capital disbursements again the proportion of capital outlay—which is almost entirely for development purposes—was very low. It was down to 34.7 per cent in 1996-99 from 42.2 in 1975-78; the all-states average came to as much as 52.2 per cent in the latest period. The per capita outlay in Bihar was only Rs. 37 in 1995-98, less than a fifth of the all-states average. The fluctuation in outlay from year to year was also very wide.

In the capital outlay, economic services generally accounted for the overwhelming proportion. However, it showed a decline from 92 per cent in 1975-78 to 76 per cent in1996-99. A major portion of the expenditure here was on irrigation and flood control, declining from 71.6 per cent to 58 per cent over

Table 3.7: Trend in Budgetary Expenditure of Bihar Vis-à-vis Other States

(Rs. million)

States	Total Expenditure: Total 1975-78 (a.a.)	Total 1996-99 (a.a.)	Per capita[a] (Rs.) 1975-78	Per capita[a] (Rs.) 1996-99	Develop Expenditure 1975-78 (a.a.)	Develop Expenditure 1995-98 (a.a.)
Bihar	7419 (6.3)	105979 (4.6)	118	1113	4030 (54.3)[b]	53332 (55.1)[b]
West Bengal	8582 (7.3)	145806 (6.3)	173	1915	4813 (56.1)	70154 (56.7)
Orissa	4349 (3.7)	72690 (3.1)	178	2080	2751 (63.3)	38822 (62.2)
Assam	2866 (2.4)	48310 (2.1)	167	1911	1746 (60.9)	26405 (57.9)
Madhya Pradesh	7752 (6.6)	144286 (6.2)	164	1898	4694 (60.6)	82840 (65.6)
Uttar Pradesh	14588 (12.4)	270348 (11.6)	147	1682	8221 (56.4)	118001 (50.3)
Andhra Pradesh	9382 (8.0)	186558 (8.0)	193	2536	6122 (65.3)	101273 (62.9)
Maharashtra	15054 (12.8)	276657 (11.9)	265	3134	8335 (55.4)	163550 (66.3)
Kerala	5135 (4.4)	94570 (4.1)	217	3006	3379 (65.8)	47689 (58.0)
All-states	117941 (100.0)	2324215 (100.0)	194	2472	70094 (59.4)	1219064 (60.1)

Per capita development total[a] 1975-78	Per capita development total[a] 1995-98	Total Revenue Expend. 1975-78 (a.a.)	Total Revenue Expend. 1995-98 (a.a.)	growth[c]	% of developmental in revenue 1975-78	% of developmental in revenue 1995-98
64.07	569.58	4307 (58.1)[b]	85555 (88.4)[b]	19.86	63.5	58.3
97.17	935.51	6141 (71.6)	101035 (81.7)	16.45	67.1	59.1
112.79	1123.00	3085 (70.9)	51172 (82.0)	16.59	69.1	61.9
101.69	1061.72	2063 (72.0)	37285 (81.8)	18.07	66.6	63.3
99.43	1109.86	5052 (65.2)	107731 (85.3)	21.32	70.0	66.1
83.12	748.40	9383 (64.3)	196529 (83.7)	20.95	66.7	53.4
126.17	1395.71	6214 (66.2)	131835 (81.9)	21.22	70.6	67.8
146.49	1879.45	10251 (68.1)	203036 (82.2)	19.81	62.6	66.6
142.81	1533.90	3868 (75.3)	69519 (84.5)	17.97	72.5	59.9
115.15	1317.66	79394 (67.3)	1668625 (86.6)	21.02	68.0	61.8

(Table 3.7 Contd.)

Capital Dis. Total		% of Development in C. D.		Per capita development (C.D.)[a]
1975-78 (a.a.)	*1995-98 (a.a.)*	*1975-78 (a.a.)*	*1995-98 (a.a.)*	*1995-98 (Rs.) (a.a.)*
3112	11244 (3.61)[c]	41.6	30.8	36.99
2441	22623 (9.27)	28.3	46.2	139.37
1264	11253 (8.90)	49.0	63.6	207.12
803	8312 (10.35)	46.5	33.9	113.31
2700	18599 (6.89)	42.9	62.8	156.51
5205	38235 (7.35)	37.7	34.0	82.42
3168	29200 (9.22)	54.8	40.9	164.64
4803	43819 (9.12)	40.0	64.7	325.76
1267	12755 (10.07)	45.5	47.4	194.63
38547	359666 (6.70)	41.7	52.4	203.58

Notes: a: per capita expenditures are based on population estimates for 1976, 1996 and 1997, respectively for 1975-78, 1995-98 and 1996-99; b: Percentage to grand total of expenditure; c : growth in multiples.

Source: As in Table 3.2.

the period. In social services, water supply and sanitation accounted for the lion's share in recent years; during 1996-99, it was to the extent of 56 per cent.

Repayment of loans to the Centre and loans and advances by the state government took away a large portion of the capital disbursements. Their combined share in 1996-99 was 60.9 per cent, rising from 55.4 per cent in 1975-78. The share of the former in it was respectively 33.8 and 32.4 per cent; at the level of all-states, repayments accounted for only 18.6 per cent in the latest period. Loans and advances by the state government—which are almost entirely for development purposes-however, had an absolute fall in the last decade, and its relative share declined from 33.9 per cent in 1988-91 to 27.1 per cent in 1996-99.

With this nature of resource deployment, development of the state naturally suffered. Development expenditure as a whole remained very small. In the aggregate of budgetary expenditure it constituted only 55.1 per cent in 1995-98 as against the all-states average of 63.3 per cent. Per capita development expenditure in Bihar stood at only Rs. 569.85 annually in 1995-98, which was 43.2 per cent of the all-states average (Table 3.7).

The plan outlays remained very low in the state. The per capita plan outlay was always much below the all-states average. The cumulative total till the end of eighth plan (March 1997) came to Rs 4,937 in Bihar, which was 66.6 per cent of the all-states average. Period-wise, in the first fifteen years (1951-66) it was Rs 132 and in the following 19 years Rs 814; in relation to the all-states average, these were respectively 72.9 per cent and 58.4 per cent. After the bifurcation of the state, the situation has worsened further. For the Tenth plan (2002-07), the outlay has been fixed at Rs. 21,000 crore, giving a per capita of Rs. 2,534 which is only 45.6 per cent of the all-states average. Jharkhand's position is substantially better, being a per capita of Rs. 5,438 which is 97.8 per cent of all-states average (GOI 2000a).

It is not only that the plan outlays were low, the proportion of revenue expenditure in them was also very high. It increased from the average of 56.90 per cent in 1987-90 to 70.12 per cent in 1990-93 and remained around this level in the following years also. The average for 1996-99 came to 70.10 per cent, which was 7.73 points higher than the all-states average; earlier, in 1987-90, it was below the latter's by 3.15 points (Gurumurthi, S. : Table 3).

This situation was primarily due to the state government's lack of interest in development, and its utter inefficiency in proper utilisation of available resources. No doubt, the Central assistance on plans was low; but even the amount provided often remained unutilised to a large extent. Over the last 50 years, special Central grants of the order of Rs. 36,000 crore could not be utilised. Bihar also forfeited a large portion of Central assistance due to its failure to provide the matching 20 per cent. In recent years, Rs 600 crore of

Table 3.8: Trend in composition of Revenue Expenditure in Bihar

(Rs. million)

Items	*1975-78 (a.a.)*	*1988-91 (a.a.)*	*1995-6*	*1996-7*	*1997-8*	*1998-9*	*1996-99 (a.a.)*	*growth*[b]
Revenue Expenditure	4307	40143	84562	82539	89565	106225	92776	21.54
Development Expend.	2736	—	50197	47898	51515	60010	53141	19.42
1. Social Services	1745	17031	32511	32218	35949	38244	35470	20.33
Education etc	1076	10752	20133	22069	25070	25628	24256	22.54
Medical, health, etc	379[a]	2490	6595	5041	5473	5855	5456	14.40
Water supply & sanitation	—	563	1119	1047	799	908	918	—
Welfare of SC, ST & OBC	—	743	1379	876	2297	1493	1555	—
Social security & welfare	125	1035	2309	1747	1026	1909	1561	12.49
Nutrition	—	83	12	75	76	4	52	—
2. Economic Services	991	12887	17686	15679	15565	21766	17670	17.83
Agriculture & allied	605	2667	4697	3675	2800	3718	3398	5.62
Crop husbandry	136	1056	954	1069	919	796	928	6.82
Soil & water conservation	21	175	55	72	97	91	87	4.14
Animal husbandry	71	447	2289	648	345	656	550	7.75
Fisheries	9	56	77	92	28	94	71	7.89
Forestry & wildlife	71	469	528	696	623	804	708	9.97
Agri. research & education	—	137	309	566	336	841	581	—
Co-operation	41	363	440	483	397	422	434	10.59
Rural development	—	3369	4192	6324	6386	12478	8396	—
Irrigation & flood control	126	3865	2318	2845	2098	2738	2560	20.32
Energy	—	2948	4360	28	1583	183	598	—
Industry & minerals	61	657	510	1053	950	555	853	13.98
of which VSI	20	—	294	754	426	304	495	24.75
Transport & communications	124	1266	1299	1550	1149	1556	1418	11.44
Civil supplies	—	—	141	17	224	191	144	—

(Table 3.8 Contd.)

Non-development expends.	1548	—	30983	34345	38030	46193	39523	25.53
1. Interest payment	592	5699	16676	14170	15360	18723	16084	27.17
2. Administrative services	616	—	8943	10323	11123	12909	11452	18.59
Distt. Administration	53	828	888	1302	724	1567	1198	22.60
Police	328	2699	5853	6656	8054	7980	7563	23.06
3. Pension	81	1671	5558	7024	7564	10242	8277	102.19

Notes: a: including water supply and sanitation; b: in multiples, between 1975-78 and 1996-99.

Source: RBIFA 1978, 1979, 1991, 1992; CMIE 1996, 2001.

special central grants for rural development were lost because the state refused to hold panchayat elections (Sahay 2000: 7).

Misappropriation of fund was also rampant in Bihar; some idea on which has been given in chapter 2. Here we may mention a case of large scale fraud going on for years. It was reported in the annual review of Bihar Treasuries for 1990-91 to 1994-95 that extensive fraud in payment of pensions was occurring in the Bhagalpur treasury, but no action was taken. Several hundred crore of rupees were lost due to payment of pension and provident fund to non-existing persons. The fraud was brought to the notice of the CAG only in 1998, and the audit report for the year contains alarming information. There was a total failure of audit in Bihar. According to rules, every treasury has to be inspected every year by the office of the AG and an annual report sent to the government for corrective action. But out of 59 district treasuries in Bihar, only eight were inspected in 1990-91, six in 1991-92, three in 1992-93, 14 in 1993-94 and nine in 1995-96 (Joseph 2000).

Thus, a basic requirement in resource mobilisation and deployment, proper control over accounts, was neglected by the Bihar government. The need for raising of resources itself loses justification if there is no proper control over their utilisation.

Panchayat Raj Institutions

The PRIs had great potential for resource mobilisation and their proper deployment for developing rural India. The Directive principles of state policy of the Constitution had stated: "The state shall take steps to organise village panchayats and endow them with such powers and authority as may be necessary to enable them to function as units of self-government." But even after five decades of development efforts, this objective remained far from being implemented. Some important steps came only after the 73rd Amendment of the Constitution, effective from April 1993. But the progress in Bihar was probably the worst. We give a brief look below into the PRIs performance in resource mobilisation and deployment.

The aggregate of revenue of all tiers of PRIs in Bihar annually averaged Rs 3973.1 million in 1995-98, constituting 2.43 per cent of all-states total. In per capita term, it was only Rs 52.97, a fifth of that for all-states (based on 1991 rural population). The growth in revenue was, however, very high in recent years, rising from Rs 359 lakh in 1990-91 to Rs 36596 lakh in 1997-98, that is, 102 times; at the level of all-states, it was merely 193 per cent. The state's share in the latter's total rose to 1.89 per cent from 0.054 per cent. In this revenue, however, there was no contribution from the PRIs' own collection; even for all-states, it was merely 3.71 per cent (GOI 2000b).

In the PRIs total revenue, the village level panchayat had no share till 1991-92, and in the following six years it varied between Rs 51290 lakh in 1993-

94 and Rs 23781 lakh in the preceding year; the average for 1995-98 came to Rs 32071 lakh, constituting 80.7 per cent of the total from all tiers. The per capita revenue came to Rs 42.75 in this period as against Rs 75.34 for all-states, that is, the former 57 per cent of the latter.

The growth in expenditure was much less. Between 1990-91 and 1997-98 it had risen only 385 per cent for all tiers, ignoring fluctuations. Actually, the expenditure started rising only from 1992-93 and reached the highest of Rs 92656 lakh in 1994-95; the average for 1995-98 came to Rs 63138 lakh, and constituted 3.59 per cent of all-states total. The per capita expenditure in Bihar came to Rs 84.16 as against Rs 279.57 for all-states, that is the former less than a third of the latter.

At village level, the expenditure annually averaged Rs 36908 lakh in 1995-98, constituting 58.5 per cent of all-tiers total. This is a high proportion; the average for all-states being only 26.9 per cent. However, in per capita term, it was much below that in all-states, being respectively Rs 49.20 and Rs 75.07 (ibid.).

BANKING RESOURCE

Outside the direct control of government, the banking system is an important instrument for mobilisation and deployment of resources according to plan priorities. However, in the first two decades, hardly any attention was paid to utilising this system. The policy of social control over commercial banks came only in December 1967, and in July 1969 14 large banks were nationalised. In 1975, the Regional Rural Banks (RRBs) were created for catering exclusively to the needs of weaker sections. In 1980, six more commercial banks were added to the nationalised sector. Measures for strengthening the co-operative credit structure were of course initiated in the fifties itself, but only half-heartedly. The banking infrastructure expanded greatly over the years. Below we give a brief look into the operation of the different types of institutions.

Co-operative Credit

Until the end of sixties, co-operative credit institutions were the only banking organisation in rural India; the credit needs of rural people used to be met by the unorganised sector of money-lenders, etc. From the beginning of 1950s, the Reserve Bank of India (RBI) began to take measures for strengthening the co-operative credit system. A number of changes came in the structure itself. However, for short-term credit it was always a three-tier system: State Co-operative Bank at the apex level, Central Co-operative Banks at the middle, and Primary Credit Societies at the base. For long-term credit, there were the Land Mortgage Banks, later renamed Land Development Banks. It was generally a two-tier system: State Land Development Banks and Primary Land Development Banks. We give a brief look into the extent of resource mobilisation and deployment by the co-operative credit system in Bihar.

At every stage, the co-operative credit system in Bihar was weak. Number of societies declined greatly by the end of seventies, and in the following years also the recovery was nominal, as evident from Table 3.9. The fall in number was mainly due to merger of weak societies, but the membership of societies also had a very low growth. Over a period of nearly three decades, 1970-96 it had risen only 152 per cent as against 262 per cent for all-India.

The volume of operation of the institutions was very low. The working capital for all types societies together had risen only 33 times between 1970 and 1998 as against 48 times for all-India; the relative share in the latter declining from 2.06 per cent to 1.41. The fall came mainly in the last decade; even in 1982 it was 2.15 per cent. The deposit mobilisation was very low. Over the entire period, it had risen only 57.7 times as against 104.6 times for all-India; Bihar's relative share declined from 2.33 per cent to 1.29 per cent.

To look at the position of grass-root level societies: the primary agriculture credit societies (PACS), constituting the largest number, failed miserably in mobilising deposits. Their total deposits had risen only 3.41 per cent between 1970 and 1985 as against 736 per cent at the national level; the relative share in the latter declining from 4.68 per cent to 0.58 per cent. In the following years, it declined further, being at only 0.13 per cent at the end of March 1997, with the amount at Rs. 81.3 million. The deposit per society came to only Rs. 11,700 in the latest year, rising from Rs. 4,484 in 1985; the former was a negligible 1.75 per cent of the national average.

On the provision of credit also the situation was not much better. Between 1970 and 1985, loans outstanding had risen by 224 per cent and another 189 per cent by March 1997; the amount in the latest year being only Rs 1809 million. Over the entire period, it was 837 per cent here as against 2534 per cent for all-India. The relative share in all-India total decclined from 2.71 per cent to 1.08 per cent. The amount outstanding per society came to Rs. 2.60 lakh in the latest year, which was 13.0 per cent of the all-India average (Table 3.9).

The non-agricultural credit societies, which operated mainly in urban areas, had a better performance. Their deposits increased by 147 per cent between 1966 and 1983, and the amount per society was higher than the national average. Bihar's share in all-India total deposit, however, declined from 3.21 per cent to 2.15, as the latter had a faster growth. In recent years, the situation has worsened much. In 1998, Bihar's share in all-India total deposit came to only 0.58 per cent; and per society it was at Rs. 146 thousand, a mere 14.1 per cent of the latter's (NABARD 2002).

On the provision of credit also the situation was similar. Between 1970 and 1998, loans outstanding had increased by only 262.4 per cent here as against 2472 per cent for all-India. In the all-India total, Bihar's share dropped to a negligible 0.31 per cent from 2.18 per cent. Loans outstanding per society were only Rs. 4.40 lakh in the latest year, less than a quarter of all-India average.

Commercial Banks

The performance of commercial banks was also far from satisfactory. Even the availability of bank offices to the people continued to be very low in Bihar. In 1969, that is, around two decades after Independence, the average population per bank office stood at 207 thousand compared with the all-India average of 65 thousand. After nationalisation also Bihar lagged behind most of the states, as may be seen from Table 3.11.

The deposit mobilisation by the scheduled commercial banks (SCBs) here had a very low growth, and Bihar's relative share in all-India total stood at only 4.40 per cent in 2001. The per capita deposit continued to be very low, always less than half the national average; in fact, it dropped to only 36.6 per cent in 2003. A noticeable feature here is, however, that the rural area's share in total deposit had a much faster growth than in most other states. In 2001, at 32.5 per cent, it was more than double that at the national level.

On the provision of credit, the situation was very depressing. The state accounted for only 1.63 per cent of the national total in 2002, declining from 2.81 per cent in 1987. The per capita credit was extremely low, declining from 21.9 per cent of the all-India average in 1977 to 15.3 per cent in 2003. A welcoming feature, as in deposit mobilisation, was a relatively large share for rural areas, although it declined over the years. Even after the fall, rural Bihar's proportion was nearly three times the all-India average (Table 3.11).

The C-D ratio continued to be extremely low and had a sharp fall in recent years. In 2003, Bihar had only 23.4 per cent as against 59.4 at the national level; earlier, the disparity was much less. The credit-plus-investment deposit ratio was also similarly placed. The rural C-D ratio had a sharp fall over the years, and the rural-urban disparity has virtually disappeared now. In the latest year, the former was higher by only 0.9 point as against 11.8 points in 1993. However, it is still much above the national average (ibid.).

Behind this distressing situation, no doubt low per capita income and low level of developmental activities are primarily to be blamed, but the quality of service provided was also not good. Bihar had one employee per 1,880 persons in 1999 as against the all-India average of 938 persons (RBI 2000; based on 1997 population estimate). Although the banks could not ignore the question of volume of business in employing more persons, the latter could have raised the former by taking a more active role.

Regional Rural Banks

The creation of RRBs was a response to the failures of the co-operative credit system and the commercial banks in assisting the weaker sections in rural areas. The co-operative credit was biased towards the landed class, and despite certain measures their operation could not be suitably modified. The commercial banks were traditionally urban-biased, and even after nationalisation

Table 3.9: Trend in Growth of Credit Societies: Bihar Vis-à-vis Other States (Rs. Lakh, unless otherwise stated)

States	No. of Societies[b]			Membership[b] (in '000)			Working capital Total[b] (Rs. million)		
	1970a	1982	1998	1970	1982	1998	1970	1982	1998
Bihar	16783 (9.1)	7207	7518 (5.5)	2983	6389	7518 (152.0)[c]	811	4505	26745 (33.0)[d]
W.Bengal	13484 (7.3)	10315	10450 (7.6)	2336	4401	4587 (96.4)	1441	7491	20562 (14.3)
Orissa	4514 (2.5)	3721	3538 (2.6)	1636	3104	3916 (139.4)	756 6	547	31847 (42.1)
Assam	3656 (2.0)	295	1509 (1.1)	425	2474	2289 (438.6)	390	10503	5585 (14.3)
Madhya Pr.	10685 (5.8)	6490	7804 (5.7)	2503	5351	9815 (292.1)	2682	1248	79868 (29.8)
Uttar Pr.	27875 (15.2)	10169	11471 (8.4)	6020	10940	16930 (181.2)	3289	20736	118001 (35.9)
Maharashtra	23429 (12.7)	24438	38983 (28.4)	6239	10792	29283 (369.4)	9285	41346	545366 (58.7)
Andhra pr.	18844 (10.3)	13138	8175 (6.0)	3105	11171	17555 (465.4)	3130	17022	131987 (42.2)
Kerala	2578 (1.4)	2264	3543 (2.6)	1908	6047	15108 (691.8)	115	11052	143953 (1251.8)
Punjab	11496 (6.3)	4132	4124 (3.0)	1563	2159	2882 (84.4)	2539	11045	73624 (29.0)
All-India	183809 (100.0)	123804	137144 (100.0)	43018	9064	155829 (262.2)	39347	209164	1892149 (48.1)

(Table 3.9 Contd.)

Deposits–b (Rs. million)			PACS Deposits		PACS Loans outstanding		PNACS deposits	
1970	1982	1998	1970	1985	1970	1985	1966	1983
145	604	8381 (57.8)[d]	293 (1776)[e]	303 (4484)[e]	1931	6260 (0.93)[e]	567 (2.57)[e]	1401 (3.05)[e]
571	1870	7917 (13.9)	72 (611)	337 (4456)	1701	12630 (1.67)	4462 (5.25)	7588 (3.17)
72	489	9459 1(131.1)	147 (3840)	437 (15635)	1975	16470 (5.89)	125 (0.69)	853 (1.00)
136	408	2994 (22.0)	54 (1663)	70 (3136)	552	870 (0.39)	146 (0.46)	257 (0.51)
245	1698	21451 (87.6)	373 (3733)	1360 (24403)	7325	31660 (5.68)	273 (0.44)	1866 (2.33)
389	3104	37560 (96.6)	475 (1788)	3612 (41990)	8052	42680 (4.96)	457 (0.39)	2294 (1.52)
1718	14027	220405 (128.3)	405 (2016)	1600 (8711)	14214	67000 (3.65)	4702 (2.09)	12840 (2.03)
201	1704	12802 (63.7)	337 (2260)	1189 (16827)	3521	27760 (3.93)	682 (0.70)	2006 (0.63)
216	2743	57440 (265.9)	879 (40681)	2735 (177874)	2979	52280 (33.99)	206 (0.53)	9174 (12.64)
373	1722	18461 (49.5)	1446 (13962)	2856 (93211)	5060	24260 (7.92)	68 (0.04)	142 (0.14)
6223	44877	651152 (104.6)	6267 (3852)	52406 (57119)	71144	432320 (4.71)	17688 (1.32)	65265 (2.59)

Notes: a : Years refer to March-end for 1998, and for all others June-end ;b : relate to all types of credit societies;c : percentage increase between 1970 and 1998;d : increase over the period, in multiples;e : per society, in Rs.

Source: Deb 1988; NABARD 2002.

Table 3.10: Trend in Scheduled commercial Banks' Operation in Bihar Vis-à-Vis other states

States	*Deposit Mobilisation (Rs. Crore)*							
	Total			*Rural*		*Per capita deposit (Rs.)*		
	1973 December	*1987 March*	*2001 March*	*1973*	*2001*	*1977*	*1998*	*2003*
Bihar	459	4771	41636 (91.1)[a]	31.1 (6.8)[b]	13597 (32.5)[b]	156	2695	4562
W. Bengal	1295	10735	68257 (52.7)	37.8 (2.9)	1033 (15.1)	571	5831	10772
Orissa	78	1316	15111 (193.7)	7.2 (9.2)	5074 (33.6)	92	2523	5446
Assam	82	1135	9864 (120.3)	10.7 (13.0)	2323 (23.6)	139	2382	4851
Madhya Pradesh.	273	3790	36691 (134.4)	21.8 (8.0)	7408 (20.2)	152	3065	6068
Uttar Pradesh	879	10380	94372 (107.4)	96.8 (11.0)	25807 (27.3)	214	3657	7127
Maharashtra	2283	19093	173831 (76.1)	48.7 (2.1)	6835 (3.9)	876	13317	26208
Andhra Pradesh	402	5786	54410 (135.3)	33.2 (8.3)	8039 (14.8)	228	4298	9679
Kerala	317	4170	45238 (142.7)	52.4 (16.5)	2299 (5.1)	356	8646	18679
All-India	10084	103112	950705 (94.3)	741.4 (7.4)	139427 (14.7)	387	6198	12450

Contd.

(Table 3.10 Contd.)

Credit Outstanding (Rs. crore) Total			Rural		Per capita			C-D Ratio* (%) June 1969		Dec. 1985	
1969	1987	2001	1987	2001	1977	1998	2003	Rural	Total	Rural	Total
52.3	1875	10005 (191.3)[a]	646 (34.4)[c]	2937 (29.4)c	61	741	1134	92.1	30.9	44.7	35.7
699.7	5485	30097 (43.0)	420 (7.7)	2415 (8.0)	395	2689	5189	2.5	108.7	42.3	49.7
16.6	1113	6265 (377.4)	368 (33.0)	2160 (34.5)	53	1140	2519	5.3	53.4	121.3	89.1
14.0	628	3193 (228.1)	169 (26.9)	800 (25.1)	63	782	1387	51.7	40.9	63.8	43.7
65.3	2334	17095 (261.8)	563 (24.1)	2911 (17.0)	83	1577	2724	10.9	58.7	83.0	60.3
172.9	4823	26651 (154.1)	1335 (27.7)	6818 (25.6)	94	1046	2067	80.4	47.4	57.6	44.7
1070.6	15549	148433 (138.6)	680 (4.4)	4997 (3.4)	666	9627	24437	56.9	92.5	82.5	76.7
146.7	4687	34429 (234.7)	1142 (24.4)	6220 (18.1)	166	3101	6058	83.0	90.1	115.1	75.4
98.7	2671	19477 (197.3)	282 (10.6)	1265 (6.5)	218	3829	8091	32.5	64.9	76.4	58.8
3608.9	66673	556436 (154.2)	9673 (14.5)	56017 (10.1)	279	3440	7392	37.5	77.4	67.9	58.5

Contd.

(Table 3.10 Contd.)

C-D Ratio 1993						Population per bank office (in'000)		
Rural	Total	1998	1999	2000	2003	June 1969	June 1981	June 2001
49.2	37.4	28.7	27.4	23.2 (34.3)[d]	23.4	207	29	21
45.7	54.3	45.7	43.4	44.9 (52.8)	48.2	87	24	18
78.2	67.0	49.4	44.2	42.8 (69.1)	46.2	212	27	16
61.9	49.3	37.8	38.7	35.5 (53.8)	17.0	198	39	22
63.5	60.9	56.7	52.2	52.5 (65.8)	46.6	116	24	18
41.9	41.5	32.7	31.1	30.9 (42.1)	30.4	119	27	20
66.2	63.7	69.8	72.6	83.4 (86.9)	93.2	44	17	15
91.4	79.5	72.4	69.1	65.5 (78.4)	62.6	75	19	15
50.9	46.5	44.7	41.8	41.7 (50.4)	43.3	35	11	10
55.3	58.9	55.3	54.8	56.0 (63.6)	59.4	65	19	15

Notes: a : growth in multiples; b : percentage to total deposit of the respective year; c : percentage to total credit of the year; d : investment plus credit-deposit ratio; *: as per utilisation

Source: RBI, Basic Statistical Returns, and Statistical Tables Relating to Banks in India, various issues.

Table 3.11: Trend in operation of Regional Rural Banks: Bihar Vis-à-vis Other states (Rs. million)

States	Deposits				Advances outstanding (Contd.)	
	Dec.1981	Sept. '90	March '99	growth[b]	Dec '81	Sept. '90
Bihar	533.8 (5.36)[a]	6118	33207 (175)[a]	62.2 (32.6)	447.8 (4.50)[c]	4250 (22.49)[c]
West Bengal	167.1 (5.66)	3380	19491 (220)	116.6 (38.9)	158.3 (5.36)	1919 (22.26)
Orissa	259.6 (6.83)	1641	11827 (140)	45.6 (20.5)	381.3 (10.03)	2362 (28.84)
Assam	72.5 (8.33)	1032	6690 (164)	92.3 (19.7)	38.9 (4.47)	950 (23.87)
Madhya Pradesh	164.5 (3.82)	3320	24015 (153)	146.0 (40.1)	207.0 (4.80)	2698 (16.85)
Uttar Pradesh	856.6 (10.23)	12043	71647 (234)	83.6 (22.9)	600.8 (7.18)	6758 (22.14)
Maharashtra	55.7 (5.51)	1005	8020 (134)	144.0 (24.3)	82.4 (8.16)	1380 (23.39)
Andhra Pradesh	354.8 (9.51)	3018	20903 (186)	58.9 (19.6)	675.0 (18.10)	4148 (36.97)
Kerala	152.5 (7.74)	903	5022 (174)	32.9 (22.5)	349.2 (17.73)	1884 (70.04)
All-India	3360.0 (7.01)	42675	266834 (182)	79.4 (26.0)	4065.9 (8.48)	35552 (24.50)

Contd.

(Table 3.11 Contd.)

States	Advances outstanding (Contd.)			C-D Ratio (%)			
	March '99	2002	growth[b]	1981	1990	1999	2002
Bihar	8229 (43)	12020 (64)c	26.8	83.9	69.5	24.8	21
West Bengal	6476 (73)	11228 (129)	70.9	94.7	56.8	33.2	34
Orissa	6196 (74)	11854 (144)	31.1	146.9	143.9	52.4	54
Assam	2118 (52)	3499 (89)	89.9	53.7	92.1	31.7	29
Madhya Pradesh	8804 (56)	13261 (81)	64.1	125.8	81.3	36.7	36
Uttar Pradesh	22047 (72)	34507 (114)	57.4	70.1	56.1	30.8	31
Maharashtra	4301 (72)	6462 (110)	78.4	147.9	137.3	53.6	52
Andhra Pradesh	13938 (124)	24603 (220)	36.4	190.2	137.4	66.7	67
Kerala	6104 (212)	10863 (315)	31.1	229.0	208.6	121.5	108
All-India	112786 (77)	185975 (130)	45.7	121.0	83.3	42.3	42

Notes: a: figures in brackets are deposit mobilisation per branch, in Rs. Lakh; b: between 1981 and 2002, in multiples; c: advances per branch, in Rs. Lakh;

d: Bihar, data for Madhya Pradesh and Uttar Pradesh include the respective new state.

Sources : RBI 1982, 1991; NABARD 2002a.

the changes that came were far from adequate. To fill-up the gaps, in 1975, therefore, the RRBs were created. The share capital of these banks were contributed jointly by the government of India, the state government concerned and the sponsoring SCB in the ratio of 50:15:35. These banks were granted many concession by the RBI. The progress was, however, very slow, as will be evident from the analysis below.

The relative performance of Bihar was very poor here also. The amount of deposit mobilised had increased only 100.7 times between December 1981 and March 2003 as against 132.6 times for all RRBs in the country. The deposit per branch was always below the national average. In 2002, it was respectively Rs 288 lakh and Rs 310 lakh (Table 3.11).

On the level of advances, the situation was worse. The total credit outstanding had increased only 26.8 times between December 1981 and March 2002 as against 45.7 times for all RRBs in the country. The amount outstanding per branch stood at Rs. 64 lakh in 2002, constituting a mere 49.2 per cent of the national average; in 1990, it was 91.8 per cent. The C-D ratio was always much below the national average; in 2002, it stood at only 21 per cent of the latter's.

From the above analysis it is apparent that the banking system in Bihar did not play the role expected of it. The potential of deposit mobilisation remained largely unexploited. No doubt, the per capita income in Bihar was very low, but it does not fully explain the situation. There is a circular relationship between deposit mobilisation, its deployment and growth of income. If the banks had played their role properly, then each of the elements would have grown much faster. Of course, there were short comings on the part of government also. The required environment did not exist, and the government rarely took any initiative. The banks were generally burdened with huge overdues and the government did not play the role expected of it. Non-performing assets constituted 24 per cent in the RRBs of Bihar as against 16 per cent at the national level in 2002. The recovery to demand ratio was only 50 per cent here compared with 71 per cent in the latter (NABARD 2000a).

When the resource mobilisation was low, both on government account and by the banking system, the development activities could not be high. In the following four chapters, we look into the pattern of growth that took place in some of the important areas, beginning with human resource development.

4

Human Resource Development

The desired pattern of economic development can be brought only with the right quality human beings. A socialist pattern of society cannot be established by man with capitalist and feudal mentality. Therefore, in any development effort, right type of education and character building must get the topmost priority. The question of skill formation is of secondary importance; it has to be ensured first that the skill is acquired by the right man, otherwise it might be used for a wrong purpose. And then, a quality mind must reside in a healthy body; in fact, the former is a prerequisite for the latter, from a long term point of view. For healthy living, proper health care facilities, both preventive and curative, are also an essential requirement. The analysis below looks into the measures taken in Bihar in the areas of education and health.

EDUCATION

The first important educational policy of the government was laid down in the Constitution itself. It was stated in the Directive Principles of State Policy: "The State shall endeavour to provide, within a period of ten years from the Commencement of this constitution for free and compulsory education for all children until they complete the age of fourteen years." (Section 45). On other aspects of educational policy, there were announcements from time to time. Great importance was attached to the quality of Secondary education as it marked the completion of education for a large majority of pupils (GOI 1972 : 239). Detailed policies were laid down in different five-year plans. In the Third Plan, for example, on general education, the main emphasis was to be on the provision of facilities for all children in the age-group 6-11, extension and improvement of the teaching of science at the secondary and University stages, development of vocational and technical education at all levels and facilities for training of teachers of every stage. There was to be a "special concentration on the education of girls" (GOI 1961: 573).

The implementation of these policies were almost totally neglected. Probably the government was afraid that if the majority become educated it will be difficult to exploit them for the benefit of the richer section of population. The allocation of fund for different purposes itself was very meagre, as will be evident from the analysis below.

Level of Expenditure

The plan outlays on education were very low in Bihar. Although the state's share in the country's total population was around 11 per cent, it never spent a commensurate proportion on education. In the all-India total of plan expenditure on it, Bihar's share declined from 9.5 per cent in the Third Plan to 7.5 per cent in the Fourth. The per capita expenditure stood at only Rs. 7.00 in the Fourth plan compared with Rs. 9.78 at the national level. In the following plans the expenditure increased considerably, but it was in terms of a much depreciated rupee. The Eighth Plan raised it to Rs. 997.7 crore, a 24-fold rise over the Fourth Plan, being Rs. 41.48 crore (GOI 1961, 1969, 1972).

The budgetary expenditure as a whole was also very low on education. In the all-India total spending, Bihar's share stood at only 5.4 per cent in 1979-82, despite having the lowest literacy rate in the country, and the maximum reached was 8.4 per cent in 1989-92. In the total budgetary expenditure of the state also education's share was generally low; the maximum reached was 24.8 per cent in 1990-91. It may be noted that, in the fifties also Bihar did not spend much. In 1956-57, for example, the total direct expenditure on education stood at only Rs. 874 lakh, constituting 5.48 per cent of all-India total (GOI 1959).

As regards the distribution of expenditure among different levels, elementary education naturally received the highest share, given the extent of illiteracy. It was always above 60 per cent, and much higher than the all-states average. The expenditure per pupil was also generally higher than in the latter. At the level of secondary education-which is no less important-however, the per pupil expenditure was very low, as evident from Table 4.1.

On university and higher education, which served mainly the richer section of population, however, the per pupil expenditure was much higher than the all-states average. In 1980-81, it was nearly three times higher. Thus, the Bihar government spent an unduly large amount in an area that could be easily self-financed to a large extent. On technical education again the expenditure was low. In 1995-96, the state spent only Rs. 1,764 per pupil as against the all-states average of Rs. 2,051. Earlier, in 1980-81, it was Rs. 675 and Rs. 1,261 respectively.

Facilities Available

With this level of expenditure–reduced further by misappropriation-naturally the facilities remained far from adequate. After more than four decades of development efforts, and despite the promises in the Constitution, the availability of schools continued to be very poor. In rural Bihar, in 1994, 35 per cent of the villages did not have a primary school; at the national level, it was 29 per cent. On habitation basis also the position was not good, as may be seen from Tab 4.2.Total number of primary schools in Bihar had risen by only 79.7

Table 4.1: Government Expenditure Per Pupil on Different Levels of Education: Bihar Vis-à-Vis Other States (Rs. at 1980-81 prices)

States	*Elementary Education*				*Secondary Education*			*University & Higher Education*		
	1980-1	*1985-6*	*1990-1*	*1995-6*	*1980-1*	*1990-1*	*1995-6*	*1980-1*	*1990-1*	*1995-6*
Bihar	171	216	349	326	333	700	752	1387	863	650
West Bengal	172	178	228	198	614	786	876	519	469	530
Orissa	132	153	268	283	800	624	671	3395	1499	905
Assam	176	209	227	329	700	588	817	585	458	365
Madhya P.	134	166	221	231	4647	1931	1010	481	347	264
Uttar Pradesh	150	204	367	255	1383	1546	893	120	215	175
Andhra Pr	189	232	225	222	448	436	369	1295	1652	749
Kerala	340	411	505	777	280	356	523	2156	1982	1536
Maharashtra	205	284	344	349	552	847	930	431	305	239
Punjab	215	273	366	349	860	1290	1382	1559	592	326
All-India	185	230	311	305	629	876	860	427	438	352

Source: GOI, Analysis of Budgetary Expenditure on Education (various issues), MHRD, Department of Education, New Delhi.

per cent between 1956-57 and 2001, from 29,692 to 53,352, as against 134.7 per cent at the national level (GOI 1959, 2002c). The available schools, moreover, did not have adequate number of rooms for instructional purpose. Ninety per cent of the primary schools had two rooms or less. Not only this, 38 per cent of the schools were without any room for instructional purpose, and a large number was using open space.

The pupil-teacher ratio has been very high in Bihar. For all areas it stood at 43.9 in 1994, which was significantly higher than the national average and highest among the Eastern states. The situation worsened further in the following years, being at 67 in 2000-01, and the difference with the national average rose to 24 points from 3.7.The rural-Urban difference was by as much as 6 points in 1994 as against only one point at the nation level. On the academic qualifications of teachers also the relative position was not good. The proportion of those with Secondary level constituted 55.67 per cent here as against 48.96 at the national level.

At Upper primary also the situation was not good. Percentage of villages not having a school with upper primary stage was found to be as much as 83.5 in 1994, 7 points above the national average. On habitation basis, only 27.1 per cent of rural population had it within the habitation. The growth in number of upper primary schools over a period of two decades was only 20.2 per cent, from 11,289 in 1980-81 to 13,571 in 2000-01, as against 74.0 per cent for all-India. Average number of rooms in the schools was also very low, being 3.67 in Bihar compared with 5.09 in all-India. As much as 26 per cent of the schools were without any room at all. The pupil-teacher ratio was also very poor, and it worsened greatly over the years, rising from 34 in1980-81 to 56 in 2000-01; at the national level, it was respectively 33 and 38.

As regards the secondary stage, even the total number of schools was very low, not to speak of their quality. Bihar had 4293 secondary schools in 1994, constituting 4.9 per cent of all-India total. Between 1956-57 and 2000-01, there was a negative growth, declining from 4,412 to 4,228. In 1994, in the rural areas, only 8.3 per cent of the habitations had a secondary school within the habitation as against 18.3 per cent at the national level. A large majority had to walk more than 2 kms. The pupil-teacher ratio was also very high. In 2000-01, it was 42 in Bihar as against 31 at the national level; in 1994, the disparity was much less, being 34.8 and 30.2.

The availability of certain ancillary facilities was extremely poor in all levels of schools. The drinking water facility was there in only 48.08 per cent of the schools in the state as against the all-India average of 52.59 per cent. For primary level, it was respectively 39.12 and 44.23 per cent. The position of urinal and lavatory facility was much worse, as evident from Table 4.2.

Enrolment

The slow growth in educational facilities, along with other deficiencies, produced a very low level of enrolment in Bihar. In 1960-61, that is, a decade

Table 4.2: Availability of Schools, Certain Facilities therein and the Pupil-Teacher Ratio: Bihar Vis-à-Vis other States

(In 1994)

States	*% of rural population having Schools within the habitation*			*% of villages not having schools with*		*Pupil-teacher ratio (all areas)*		*Rooms for instructional purpose (contd.)*	
	for all	*Primary for SCs*[a]	*Upper primary (all)*	*Primary stage*	*Upper primary*	*Primary*	*Upper primary*	*Primary two rooms or less (% of schools)*	*Schools average No.*
Bihar	77.2	57.3	27.1	35.1	83.5	43.9	41.3	90.3 (38.4)[b]	1.23
W. Bengal	61.2	58.8	14.2	28.9	86.3	43.6	32.4	63.8 (11.7)	2.19
Orissa	76.1	67.8	34.2	33.6	79.8	36.3	30.0	66.3 (2.7)	2.35
Assam	66.3	72.7	22.4	30.9	76.1	32.2	18.3	82.1 (19.0)	1.42
Madhya P.	84.7	84.0	31.4	22.6	84.0	41.5	29.2	70.6 (10.2)	2.18
Uttar P.	60.5	47.0	21.7	46.4	85.8	37.6	20.5	65.4 (3.9)	2.65
Andhra P.	92.4	82.1	43.0	11.7	69.6	46.9	35.6	83.5 (6.2)	1.82
Kerala	76.7	59.2	50.5	4.1	10.4	37.4	34.5	10.8 (2.0)	5.91
Punjab	90.8	90.9	45.4	16.8	76.3	44.6	23.6	53.6 (5.2)	2.89
All-India	77.8	64.3	37.0	28.8	76.7	40.2	32.6	70.5 (10.6)	2.28

(contd.)

(Table 4.2 Contd.)

Upper Primary			Secondary Schools			% of schools (all levels) having facilities for (all areas)				% of villages having NFE Centre
3 or less (%)	Average no.	with in 2 kms (rural areas)	Total no.	P-T ratio (all areas)	% having science lab.	Drinking water	Urinal	Separate Urinal for girls	Lava-tory	
47.2 (26.0)[b]	3.67	42.1 (8.3)[c]	4293 (4.9)	34.8	67.2	48.1 (39.1)[d]	11.3 (3.4)[d]	5.6	14.5	1.64
8.2 (2.9)	4.95	57.7 (9.6)	5845 (6.7)	37.9	41.6	64.2 (59.5)	33.4 (22.1)	15.9	21.3	0.00
63.7 (0.6)	3.29	51.0 (18.6)	5355 (6.1)	19.9	15.1	33.5 (24.9)	17.2 (6.7)	10.2	9.0	19.97
58.5 (5.8)	3.69	51.0 (9.7)	3447 (4.0)	21.7	6.2	28.6 (19.8)	21.9 (12.0)	9.2	5.4	27.83
57.7 (6.0)	3.95	26.5 (11.3)	5580 (6.4)	27.3	57.0	41.6 (34.4)	28.2 (18.4)	15.3	15.2	26.96
57.1 (8.7)	3.91	31.8 (6.2)	6839 (7.8)	35.0	60.4	60.0 (55.5)	34.0 (25.3)	19.1	24.2	28.50
32.9 (0.0)	5.17	48.0 (27.9)	7257 (8.3)	32.2	45.0	41.2 (31.4)	17.8 (7.3)	13.8	15.1	54.28
7.2 (1.0)	11.86	62.7 (29.6)	2478 (2.8)	29.9	81.0	83.3 (76.2)	88.4 (81.4)	66.6	55.8	1.16
59.9 (1.7)	4.51	64.1 (33.1)	2898 (3.3)	29.3	70.6	90.2 (87.7)	63.0 (52.5)	36.6	34.1	0.00
39.4 (6.7)	5.09	45.5 (18.3)	87238 (100.0)	30.2	59.7	52.6 (44.2)	31.5 (18.9)	19.5	20.3	15.57

Notes: a: predominantly habituated by SCs; b: percentage of schools with no room for instructional purpose ; c: percentage of schools within the habitation;
d: relate to primary schools.
Source : NCERT 1998: I, II, IV, V.

Table 4.3: Trend in Growth of Enrolment as Percentage to Population in the Age-group: Bihar Vis a Vis other States Classes I–V

States	*1960-61*			*1979-80*			*1994*		
	Boys	*Girls*	*Total*	*Boys*	*Girls*	*Total*	*Boys*	*Girls*	*Total*
Bihar	80.0	26.9	53.5	104.2	47.4	76.7	77.2	47.4	63.1
West Bengal	80.8	48.4	65.6	104.4	69.7	87.4	88.3	77.7	83.1
Orissa	71.6	23.9	47.8	96.5	66.9	82.2	104.8	84.6	94.8
Assam[a]	73.6	48.0	61.7	90.0	67.1	78.8	93.1	79.6	86.4
Andhra Pradesh	74.0	46.2	60.3	93.8	67.7	81.0	81.5	70.2	75.9
Kerala	118.0	99.7	108.8	103.4	102.2	102.8	98.9	95.7	97.3
Madhya Pradesh	73.5	19.3	47.0	84.9	43.2	64.8	99.4	77.3	88.6
Uttar Pradesh	68.6	19.9	45.4	91.0	45.1	68.9	74.6	50.6	63.4
Maharashtra	89.0	56.6	73.3	124.4	97.5	111.4	98.5	91.0	94.9
Punjab	84.0	36.3	61.8	118.1	107.6	113.0	86.2	81.5	84.0
All-India	80.5	40.4	61.1	100.2	65.9	83.6	90.0	73.1	81.8

Contd.

(Table 4.3 Contd.)

Classes VI-VIII									Proportion of children aged 5-14, attending Schools in 1993-94 (Rural areas)[b]		
1960-61			1979-80			1994					
Boys	Girls	Total	Boys	Girls	Total	Boys	Girls	Total	Boys	Girls	Total
34.3	4.2	19.4	41.0	13.8	27.8	40.6	20.7	31.6	58.4	38.6	49.7
30.3	10.7	21.1	49.4	33.8	41.7	50.6	38.4	44.7	68.9	61.2	65.2
13.8	2.0	7.9	39.0	18.9	29.2	59.5	40.6	50.1	66.9	54.0	60.7
37.4	16.0	27.4	48.6	32.7	40.7	60.7	52.0	56.5	75.8	72.6	74.4
23.9	7.2	15.6	27.8	14.8	21.4	49.2	35.5	42.7	68.0	50.8	59.3
59.4	41.3	50.3	91.8	85.3	88.6	96.6	94.8	95.7	92.5	93.9	93.2
26.6	5.5	16.3	45.0	15.5	30.8	65.3	38.8	52.8	61.4	44.2	53.5
30.9	5.0	18.6	53.3	18.7	36.8	54.6	30.5	43.6	66.7	44.5	56.8
40.7	15.5	28.5	58.8	33.7	46.5	73.3	60.9	67.4	82.8	73.0	78.1
38.8	16.3	28.3	68.4	48.4	59.0	65.7	60.5	63.3	79.6	72.8	76.5
34.3	10.8	22.8	52.0	27.7	40.2	62.1	45.4	54.2	70.3	55.	63.3

Notes: a: for Assam, in 1979-80 the primary stage refers to classes I-IV; b: these are NSSO data, the NCERT data show higher percentages.
Source: GOI 1961: 604, 605; 1981: 362, 364; NCERT 1998: IV; NSSO 1997.

after economic planning began, enrolment as percentage to population in the age-group 6-11 was only 53.5 as against the national average of 61.1. The situation was particularly depressing for girls. Their proportion this year was only 26.9 per cent as against 40.4 per cent for all-India. In the following years, it worsened further; and stood at respectively 47.4 and 73.1per cent in 1994, and 60.5 and 85.9 in 2000-01. Even for boys and girls together, Bihar had only 65.7 per cent in the latest year as against 95.7 for all-India.

At the level of upper primary, the disparity with the national average was still wider. In 2000-01, for girls the enrolment ratio stood at only 25.2 per cent, half the national average; for boys and girls together, it was respectively 37.4 and 58.6 per cent. Four decades earlier, in 1960-61, the relative position was better, as may be seen from Table 4.3.

The proportion of children attending school in Bihar continued to be very low. For the age group 5-14, in 1993-94, in the rural areas it stood at only 49.7 per cent compared with 63.3 per cent at the national level. For girls, the situation was much worse, as may be seen from the Table. An NSSO study in 1995-96 found that only 41.2 per cent of persons aged 5-24 were attending any educational institution (general) in Bihar as against 49.8 per cent at the national level. The position of females was much worse. In rural Bihar only 26.4 per cent were attending any educational institution as against 38.1 per cent in rural India. The break-up reveals a horrifying situation. In the age-group 6-10, only 43 per cent were found to be attending school here as against 69 per cent at the national level (NSSO 1998a). The picture of net attendance was very depressing (Table 4.4).

The drop-out rate, particularly at the primary stage, was very high. In rural Bihar it stood at 41.0 per cent in 1995-96 as against 33.2 in rural India. The situation appears to be deteriorating rapidly. In 2000-01, rural-urban combined, the gross drop-out rate stood at 59.5 per cent as against the national average of 40.7 per cent; for classes I-VIII, it was respectively 75.0 and 53.7 per cent. To realise the gravity of the situation, it is necessary to look into the extent of never-enrolled. In 1995-96, for males, Bihar had 39.6 per cent in the age-group 5-24 and for females 64.2 per cent (Table 4.4 and GOI 2002c).

Reasons Behind

Behind this distressing educational scenario of Bihar, many factors have operated. Apart from the low level of facilities noted earlier, weak motivation of teachers, low quality curriculum, poverty of the people and inability of parents to perceive the benefit from education are important. We may note here the findings of the 52nd Round of NSS (1995-96) on this.

On dropping-out in rural Bihar, the factors found important were 'parents not interested in studies', 'child not interested', 'education not considered useful', 'has to participate in economic activities', 'financial constraints', 'needed for attending to domestic activities' and 'inability to cope with studies'. The first one accounted for 21.7 per cent of the cases, followed by financial constraints

17.0 per cent, parents not interested 11.8 per cent and education not considered useful 11.4 per cent. Thus, these four reasons together explained 62 per cent of the total drop-out cases. For females, the most important reason was found to be 'need for attending to domestic activities', 23.5 per cent of the cases, followed by 'parents not interested' 15.7 per cent and 'child not interested' 13.7 per cent. For non-enrolment, the most important reason was parents not interested in studies, accounting for 36.1 per cent of cases, followed by 'financial constraints' 21.3 per cent and 'child not interested' 12.6 per cent. In case of females, the first one accounted for a larger proportion.

Studies conducted by the NCERT on drop-out by female students found a sense of insecurity preventing many adolescent girls from continuing with their education. It has been pointed out that absence of women teachers acts as a deterrent. One study also noted that sheer hunger and lack of basic nourishment force many young girls to drop out of schools; they suffer frequent bouts of illness because of malnourishment. The low priority accorded to girls vis-à-vis their brothers as far as health care is concerned is an important contributor to it (Statesman 2001f).

The government's efforts to overcome these problems were insignificant. The relative position of Bihar on some of the incentive measures may be seen from Table 4.5. The provision of scholarship covered only 3.5 per cent of the students in age group 5-24 in 1995-96 as against 6.8 per cent at the national level. In neighbouring Madhya Pradesh, it was as much as 18 per cent. On the costliest item, books also a very low proportion of students were benefited. Free or subsidised supply covered only 5.7 per cent here compared with the national average of 25.6 per cent. As regards supply of stationary, only 1.5 per cent of the students got it as against 3.9 per cent in all-India.

Probably the most effective instrument for attracting students to schools would have been the provision of midday meals. But it could be launched only in 1995, and then also the coverage remained only 3.4 per cent of students compared with 17.9 per cent at the national level. This useful scheme has been almost a total failure in most of the states. Feeding a large number of primary students in an environment of corruption and inefficiency is not an easy task. Seeing the extent of mismanagement and short-cuts adopted, recently the Supreme Court had to order making the provision of cooked meals mandatory (Statesman 2001g).

The extent of resources and commitment required for fulfilling the Constitutional directive of compulsory education up to the age of 14 is bound to remain unachieved for many more years to come, given the quality of government the state is burdened with. There is need for radical changes in many directions to make it possible. Physical facility, quality of teaching, proper curriculum, financial assistance to BPL families, and convincing the parents of the need for education, all these will require a level of commitment from the government that is unthinkable in the present situation. It may be noted here

Table 4.4: Net Attendance, Drop-out Rate and the proportion of Never-enrolled in Bihar Vis-à-Vis other States

(in 1995-96)

States	Net attendance Ratio (%)				% of Drop-out (all areas)			% of never-enrolled[b] (Rural areas)	
	I-V	VI-VIII	IX-X	All stages Combined	Primary	Middle	Secondary	Male	Female
Bihar	41 (39)[a]	33 (31)[a]	20 (17)[a]	40.4 (43.0)[a]	39.4	26.4	16.3	39.6	64.2
West Bengal	66 (64)	33 (28)	15 (10)	62.2 (64.7)	41.4	37.8	14.9	26.3	35.0
Orissa	61 (60)	45 (43)	33 (29)	56.1 (56.5)	47.5	15.7	30.1	21.8	39.5
Assam	72 (72)	43 (42)	34 (33)	61.9 (62.3)	36.1	23.0	30.5	20.9	25.9
Andhra P.	70 (66)	41 (36)	30 (24)	61.2 (66.7)	38.5	23.1	24.9	24.0	38.8
Kerala	91 (91)	76 (76)	60 (57)	67.7 (69.3)	3.3	16.4	54.5	1.3	2.9
Madhya P.	63 (59)	35 (28)	14 (8)	38.5 (58.7)	28.0	21.5	5.5	30.9	49.8
Uttar Pradesh	59 (58)	33 (31)	19 (16)	48.7 (49.2)	26.6	24.6	30.5	27.2	54.2
Maharashtra	85 (85)	55 (49)	38 (35)	63.5 (67.9)	18.9	21.7	40.2	11.0	19.4
Punjab	81 (80)	59 (57)	33 (30)	44.0 (42.4)	29.2	32.6	17.3	11.3	15.2
All-India	66 (63)	43 (39)	26 (22)	56.2 (58.1)	30.4	26.2	28.7	23.5	40.6

Notes : a: relate to rural areas; b : refer to age 5-24 years.
Source: NSSO 1998a.

that, although the state has 20.15 lakh children out of school, under the Sarva Shiksha Abhijan it could spend only 60.9 per cent of the total of Rs. 560 crore available in 2004-05 (Statesman 2005).

ADULT EDUCATION

For raising the level of literacy in the country, there was an urgent need for rapidly expanding the non-formal education system. But until early eighties, it did not receive any attention worth the name. The Third and Fourth Five-year plans talked of mobilising local community resources and voluntary efforts. It was to develop as extension activities by educational institutions, primarily village school. The National Board of Adult Education was set up to advise the government and organise the activities. From the Fifth Plan onwards, the work was given some greater attention and it was also included in the Minimum Needs Programme.

A significant boost to this work, however, came only in the Seventh Plan, with the launch of the National Literacy Mission in 1988. The NLM was to impart functional Literacy to 100 million non-literate persons in the age-group 15-35 in a time-bound system. Till March 1998, 434 literacy projects were sanctioned covering 442 districts in the country, out of 577. The literacy projects were of three types: Literacy campaign (LC), Post Literacy Campaign (PLC) and Continuing Education Projects (CEP).

The Progress of NLM in Bihar was very poor, as evident from Table 4.6. Total number made literate over the last 10 years, from May 1988 to March 1998, was only 5.23 lakh, constituting 7.2 per cent of all-India total. A number of smaller states had much higher achievements. The performance of TLC in particular, was very poor. In the total number made literate under the NLM, its share was 43.2 per cent as against 72.3 per cent at the national level.

Component-wise, on the literacy phase, the achievement was only 22.9 per cent of the target, around half the proportion at the national level. Among the selected states, all but two had better performance. As regards the post-literacy phase, of the target set, the enrolment was a fifth, and those completing the phase I was a mere one-tenth; at the national level, 40 per cent of the target was achieved.

The performance varied widely from district to district. While three districts—Dumka, Madhepura and Dhanbad—had more than 60 per cent achievement, for Begusarai, Darbhanga, Saharsa and Ranchi it was 20-40 per cent. The lowest performance was in Muzaffarpur and Khagari a less than 10 per cent at level III even after 18 months of sanction.

Behind the poor performance in adult literacy an important factor was the adverse social situation. Caste rivalry, domination of landlords and in certain areas reluctance to employ as daily workers those attending the literacy classes prevented the programme from having any noticeable success. The agencies entrusted with the work also did not do it with the level of sincerity required.

Table 4.5: Provision of Scholarship, Free Education, Midday Meals, etc in Bihar Vis-à-Vis other states (% of students of age 5-24 years)

States	*Scholarship*	*Free Education*			*Free or Subsidised*		*Midday*
		Primary	*Middle*	*Sec. & H.S.*	*Books*	*Stationery*	*meals*
Bihar	3.5 (3.8)[a]	78.4 (8.31)[a]	75.7 (79.1)[a]	65.8	5.7	1.5	3.4
West Bengal	4.5 (5.8)	91.8 (96.7)	91.3 (94.6)	83.7	57.6	3.1	.4.4
Orissa	5.5 (5.5)	94.9 (97.5)	87.8 (88.8)	61.2	11.0	2.9	48.9
Assam	1.6 (1.5)	95.1 (96.3)	93.3 (95.9)	75.6	70.1	10.2	25.1
Andhra Pradesh	2.5 (2.6)	71.5 (82.1)	66.7 (80.9)	54.1	44.6	6.1	12.6
Kerala	9.2 (9.6)	80.5 (82.7)	84.1 (86.0)	71.4	4.9	3.4	30.4
Madhya Pradesh	18.0 (20.8)	85.2 (92.3)	79.5 (88.4)	71.1	29.2	3.6	23.7
Uttar Pradesh	6.5 (7.4)	60.7 (67.7)	57.1 (62.5)	60.6	0.6	0.4	4.4
Maharashtra	2.1 (2.3)	81.7 (92.9)	64.5 (74.4)	46.6	12.8	5.1	10.7
Punjab	11.3 (13.8)	56.3 (68.7)	51.8 (64.2)	15.6	21.1	2.3	8.7
All-India	6.8 (7.8)	76.0 (84.0)	71.4 (79.9)	57.4	25.6	3.9	17.9

Notes : a : relate to rural areas.
Source: NSSO 1998[a].

HEALTH AND FAMILY PLANNING

The government's policies on health and family planning were on the whole beyond reproach; the problem was with implementation. The Third Five-year Plan document stated the objectives on health and family planning as "ensuring a certain minimum of physical well-being and to create conditions favourable to greater efficiency and productivity". There was to be an emphasis on preventive public health services, and specific programmes formulated " for improvement of environmental sanitation, specially rural and urban water supply, control of communicable diseases, organisation of institutional facilities... and provision of services such as maternal and child welfare, health education and nutrition". The Plan also intended to give a very "high priority to family planning".

In 1977, the government announced the policy of 'Health for all by 2000 A.D', along with the long-term objective of stabilizing population by reducing net reproduction rate to one by 1995. The Sixth Plan document stated the strategy to be followed in the next two decades as:

(i) Emphasis to shift to rural areas and a combination of preventive, promotive and curative measures built-up starting from village level; (ii) Each primary Health centre (PHC) was to serve a population of 30,000 and a sub-centre 5,000, with relaxation for Hill areas; (iii) Proper coordination of programmes under education, water supply and sanitation, control of communicable diseases, family planning, nutrition, etc, for obtaining optimum results; (iv) Adequate number of medical and paramedical manpower was to be trained, and education and training given a suitable rural orientation; and (v) The people were to be involved in tackling their health problems and ultimately they were to supervise and manage their own health programmes.

The specific targets laid out for the year 2000 were : infant mortality per 1000 live births to come down to below 60, crude death rate to 9, life expectancy at birth to 64 and crude birth rate to 21.

We have noted in chapter 2 that on every indicator of health Bihar presented a very gloomy picture and none of the specific targets could be reached by the end of nineties. Below we look into the level of expenditure in different areas and the extent of facilities created over the years.

Pattern of Expenditure

The expenditure on health and family planning in Bihar was very low, at least till mid-seventies. The total expenditure increased from Rs. 13.10 crore in the Second Five-year Plan to Rs. 20.43 crore in the Fourth; in real term, this was actually an absolute fall. The Fifth Plan registered a three-fold rise over the preceding plan, being at Rs. 60.20 crore. The growth in the following plans was also substantial and reached Rs. 1622.38 crore in the Ninth. In the total expenditure, the share of water supply and sanitation was more than half in most of the plans, with the highest at 70 per cent in the Fourth Plan.

Table 4.6: Progress under the NLM since Inception : Bihar Vis-à-vis Other States (As at 31.3.1998)

States	Total no. made Literate (in '000)	of which under the TLC (%)	Level of Achievement (in '000 nos.)					
			Literacy Phase			Under Post-Literacy		
			Target	Enrolment	Achievement[a]	Target	Enrolment	Achievement[b]
Bihar	5231 (7.2)	43.2	9853	5953	2259 (22.9)[c]	2590	533	269 (10.4)[c]
West Bengal	8972 (12.4)	92.0	149292	11388	8253 (57.7)	7848	3881	2582 (32.9)
Orissa	2440 (3.4)	85.9	5493	4242	2097 (38.2)	2532	1816	850 (33.6)
Assam	1240 (1.7)	31.9	3296	1762	396 (12.0)	136	63	53 (39.0)
Madhya Pradesh	5779 (8.0)	73.3	12589	10090	4238 (33.7)	1501	1046	497 (33.1)
Uttar Pradesh	8638 (11.9)	53.6	18915	12989	4626 (24.5)	1224	885	598 (48.9)
Andhra Pradesh	8287 (11.4)	88.0	14162	12551	7290 (51.5)	6951	5542	3688 (53.1)
Kerala	1560 (2.2)	86.2	2417	1782	1345 (55.6)	1222	1100	401 (32.8)
Punjab	609 (0.8)	45.2	1981	757	275 (13.9)	438	325	73 (16.7)
Maharashtra	5851 (8.1)	65.1	6408	5680	3807 (59.4)	2078	1860	1561 (75.1)
All-India	72557 (100.0)	72.3	126324	96576	52473 (41.5)	4241	30148	16977 (40.0)

Notes : a : At level III; b : PL-I completed; c : % in relation to target.
Source: GOI 1998.

Table 4.7: Relative Position of Bihar on Budgetary Expenditure under Health

States	*Total Expenditure (Rs. lakh)*		*Per capita (Rs.)*			*Total Revenue*	
	1975-78 (a.a.)	*1995-98 (a.a.)*	*1975-78*	*1995-98*	*Growth*	*1960-1*	*1980-1*
Bihar	4462 (84.9)[c]	71307 (94.0)[c]	6.68	76.19	11.41	653 (1.41)[b]	5441 (7.78)[b]
West Bengal	8335 (91.7)	87506 (98.5)	15.82	116.69	7.37	882 (2.52)	10961 (20.08)
Orissa	2984 (93.2)	44346 (89.8)	12.06	128.28	10.64	259 (1.48)	4087 (15.50)
Assam	2018 (89.1)	33584 (98.3)	10.72	135.04	12.60	304 (2.74)	2326 (11.69)
Madhya Pradesh	5797 (95.7)	93068 (97.1)	11.66	124.69	10.69	556 (1.72)	6878 (13.18)
Uttar Pradesh	7868 (96.6)	162390 (95.8)	7.57	102.99	13.61	740 (1.00)	11162 (10.07)
Kerala	5050 (80.8)	57776 (96.2)	20.53	185.83	9.05	445 (2.63)	5709 (22.43)
Andhra Pradesh	6731 (89.8)	106161 (99.8)	13.76	146.31	10.63	756 (2.10)	8762 (16.36)
All India[a]	85319 (89.5)	1478997 (90.2)	13.77	157.42	11.43	10768 (2.45)	118881 (17.35)

(Contd.)

(Table 4.7 Contd.)

Expenditure (Rs. Lakh)			Hospitals &Dispensaries[d]			National Disease Programme[d]		
1992-3	1998-9	Growth (1960-99)	1960-1	1980-1	1992-3	1960-1	1980-1	1992-3
38564 (42.62)[b]	58550 (61.48)[b]	89.7 (43.6)	30.3 (0.43)[b]	51.9 (4.04)[b]	15.1 (6.42)[b]	36.9 (0.52)[b]	12.9 (1.01)[b]	11.5 (4.92)[b]
42787 (59.85)	113270 (148.77)	128.4 (59.0)	20.6 (0.52)	48.3 (9.70)	38.9 (23.30)	1.5 (0.04)	8.7 (1.75)	9.4 (5.61)
17151 (52.05)	40120 (114.79)	154.9 (77.6)	43.0 (0.64)	45.7 (7.09)	24.6 (12.81)	23.2 (0.34)	8.7 (2.90)	12.5 (6.48)
13644 (59.37)	23120 (91.46)	76.1 (33.4)	34.6 (0.95)	58.3 (6.82)	24.5 (14.56)	10.3 (0.28)	17.3 (2.02)	9.9[e] (—)
33718 (48.33)	——	——	45.0 (0.77)	44.6 (5.89)	28.6 (13.81)	15.4 (0.27)	15.5 (2.05)	9.9 (4.78)
73788 (50.44)	123390 (76.78)	166.7 (76.8)	35.2 (0.35)	39.4 (3.97)	30.1 (15.18)	4.6 (0.05)	19.4 (1.96)	18.8 (9.50)
23013 (76.86)	54530 (173.33)	122.5 (65.9)	55.6 (1.46)	54.2 (12.17)	42.2 (32.41)	1.2 (0.03)	5.2 (1.18)	4.6 (3.51)
42216 (60.51)	103880 (141.22)	137.4 (67.2)	56.2 (1.18)	46.9 (7.67)	32.0 (19.38)	14.2 (0.30)	15.0 (2.46)	16.8 (10.20)
620391 (70.15)	1268380 (134.90)	117.8 (55.1)	39.7 (0.97)	43.3 (7.51)	27.3 (19.41)	26.0 (0.64)	13.0 (2.25)	10.8 (7.60)

Notes: a: the data on total expenditure and the revenue expenditure for 1998-99 refer to all-states, not All-India; b : per capita expenditure in Rs.; c: percentage of revenue expenditure to total; d: percentage share of total revenue expenditure; e : relates to 1991-92.

Source: Quoted in Duggal 1995; CMIE 2001.

The relative position of Bihar among the states may be seen from Table 4.7. The aggregate of budgetary expenditure on health, etc had risen at a relatively low rate here, and the per capita level remained half the all-states average in 1995-98. Among the eastern states, Bihar's was the lowest. The revenue expenditure, which generally accounted for around 90 per cent of the total, was also in a similar position. The per capita expenditure had risen only 43.6 times between 1960-61 and 1998-99 compared with 55 times at the national level. In the last few years, the situation appears to have deteriorated further. During 2000-03, the annual average of expenditure came to Rs. 624 crore, and constituted only 4.66 per cent of the all-states total. On per capita basis, it was Rs. 56.83 as against Rs. 132.38 for all-states; that is, the former only 42.9 per cent of the latter (CMIE 2004a).

In the revenue expenditure, the proportion for hospitals and dispensaries was generally the highest, followed by family welfare and national disease programme. However, the per capita expenditure on hospitals and dispensaries remained small. Even with a share of as much as 52 per cent in 1980-81, it came to only Rs. 4.04, around half the all-states level. The proportion going to family welfare showed a significant rise over the years, but the per capita expenditure remained below the all-states average. Even in the year with highest proportion, 1985-86, it was only Rs. 3.79 as against the all-India average of Rs. 6.49. The allocation to national disease programme-which is influenced by the actual incidence of diseases-had a sharp fall over the years. In 1960-61, 37 per cent of the total expenditure went to it but in 1992-93 it was only 11.5 per cent. The per capita expenditure was always much below the national average (Table 4.7). As regards the MCH activities, it was probably the most neglected here. In 1985-86, the state spent a mere Rs. 2.83 million on it, constituting 2.33 per cent of all-states total. In 1992-93, it rose to Rs. 10.70 million, but the relative share declined further to only 1.85 per cent.

On medical education and training also the state spent a very low amount. The proportion given to it was always much below the national average. The amount spent in 1992-93 stood at Rs. 284 million, and constituted 6.2 per cent of the all-states'. The health administration too received a scanty amount. In 1992-93, the per capita expenditure came to Rs. 1.80 as against Rs. 3.22 at the national level.

State of Infrastructure

With this level of expenditure, naturally the infrastructural situation remained far from satisfactory. The availability of health centre, dispensaries, etc to the people of Bihar was very low. In 1991, per lakh population, there were only 3.33 PHCs, which was below the national average. On sub-centres, dispensaries and hospitals also the situation was similar, as may be seen from Table 4.8. The availability of beds in Bihar was extremely low, and all were concentrated in urban areas.

Table 4.8: Availability of Medical Infrastructure and Personnel : Bihar Vis-à-vis Other States (Number per lakh population)

States	*Primary Health Centres*		*Sub-centres*		*Dispensaries*		*Hospitals*	
	1961	*1991*	*1971*	*1991*	*1966*	*1991*	*1966*	*1991*
Bihar	0.84	3.33	6.95	19.74	1.39 (14.03)[a]	0.49 (3.62)[a]	0.31 (2.47)[a]	0.35 (1.95)[a]
W. Bengal	0.63	3.13	3.99	15.95	1.30 (4.06)	0.81 (2.19)	0.67 (1.86)	0.61 (1.51)
Orissa	0.68	3.75	7.71	19.89	1.41 (16.85)	0.62 (3.12)	0.92 (5.40)	0.91 (3.92)
Assam	0.63	2.23	2.86	25.78	5.51 (62.66)	1.46 (12.02)	1.10 (4.90)	1.20 (4.74)
Madhya Pradesh	0.74	2.33	6.88	23.45	1.02 (5.91)	0.42 (0.99)	0.40 (1.86)	0.61 (2.48)
Uttar Pradesh	0.80	3.27	4.50	18.09	0.49 (1.84)	1.26 (4.81)	1.04 (4.94)	0.53 (2.38)
Maharashtra	0.78	3.41	8.01	19.41	2.22 (5.47)	1.69 (2.61)	0.87 (2.78)	2.67 (5.78)
Andhra Pradesh	0.65	2.64	3.55	16.26	2.69 (12.30)	0.27 (0.77)	0.93 (3.71)	1.75 (4.71)
Kerala	0.58	4.27	8.93	23.85	1.07 (6.54)	6.04 (16.24)	0.55 (1.46)	7.02 (7.80)
All-India	0.75	3.55	6.36	20.90	1.92 (8.14)	3.25 (5.38)	0.81 (2.68)	1.32 (3.51)

Average No. of Villages Covered by a (as on 31.12.97)		*Beds*		*Doctors*		*Nurses*	
Sub centre	*PHC*	*1961*	*1991*	*1971*	*1991*	*1971*	*1991*
4.56	30.56	22.33	32.70 (3.07)[b]	18.54	30.55	6.52	10.29
4.82	24.36	83.22	80.14 (15.42)	58.02	61.38	11.38	25.26
7.93	34.76	31.32	44.64 (11.05)	19.70	35.19	7.49	50.23
4.68	39.88	31.43	56.98 (20.10)	32.05	47.08	11.04	10.18
5.99	39.43	30.75	38.27 (4.38)	11.53	16.92	9.55	88.00
5.60	29.62	35.76	38.20 (6.93)	14.59	23.91	3.86	9.24
4.16	23.84	69.94	144.64 (26.32)	45.28	62.72	39.10	48.64
2.52	19.91	55.78	64.55 (12.55)	22.18	49.67	16.66	23.34
0.27	1.45	71.42	263.20 (202.94)	27.09	56.72	19.43	78.41
4.29	25.57	52.28	78.70 (22.26)	27.57	47.19	14.71	36.88

Notes: a : figures in brackets here refer to number in urban areas; b : number in rural areas.
Source: Quoted in Duggal 1995; GOI 2000.

In recent years also the situation has not shown any improvement, except for the availability of sub-centres. In 1999, there were 15.54 sub-centres per lakh population as against 14.37 at the national level; on PHCs, it was respectively 2.32 and 2.45, and on CHCs 0.16 and 0.31 (based on the estimated population of 1997). The average rural area covered by them were respectively 11.50, 77.02 and 1149.55 sq km as against 22.81, 136.31 and 1067.10 sq km at the national level (GOI 2000i). Number of dispensaries per lakh population stood at only 0.39 in 1998 as against 2.45 at the national level; and for hospitals, 0.30 and 1.63, respectively. The availability of beds increased to 39 as against 94 for all-India (based on 2001 population ;GOI 2000).

As regards personnel, the availability of doctors was always much below the national average. In 1991, it stood at 30.55 per lakh population compared with 47.19 in all-India. In 1999, number of doctors per PHC was only 0.96 here as against 1.10 in all-India. On the indigenous systems and homeopathy, however, Bihar has a relatively large number of doctors. In 2001, there were 146.7 doctors per lakh population as against 67.1 in all-India (GOI 2003d). On the availability of nurses, the situation was very poor. In 1991, per lakh population, it was only 10.29, less than a third of the national average. The health workers in rural areas was also scarce. In 1985, as against the requirement of 17,008 health worker's (female)/ANM), only 7,541, that is, 44.3 per cent, were in position. On male health worker, the situation was still worse; against the requirement of 14,799, only 1,761 were in position this year. After 14 years, in 1999, also the figures have remained the same (Table 4.8; GOI 2000i, 2003).

Incidence of Diseases and Measures

In this background, the incidence of certain diseases in Bihar could not but be high. In 1992-93, it was found that, per lakh population, 595 persons were suffering from tuberculosis, 712 from impairment of limbs, 479 persons from complete blindness and 123 from leprosy; all these were higher than the national averages. The proportion of children and married women suffering from anaemiah were also very high. In 1998-99, 81 per cent of children under age 3 were affected by it as against the national average of 74 per cent, and for married women at 63.4 and 51.8 respectively (IIPS 1995, 2000; CMIE 1996a).

Although the diseases are caused by a variety of factors, lack of adequate preventive measures was an important reason. The maternal and child health activities were at a very low level here. The coverage was generally the lowest among the states. Per thousand pregnant women, number registered for pre-natal care was only 99 in 1995-96 as against the all-India average of 455; delivery in health institutions per 1000 deliveries at 95 and 254, respectively; and per 1000 mothers, number registered for post-natal care 74 and 271 (NSSO 2000).

The immunization programme for children to control vaccine preventable diseases had a very low level of achievement here. Percentage of children aged 12-23 months fully immunized (against tuberculosis, DTP, polio and measles) was only 11.0 in 1998-99 as against 42.0 at the national level; complementary feeding of infants covered 15 and 33.5 per cent, respectively; and percentage of births receiving IFA for three or more months 19.8 and 47.5. On prophylactic against nutritional anaemiah and blindness also the achievements in relation to target were very low. On the former, the coverage in 1993-94 for children was only 8.1 per cent and on women 27.1 per cent as against 66.2 and 79.9 at the national level (IIPS 2000, 1995). The nutritional deficiency was very high in Bihar. The proportion of malnourished children (1-5 years) was found to be 56.1 per cent (moderate and severe) in 1998 as against 41.4 in India (GOI 2003).

Unhygienic living condition is no less important a factor behind the diseases. But the government's attention towards it was negligible. On rural sanitation, the state government was spending a small sum under the minimum needs programme; and since 1986, it was supplemented by the centrally sponsored rural sanitation programme (CRSP). But the funds allotted for it remained largely unutilised. In 1999-00, for example, the total expenditure on both the programmes together came to only Rs 5.47 lakh till the end of October, against the allocation of Rs 15.86 crore under the CRSP and Rs 2 crore under the MNP (GOI 2000h). This is the situation despite the absence of a latrine facility for the vast majority of the population, as noted in chapter 2.

In this situation what is urgently needed is not only a larger allocation of fund on different health facilities but also greater attention to their utilisation. We may note here some recent instances of misappropriation and inefficient utilisation of fund, as brought out by the CAG report for the year ending March 1999 (Statesman 2001G).

On the implementation of the Integrated Child Development Service, the report notes cases of "diversion and misuse of funds" and "failure to spend large amounts". Bureaucrats and ministers used the money meant for the scheme for their personal expenditure, and there were also instances of fictitious payments. About Rs. 200 crore are alleged to have been misused by those connected with the execution of the scheme. On the underutilisation of fund, it is reported that the project coordinator of Patna had closing balance ranging between Rs. 1.73 crore and 48.68 crore in the cash book at the end of every year. Furthermore, during 1992-94, the state government failed to release 43 per cent of the funds it received from the Centre on the scheme.

FAMILY PLANNING

Population control has to form an integral part of any development effort, if it is to be sustainable. There is a limit to which the natural resources can be exploited without endangering the ecological balance. No government can provide the wherewithal of survival even on a modest standard of living to a rapidly rising population. But Bihar's performance in controlling population growth was extremely poor, as noted in chapter 2. For many years, the birth rate had in fact shown a rise rather than a fall. Below we give a brief look into the trend in some of the variables that generally affect the birth rate.

The fertility rate in Bihar had a very slow decline over the years, and always remained substantially above the all-India average. In 1996, with 4.5 per

Table 4.9: Trend in Selected Variables Affecting the Birth Rate : Bihar vis-à-vis Other States

States	Mean age at effective marriage Female		% of women ages 20-24 married before 18	Total Fertility Rate (Per woman)					Contraceptive prevalence*	
	1961-2	1996	1998-99	1961-6	1971-6	1980-2	1990-2	1996	all Methods	modern permanent
Bihar	15.87	18.6 (18.5)[a]	71.0	6.31	6.09	5.7	4.6	4.5	24.5	20.2
West Bengal	14.72	19.4 (18.9)	45.9	6.72	5.27	4.2	3.2	2.6	66.6	33.8
Orissa	16.29	19.6 (19.5)	37.6	6.07	5.58	4.2	3.3	3.1	46.8	35.6
Assam	16.80	20.0 (19.8)	40.7	—	5.5[b]	4.1	3.4	3.2	43.3	16.6
Madhya P.	15.79	18.9 (18.4)	64.7	6.56	5.94	5.2	4.6	4.1	44.3	38.0
Uttar P.	16.24	19.4 (19.2)	62.4	6.33	6.33	5.8	5.2	4.9	28.1	15.6
Andhra P.	15.23	17.9 (17.5)	64.3	5.51	5.15	3.9	3.0	2.5	59.6	57.0
Kerala	18.17	22.0 (22.0)	17.0	5.04	3.79	2.9	1.8	1.8	63.7	51.0
Maharashtra	15.56	19.4 (18.5)	47.7	5.66	4.86	3.7	3.0	2.8	60.9	52.2
Punjab	16.86	20.7 (20.5)	11.6	6.01	4.63	4.0	3.1	2.8	66.7	30.8
All-India	16.02	19.4 (19.0)	50.0	5.35	4.45	4.5	3.7	3.4	48.2	36.0

(Contd.)

(Table 4.9 Contd.)

% effective CPR due to all methods					% of ever married women ages 15-49[c]	
1980	*1985*	*1990*	*1995*	*1998*	*Illiterate*	*exposed to any media*
12.4	17.2	26.3	22.4	20.9	68.8	27.3
21.4	27.3	33.1	35.7	33.8	43.0	61.4
26.9	32.8	40.7	40.6	39.0	48.6	44.3
19.3	24.9	28.2	22.6	17.6	43.5	52.6
21.7	29.5	39.4	48.0	47.7	58.5	54.8
11.5	17.1	33.3	37.1	39.1	60.6	45.3
25.6	32.0	42.9	49.4	46.1	56.4	76.3
28.9	38.1	54.4	50.7	41.3	9.2	88.5
34.5	51.8	54.4	54.1	50.7	36.6	70.4
23.5	48.9	73.2	79.1	68.9	31.0	82.0
22.3	32.1	43.3	45.8	45.4	49.1	59.7

Notes : a : relate to rural area; b : refers to 1970-72; c: at the time of the survey in 1998-99; * : percentage of currently married women ages 15-49 using family planning methods at the time of survey (1998-99); modern permanent methods are male/female sterilization;
Source: GOI 1999a; IIPS 2000; Rele 1987.

woman, it was the second highest among the states. In the sixties, the relative position was better, being lower than in three of the states. Early marriage continued to be highly prevalent here. The mean age at effective marriage stood at 18.6 in 1996, below the national average. The National Family Health Survey (NFHS) of 1998-99 found that 71.0 per cent of women aged 20-24 were married before age 18; the national average stood at only 50.0 per cent (Table 4.9).

The use of contraceptive was very low in Bihar. Only 24.5 per cent of the currently married women were found to be using family planning methods in 1998-99, which was half the national average. Modern permanent methods were being used by only 20.2 per cent here as against 36 per cent at the National level. The cumulative number of sterilization till March 2001came to 75.6 per thousand population as against 118.6 for all-India. Naturally, the effective couple protection rate continued to be very low, and recorded a fall from 26.3 per cent in 1990 to 20.9 in 1998 (Table 4.9; GOI 2002).

Female illiteracy is probably the most important factor behind this distressing situation. Percentage of illiterate among the ever married women ages 15-49 was found to be 68.8 in 1998-99, 20 points higher than the national average. The reach of media was also very low. Only 27.3 per cent of the women were exposed to any media in Bihar as against the national average of 59.7 per cent. Part of the reason behind this is of course the poverty of the people. In 1998, only 7.0 per cent of the rural households were possessing a TV set as against 18.4 per cent in rural India. Even a radio set was there with only 30.5 per cent of the households, just equal to the national average (NSSO 2000).

The quality of service provided by the family welfare department is also very poor here. The NFHS-I (1992-93) found the quality of care during sterilization to be very good only in 35.9 per cent of cases as against 42.6 at the national level. Another indicator of poor service is that, the percentage of illiterate women (ages 13-49) using any contraceptive method was found to be only 17.6 here as against the national average of 33.9 (IIPS 1995). The level of birth registration in Bihar was only 17.6 per cent in 1998 as against 56.0 per cent in all-India (GOI 2003b).

As the motivation towards family planning depends on a variety of factors like female literacy, chances of child survival, availability of a good health care system, level of income and the source of livelihood, there is need for vigorous action on a variety of directions. A recent study on fertility has concluded thus. "Higher levels of female education and access to good health care are important correlates of lower infant mortality and fertility rates, along with income." (Measham 1999: 1367).

5

Agricultural Transformation

Although the agricultural sector is of critical importance for the entire country, it is particularly important here because of the high proportion of agricultural labourers. In the state's total rural population, they constituted 39.9 per cent in 1951 compared with 34.4 per cent at the national level. Even the agricultural population as a whole was high here, constituting 90.5 per cent of the state's total this year, which was the highest among the states. There has not been any noticeable change over the years.

The object of this chapter is to look into how the agriculture and allied sectors progressed over the last five decades. The analysis is divided into two parts: the first dealing with agriculture proper, and the second with the allied sectors like animal husbandry, fishery and forestry.

AGRICULTURE

The growth rate of agricultural production in Bihar was always less than that at the national level. The compound annual growth (CAGR) declined from 2.97 per cent during 1952-53 to 1964-65 to 1.39 per cent during 1968-69 to 1981-82. In the following decade it recovered considerably, but in the nineties again there was a sharp fall, to as low as (-)1.4 per cent during 1991-92 to 1996-97. The annual average value of output had risen only 34.3 per cent between 1962-65 and 1992-95, which was around a quarter of that at the national level. Bihar's share in all-India total production declined from 6.95 per cent in 1962-65 to 4.19 in 1992-95. The growth in productivity was extremely low, particularly in the first phase of the green revolution. Between 1970-73 and 1980-83, the yield per hectare in value term had a CAGR of only 0.10 per cent compared with 1.80 per cent at the national level. The output per hectare in Bihar was only 76.9 per cent of the national average in 1992-95, declining from 98.4 per cent in 1962-65 (GOI 1969:119; Sawant and Achuthan 1995; RBI 1998: I).

The low value of agricultural output is partly due to the fact that an overwhelming proportion of the land was in food grains production. The percentage of grass cropped area (GCA) under it was 91.7 in 1960, 92.6 in 1970 and 92.0 in 1990. There was not a single major state with such heavy reliance on food grains. Below we give a brief look first into the pattern of growth in this group of crops.

Food grains

Bihar's performance in food grains production was on the whole very poor. In the post-green revolution period, it had increased by only 4.8 per cent during 1968-83 as against 30.0 per cent for all-India. In the following years the growth improved significantly, being at 58.1 per cent in 1980-98 compared with 45.8 per cent at the national level. Bihar's relative share in all-India production was, however, still only 7.04 per cent as against 8.05 per cent in 1968-71. In the last few years, however, there has been considerable improvement. The annual average production in 2000-03 came to 13,625 thousand tonnes (including Jharkhand) and constituted 10.42 per cent of all-India total. The per capita food grains production was, however, still below the national average, being respectively, 124 kg and 127 kg. The yield rate continued to be very low, generally below the national average. During 2000-03, Bihar had 1611 kg/ha and Jharkhand 1,202 kg as against the all-India average of 1,643 kg (Table 5.1; CMIE 2005).

Among food grains, the most important crop was rice, always accounting for more than half of the total area. Its performance was, however, very poor. The yield rate was virtually static till early eighties and in the following years also the growth was not much; it continued to be below the national average. The area under rice showed a continuous decline, even when the yield rate rose. The production registered an absolute fall in the first period, 1968-71 to 1980-83, and showed a substantial rise in the second. Bihar's share in all-India production declined from 10.9 per cent in 1968-71 to 8.6 in 1995-98. After the division of the state, in 2000-03, the production annually averaged 70.46 lakh tonnes (including Jharkhand) and the share in all-India total declined to only 4.35 per cent. The yield rate in this period was 1447 kg in Bihar and 1216 kg in Jharkhand.

The next important crop in terms of acreage is wheat, and its performance was significantly better. The yield rate was doubled over the period, rising from 1053 Kg/ha in 1968-71 to 2057 kg in 1995-98. However, here also it remained much below the national average. The area under the crop increased greatly over the years, and stood at 23.5 per cent of the total under food grains, rising from 12.0 per cent. Bihar's share in all-India total production of wheat rose to 6.6 per cent in 1995-98 from 5.9 in 1968-71.

Maize also accounted for a substantial acreage, despite a noticeable fall over the years. In the all-India total acreage under maize, Bihar's share decreased

Table 5.1: Trend in Area, Production and Yield Rate of Different Food grains: Bihar Vis-à-Vis Other States

States	*Food grains Total (Contd.)*								
	1968-71 (a.a.)			*1980-83 (a.a.)*			*1995-98 (a.a.)*		
	A	*P*	*Y*	*A*	*P*	*Y*	*A*	*P*	*Y*
Bihar	9881	8099	820	9388	8489	904	8959	13423	1498
W.Bengal	6041	7339	1215	5888	6894	1171	6523	13664	2095
Orissa	5672	5189	915	6633	5294	798	5505	6090	1103
Assam	2268	2152	949	2529	2633	1041	2726	3557	1305
Madhya P.	16779	10050	599	17795	12521	704	17667	18324	1037
Uttar P.	19485	17809	914	20256	25239	1246	20427	40860	2002
Andhra P.	9284	7217	777	8917	10859	1218	6857	12094	1759
Maharashtra	13255	6553	494	13948	9843	706	13413	11972	889
Punjab	3799	6832	1798	4947	13125	2653	5759	20836	3618
All-India	122772	100645	820	126967	130801	1030	122814	190703	1551

% increase over the period				*% of GCA (1995-98)*	*Rice (Contd.)*					
P		*Y*			*1968-71 (a.a.)*			*1980-83*		
I	*II*	*I*	*II*		*A*	*P*	*Y*	*A*	*P*	*Y*
4.81	58.13	10.24	65.71	89.1 (91.7)[a]	5398	4454	827	5139	4319	830
-6.06	98.20	-3.62	78.9	72.5 (85.4)	4937	6247	1267	5083	6083	1193
2.03	15.04	-12.79	38.22	59.9 (91.8)	4439	4452	1003	4136	3715	900
22.32	35.11	9.69	25.36	69.0 (76.8)	2137	2097	983	2279	2447	1073
24.58	46.35	17.53	47.30	70.2 (84.6)	4364	3301	753	4836	3635	750
41.72	61.89	36.32	60.67	78.9 (77.6)	4539	3385	747	5248	5704	1087
50.46	11.37	56.76	44.4	52.1 (78.0)	3292	4609	1400	3867	7517	2040
50.20	21.63	42.91	25.92	62.5 (71.5)	1373	1488	1087	1502	2248	1497
92.12	58.75	47.55	36.37	74.0 (78.3)	371	574	1537	1256	3708	2947
29.96	45.80	25.61	50.58	65.5 (77.8)	37413	40805	1090	39707	51332	1293

Contd.

(Table 5.1 Contd.)

1995-98 (a.a.)			Wheat 1968-71 (a.a.)			1980-83 (a.a.)			1995-98 (a.a.)		
A	P	Y	A	P	Y	A	P	Y	A	P	Y
5027	6898	1398	1185	1239	1053	1709	2311	1350	2101	4320	2057
5885	12587	2141	250	523	2027	254	489	1923	352	792	2249
4500	5623	1248	14	18	1313	66	123	1867	5.0	6.4	1293
2495	3367	1350	13	8	603	103	118	1147	86	107	1247
5381	542	1007	3212	2272	707	3421	3419	997	4289	7269	1695
557	11433	2041	3508	6697	1210	8060	13797	1710	9053	22967	2537
376	9403	2490	15	6	367	17	10	587	11	7.8	740
140	2524	1694	873	423	483	1077	908	840	749	913	1215
220	7333	3332	2182	4822	2210	2925	8462	2890	3251	12970	3988
4329	80415	1861	16942	20859	1230	22663	38853	1713	25865	65931	2250

Maize 1968-71 (a.a.)			1980-83 (a.a)			1995-98 (a.a.)			Ragi (Contd.) 1968-71 (a.a.)		
A	P	Y	A	P	Y	A	P	Y	A	P	Y
967	999	1030	844	859	1020	729	1405	1918	178	90	507
49	44	903	52	58	1113	41	107	2599	9.7	7.7	793
70	58	833	167	174	105	51	61	1173	146	148	1020
22	12	550	21	12	600	19	14	709	—	—	—
611	465	767	787	762	971	846	1065	1259	19	5.1	270
1505	1442	957	1161	912	787	1077	1564	1450	236	176	740
247	306	1240	328	700	2133	363	1050	2889	314	251	800
44	50	1160	79	128	1623	268	380	1405	222	172	777
533	813	1527	341	590	1740	168	337	2005	—	—	—
5810	6287	1083	5887	6801	1153	6187	10373	1673	2498	1973	

Contd.

(Table 5.1 Contd.)

						Small Millets (Contd.)					
1980-83 (a.a.)			1995-98 (a.a)			1968-71 (a.a.)			1980-83 (a.a.)		
A	P	Y	A	P	Y	A	P	Y	A	P	Y
161	94	577	79	73	922	229	98	430	133	48	360
16	9.3	597	13	14	1128	13	8.0	713	9.7	6.7	690
308	249	810	78	47	600	166	76	480	226	114	490
—	—	—	—	—	—	—	—	—	—	—	—
20	5.4	267	13	3.8	291	1653	375	227	1447	313	217
166	155	940	142	185	1305	538	333	620	327	209	637
252	255	1013	115	132	1148	818	231	283	477	229	410
224	218	970	153	153	999	214	87	410	188	78	417
—	—	—	—	—	—	—	—	—	—	—	—
2516	2535	1003	1755	2385	1359	4754	1841	390	3754	1480	393

						Arhar					
1995-98 (a.a.)			1968-71 (a.a.)			1980-83 (a.a.)			1995-98 (a.a.)		
A	P	Y	A	P	Y	A	P	Y	A	P	Y
46	25	556	166	142	860	88	91	1037	68	72	1065
5.9	4.1	678	30	23	763	25	21	853	3.6	2.5	704
51	25	489	40	24	613	101	69	663	148	91	609
—	—	—	3.9	2.7	700	7.4	5.3	717	6.5	4.6	711
895	232	258	496	345	693	518	374	720	386	293	764
134	135	1009	590	695	1183	506	650	1280	489	515	1050
83	57	673	183	78	430	239	50	207	333	99	292
106	68	639	634	320	510	697	395	567	1037	584	562
—	—	—	1.7	1.0	777	16	16	963	11	9.2	826
1598	717	448	2618	1847	707	2924	1961	667	3440	2272	659

(Contd.)

(Table 5.1 Contd.)

Gram								
1968-71 (a.a.)			1980-83 (a.a.)			1995-98 (a.a.)		
A	P	Y	A	P	Y	A	P	Y
240	163	680	187	135	727	131	103	794
162	124	760	78	50	647	29	25	872
23	14	597	43	26	620	34	22	644
—	—	—	—	—	—	—	—	—
1577	835	530	2074	1356	650	2589	2234	864
2195	1622	740	1524	1248	823	931	759	820
70[b]	23	327	53	21	393	113	84	744
377	110	293	442	158	357	727	388	532
375	300	787	208	109	517	16	14	607
7565	5018	663	7284	4753	657	7175	5559	774

Notes: a: relate to 1960; b: relates to 1970-73; A: area in thousand hectares; P: production in thousand tonnes; Y : yield in kg per hectare. I: refer to the growth between 1968-71 and 1980-83; II: between 1980-83 and 1995-98.

Source: CMIE 1995, 2000.

to 11.8 per cent in 1995-98 from 16.6 per cent in 1968-71. The production also declined in the first fifteen years, with both area and yield rate registering a substantial fall. In the following years there was a noticeable growth in yield rate, and it became 15 per cent higher than the national average in 1995-98 as against lower earlier. Bihar's share in all-India production of maize stood at 13.5 per cent in the latest period, declining from 15.9 per cent in 1968-71 (Table 5.1).

Small millets and ragi were the two other important crops in cereals; but both had a sharp fall in acreage. The area under the former in 1995-98 was reduced to a fifth of the earlier level, and in the latter to less than half. The production also had sharp declines as the improvement in yield could not compensate for the fall in acreage. The yield rate in millet had an absolute fall in the first period, and in ragi a growth of only 82 per cent over the entire period.

In pulses, the important crops were gram and arhar. Both had, however, recorded a sharp fall in acreage. The area under the latter in 1995-98 was only 41 per cent of that existing in 1968-71, and in the former 55 per cent. Consequently, despite a substantial rise in yield rate, the production declined. The yield rate was particularly high in arhar. In 1995-98, at 1065 kg/ha, it was 62 per cent higher than the national average, and highest among the selected states.

Non-food grains

As food grains took away most of the cropped area, naturally very little was left for non-food grains. During 1994-97, the annual average of area under them was only 966 thousand hectares, constituting 1.5 per cent of all-India total. The important non-food grains grown in Bihar are sugarcane, jute and mesta, potato, rapeseed and mustard, linseed, niger seed, sesamum, tobacco, sweet potatoes, banana and onions. Group-wise, oilseeds accounted for the largest acreage. Below we give a brief look into the pattern of growth over the years.

None of the non-food crops showed any consistency in growth of yield rate or acreage. In oilseeds, the most important crop rapeseed and mustard, had recorded an absolute fall in area during 1980-83 over 1968-71, and then had a substantial rise by early nineties. In the last one decade, the area under it was generally around 104 thousand ha. Production also had a similar pattern. Ignoring fluctuations, over the entire period of three decades, there was only a 76 per cent rise. The yield rate rose to the highest of 877 kg/ha in 1990-93 and generally remained below the national average. In linseed, the acreage declined and so also the production, as the growth in yield rate was nominal. The former had declined from 92 thousand ha in 1980-83 to 60 thousand ha in 1995-98. The yield rate in the crop was, however, much higher than the all-India average; in 1995-98, it was respectively 541 kg/ha and 341 kg. Niger seed showed a continuous growth in yield but the production declined due to a sharp fall in acreage. The yield rate was more than double the national average in 1995-98, being respectively 606 kg and 286 kg. The area under the crop stood at only 24.7 thousand ha in the latest period, declining from 42 thousand ha in 1980-83. In sesamum also the yield was higher than the national average, but production declined due to a noticeable fall in acreage. The area under it averaged 19 thousand ha in 1995-98, declining from 32 thousand ha in 1968-71. The yield rate was 447 kg in the latest period compared with 317 kg at the national level. Groundnut was also grown in a small way, with the acreage averaging 5.4 thousand ha in 1995-98; and the yield rate at 1092 kg was higher than the national average.

Sugarcane, which generally had the largest acreage among non-food grains, showed a very uneven growth. In 1995-98, the area under it averaged 124 thousand ha, declining from 160 thousand ha in 1968-71. The yield rate fluctuated continuously, and was always much below the national average. In 1995-98, it stood at 44976 kg as against 68477 kg in all-India. The next important crop jute, had a much better performance. Both the area and the yield rate showed a noticeable growth. The area had risen to 144 thousand ha in 1995-98 from 123 thousand in 1968-71. The yield rate was doubled over the period, rising from 884 kg to 1613 kg. However, it remained much below the national average. The production of jute was doubled over the period of three decades. The allied product mesta had a considerable fall in acreage in recent years, and stood at 18.5 thousand ha in 1995-98. The yield rate increased substantially and was always higher than the national average. The performance in tobacco was very poor. The yield rate declined continuously, but then also the area under it increased and stood at 18.6 thousand ha in 1995-98.

Among spices, chillies continued to be the most important crop despite a sharp fall in area. The yield rate also declined in the nineties and the production was down to a quarter of the level in 1968-71. The area under the crop was only 6.1 thousand ha in 1995-98, declining from 20.1 thousand in 1968-71. The yield rate in the latest period was 786 kg as against the national average of 1028 kg. Turmeric and coriander also did not perform well, both registering a sharp fall in production. The areas under them declined continuously and the yield rate remained much below the national average. The former, with an acreage of 3.0 thousand ha in 1995-98, had an yield rate less than a quarter of the national average.

In vegetables and fruits, Bihar's position was relatively good. In 1992-93, the state's share in all-India total acreage under vegetables was 17.4 per cent but in production it was 22.8 per cent; with 887.3 thousand hectares under the crops, the state produced 16,200.4 thousand tonnes. In fruits, with 271.2 thousand ha, 3359 thousand tonnes were produced. In the national total, these were respectively 8.5 per cent and 10.2 per cent (CMIE 1996b).

Among vegetables, potatoes recorded a noticeable growth in acreage; and in 1995-98, with 171.5 thousand ha, it was the highest among all non-food grain crops. The yield rate however declined, and stood at only 8990 kg in 1995-98, which was around half the national average. Sweet potatoes had a sharp fall in acreage, down to only 19 thousand ha in the latest period from 77 thousand ha in 1968-71. The yield rate improved considerably, and became higher than the national average from lower earlier. The production was down to a third of what it was earlier. Among other vegetables, Onions became quite important in recent years, with a substantial growth in yield rate, although it remained much below the national average. The area under the crop stood at 18.3 thousand ha in the latest period.

Among fruits, banana was the most important, crop, and it recorded a spectacular growth in recent years. The area under it was nearly quadrupled over the period of three decades, and stood at 27 thousand ha in 1995-98. The production multiplied 14 times, with a 3.7-fold rise in yield rate. The growth however, came mainly in the nineties. The potential still remains largely unexploited; the latest yield rate was only 20,006 kg as against 29,747 kg at the national level (CMIE 1995, 2000).

District-wise Disparity

It was not only that among the states Bihar's performance was one of the worst, within the state also there were wide disparities inter-district. We may note here the pattern of growth in yield rate in three of the important food grains.[1]

In rice, there were even negative growth in yield in four of the districts– Begusarai, Madhubani, Godda and Deogarh—and three had less than 2 per cent; on the other hand, six districts had above 50 per cent growth. The yield rate in 1990-93 stood at as much as 1682 kg/ha in Rohtas as against less than 600 kg in Khagaria and Begusarai, that is, the latter only 35.0 per cent of the former. There was a nominal reduction in disparity over the years; in 1981-84, the lowest was 32.7 per cent of the highest. There were a number of districts with very low productivity but having a substantial acreage under the crop. As regards the latest situation, the disparity appears to have increased. In 1997-99, on winter rice, the lowest yield was 692 kg/ha in Khagaria and the highest at 2397 kg in Buxar, with the state average at 1384 kg. The lowest was thus only 28.9 per cent of the highest.

In wheat, the disparity was somewhat less. In 1981-84, the annual average yield was 2029 kg/ha at the highest in Deogarh as against the lowest of 836 kg in Gumla, with the state average at 1437 kg; the lowest was thus 41.2 per cent of the highest. After more than a decade, in 1990-93, the disparity showed an increase-the lowest declining to 37.7 per cent of the highest; the former was 839 kg in Palamau and the latter 2226 kg in Patna. The growth in yield over the period was negative in four of the districts—Godda, Deogarh, Palamau and Vaishali—as against the highest of 81.5 per cent in Gopalganj. In more recent years again, the disparity has fallen. In 1997-9, the highest was 2645 kg/ha in Patna and the lowest at 1322 kg in Garhwa—that is, the latter 50.0 per cent of the former.

In maize, the third important crop, the district-wise variation was much wider. The highest yield rate in 1990-93 was 2470 kg in Khagaria and the lowest at 715 kg in Palamau—that is, the latter only 29 per cent of the former. In 1981-84, the highest was 2097 kg and the lowest at 513 kg—that is, the latter 24.5 per cent of the former; a reduction of only 4.5 points over a period of more than a decade CMIE 1996b).

CAUSAL FACTORS

Behind this depressing performance in agriculture, many factors have operated. Some of them are natural, like soil quality, topography, extent of rainfall, etc, but the man-made factors are also no less responsible. Inefficient management of the available resources made the situation worse than what it would have been otherwise. In the motivation towards better utilisation of the land, the first critical requirement is the right pattern of land holding, and then there is the need for proper irrigation facility, availability of other inputs and credit, extension services and the marketing facilities. All these require the right attitude from the side of the government, and the allocation of resources accordingly. Below we give a brief look into the position of all these factors in Bihar, beginning with the availability of land resource.

Land Availability and Utilisation

The cultivable land in Bihar is relatively low, and that too has not been utilised properly. The net cropped area (NCA) as percentage to the state's total reporting area (RA) was only 42.2 in 1995-96 compared with the national average of 46.6. Bihar is one of the few states that showed an absolute fall in the NCA, from 8276 thousand ha in 1971-72 to 7321 thousand in 1995-96. Bihar's share in the all-India total of NCA was only 5.1 per cent in the latest year, and the NCA per thousand population came to 77.1 hectares, less than half the national average.

The cropping intensity was also low. In fact, the ratio between the GCA and the NCA had registered a fall from 1.41 in 1962-65 to 1.29 in 1972-73, and in the following years also the recovery was not much. The average for 1996-99 came to 1.36, which was the lowest among the eastern states as against the highest in the sixties. The GCA per thousand population was down to 105.6 hectares in 1995-96 from 189.6 hectares in 1971-72 (Table 5.2; CMIE 2002a).

The proportion of RA not available for cultivation was high here, rising from 11.79 per cent in 1955-56 to 19.28 in 1995-96; at the national level, it declined from 14.68 to 13.57 per cent. The amount of fallow land was also high, being as much as 16.7 per cent of the RA in the latest year-more than double that at the national level. In the all-India total of fallow land, Bihar's share was 12.2 per cent. Thus, there was enough scope for raising the land availability.

The Land-Holding Pattern

The land reform was the first vital step necessary for raising agricultural productivity, and also for reducing rural poverty. There was need for drastically reducing the concentration in land-ownership and bringing an equitable distribution. Possession of land in rural areas is not only a symbol of economic strength but also of social status. Uncertainty of tenure and high rents were great obstacles in the way of bringing out the best in the farmer. Fragmentation of holdings also needed attention as it stood in the way of deriving the economies of scale. Bringing any significant change in the existing land-holding system was, however, not an easy job in the given socio-economic power balance, as will be evident from the analysis below.

Abolition of *Zamindari* System

At the time of Independence, there was an extreme concentration of land ownership in Bihar. While 87.67 per cent of the households, with 20 acres and below, accounted for 48.61 per cent of the area, for the remaining 12.33 per cent—with 20.01 acres and above—it was 51.39 per cent. The top 3.13 per cent of households owned 29.67 per cent of the area as against only 9.35 per cent of area by the bottom 40.52 per cent. The change after the abolition of zamindari system was not significant. The top 11.41 per cent of households—with above 20 acres—owned 42.46 per cent of the area, and the top 2.09 per cent—with above 50 acres—16.70 per cent. The share of the bottom 39.82 per cent of households was 10.71 per cent of the area, a nominal rise over the earlier level (Ojha 1980: 186).

This level of achievement was not a surprise, given the clout of the landlords. The process of enactment of the legislation itself faced tremendous obstacles. The Act originally passed in 1948 was strewn with many loopholes and had to be replaced by a new bill within a short period. The new bill, however, could not be passed immediately due to opposition from the zamindars, and this was despite the Congress party having an absolute majority in the legislature. It had to be sent to a select committee. And when the bill was passed, it was challenged in the High Court. The verdict went in favour of zamindars, and the constitution of India had to be amended suitably in 1951. The problem was not over; the zamindars challenged the very validity of this amendment in the Supreme Court. The state authorities finally won the legal battle, and in 1952 the zamindars were directed to submit all their rent-rolls and related village records. But the zamindars refused to supply the village papers and in 1954 again approached the courts individually to prevent the government from taking over their estates. Court injunctions were issued and the implementation of the Act could not proceed. The delay helped the zamindars to make paper partition of joint-family properties by bribing the village officials into falsifying crucial records.

The Act itself largely favoured the zamindars. The government deliberately allowed a substantial portion of lands to be retained by them for private cultivation. The Act permitted the zamindars to retain their *sir* and *khudkast* lands, which were estimated at 3.46 million acres out of a total cultivated area of 24.48 million acres—that is, 14.1 per cent (GOI 1945 : 268). If the evictions and coercive transfers that took place in the intervening period are considered the amount of land retained by the zamindars would not be less than a fifth of the total.

The Ceiling Legislation

The imposition of ceiling on land-ownership and the distribution of surplus were unduly delayed even to start with. The Bihar Land Reforms (Fixation of Ceiling Area and acquisition of Surplus Land) Act itself was passed only in 1962, though this question was talked about since the beginning of Independence. A bill to impose ceiling on Land-ownership was proposed in 1955, but it met with serious opposition and had to be sent to the Select Committee. There was no further progress on it until 1959, when the Congress Working Committee pressed the government to implement the Nagpur Resolution.

As in case of the Bihar Abolition of zamindari Act, here also the landed class influenced the legislation and high ceilings were fixed along with a variety of exemptions. The ceiling varied between 20 acres in case of land irrigated by flow irrigation work and 60 acres for hilly, sandy or surplus homestead land. In addition, a land-holder could retain any land forming part of its homestead not exceeding 10 acres, and also any land constituting an orchard, *bansbari*, *Kharhur* or pasturage not exceeding 15 acres. Exemptions were also allowed to several categories of land including lac production farms, sugarcane farms and land held by public religious institutions. The ceiling was fixed on the basis of an individual land-holder, and therefore, a family could be entitled to a very large holding if there were more than one adult member.

Although the Act was enforced from April 1962, the actual administrative work did not start before 1965, and till December 1966 only 1,790 returns were filed showing a surplus of 7,797 acre of land. Large-scale *mala fide* transfers greatly reduced the quantum of surplus. According to one estimate, the fictitious transfers alone were of the order of five lakh acre (Ojha 1980: 125). There were many conflicting and vague provisions in the Act which encouraged the

Table 5.2: Pattern of Land use in Bihar Vis-à-vis other States

States	Reporting area ('000 ha)	Net cropped Area ('000 ha)				GCA / NCA			
		1971-2	1995-96	% to RA 1995-6	per'000 pop. (in ha) 1995-6	1962-65	1972-3	1980-82	1995-6
Bihar	17330 (5.7)	8276	7321 (5.1)	42.24	77.1	1.41	1.29	1.33	1.37
W.Bengal	8846 (2.9)	5463	5462 (3.8)	62.82	74.5	1.18	1.25	1.32	1.64
Orissa	15540 (5.1)	5765	6210 (4.4)	39.88	181.2	1.21	1.23	1.41	1.56
Assam	7852 (2.6)	2321	2780 (2.0)	35.44	113.0	1.19	1.30	1.24	1.42
Madhya P.	44342 (14.5)	18461	19752 (13.9)	44.54	273.8	1.13	1.12	1.16	1.27
Uttar P.	29797 (9.8)	17317	17399 (12.2)	58.39	115.9	1.28	1.33	1.43	1.48
Gujarat	18822 (6.2)	9762	9609 (6.8)	51.05	215.4	1.05	1,06	1.13	1.05
Punjab	5033 (1.7)	4076	4139 (2.9)	82.24	191.6	1.29	1.45	1.64	1.87
Andhra P.	27440 (9.0)	11269	10637 (7.5)	38.76	148.3	1.11	1.11	1.15	1.23
All-India	305005 (100.0)	139721	142215 (100.0)	46.64	155.3	1.15	1.18	1.24	1.31

GCA per '000 population		Fallow land ('000 ha) 1995-6	Land not available for cultivation (%)	Land under Forest[a]	
1971-2	1995-6			1970-1	1995-6
189.6	105.6	2901 (16.7)[a]	19.28	16.8	17.02 (2949)[d]
161.8	122.5	251 (2.9)	18.88	13.5	13.76 (1196)
313.2	282.1	564 (3.6)	9.06	43.3[b]	36.75 (5722)
197.6	160.0	144 (1.8)	31.22	37.0[c]	25.63 (2012)
501.6	347.1	1528 (3.4)	9.54	38.1	33.08 (14670)
260.6	171.8	1933 (6.5)	11.80	16.8	17.33 (5164)
392.5	226.0	765 (4.1)	19.83	8.9	10.03 (126)
422.4	358.9	75 (1.5)	9.68	4.2	5.76 (290)
290.8	181.9	4235 (15.4)	16.95	23.5	22.41 (6148)
301.3	203.7	23822 (7.8)	13.57	22.8	22.57 (68826)

Notes : a: percentage to the state's reporting area; b : relates to 1968-69; c: including Mizoram ; d : area in '000 ha.
Source : CMIE 1996b, 1999; GOI 1976a.

adoption of fraudulent methods. The absence of up-to-date land records also helped in undoing the objective of the legislation.

To remove the deficiencies, some major changes were made in the Act in 1973. The unit of ceiling on holding was changed from individual to family consisting of not more than five members. The level of ceiling for various categories of land was also lowered. Now the minimum was reduced to 15 acres and the maximum to 45 acres. There was also a drastic reduction of the additional areas that could be retained over and above the ceiling. The time limit for submission of return and also of land selection was drastically cut.

The amendment, however, did not bring any radical change in the overall situation as large-scale *mala fide* and *benami* transfers had already taken place. The government had fixed a target of acquiring at least 50,000 acre under the amended Act by June 1975 but hardly 13,000 could be acquired. In the following years also there was no noticeable improvement. The area declared surplus rose to 96.2 thousand hectare in 1982, and after another 13 years, in 1995, to 197.9 thousand ha-constituting 6.6 per cent of all-India total. In taking possession of land the situation was much worse, as may be seen from Table 5.3.

The potential of acquiring more surplus land was immense. Initially the area of land to be acquired under the ceiling legislation was estimated at 5.26 lakh hectare. But the state government fixed the target at only 3.64 lakh (Prasad 1991 : 369-70). And even that could not be declared surplus. The concentration of land ownership continued to be high. In 1982, the share of those with 15 acres and above in total number of holdings was 1.35 per cent but their share in total area stood at 15.34 per cent; for medium holdings (5.00-14.99 acres) the proportions were respectively 9.59 per cent and 37.79 per cent (Sharma 1994).

The acquired surplus land were to be distributed on a preferential basis first to landless agricultural labourers, followed by those having five acres or less of class I land. As the quantum of land taken possession was meagre, naturally the distribution proved utterly inadequate. The cumulative total of land distributed increased from 57.4 thousand hectare till 1982 to 119.4 thousand in 1995. Bihar's share in all-India total distributed declined from 7.5 per cent to 5.8 per cent. In the following four years, some e significant progress came; the quantum distributed till September 1999 rose to 308.5 ha and the relative share to 5.9 per cent. In neighbouring W. Bengal, more than three times as much could be distributed by the latest year. The number of beneficiaries came to only 3.80 lakh, around a seventh of that in West Bengal (Table 5.3).

The value of even this redistribution is much less than what appears on the face of it. The quality of land distributed was very poor, as the surplus land-holder had the freedom to select the land. According to rough official estimates, about 50 per cent of the 2 lakh acres acquired till 1977 were sandy, hilly, forest

Table 5.3: Relative Position of Bihar on Area Declared Surplus, taken Possession and Distributed (in '000 ha)

States	*Declared surplus*		*Possession taken*		*Distributed*		*No of beneficiaries (in '000)*		*Distribution per beneficiary (hectare)*	
	1982	*1995*	*1982*	*1995*	*1982*	*1995*	*1982*	*1995*	*1982*	*1995*
Bihar	96.2	197.9	59.8	168.0	57.4	119.4	156.8	359	0.37	0.33
W.Bengal	66.7	514.4	45.7	486.4	25.3	383.7	176.5	2085	0.14	0.18
Orissa	55.5	70.4	49.1	66.4	41.4	61.9	78.2	133	0.53	0.47
Assam	155.6	247.7	124.3	233.1	89.8	199.1	253.5	434	0.35	0.46
Madhya P.	149.8	117.8	114.0	105.2	114.0	74.9	76.9	72	1.48	1.04
Uttar P.	114.5	220.6	105.7	207.6	94.5	150.1	190.5	324	0.50	0.46
Karnataka	113.0	110.5	45.6	64.8	25.6	47.3	13.1	30	1.95	1.58
Kerala	48.8	55.4	32.7	38.4	21.5	25.9	85.9	144	0.25	0.18
Gujarat	59.3	99.6	25.1	64.3	3.3	53.4	2.0	31	1.70	1.72
Punjab	18.8	53.8	6.5	42.5	5.1	41.7	3.0	27	1.70	1.54
All-India	1614.7	2971.7	1102.4	2624.5	767.3	2067.6	1366.3	4957	0.56	0.42

Source: CMIE 1995; Deb 1986: Table III.2.

Table 5.4: Trend in the Extent and Nature of Tenancy: Bihar Vis-à-Vis Other states

States	*Extent of Tenancy*				*Terms of Lease (%)*					
	% of tenant holding		*% share of total area*		*Share of Produce*		*Fixed Money*		*Fixed produce*	
	1981-2	*1991-2*	*1981-2*	*1991-2*	*1981-2*	*1991-2*	*1981-2*	*1991-2*	*1981-2*	*1991-2*
Bihar	19.7	5.6	10.3	3.9	73.3	43.5	6.5	9.5	3.6	12.8
West Bengal	23.1	14.4	12.3	10.4	5.6	46.5	2.8	8.6	11.9	11.7
Orissa	18.2	16.9	9.9	9.5	42.0	50.9	5.1	19.7	8.1	4.7
Assam	12.9	10.1	6.4	8.9	8.8	28.9	15.4	17.0	8.4	4.0
Uttar P.	20.5	15.5	10.2	10.5	50.1	46.5	8.6	9.2	4.9	15.2
Madhya P.	8.0	9.0	3.6	6.3	27.8	24.9	1.7	15.3	1.1	21.4
Andhra P.	13.8	14.1	6.2	9.6	8.8	28.9	13.0	25.9	11.1	26.8
Kerala	6.7	5.2	2.6	2.9	13.2	2.1	3.4	15.9	0.0	0.0
Punjab	21.3	15.9	16.1	18.8	39.9	11.3	42.1	49.2	4.6	18.2
India	15.2	11.0	7.2	8.3	41.9	34.4	10.9	19.0	6.3	14.5

Source: NSSO 1997a.

and even land eroded by rivers. (Singha 1978 : 1759). An even bigger deception was that the land was not distributed free to the landless but was sold to them. In fact, the state made a profit out of the land redistribution. For instance, for an acre of class I land, the state gave the landlord Rs. 900 but took from the landless allottee Rs 1500, apart from the land rent. The cruelty was blatant when the landless peasant did not get possession of the land, either because it was unfit for cultivation or the landlord prevented him from going to the plot.

The ceiling legislation was primarily an eye wash. The government did not want to take any measure that would harm the landed class and benefit the landless. There are tell-tale evidences of the government's disinclination towards implementing the law. To cite a recent instance : on July 3, 2000, when the Bihar Assembly was discussing the land reform issue, there were only 40 members present in the 324-member house. And strangely, more than ten members were slumbering when the discussion was going on. At the end of the debate, the land reforms minister reeled off some statistics which were reported to be being repeated for many years (Statesman 2000h: 6).

Tenancy Reform

The tenancy system in Bihar had been guided by the Bihar Tenancy Act, 1885, which classified the tenants into three classes : Occupancy *raiyats*, non-occupancy *raiyats* and under-*raiyats*. There was also a number of special type of *raiyots*. An occupancy *raiyat* could not be ejected from his land so long as he observed the norms laid down by the law. The rights were heritable and transferable. In the tribal areas, however, the right of transfer was restricted. Generally, an occupancy raiyat enjoyed the privileges of fair rent and fixity of tenure. A non-occupancy raiyat, on the other hand, was very inseoure, as he could be ejected from the land under certain situations. The rights of such a raiyat were neither hereditary nor transferable. The under-raiyats were those who held the land under a raiyat and their rights were also neither hereditary nor transferable. As a matter of custom an under-raiyat paid a much higher rate of rent than the raiyat under whom he held the land.

The Act of 1885 was amended once in 1938 and again in 1955. The later amendment made some special provisions for protecting the interests of the under-raiyats. It introduced a limit on the maximum produce recoverable from him, put restriction on payment of certain kinds of rent, provided for the acquisition of the right of occupancy and restoration in case of unlawful ejection. The amendment also provided for a Conciliation Board to resolve dispute between a landlord and an under-raiyat. For the scheduled castes, scheduled tribes and the backward classes special protection was provided. There were also some general provisions for saving the tenants from unlawful harassment, like entitlement to a receipt on payment of rent. With regard to the share of

Table 5.5: Trend in Distribution of operational Holdings by Size Categories: Bihar Vis-à-vis other States

(percentages)

States		Marginal (one ha or less)		Small (1.01-2.00)		Semi-Medium 2.01-4.00		Medium (4.01-10.00)		Large (10.01 & above)	
		No	Area	No	Area	No	Area	No	Area	No	Area
Bihar	(a)	58.86	18.14	23.32	26.22	12.85	28.92	4.52	21.01	0.45	5.71
	(b)	76.76	29.01	13.68	25.14	6.86	23.69	2.48	18.24	0.22	3.92
W.Bengal	(a)	61.21	24.80	22.80	28.92	12.94	31.06	2.98	14.58	0.07	0.64
	(b)	80.69	39.98	13.43	30.69	5.00	22.06	0.88	7.27	0.00	0.00
Orissa	(a)	54.52	18.60	25.78	27.32	13.90	27.06	5.25	21.56	0.55	5.46
	(b)	59.99	22.09	24.34	30.16	12.02	27.87	3.36	16.20	0.29	3.68
Assam	(a)	52.40	21.64	30.23	34.90	14.30	30.54	2.99	12.20	0.08	0.72
	(b)	70.78	34.24	19.99	31.22	7.53	22.92	1.51	9.07	0.19	2.55
India	(a)	45.77	9.21	22.38	14.80	17.66	22.52	11.11	30.49	3.08	22.98
	(b)	62.79	15.60	17.79	18.70	11.99	24.13	6.10	26.37	1.33	15.20

Notes : (a) refers to 1970-71 ; (b) 1991-92.
Source: As in the preceding Table.

produce rent, the amendment provided that the landlord is not entitled to more than seven-twentieth of the produce, after the customary deductions.

Apart from the Bihar Tenancy Act applicable to the whole of Bihar, there were special laws for the districts of Santhal Pargana and Chotanagpur division. A comprehensive Act to protect the various interests of the Santhals was passed in 1949, and the Chotanagpur Tenancy Act was there since 1908. An important objective of these Acts was to prevent the alienation of land belonging to the tribal. Transfer of land to a non-tribal was prohibited and there could not be any ejection of a raiyat from his land without an order from the deputy commissioner.

All these regulations were, however, rarely of any use to the under-raiyats or to the tribals. Illegal eviction of tenants continued on a large scale, mostly in the name of voluntary surrender or abandonment. An evicted tenant did not like to go to a law court or to a Conciliation Board for various reasons. The Conciliation Boards were generally pro-landlord biased and so also the officials. For recognising the rights of *bataidars*, there was always insistence on rent receipts, but the landlords never issued it (Ojha 1980: 86). To cope with the problem of ejection, the Act of 1955 was completely amended in 1970. The collectors were empowered fully not only to restore possession to the tenants evicted unlawfully but also to take steps to prevent eviction when threatened. The legal provisions however, did not deter the landlords from ejecting the under-raiyats and it continued as ever. The provisions regarding crop-sharing were also largely violated.

The incidence of tenancy, however, appears to have declined considerably in recent years, as evident from Table 5.4. In 1981-82, Bihar had a significantly higher proportion of tenant holdings than at the national level but in 1991-92, it was down to half that in the latter. The proportion of total area under tenancy dropped to only 3.9 per cent from 10.3 per cent over the period. The authenticity of this data may, however, be doubted. In Bihar, still a large proportion of tenancy is oral. As regards the terms of lease, some significant changes have taken place over the years. The importance of the share of produce system has declined noticeably, whereas the fixed produce and fixed money system have gained considerably (Table 5.4).

Size of Operational Holdings

Consequent on the land reform measures, the size of operational holdings—which has an impact on operational efficiency—has undergone significant changes. The proportion of marginal holdings increased from 58.9 per cent in 1970-71 to 76.8 per cent in 1991-92 and further to 80.1 per cent in 1995-96; at the national level, the proportion in the latest year was only 61.6 per cent (Table 5.5; CMIE 2004b). Within the marginal holdings again, the proportion of lower sizes is very high here; in the total number of holdings, those with below 0.40 ha constituted 52.03 per cent in 1991-92 compared with 37.70 per cent at the national level. In total area, the share of marginal holdings rose to 29.0 per cent in 1991-92 and further to 36. 2 in 1995-96,from 18.1 in 1970-71; at the national level, the proportions were much lower; in the latest year only 17.2 per cent. In this situation, naturally all other size-classes accounted for a relatively low proportion (ibid.).

Along with a high proportion of sub-marginal holdings, Bihar's holdings were also highly fragmented. In 1981-82, the average number of parcels for all sizes of operational holdings was 6.27 and the average area per parcel at 0.16 hectare; the national averages were, respectively, 4.04 parcels and 0.41 hectare. There was not a single state with this level of fragmentation. The progress in consolidation of holdings was nominal. The area consolidated till October 1983 was only 8.87 per cent of the net cultivated area in the state as against the all-India average of 35.56 per cent (Thangaraj 1995; Haque and Sirohi 1986:102).

Provision of Inputs

Given the right motivation for proper utilisation of the land, optimum exploitation of the potential requires adequate and timely availability of water and other inputs. Too much dependence on nature will not only lead to low productivity but also wide fluctuations from year to year. Below we look briefly into the provision of different inputs like irrigation water, fertilizers, high-yielding seeds, etc.

Irrigation Facility

Bihar gets a substantial amount of rainfall, but it is concentrated in the four months of mid-June to mid-October. The annual average rainfall during 1995-97 (three years) came to 1371.2 mm in the plateau region and 1186.8 mm in the plains. The year-to-year variation was sometimes quite high. Thus in the last seven years, the minimum in the plains was 780.5 mm in 1992 and the maximum at 1347.6 mm in 1997. Although in relation to the all-India average the quantum of rainfall here is not low, in the eastern region it gets the lowest amount (GOI 1999).

The growth of irrigation facility was relatively fast. The NCA under irrigation increased from 1904 thousand ha in 1957-58 to 2155 thousand in 1970-71 and 3680 thousand in 1995-96-that is, a growth of 93.3 per cent over the entire period. The irrigated area constituted an average of 48.7 per cent in 1996-99, rising from 28.8 per cent in 1971-72 and 22.6 per cent in 1959-60. All these were substantially higher than the national average, as evident from Table 5.6.

Crop-wise, the coverage was naturally the highest in food grains—rising from 26.9 per cent of the cropped area in 1973-74 to 47.1 per cent in 1995-96. Among food grains, the irrigated areas were largely confined to wheat, maize and rice. In the latest year, 88.4 per cent of the wheat areas were irrigated as

Table 5.6: Trend in Irrigation Facility, Potential and Development: Bihar Vis-à-vis Other states

States	*Net Irrigated Area as % to Net sown Area*				*Percentage of Irrigated Area to total area under the crop (Contd.)*					
					Total cereals		*Pulses*		*Total Food-grains*	
	1959-0	*1971-2*	*1995-6*	*1993-96*	*1973-4*	*1995-6*	*1973-4*	*1995-6*	*1973-4*	*1995-6*
Bihar	22.6	28.8	50.3	48.6	31.9	52.2	1.0	2.2	26.9	47.1
West Bengal	25.8	27.3	35.0	35.0	28.3	29.9	5.7	3.2	25.5	28.6
Orissa	17.4	14.8	33.7	33.4	20.6	33.2	—	6.8	17.4	25.4
Assam	28.1	24.6	20.6	20.8	33.6	33.6	9.3	9.3	32.6	32.6
Uttar Pradesh	30.1	40.4	67.1	67.2	37.4	70.3	24.2	27.5	35.0	64.3
Madhya Pradesh	5.8	8.9	30.0	28.9	10.7	32.7	2.9	21.2	8.5	29.3
Andhra Pradesh	27.1	26.6	38.8	38.2	43.4	69.9	0.1	1.2	36.9	53.8
Kerala	18.7	20.1	15.1	15.2	59.3	48.8	—	—	56.8	46.7
Punjab	40.1	72.5	92.9	93.3	83.7	96.6	29.5	72.5	78.0	96.1
All-India	18.1	226	37.6	37.0	28.3	47.1	7.9	13.0	24.6	40.5

Total oilseeds		*Source of Irrigation[a] (% of total irrigated area)*						*Ultimate Irrigation Potential (in '000ha)*	
		Canals		*Wells*		*Tanks*			
1973-4	*1995-6*	*1973-4*	*1995-6*	*1973-4*	*1995-6*	*1973-4*	*1995-6*	*Major & Medium*	*Minor*
4.3	20.6	38.7	29.9	30.9	49.6	3.5	3.8	6500 (11.1)	6847
—	70.9	64.5	37.5	1.1	37.3	20.3	13.8	2300 (3.9)	4618
4.5	13.9	63.6	45.4	15.4	40.0	21.1	14.6	3600 (6.2)	5203
—	—	63.3	63.3	—	0.0	—	0.0	970 (1.7)	1900
12.1	51.4	33.7	26.3	57.8	69.9	4.4	0.5	12500 (21.3)	17999
1.5	7.2	43.3	30.3	41.1	53.4	7.2	3.5	6000 (10.3)	11932
11.9	17.6	45.5	37.3	19.7	40.2	31.3	18.1	5000 (8.6)	6260
—	17.9	50.8	31.3	1.1	21.3	16.6	14.3	1000 (1.7)	1679
40.1	88.8	43.3	35.2	56.5	61.3	—	—	3000 (5.1)	2967
8.5	26.1	40.0	32.0	40.7	55.7	12.0	5.8	58465 (100.0)	81428

(Table 5.6 Contd.)

Potential created in (in '000 ha) Major & medium (March-end 1997)	Minor (March 1991)	Level of ground water development (%) (1997)	1997-2000 IPC	IPU
2802.50 (43.1)[b]	4608 (67.3)b	19.19	213.41	122.15 (57.2)[c]
1444.08 (62.8)	2694 (58.3)	24.18	481.41	433.44 (90.0)
1557.75 (43.3)	1204 (23.1)	8.42	211.48	363.2 (171.7)
196.67 (20.3)	558 (29.4)	4.48	12.94	9.24 (71.4)
7059.00 (56.5)	17740 (98.6)	37.67	2111.05	1050.91 (49.8)
2317.60 (38.6)	2500 (21.0)	16.49	120.10	86.70 (72.2)
3045.10 (60.9)	2817 (45.0)	23.64	488.12	466.39 (95.5)
513.31 (51.3)	498 (29.7)	15.28	127.07	125.45 (98.7)
2512.85 (83.8)	3256 (109.7)	93.85	64.09	81.13 (126.6)
32957.14 (56.4)	48420 (59.5)	31.92	5170.31	3943.10 (76.3)

Notes : a : under 1973-74, data relate to 1967-68 in case of W.Bengal, and 1953-54 for Assam; b: figures in brackets are percentages of ultimate potentials in the respective area; the ultimate potentials are reassessed figures as given in GOI 2000c; c: percentage of IPC; IPC : irrigation potential created; IPU : potential utilised.

Source: GOI 1977, 2000, 2000c, 2001a: 35; CMIE 1999.

against 40 per cent in the other two crops; at the national level, the proportions were, respectively, 86.6, 22.7 and 50.1 per cent. For cereals as a whole, the coverage in Bihar stood at 52.2 per cent this year, higher than the national average. Pulses, on the other hand, had an extremely low coverage.

Among other crops, in oilseeds, even after a significant growth, the coverage remained much below the national average. Within oilseeds, the most important crop rapeseed and mustard had only 33.3 per cent of the area irrigated in 1995-96 as against 66.3 per cent at the national level. In sugarcane, with the highest acreage in cash crops, until recently only 22.4 per cent of the area had the facility compared with 88.5 per cent for all-India. Tobacco, a much less important crop, on the other hand had 73.7 per cent coverage.

As regards the source of irrigation, in the total area irrigated the share of canals has declined over the years whereas that of wells registered a significant growth. In both of them, however, the proportion is less than at the national level. In 1995-96, wells irrigated 49.6 per cent of the total here as against 55.7 per cent at the national level; for canals, it was respectively 29.9 per cent and 32.0 per cent. Tanks always played a very insignificant role (Table 5.9).

District-wise, there was wide disparity in the provision of irrigation facility. More than two decades after Independence, in 1968-71, seven districts (out of 17) had a coverage of less then 10 per cent of the cropped area as against the state average of 24.0 per cent; for three districts, Dhanbad, Ranchi and Muzaffarpur, it was less than 5 per cent. South Bihar (present Jharkhand) as a whole remained totally neglected. Their coverage at the highest was 10.6 per cent in Palamau (GOB 1973).

After another three decades, in 1997-98, also South Bihar remained more or less in the same position. Out of the 18 districts, seven had less than 5 per cent of the GCA irrigated and 12 districts with less than 10 per cent as against the state average of 47.0 per cent. In the rest of Bihar also the disparity was not small. There were three districts—Nalanda, Bhabhua and Rohtas—with more than 90 per cent of the GCA irrigated as against only 17.4 per cent in Jamui and 25 per cent in Kishanganj, Munger and Sitamarhi. Region-wise, the irrigation facility continued to be much inferior in North Bihar than in the central part (office record).

This situation persisted despite Bihar having a good irrigation potential. The state accounted for 11.1 per cent of the country's total potential in major and medium irrigation as may be seen from Table 5.6, but the potential created till the end of March 1997 was only 43.1 per cent of the ultimate potential; at the national level, it averaged 56.4 per cent. In minor irrigation, Bihar accounted for 8.4 per cent of the country's potential, of which 67.3 per cent were created by March 1991. The development of ground water is still very low here. At the end of March 1997, it was to the extent of only 19.2 per cent as against 31.9 per cent at the national level.

The created irrigation potential were also rarely utilised to the optimum level, particularly in case of major and medium projects. For example, the potential created during 1997-2000 could be utilised to the extent of only 57 per cent in Bihar compared with the national average of 76 per cent. The utilisation was better in the other eastern states also (Table 5.6).

This situation is largely due to lack of proper drainage system and inefficient distribution. The government has so far failed to construct field channels in adequate number, and where these are available the maintenance is generally very poor. The under-utilisation is also partly due to the peasants' ignorance of the cropping pattern conducive to irrigated farming. The command Area Development Authorities were set up in mid-seventies to bridge the gap between potential created and that utilised but their performance remained far from satisfactory.

It is largely due to this inefficient water management, the yield rate from irrigated land in Bihar is much less than in many other states. In 1990-91, in case of rice, the irrigated land in Bihar gave a yield rate of only 1225 kg/ha as against the all-India average of 1972 kg. The disparity between irrigated and unirrigated land was low in Bihar. The rice yield in unirrigated land this year was 897 kg/ha-that is, 73.2 per cent of that in irrigated land; at the national level, it was 1046 kg, that is, 53.0 per cent. Similar was the situation with regard to wheat (CMIE 1996b).

OTHER INPUTS

Fertilizers

Nutrient management is a complex task. There is need for an integrated nutrient use system involving balanced use of chemical fertilizers, micro-nutrients, green manure and conservation of organic resources and recycling of crop residues. Given the level of expertise with the majority of our farmers, the situation is far from satisfactory. However, due to lack of appropriate data, no detailed analysis is possible. We are looking primarily to the spread in use of chemical fertilizers in Bihar.

The growth in use of chemical fertilizers has been very disappointing here. In 1962-65, the annual average consumption stood at only 2.96 kg per hectare, which was a mere 68 per cent of that at the national level. After two decades, in 1980-83, the relative position worsened; at 27.46 kg/ha, it was only 64 per cent of the latter's. In recent years, however, there has been considerable improvement, as may be seen from the Table.

The use of rural and urban compost was very low here. Their production stood at the annual average of 24.044 lakh tonnes during 1994-97, and constituted 1.81 per cent of all-India total; in the eastern region, West Bengal and Orissa had much higher production (FAI 2003).The cow dung is used here largely as fuel. In 1999-00, 24.2 per cent of the rural households and 21.8 per cent of the urban households were using it as the primary source of energy for cooking (NSSO 2001). Number of bio-fertiliser plants was also only 3 in 1999 as against 12 in Uttar Pradesh.

District-wise, the consumption of fertilizers varied widely, and it was not solely due to variation in the irrigation facility. There were some districts with low use despite having a relatively good irrigation facility. In 1977-80, for example, Gaya with the highest proportion of cropped area irrigated, had a consumption of only 22.41 kg/ha. Saran with a much lower level of irrigation facility on the other hand, had a significantly higher level of fertilizer use. Region-wise, South Bihar had a very low level of consumption, only 5.18 kg/ha in this period as against 16.56 kg at the state level. Within the region again, the lowest was in Singhbhum, only 2.55 kg/ha, although the proportion of irrigated area was not the lowest here (Chadha 1987). Obviously, the benefit of higher irrigation facility was neutralised by some adverse factors. The district-wise variation in consumption is still very high. In 2001-02, out of 55 districts, 9 had consumption between 25 and 50 kg/ha as against one with above 200 kg and three with 150-200 kg (FAI 2003).

The availability of fertilizer was probably not easy in Bihar. Number of fertilizer depots was relatively low. Per thousand hectares it came to 1.75 in 1993, which was not only less than the national average, among the eastern states it was the lowest. In recent years also the situation was not better. At the end of March 2003, Bihar had only 4390 fertiliser sale points, constituting 1.55 per cent of all-India total; even Assam had a larger number. Moreover, 90.5 per cent of these were privately owned as against 75.6 per cent at the national level. The share of cooperatives in distribution of total fertilisers declined from 22.0 per cent in 1990-91 to 1.53 per cent in 1995-96, and in the following years varied between 8.36 and 14.74 per cent (Bhatia 1999; FAI 2003).

The soil testing facility was also very poor. In 2000-01, the total analysing capacity of soil testing laboratories in Bihar stood at only 411.50 thousand number of samples, constituting 5.14 per cent of all-India total. The utilisation of even this facility was extremely low; this year, it was to the extent of 7.2 per cent as against 55.6 per cent at the national level. The fertiliser quality control situation was also very depressing. The annual capacity of quality control laboratories totalled only 2000 samples in 2002-03, constituting 1.60 per cent of all-India total; and even this capacity could be utilised to the extent of only 13.2 per cent this year. The extension service was also very poor. Number of agricultural extension worker per million rural population stood at 56 in 1993 as against 95 for all-India.

Improved Seeds

Availability of quality seeds is a basic requirement for increased agricultural production, although it must be associated with proper application

Table 5.7: Trend in use of Fertilizers and HYV Seeds: Bihar Vis-à-Vis Other States

States	*Consumption of Fertilizers (in kg/ha)*								
	1962-65 (a.a.)	*1980-83 (a.a.)*	*1990-91*	*1995-6*	*1996-7*	*1997-8*	*1998-9*	*1996-99 (a.a.)*	*2001-03 (a.a.)*
Bihar	2.96	27.46	56.8	71.9	77.5	84.8	95.3	85.9 (103.4)	87.5*
W.Bengal	4.72	48.02	90.3	94.5	98.9	107.7	106.4	104.3 (125.5)	122.8
Orissa	1.20	13.78	20.9	24.6	30.5	35.4	42.4	36.1 (43.4)	37.2
Assam	0.26	4.15	—	12.5	14.0	17.9	18.7	16.9 (20.3)	40.0
Madhya P.	0.82	11.78	35.4	33.0	38.2	48.1	48.9	45.1 (54.3)	38.0*
Uttar P.	40.6	75.36	90.1	101.0	105.9	116.0	121.2	114.4 (137.7)	128.4*
Maharashtra	2.41	26.83	66.4	64.4	61.2	73.9	76.0	70.4 (84.7)	74.7
Kerala	15.40	45.66	84.4	66.3	62.1	72.7	60.2	65.0 (78.2)	63.6
Punjab	7.84	192.07	171.2	163.0	154.0	167.6	176.6	166.1 (199.9)	172.9
Andhra P.	9.67	58.20	133.3	134.3	131.9	126.4	137.8	132.0 (159.0)	139.2
All-India	4.33	42.62	72.4	74.4	75.5	85.4	88.5	83.1 (100.0)	88.1

Area under HYV Seeds ('000 ha)					
1971-74[a] (a.a.)	*1987-90 (a.a.)*	*1994-5*	*1995-6*	*1996-7*	*1994-97 (a.a.)*
2185	4430	5780	5950	6750	6160 (61.5)[b]
1069	3164	4140	4700	4810	4550 (50.7)
383	2120	3020	3150	3140	3103 (32.1)
335	1202	1300	1360	1540	1400 (35.6)
1193	5524	7400	7790	7800	7663 (30.0)
3941	11937	14310	14700	14970	14660 (56.8)
1423	6895	7730	7920	8960	8203 (38.5)
277	223	170	160	400	243 (7.9)
2277	4971	5580	5410	5420	5470 (70.6)
1549	4241	4850	4010	4700	4520 (34.7)
22114	58431	70930	72310	76430	73223 (39.2)

Notes: a: for five major cereals (rice, jowar, bajra, maize and wheat); b: percentage of grass cropped area; *: refer to the undivided states.
Source: GOI 1983, 1976a; CMIE 1996b, 2000; FAI 2003.

Table 5.8: Use of selected Agricultural Machinery and Implements and Consumption of Electricity: Bihar Vis-à-Vis other states

State	No. of pump sets per '000 ha			No. per 10,000 ha (1992)		No. per 100 households (1992)			Electricity consumption in agri. (mkwh)	
	1962-65 (a.a.)	1980-83 (a.a.)	1994-97 (a.a.)	Tractor	Power tiller	Plough	Harrow	Seed drill	1973-74	1996-97
Bihar	0.92	49.76	26.67	59	25	65.3 (9.91)[a]	21.32	0.40	74 (2.75)b	1331 (12.39)b
W. Bengal	0.80	37.36	11.27	37	86	44.9 (2.82)	32.02	0.56	30 (0.59)	1372 (9.73)
Orissa	0.19	2.82	7.11	5	2	85.8 (8.68)	26.66	0.72	8 (0.51)	722 (6.86)
Assam	0.11	0.52	0.93	0	23	105.1 (2.34)	74.34	4.41	2 (0.53)	46 (2.49)
Madhya P.	1.05	21.36	45.22	73	12	88.9 (5.48)	21.92	11.40	126 (4.96)	8876 (36.43)
Uttar P.	1.45	63.93	29.44	215	58	68.5 (23.96)	6.50	0.94	841 (20.26)	9846 (37.08)
Kerala	4.36	45.41	1022.00	3	15	3.46 (0.57)	1.45	0.56	92 (5.13)	329 (4.39)
Andhra P.	5.43	62.37	129.57	48	1	39.2 (4.06)	25.51	5.41	588 (23.8)	8210 (49.64)
Punjab	8.20	157.69	2584.00	1024	584	28.2 (17.76)	7.59	6.14	710 (25.60)	6348 (35.55)
All-India	4.58	49.16	59.66	109	41	57.0 (11.13)	23.96	6.48	6310 (12.56)	84331 (30.80)

Notes: a: number of iron plough per 100 households; b: percentage share in total electricity consumption in the state.
Source: GOI 1999, 1983, 1976a; CMIE 1996b, 2000; NSSO 1998b.

of other inputs in order to get the optimum result. Among the quality seeds, particularly important is the use of high-yielding variety (HYV) that brought the green revolution in the country. The analysis is, therefore, focussed on the spread of HYV seeds in Bihar.

On the adoption of HYV seeds, the state's performance was relatively good. By 1971-74, the coverage of the state's total GCA reached 20.45 per cent. In the following years also the growth was quite fast, and reached 61.5 per cent in 1994-97. In relation to the national average, this is a good performance, as may be seen from Table 5.7. However, in the all-India total area under HYV, the state's share declined from 9.9 per cent to 8.4 per cent over the period.

Crop-wise, the spread of HYVs was largely confined to wheat, rice and maize. In 1979-81, for example, the coverage of wheat area was to the extent of 74.8 per cent as against only 21.9 per cent for rice and 35.9 per cent in maize. These three crops together accounted for around 70 per cent of the total area under HYVs.

The yield rate from HYV was relatively low in Bihar. In rice, it gave a yield rate of only 1,598 kg/ha in 1990-91 as against the national average of 2,192 kg. The difference with low-yielding varieties (LYV) was not much as the overall yield rate for rice this year was 1218 kg in Bihar. In wheat also the state's performance in HYV was disappointing. The yield rate here was 1,502 kg/ha compared with 1,967 kg at the national level. The overall yield rate was higher, being at 1561 kg, signifying that the LYVs gave a higher return (CMIE 1996b). The low yield of HYVs is probably due to the poor cultural practices followed.

On the provision of adequate supply of certified/HYV seeds also there were many deficiencies. The Seeds Act was passed in India only in 1966 and became effective from October 1969. A subsidy scheme for encouraging the use of certified seeds came only in 1975-76, and the State Seeds Corporation was established in 1980-81. Thus, everything moved very slowly. The performance of the corporation was also far from satisfactory. The growth in production of certified seeds was negligible except for paddy, wheat and gram.

Bihar has been dependent on outside sources for most of its quality/improved seeds. The foundation and breeder seeds of the suitable varieties are not available in the state, and consequently the seed replacement rate is far less than the defined norm. In rice, for example, the replacement rate in recent years was 5 per cent and in wheat 10 per cent as against the norm of 20 per cent. Due to the shortage of certified seeds many farmers produced their own seeds and also exchange seeds, but the facility of seed testing laboratory is utterly inadequate.

Plant Protection Measures

The need for protection of plants became more important with the coming of the 'green revolution' technology. As the new agriculture required much higher investment, any loss of crop began to prove too costly, and therefore, the greater need for protecting them. Plant protection generally involves four types of activities: seed treatment, weed control, post-sowing prophylactic treatment and aerial spraying of pesticides. The use of different methods varied from situation to situation. Due to lack of reliable data on the use of most of the methods, we note here only the position of pesticides in some of the years.

The use of pesticides in Bihar was quite low. In 1976-77, 19.8 per cent of the cropped areas in Bihar were estimated to have suffered from pests and diseases but the area treated with pesticides was only 7.2 per cent (Prasad 1998: 284). During 1985-88, the annual average consumption of pesticides in Bihar came to 2,250 tonnes, constituting 3.35 per cent of all-India total. In recent years, the use of pesticides has fallen noticeably, from 1383 tonnes in 1995-96 to only 834 tonnes in 1998-99. Per hectare of GCA, the consumption declined from 0.28 kg in 1987-88 to 0.08 kg in 1998-99; the national average in the latest year was 0.26 kg (CMIE 1996b; GOI 2003c).

The use of pesticides is mainly in the irrigated areas. In 1976-77, for example, the consumption in irrigated areas was 0.73 kg/ha as against 0.23 kg in non-irrigated areas. Farm size-wise, generally larger holdings used more pesticides than the smaller ones. In 1976-77, in the irrigated areas, large holdings used 0.84 kg/ha as against 0.37 kg by small holdings. The use was naturally influenced by the means of the farmer.

The supply and use of pesticides suffered from many deficiencies. The Insecticides Act, 1968 came into operation only in 1971, and even now control over the manufacture, distribution and transport of insecticides is far from satisfactory. The extension services are also very weak in Bihar. Increasing use of pesticides without proper care has caused contamination of soil, air and water, besides affecting the crop plants and produce.

Since mid-eighties, therefore, need-based use of plant-protection measures instead of prophylactic treatment has been emphasised. Pesticides were to be used only when the pest population increased beyond the economic threshold level. Natural methods like use of parasites and predators and mechanical devices were expected to be used on a much larger scale, but there has not been any noteworthy progress.

Use of Implements

Given the poverty of the population and the extremely small size of holdings, use of machinery and implements could not be high. Looking to bullock-operated implements first, even on the quality of plough used the situation was very depressing. In 1987, number of iron ploughs per thousand hectares of NCA came to only 21.1 as against 65.1 at the national level. Per hundred households, in 1992, it numbered 9.91 and 11.13, respectively. On the use of seed drill, the situation was still worse. In 1987, there were only 3.3 per thousand ha as against 47.5 at the national level (GOI 2000). In 1992, per 100 households, it was respectively 0.40 and 6.48. On the use of harrow, however, the situation was not so bad, as may be seen from Table 5.8.

As regards machine-operated implements, even on the use of pump sets, the situation was very depressing. Number used per thousand ha rose to 49.76 in 1980-83 but declined again to only 26.67 in 1994-97; the latest is less than half the national average. The fall in use is at least partly due to the irregularity in supply of electricity, and the high price of diesel oil which has often to be purchased from the black market. The use of tractor and power tiller was also similarly placed. Among other instruments, only the harvester and thresher had a relatively high use (Table 5.8).

The low growth of mechanisation in Bihar's agriculture is reflected in the level of electricity consumption. In 1996-97, the total consumption in agriculture came to only 1331 million kWh, constituting 1.57 per cent of all-India total. In the state's total, the share of agriculture stood at only 12.4 per cent, less than half that at the national level. Two-and-half decades earlier, in 1973-74, the relative position was far worse (Table 5.8).

Institutional Credit

Easy availability of credit is a prerequisite for agricultural growth, particularly in a situation where the farmers are very poor. But the role of the organised banking system here has been far from satisfactory. The total flow of credit to Bihar's agriculture in 1996-97 was only Rs 454.3 crore, constituting 1.7 per cent of all-India total. The credit per hectare came to Rs. 453, less than a third of the national average. Earlier, in 1986, the relative position was significantly better, as evident from table 5.9. Below we give a brief look into the role of different institutions.

Co-operative Credit

Despite being the oldest form of organised banking in rural areas, the co-operative credit institutions in Bihar did not play any important role in providing credit to agriculture. In 1996-97, the aggregate of ground level credit to it from the State and Central co-operative Banks stood at only Rs 79.44 crore, constituting 17.5 per cent of the total from all institutions. In the all-India total, this was a mere 0.78 per cent.

In the provision of credit, the most important institution is the primary agricultural credit societies (PACS), followed by Central co-operative Banks (CCB). The share of the former in total credit was generally above 60 per cent. The growth in credit flow was, however, very low. The short-and medium-term credit together stood at Rs. 57.04 crore in 1994-95, rising from Rs. 16.08 crore in 1977-78 and Rs. 9.74 crore in 1965-66, that is, only a 6-fold rise over the entire period; at the national level it was 26.5 times, and consequently Bihar's relative

Table 5.9: Trend in Credit to Agriculture from the Banking System : Bihar Vis-à-Vis Other States

States	Total credit to agriculture From all agencies (Rs. crore)			Sch. Comm. Banks' Direct Agri. Advances Outstanding (Rs. Crore)			
				As on March 1980		As on June 1997	
	30.6.1986	1996-7	per ha* Rs.	Total	Short-term	Total	Short-term
Bihar	697 (4.6)	454.3 (17.2)	453	87.8 (4.6)	17.75 (20.2)[a]	740.2 (3.6)	154.3 (20.8)[a]
W.Bengal	515 (3.4)	733.2 (2.78)	817	s91.9 (4.8)	40.91 (44.5)	803.0 (3.9)	410.6 (51.1)
Orissa	563 (3.7)	451.3 (1.71)	290	35.1 (1.8)	20.40 (58.1)	386.3 (1.9)	206.1 (53.4)
Assam	180 (1.2)	38.8 (0.15)	49	5.4 (0.3)	2.71 (50.0)	217.1 (1.1)	121.2 (55.8)
Madhya P.	966 (6.3)	1661.2 (6.29)	375	109.4 (5.8)	14.00 (12.8)	1321.1 (6.5)	226.2 (17.1)
Uttar P.	1924 (12.6)	2562.6 (9.70)	994	219.6 (11.6)	38.48 (17.5)	2087.3 (10.2)	513.6 (24.6)
Maharashtra	1609 (10.6)	2814.7 (10.66)	915	158.9 (8.4)	57.46 (36.2)	1802.7 (8.8)	536.3 (29.7)
Kerala	920 (6.0)	1332.2 (5.05)	4348	96.5 (5.1)	70.22 (72.7)	1082.5 (5.3)	708.4 (65.4)
Andhra P.	1601 (10.5)	3686.0 (13.96)	2826	280.5 (14.8)	228.99 (81.6)	2511.3 (12.3)	1789.4 (71.3)
Punjab	866 (5.7)	2396.5 (9.07)	3091	156.2 (8.2)	26.71 (17.1)	1433.8 (7.0)	325.5 (22.7)
All-India	15228 (100.0)	26411.3 (100.00)	1416	1900.7 (100.0)	829.50 (43.6)	20396.2 (100.0)	8766.4 (43.0)

(Contd.)

(Table 5.9 Contd.)

per hect. of GCA (Rs.) Short term	Total	RRB's Agri. Advcs. Outstanding March 1996 Total (Rs. lakh)	per hect (Rs.)	June 1986 per hect (Rs.)	PACS Amount outstanding (Rs. lakh) March 1996	% of overdue 1970	1985	LDBs' loans to borrowers (Rs. Crore) 1993-97 (a.a)
154	739 (320)[b]	21406 (32.3)[c]	229	98	14082 (1.24)	50	90	18.17 (1.09)
458	895 (447)	11466 (24.9)	134	55	21397[d] (1.89)	56	66	46.04 (2.77)
213	400 (217)	16693 (42.8)	177	78	26137 (2.31)	63	52	12.76 (0.76)
308	551 (186)	173 (37.1)	178	35	—	82	75	—
90	528 (196)	26563 (49.9)	112	33	—	39	51	67.32 (4.05)
199	809 (358)	73234 (46.9)	285	65	—	34	48	282.15 (16.96)
251	845 (386)	14602 (54.4)	69	15	233616 (20.64)	40	40	148.40 (8.92)
2311	3531 (1290)	15270 (43.7)	501	182	184049 (16.27)	24	18	140.19 (8.43)
1372	1925 (785)	52104 (54.1)	409	114	165599 (14.64)	43	34	—
420	1850 (912)	6012 (51.2)	80	8	75610 (6.68)	39	42	189.35 (11.38)
470	1093 (-.)	346651 (46.2)	187	—	1131464 (100.00)	38	42	1663.56 (100.00)

Notes: a: percentage share of total; b: as on 30.6.1986; c: percentage share of agriculture in total advances; d : relates to 1991-92; *: based on GCA of 1995-96.

Source: NABARD 1998, 1999; RBI 1982, 2000a, 1996, 1990; GOI 2000.

share dropped to 0.69 per cent from 3.10 per cent. In the credit outstanding, the state's share stood at 1.24 per cent in March 1996.

The PACS are in a very poor shape in Bihar. Average membership per society stood at only 888 in 1993-94 compared with the national average of 1,458. The transaction cost per Rs. 100 of loan averaged Rs. 79.90 during 1993-94 to 1996-97 as against Rs. 18.90 at the national level. The performance in loan recovery was extremely poor. The overdue as percentage to amount outstanding reached as much as 90 in 1985 and presently also it is very high.

On the provision of long term credit also the situation was not good. The State Land Development Bank had provided an annual average of Rs. 18.17 crore during 1993-97, which was 1.09 per cent of all-India total. Around three decades earlier, at June-end 1970, the amount outstanding stood at Rs. 8.08 crore, constituting 5.52 per cent of all-India total (RBI 1971). The performance in loan recovery is very low. In 1996-7, it was 35 per cent of demand as against 60 per cent at the national level.

Commercial Banks

The most resourceful group of banks, the scheduled commercial banks (SCBs), did not enter the rural areas until two decades after Independence. In December 1970, the RBI issued a set of guidelines to the commercial banks for financing agricultural development. Gradually, a network of branches was opened in rural areas. The progress in lending to rural Bihar was, however, very slow. At the end of June 1997, the SCBs' direct advances to agriculture stood at Rs. 740 crore, constituting 3.6 per cent of all-India total. This is a fall from the level existing in 1980 (Table 5.9).The agricultural advances per hectare of GCA stood at only Rs 739 in the latest year, 68 per cent of that at the national level.

In the aggregate of credit to agriculture, the share of short-term was very low in Bihar-generally constituting a fifth as against more than two-fifths at the national level. The state's share in all-India total provision of short-term credit declined from 2.14 per cent in 1980 to 1.76 per cent in 1997. The credit outstanding per hectare of GCA came to only Rs 154 in 1997, which was less than a third of the national average. On the provision of term loans also the situation deteriorated. Bihar's share in all-India total declined from 6.54 per cent to 5.04 per cent over the period.

As regards the RRBs, sponsored by the commercial banks, the performance appears to be better. At the end of March 1996, the agricultural advances outstanding from them stood at Rs 214.06 crore, and constituted 6.18 per cent of all-India total. The credit outstanding per hectare was Rs. 229 here compared with the national average of Rs 187. Earlier, in 1986, also the state was in a similar position (Table 5.9). However, the RRBs' attention to agriculture is relatively low here. In the aggregate of advances outstanding from them in

1996, the share of agriculture was only 32.3 per cent compared with 46.2 per cent at the national level.

Agricultural Marketing

Outside the production system, availability of proper marketing facilities is a great incentive towards increased production. Farmers must have a reasonable assurance about remunerative prices. In this direction, there is need for proper market places, assembling, storing, grading, transportation, financing and other facilities. Fixation of minimum support/procurement prices and proper arrangement for procurement also play an important role in inducing farmers to go for increased production.

All these are, however, in an extremely poor state in Bihar. To look at the quality of market places first: The number of markets available was no doubt relatively good but the facilities within them were far from satisfactory. Between 1963 and 1982, number of wholesale markets increased from 314 to 672 and the regulated ones in them from 63 to 120. In the following years, the latter had a much faster growth. In 1992, it reached 828 and constituted 12.5 per cent of all-India total. The number of sub-markets rose to 706 this year which was 15.9 per cent of the national total; sixteen years back, in 1976, there were only 76 such markets, constituting 4.6 per cent. For all types of markets together, Bihar had 2.5 markets per 100 sq km in 1993 as against the national average of 2.4. In the eastern region, Bihar had the highest number.

The markets were, however, hardly of any use to a vast majority of the farmers. A large number of middlemen are present in the marketing system, and they successfully manipulate the market forces. Advances at the time of sowing for purchase of inputs are given to the farmers by the middlemen, after fixing the price at which the produce would be purchased. In the markets malpractices are rampant, particularly in the unorganized ones. There is no transparency in the transactions. The traders are so organised and wield so much power that they get brokerage from both the sellers and buyers. Nearly 40 per cent of the price is grabbed by them. A product is sold four to five times as it moves from the lower to the higher rung in the ladder of the traders. In weights and measures also the farmers are duped. And then there are a number of illegal deductions (Prasad 1998: 434). No doubt, certain measures like passing the Bihar Agriculture Produce Act, 1960 and the Standards of Weights and Measures Enforcement Act, 1985 were taken but the situation did not improve much.

For raising the bargaining strength of farmers, the government encouraged the setting up of co-operative agricultural marketing societies. But the progress was very small, particularly for poor farmers. Number of PAMS increased from 218 in 1963 to 473 in 1988-89-that is, by only 117 per cent over the period. As the growth at the national level was much higher, Bihar's relative share declined from 7.0 per cent to 1.69 per cent. The value of agricultural produce marketed by the societies stood at only Rs 18.23 crore in 1976-77, constituting 1.5 per cent of the all-India total.

The storage and transportation facilities in Bihar continued to be very poor. In 1993, the storage facility as percentage to total food grains production stood at only 3.0 as against the all-India average of 21.4. The latest position is also far from satisfactory. At the end of March 2003, the storage capacity (in the erstwhile Bihar) with the co-operative sector totalled 571.5 thousand tonnes, constituting 4.10 per cent of all-India total; and the Food Corporation of India had 519.1 thousand tonnes and 1.95 per cent respectively (Bhatia 1999; FAI 2003). The lack of storage space often hampers the procurement operation of the FCI. Recently, the situation became so desperate that the farmers threatened to go for growing marijuana in place of paddy. Thousands of sacks of paddy remained piled up at different procurement centre. The Scarcity of cold storage facility often leads to huge wastage of perishable commodities.

As regards the transportation system, the relative position has worsened noticeably over the years. Road length per thousand sq km of area was nearly double the all-India average in 1975–being respectively 69 and 36 km—but in 1998-99 it was much below the latter's, respectively 514.35 km and 768.42 km. And then, the proportion of unsurfaced road continued to be very high. In the latest year, it was respectively 61.89 and 42.65 per cent. The rural situation is extremely poor. Percentage of villages connected with all-weather roads stood at only 35 in 1996. The availability of transport vehicles was also very low. In 1999-00, Bihar had only 5.01 vehicles per sq km of geographical area as against 14.72 at the national level. On railways also the situation was not good. The route length has shown a noticeable decline over the years. Per thousand sq km of area, it was down to 19.80 km in 2000-01 from 30.68 km in 1992-93; at the national level, it has remained static at 19 km (GOA 1979; CMIE 1999a, 2003).

On the problems of agricultural production in Bihar, one cannot but note the losses caused by devastating floods almost on a regular basis. In 1987, 30 million people were affected by floods and crops worth Rs. 680 crore were destroyed. In the years 2000 and 2001, crops and property worth Rs 875 crore were destroyed, with people affected at 12 million (Statesman 2001 h : 2; Bhagirath 2001; GOB 1988). North Bihar with a population of 40.58 million (1991) and an area of about 54 lakh hectares is the most affected part. The total flood prone area of the state increased from 25 lakh ha in 1954 to 68 lakh in 1994 (Mishra 1997); presently it is estimated at 42.6 lakh ha, constituting 12.7 per cent of all-India total (Bhagirath 2001: 35).

The government's efforts at flood control are almost totally ineffective. The length of embankment along the rivers no doubt increased from only 160 km in 1954 to 3465 km in 1992 but breaches in the embankments became common over the years. The breaches in the Kosi embankment, near Nauhatta in Saharsa, in September 1984 had inundated over 70,000 hectares of land and uprooted over 4.5 lakh trees in just one stroke. As the construction of embankments failed to bring any relief to the people, many proposals for construction of large dams on the rivers in Nepal came but very little could be implemented. The Kosi project and the Gandak project that started in 1955 and 1964, respectively, are yet to be completed.

ALLIED ACTIVITIES

Animal Husbandry

Among the allied activities, animal husbandry plays a very important role in rural areas. It provides a variety of animal products consumed as food, like milk, milk products, eggs and meat. It also provides wool and by-products of slaughter houses such as hides and skins, bones, etc. There are a number of other uses: Cattle provide draught / motive power on a significant scale—in the work of cultivation, and in the bullock—cart as an important means of rural transport in interior areas-and there is the use of cow-dung as fuel and manure. Generation of bio-gas using cow-dung is an important recent development.

The animal husbandry is generally divided into two groups: livestock and poultry. The former comprises primarily of cattle, sheep, goats, buffalo, pigs, horses and camels. The growth in number of livestock in Bihar over the years has not been much. Between 1951 and 1992, that is, a period of four decades, the total number had risen by only 81.2 per cent—from 264.5 lakh to 479.3 lakh. However, at the national level also the growth was low, and consequently Bihar's share in the latter rose to 10.18 per cent from 9.84 (GOI 1959, 2000d). Below we give a brief look into the pattern of growth in some of the important livestock.

Cattle and Buffalo

Among the cattle, male ones are used in the tasks of cultivation, or alternatively as pack animal, and the female cattle for yielding milk. The growth in number of cattle was relatively high in Bihar. Between 1972 and 1992, as may be seen from Table 5.10, it was nearly doubled as against a 60 per cent rise at the national level. The state's share in all-India total rose to 10.8 per cent from 8.7. The females among them had a much faster growth-by 174 per cent compared with 93 per cent in all-India. Despite this, male-female ratio remained high. The proportion of female in total number stood at 47.6 per cent in 1992 as against the national average of 50.3. Not only this, the proportion of milch cattle in them and those in milk were very low in Bihar.

In the cattle population, the cross-bred which has higher milk yield, constituted a negligible proportion. In 1992, it was only 0.86 per cent as against the national average of 7.44 per cent. In the total number of females also, the cross-bred constituted only 51.8 per cent here compared with 69.4 per cent at the national level. Even in the eastern region, Bihar's was the worst position. In

Table 5.10: Pattern of Growth in Cattle and Buffalo Population: Bihar Vis-à-Vis Other States (Number in '000)

States	CATTLE (contd.) 1972a		1992			
	Total no.	Females	Total no.	Females	Cross-bred Total no.	Females
Bihar	11146 (8.7)	3851 (34.6)[b]	22154 (10.8)	10543 (47.6)[b]	191 (0.86)[c]	991 (51.8)[b]
W.Bengal	8382 (6.6)	3643 (43.5)	17453 (8.5)	9723 (55.7)	960 (5.50)	740 (77.1)
Orissa	8445 (6.6)	3781 (44.8)	13841 (6.8)	6794 (49.1)	600 (4.33)	428 (71.3)
Assam	3915 (3.1)	1654 (42.2)	10118 (4.9)	5091 (50.3)	325 (3.21)	230 (70.8)
Madhya P.	17463 (13.7)	7858 (45.0)	28688 (14.0)	13522 (47.1)	208 (0.73)	144 (69.2)
Uttar P.	20390 (15.9)	6696 (32.8)	25635 (12.5)	10974 (42.8)	2498 (9.74)	1049 (42.0)
Andhra P.	9363 (7.3)	3872 (41.4)	10946 (5.4)	4731 (43.2)	484 (4.42)	376 (77.7)
Kerala	2856 (2.2)	2076 (72.7)	3524 (1.7)	3002 (85.2)	1759 (49.91)	1555 (88.4)
Punjab	2324 (1.8)	912 (39.2)	2909 (1.4)	1841 (82.5)	1628 (55.96)	1180 (72.5)
All-India	127868 (100.0)	53409 (41.8)	204584 (100.0)	102988 (50.3)	15215 (7.44)	10557 (69.4)

CATTLE % increase in		BUFFALOES 1972[a]		1992		% increase in		% of milch Cattle in (1992)	
Total no	Females	Tot. no.	Females	Tot. no.	Females	Tot. No.	Females	Tot. female cattle	milk
98.8	173.8	2535	1817 (71.7)[b]	5352 (6.4)	3877 (72.4)[b]	111.1	113.4	47.5	35.9
108.2	166.9	711	189 (26.6)	1012 (1.2)	335 (33.1)	42.3	77.2	36.2	92.0
63.9	79.7	1017	387 (38.1)	1536 (1.8)	693 (45.1)	51.0	79.1	57.6	47.1
158.4	207.8	343	142 (41.4)	959 (1.1)	506 (52.8)	179.6	256.3	53.2	65.6
64.3	72.1	3652	2505 (68.6)	7970 (9.5)	5414 (67.9)	118.2	116.1	63.0	49.4
25.7	63.9	8164	6537 (80.1)	20084 (23.9)	15213 (75.7)	146.0	132.7	57.9	58.6
16.9	22.3	4757	3416 (71.8)	9150 (10.9)	7799 (85.2)	92.3	128.3	50.4	59.6
23.4	44.6	374	148 (39.6)	296 (0.35)	180 (60.8)	(-)20.9	21.6	53.3	65.6
25.2	101.9	2178	1910 (87.7)	6008 (7.1)	5376 (89.5)	175.8	181.5	55.8	69.8
60.0	92.8	36678	28612 (78.0)	84206 (100.0)	66855 (79.4)	129.6	133.7	56.1	54.6

(Table 5.10 Contd.)

% of cross-bred in (1992)		% of milch buffaloes in (1992)		Working Bovine per 100 Hects. of operated area	
total no. of Milch cattle	total no. in milk	total female buff.	milk	1971-2	1991-2
1.18	1.94	62.5	39.1	90	115
11.29	8.97	63.9	75.7	125	115
6.08	8.30	56.0	53.1	115	122
4.50	4.61	52.0	62.4	141	157
1.02	1.40	63.7	60.6	59	67
9.21	9.86	61.9	64.0	103	63
9.01	10.76	57.2	71.5	66	63
52.59	55.52	80.6	50.3	42	9
62.45	63.51	20.9	20.2	47	20
10.02	12.71	60.2	64.3	68	59

Notes: a: cattle over three years of age; b: percentage of females in respective category's total number; c: percentage of cross-bred in total cattle.
Source: GOI 1977, 2000; NSSO 1998c.

the milch cattle again, the share of cross-bred was extremely low (Table 5.10) Thus, in terms of milk production, Bihar's management of the cattle population was the worst among the states. And this was despite a continuously rising pressure of cattle on land. Number of cattle per hectare of NSA rose to 3.09 in 1992 from 1.35 in 1972; the all-India average in the latest year was only 1.44.

In recent years, the situation has deteriorated further. The latest livestock survey in 1997, has found the total number of cattle in Bihar at 245.98 lakh, a 11 per cent rise over 1992 as against an absolute fall at the national level. Number of cattle per hectare of NSA has risen to 3.32 whereas for all-India it has declined to 1.40. Total number of cross-bred has risen to 3.69 lakh, a 93 per cent rise over 1992; their share in total cattle is now five times higher, being 4.56 per cent (GOI 2004a).

With regard to buffaloes—which are kept mainly for milk production—also the situation was no better. The growth in number of buffaloes was only 111 per cent between 1972 and 1992, compared with 130 per cent at the national level. Bihar accounted for only 6.4 per cent of all-India total number in the latest year. The proportion of females in them was also low—being 72.4 per cent in 1992 as against 79.4 per cent at the national level. A more disappointing aspect is that, Bihar had a very high proportion of dry buffaloes. The proportion in milk was only 39.1 per cent in the latest year compared with 64.3 per cent in all-India.

The bovine population in Bihar was used largely for work purposes, as evident from Table 5.10. This naturally had an adverse impact on the growth in milk production. Between 1971-72 and 1995-96, milk production in Bihar had risen only 89.8 per cent as against 194.2 per cent at the national level. The per capita production in the latest year was less than half the national average. Bihar's share in all-India total production declined continuously from 11.03 per cent in 1956 to 7.8 in 1971-72 and 5.0 per cent in 1995-96 (Table 5.11). There has not been any improvement in more recent years also. In 2001-02, with the production at 40.68 lakh tonnes, the relative share came to 4.81 per cent (GOI 204b).

In the aggregate of milk production, the share of buffalo was relatively low in Bihar. In 995-96, it stood at 51.0 per cent, which was below the national average. The remaining portion came from cows and goats–contributing respectively 37.7 per cent and 11.3 per cent; at the national level, the former contributed 39.4 per cent and the latter only 4.1 per cent.

The low level of milk production in Bihar is not only because of the unfavourable composition of bovine population but also due to the low yield per animal. For indigenous cattle, it was found to be only 1.665kg /day in 1987-88 as against 3.202 kg in Punjab and more than 2 kg in a number of states. For cross-bred cattle, Bihar had 4.945 kg compared with 7.943 kg in Gujarat. In buffalo also Bihar's yield rate was relatively low (Patel 1993).

Table 5.11: Trend in Milk Production: Bihar vis-à-vis other States

(In lakh tonnes)

States	*1971-2*	*1981-2*	*1995-6*		
			Total	*% share of buffaloes*	*% increase 1971-96*
Bihar	17.5 (31.0)[a]	20.4 (29.2)[a]	33.2 (35.0)[a]	51.0	89.7 (12.9)
W.Bengal	4.9 (11.1)	17.8 (32.6)	33.4 (45.6)	8.6	581.6 (310.8)
Orissa	3.4 (15.5)	3.2 (12.1)	6.5 (18.9)	19.6	91.2 (21.9)
Assam	1.5 (10.3)	5.2 (28.9)	7.0 (28.4)	-	366.7 (175.7)
Madhya P.	11.7 (28.1)	23.9 (45.8)	51.2 (71.0)	50.9	337.6 (152.7)
Uttar P.	43.0 (48.7)	59.5 (53.7)	118.8 (79.1)	66.5	176.3 (62.4)
Andhra P.	11.3 (26.0)	24.2 (45.2)	42.6 (59.4)	79.0	277.0 (128.5)
Kerala	2.8 (13.1)	9.5 (37.4)	21.9 (70.9)	3.9	682.1 (441.2)
Punjab	21.4 (157.4)	34.9 (307.3)	64.2 (297.4)	71.9	200.0 (88.9)
All-India	225.0 (41.0)	343.0 (50.2)	661.9 (72.3)	53.8	194.2 (76.3)

Note: a: per capita production in kg.
Source: CMIE 1996b, GOI 2000, 2000d.

The low yield is primarily due to lack of proper feeding and maintenance and inferior quality of the breed. While the poverty of the people is an important reason behind this situation, the government's efforts at provision of facilities were also very inadequate. For example, at the end of March 1998, Bihar had only 62 veterinary hospitals / polyclinics, constituting 0.80 per cent of all-India total (GOI 2000e).

Other Livestock

Among other types of livestock, goats, sheep and pigs are relatively more important in Bihar. Goats find a regular place in the farm livestock of the poorer families, particularly in certain castes and communities. The growth of goat population was relatively high. Between 1972 and 1992, it had risen by 137 per cent—from 73.6 lakh to 174.6 lakh—compared with only 57 per cent at the national level. Bihar's share in all-India total rose to 16.4 per cent from 10.9 over the period. Goats provide some milk but their main contribution is in the provision of meat and hides and skins. Reliable data on meat production is not available, but on milk output the contribution was relatively good, as noted earlier.

On sheep farming, which is localized to certain areas, Bihar's position is not good. Over the period of two decades, 1972 to 1992, number of sheep had increased by only 72 per cent, from 9.83 lakh to 16.89 lakh. Although this growth is higher than at the national level, being only 36 per cent, Bihar's share in all-India total stood at only 3.3 per cent in the latest year. The quality of sheep reared is not good. In 1992, in the total number, cross-bred constituted only 2.55 per cent as against 4.75 per cent at the national level. The production of wool increased from 5.47 lakh kg in 1972 to 11 lakh in 1989-90 but in the following years it stagnated; in 2001-02, at 13.4 lakh kg, it constituted 2.64 per cent of all-India total. The yield per sheep was very low and the wool was of inferior quality.

The position of pig farming is also not good. It is confined to certain communities and is reared mainly for the purpose of meat. There has not been any noticeable growth in number of pigs over the years. Till 1966 it remained almost static at around 6 lakh, and then gradually rose to 11.3 lakh in 1987. Bihar's share in all-India total stood at 8.8 per cent in the latest year.

Poultry Development

Traditionally poultry rearing was confined to certain communities, and was done primarily on a household basis. But in recent years there has been considerable expansion as a commercial activity. The development of poultry is, however, still very low in Bihar. The growth in number of birds was much below that at the national level. Between 1972 and 1992 it had risen by only 40.6 per cent as against 121.6 per cent at the national level. Bihar's share in the latter

Table 5.12: Trend in Growth of Poultry Population and in Egg Production: Bihar vis-à-vis Other States

States	Poultry (no. in '000) 1972	1992			Egg Production Total No. (million)			Per capita No.
	Total	Fowls	Ducks	Total	1987-8	1994-5	1995-6	1995-6
Bihar	12560 (9.1)	15562 (3.0)[a]	753 (4.3)[b]	17655 (5.7)	1311 (7.4)	1398 (5.4)	1400 (5.1)	14.7
W.Bengal	15492 (11.2)	27474 (20.2)	5619 (15.0)	37407 (12.2)	2155 (12.1)	2500 (9.6)	2568 (9.4)	35.0
Orissa	8452 (6.1)	12279 (5.8)	194 (1.5)	13062 (4.3)	343 (1.9)	574 (2.2)	585 (2.2)	17.1
Assam	8879 (6.4)	11665 (14.8)	1596 (9.7)	16394 (5.3)	438 (2.5)	460 (1.8)	470 (1.7)	19.1
Madhya p.	6701 (4.8)	11639 (23.3)	47 (0.4)	11800 (3.8)	606 (3.4)	1145 (4.4)	1995 (7.3)	27.7
Uttar P.	3920 (2.8)	10422 (33.2)	152 (1.4)	10790 (3.5)	398 (2.2)	627 (2.4)	671 (2.5)	4.5
Andhra P.	19047 (13.7)	49373 (57.2)	69 (0.1)	49884 (16.2)	3241 (18.2)	5435 (20.9)	6027 (22.2)	84.0
Kerala	12207 (8.8)	20798 (10.9)	724 (3.30)	21907 (7.1)	1440 (8.1)	1916 (7.4)	1987 (7.3)	64.3
Punjab	3017 (2.2)	18308 (87.2)	6 (neg.)	18331 (6.1)	1328 (7.5)	2438 (9.4)	2510 (9.2)	16.2
All-India	138544 (100.0)	284025 (34.8)	10604 (3.5)	307069 (100.0)	17795 (100.0)	25975 (100.0)	27198 (100.0)	29.7

Notes: a : percentage of improved fowls; b : percentage to total number of poultry.

Source: GOI 1977, 1999, 2000, 2000d; CMIE 1996b.

declined to 5.7 per cent from 9.1 per cent; in 1951, it was as much as 14.3 per cent. The productivity continued to be very low. Total production of eggs increased from 147 million in 1951 to 553 million in 1976-77 and 1400 million in 1995-96, that is a growth of 9.5 times over the 45-year period. As the growth at the national level was much higher, Bihar's relative share in the latter's total declined to 4.9 per cent in 1995-96 from 7.4 per cent in 1987-88. Per capita annual production here came to half the national average in the 1995-96 (Table 5.12). In the last few years, the situation has deteriorated further. The production in 2001-02 was 1565.6 million and the relative share at 4.60 per cent; the growth over the seven-year period was only 11.8 per cent here as against 25.1 per cent for all-India (GOI 2004b).

The low level of growth in poultry is due to a number of reasons. The modern techniques of using the hybrid birds have made little progress here. Percentage of improved fowl in the total stood at only 3.0 in 1992 as against the all-India average of 34.8. In ducks, the proportion of improved variety was still lower—only 1.73 per cent. The government's efforts at developing the poultry sector were hardly noticeable. The intensive egg and poultry production-cum-marketing centres were very ill-equipped. Attempts at developing the co-operative sector were also not much of a success. The availability of feed and health-care facilities was far from adequate. The provision of extension services was negligible in most part of the state. Due to all these, the poultry rearing was confined to a few districts. In 1982, four districts—Singhbhum, Ranchi, Santhal Pargana and Purnea—together accounted for 60 per cent of the total number of poultry, 90 lakh out of 150 lakh (GOB 1984).

The animal husbandry sector as a whole did not get the attention it deserved. The fund allocation for it continued to be very low. In the last four five-year plans, sixth through ninth, the aggregate of outlay was Rs. 133.28 crore. The allocation for the ninth plan was Rs 38.26 crore, declining from Rs 45 crore in the preceding plan. In the grand total of plan outlay, animal husbandry's share declined from 0.35 per cent to 0.23 per cent (GOB 2000). The annual average of revenue expenditure during 2000-03 came to only Rs. 93 crore, constituting 4.57 per cent of all-states average (CMIE 2004a). Given the nature of control over spending, these were almost nothing in the vastness of problems.

Fishery Development

Bihar does not have a very high level of water resources for developing the fishery. As evident from Table 5.13, the state accounts for only 1.72 per cent of the all-India total length of rivers and canals. The share of reservoirs, tanks and ponds etc were also small. In the former it was 2.94 per cent and in the latter 4.51 per cent.

However, even the available resources have not been utilised properly, and consequently, the fish production remained small. The rate of growth was

Table 5.13: Water Resources and the Trend in Fish Production: Bihar Vis-à-Vis other States

States	*Water Resources*				*Fish Production (in '000 tonnes)*			
	Rivers & Canals (Km)	*Reservoirs (lakh ha)*	*Tanks& ponds (Lakh ha)*	*Flood plain, lakes etc (lakh ha)*	*1967-69[a] (a.a.)*	*1984-87 (a.a.)*	*1991-94 (a.a.)*	*1996-99 (a.a.)*
Bihar	3200 (1.72)	0.60	0.95	0.95	48.7 (3.2)	125.1 (4.4)	183.3	220.2 (4.1)
W.Bengal	2526 (1.36)	0.17	2.76	0.42	222.3 (14.8)	433.6 (15.1)	765.7	960.7 (18.0)
Orissa	4500 (2.42)	2.56	1.15	1.80	25.2[b] (1.7)	104.3 (3.6)	209.4	290.2 (5.4)
Assam	4820 (2.60)	0.02	0.23	1.10	25.2[c] (1.7)	50.2 (1.7)	140.5	155.1 (2.9)
Madhya P.	20661 (11.12)	2.94	1.19	-	7.7 (0.5)	34.4 (1.2)	50.2	115.1 (2.2)
Uttar P.	31200 (16.80)	1.50	1.62	1.33	15.2 (1.0)	66.9 (2.3)	122.4	164.1 (3.1)
Andhra P.	11514 (6.20)	2.34	5.17	-	160.4 (10.7)	239.1 (8.3)	284.8	381.0 (7.1)
Kerala	3092 (1.66)	0.30	0.30	2.43	342.2 (22.7)	357.1 (12.4)	573.2	621.4 (11.7)
All-India	185734 (100.00)	20.41	21.05	7.95	1505.0 (100.0)	2873.1 (100.0)	4400.9	5332.9 (100.0)

Notes: a: refer to calendar years; b: excluding marine production; c: including estimates for Mizoram and Meghalaya.
Source: GOI 2000e, 1976a, 2000; CMIE 1996b.

not bad; over the long period of three decades, between 1967-69 and 1996-99, fish production had risen by 352 per cent here as against 254 per cent at the national level. But as the base was very small, the state accounted for only 4.1 per cent of all-India total in the latest period, rising from 3.2 per cent in 1967-69. Even the growth rate was very low in the last decade or so. Between 1984-87 and 1996-99, production here rose by only 76 per cent compared with 86 per cent at the national level (Table 5.13).

If the comparison is with the country's inland production only, then the situation is not so bad. The state accounted for 10.5 per cent of total inland production in 1996-97, rising from 8.0 per cent in 1967-69. However, in recent years the situation has deteriorated considerably. The production declined from 249.8 thousand tonnes in 1996-97 to 222.2 thousand in 2000-01; the latest is only 7.8 per cent of all-India total, although the state remains the second largest producer (GOI 2004a).

The low growth in fish production was primarily due to the low level of fish culture practised. The increase came mainly from extensive type of cultivation; intensive pisciculture has hardly touched Bihar. The output from reservoirs continued to be very low. The stocking of reservoirs with fry and fingerlings were not done on a regular basis. Fish seed farms of suitable size have not been constructed near the bigger reservoirs. In the net work of irrigation canals docks have not been constructed at suitable distances and, therefore, substantial areas could not be made available for culture. Even in the areas where fish culture is practised, the level of culture is generally very low.

The government's efforts at developing the fishery were meagre. A large number of *dhars* in Saharsa and Purnea known for their rich fisheries got silted progressively and there was no effort to desilt them and convert into good fisheries. The tanks and lakes *(jheels)* taken over from the erstwhile zamindars were also not looked after properly by the revenue department. The production of fish seed did not get the needed attention from the government. The targets often remained unachieved. For example, at the end of Seventh Plan, in 1990, it was to be 800 million number but only 500 million could be produced.

The governmental inefficiency often stood in the way of development of fishery. To give one example: In 1981, the government underwrote the World Bank assisted fisheries development project to be operative in certain districts. But completion of the formalities alone took four years, and the work could start only in 1988-89, and that too after Central intervention. Moreover, due to erratic financial support all the districts could not be covered by the project.

Forestry

Forests perform at least three sets of functions: (i) ecological security, (ii) provision of fuel and fodder to the local population, and (iii) raw materials to industries. To serve these needs properly on a continuing basis, there must be

Table 5.14: The State of Forest Area and the Trend in Revenue and Expenditure: Bihar Vis-a Vis other States

States	*Forest Area (sq km) (1997)*					*Revenue (Rs lakh)*		*Expenditure (Rs lakh)*	
	Total Recorded	*Actual Forest cover*	*Dense forest (% of AFC)*	*per capita forest (Ha)*	*Reserved area (% of TR)*	*1972-73*	*1995-96*	*1972-73*	*1995-96*
Bihar	29226	26524 (90.8)[a]	50.1	0.03	17.3 (17.3)[d]	540	4721 (8.7)[ce]	326	2092[b] (6.4)[c]
W. Bengal	11879	8349 (70.3)	42.6	0.01	59.4 (59.1)	412	4352 (10.6)	322	9129 (28.4)
Orissa	57184	46941 (82.1)	55.6	0.15	47.4 (40.2)	797	6807 (8.5)	313	5719 (18.3)
Assam	30708	23824 (77.6)	65	0.11	59.4 (57.2)	438	1726 (3.9)	180	5468 (30.4)
Madhya P.	154497	131195 (84.9)	63.1	0.20	53.5 (47.5)	3644	55717 (15.3)	999	40279 (40.3)
Uttar P.	51663	33994 (65.8)	67.5	0.02	70.5 (66.8)	2466	9847 (4.0)	952	15219 (16.0)
Andhra P.	63814	43290 (67.8)	53.2	0.07	79.1 (70.2)	965	14405 (14.9)	569	8750 (15.4)
Kerala	11221	10334 (92.1)	81.8	0.04	98.4 (79.8)	1033	16077 (15.6)	359	7812 (21.8)
Maharashtra	63842	46143 (72.3)	51.2	0.06	75.8 (59.9)	1840	13729 (7.5)	1346	23165 (17.2)
All-India	765210	633397 (82.8)	58.0	0.07	54.4 (47.0)	16841	169028 (10.0)	9257	199341 (21.5)

Notes: a :percentage of total forest area; b : relates to 1993-94; c : growth in multiples; d: Percentage of reserved area in 1972-73; e: the revenue collected in 1993-94 was much higher, being Rs. 6977 lakh.

Source: GOI 1999, 2000d, 1976, 1976a.

adequate measures for protection and development of forests at the right time. The National Forest Policy of 1952 had expected the forests to constitute at least a third of the total land area.

The forests of Bihar are, however, in a deplorable condition. It is not only that the proportion of area under forest is low, the health of the forest is also very poor. The total area under forest in Bihar stood at 29.49 lakh hectares in 1995-96, constituting 17.02 per cent of the state's total area, and only 4.28 per cent of the country's total. The per capita forest area here works out to 0.031 hectare against 0.075 for all-India. Over the past four decades, the area under forest has fallen considerably; in 1955-56 it stood at 32.15 lakh hectares, and constituted 19.3 per cent of the total area (Table 5.14; GOB 1959).

The density of the forest has fallen sharply over the years. The areas that were considered stable a few decades ago have now become ecologically fragile with large chunks turning barren. The dense forest area constituted only 50.1 per cent of the actual forest cover in 1997 as against the all-India average of 58.0. The forests can produce only 1.2 cubic metres of timber per hectare against the potential of 3 cubic metres.

The distribution of the forest area in Bihar is very uneven. North Bihar accounted for only 3.3 per cent of total forest area in 1955-56 and was halved by 1992-93, being at 1.6 per cent; the proportion in South Bihar decreased from 14.8 per cent to 11.7 in this period. Chotanagpur and Santhal Parganas, which accounted for the balance of forest areas, were the worst sufferer; their share declined from 81.8 per cent to 27.5 per cent.

The decrease in forest wealth was due to a multiplicity of factors. The forests were exploited ruthlessly ignoring the need for their regeneration. The demands on the forest increased greatly both due to population pressure and the greed of the richer section of population. The local inhabitants had to depend on forest for their sustenance, in the absence of any alternative means of livelihood. Overgrazing of forests by cattle and reckless collection of fuel wood contributed greatly to the destruction. Even in 1999-00, 63.4 per cent of the rural households and 25.7 per cent of the urban households were using firewood and chips as the primary source of energy for cooking (NSSO 2001). The exploitation for industrial materials also accelerated. Mining activities caused degradation of the forest area to an alarming extent; large areas became barren due to the mine spoils. It may also be noted that even in 1973 Bihar had the lowest proportion of reserved area among the states, being only 17.3 per cent, rising from 11.2 per cent in 1956. The protected area was also only 5 per cent of total.

The revenue of the forest department had risen at a much faster rate than the expenditure. Between 1972-73 and 1993-94, the former had risen 12.9 times while the latter only 6.4 times; at the national level, the growth in expenditure was more than three times as much. Among the selected states, Bihar had the lowest growth. If a longer period is considered, the continued neglect of the forest appears more glaring. In relation to 1954-55, the revenue collection increased 91-fold whereas the expenditure only 32 times (the former stood at Rs. 76.33 lakh and the latter at Rs. Rs 65.14 lakh in 1954-55). Bihar's share in all-India total expenditure declined from 3.52 per cent in 1972-73 to 1.47 per cent in 1993-94. Only in the last few years, there has been a noticeable growth in the revenue expenditure on forest. The average for 2000-03 came to Rs. 228.3 crore and constituted 6.5 per cent of the all-states average (CMIE 2004a).

The plan expenditure on forest increased only in recent years. During the Third Plan, it was only Rs 2.54 crore and constituted 6.81 per cent of the aggregate for agricultural programmes. In the Sixth Plan, although the expenditure rose to Rs 18.00 crore, the relative share was down to 3.06 per cent. Only in the Eighth Plan, an appreciable increase came, to Rs 161.20 crore and 18.77 per cent of the total (GOB 1984, 1985, 2000).

It was not only that the expenditure on forestry was low it was further reduced by misappropriation of funds and callousness in implementation of schemes. The officials did not stop there; they made money through illegal transactions also. Illegal felling of trees continued to be a common phenomenon. In the looting of the forest, everybody from the circle officer up to the Minister participated. The growth in plantation activities remained very low until recent years. The cumulative total of plantation area stood at only 1326 thousand ha between 1951 and 1999, constituting 4.25 per cent of all-India total. In this, the share of block plantation area was 71.0 per cent and the balance from seedlings distributed (GOI 2003c).

To combat the ruthless exploitation of forest, some new initiatives were taken in recent years. The National Forest Policy of 1988 called for discontinuation of commercial exploitation of forests for/by industries; their maintenance was to be for conservation of soil and environment, and to meet the subsistence requirements of local people. The states were asked by the Centre in1990 to adopt the system of Joint Forest Management, in pursuant to this policy. Along with other states, Bihar has also launched the JFM system. The progress is, however, far from satisfactory, and illegal felling of trees has not stopped. Given the quality of officials and the socio-economic environment, it is futile to expect much from the present policy.

Note

1. The data are, however, not exactly comparable in every case as the number of districts, and consequently their boundaries, were not always the same. In early eighties there were 34 districts and at the time of 1991 census it was 42. Presently there are 55 districts, of which 18 have gone to the Jharkhand state.

6

Pattern of Industrial Growth

Bihar, until the separation of Jharkhand area, was rich in mineral resources. But the industrial performance of the state had been very dismal, as has been noted in chapter 2. The contribution of manufacturing to SDP here was always much below that at the national level. In this chapter, we look into the pattern of growth in different sectors of industry over the years, beginning with the factory sector. The causal factors behind the poor performance have also been looked into.

Factory Sector

In industrial production, the factories registered under the Factories Act, 1948 account for the largest share of output. The units covered are those using power and employing at least 10 workers, and those not using power but employing 20 or more workers. The factory sector of Bihar presented a very dismal picture. The trend in relative position of the state on different aspects of growth may be seen from Table 6.1.

The value of output of the sector had risen only 118-fold in current prices over a period of nearly four decades, between 1960 and 1997-98, as against double this rate at the national level. Consequently, Bihar's share in all-India total production was halved over the period-declining from 7.0 per cent to 3.5 per cent. The per capita output stood at only Rs 3,038 in the latest year, which was 35 per cent of the national average; two decades earlier, in 1977-78, it was 54 per cent and still earlier, in 1955, at 80.4 per cent (GOI 1959). The downhill journey is non-stop; in 1999-00, the per capita production came to only Rs. 2636 as against the all-India average of Rs. 8743, that is, the former 30.1 per cent of the latter (GOI 2002d).

The growth of employment in the sector has stopped for many years. There was an absolute fall in 1997-98 over 1977-78, as against a 41 per cent rise at the national level. In 1999-00, only 2.72 lakh persons were employed in the sector, constituting 3.33 per cent of all-India total. Productivity of the employees was, however, not bad until recently. Per employee it was significantly higher than the national average in 1997-98, to the extent of 27.5 per cent; but in 1999-00 became lower, albeit nominally, being respectively Rs 10.64 lakh and Rs, 10.99 lakh. The fixed capital per employee continues to be significantly higher, being respectively Rs 5.59 lakh and Rs 4.92 lakh. The total emolument per employee is also high. In 1997-98, it was as much as Rs 74 thousand, 42 per cent higher than the national average; the disparity, however, narrowed down to 32 per cent in 1999-00, being respectively Rs 77.2 thousand and 58.5 thousand (Table 6.1 and ibid.).

The capital-output ratio showed a noticeable fall over the years. In 1997-98 it was down to less than half the level in 1977-78, and became less than the national average as against much higher earlier. However, in 1999-00 again it became substantially higher, being respectively 0.52 and o.45. The net value added to output improved noticeably over the years, and the advantage over the national average increased greatly. In 1999-00, Bihar's ratio stood at 0.30 as against 0.17 at the national level.

Structural Change

As regards the industry-wise composition of the factory sector, it is heavily concentrated on a few items. Five industries—basic metal and alloys, rubber, plastic etc, transport equipment, electricity and machinery and equipment—together accounted for 85.6 per cent of total output in 1989-90. After five years, in 1993-94—that is, in the period of industrial reform—also their combined share remained more or less the same. Among them, however, some significant changes have come. The relative share declined for four of them whereas the electricity industry registered a nearly three-fold rise.

Being a metallic-mineral rich state, basic metal and alloys continued to dominate the industrial scenario of Bihar. Its relative share in the aggregate of output stood at 44.1 per cent in 1989-90 and declined to 40.2 in 1993-94. The share in total employment decreased from 32.8 per cent to 29.4 per cent in this period. The productivity of the employees declined despite a noticeable rise in value of fixed capital. In the factory sector's aggregate of fixed capital, its share rose to 60.2 per cent in 1993-94 from 54.1 in 1989-90. The fixed capital per employee increased by 228 per cent between 1989-90 and 1996-97 but the output per employee had risen only 163 per cent. The net value added to output ratio had also shown a decline (CMIE 1997; GOI 2000g).

The second important industry in Bihar is rubber, plastic etc, and its performance was also very poor. In the aggregate of factory sector's output its share declined to 11.3 per cent in 1993-94 from 16.5 in 1989-90. The output per employee had a very low growth. Between 1989-90 and 1996-97, it increased by only 37 per cent, with fixed capital rising by 28 per cent. The industry's share in the sector's aggregate of fixed capital was down to 2.75 per cent in 1993-94 from 4.47 per cent in 1989-90. The net value added to output continued to be very low, and stood at only 0.11 in 1996-97.

Table 6.1: Pattern of Growth in the Factory Sector : Bihar Vis-a-Vis other States

States	*Value of Output (Rs crore)*			*Per Capita (Rs)*	*No. of Employees ('000)*				
	1960	*1977-78*	*1997-8*	*1997-8*	*1960*	*77-8*	*97-8*	*A*	*B*
Bihar	245 (7.0)	2130 (5.5)	28935 (3.5)	3038 (331)[a]	166	373	275	124.7	(-)26.3
W. Bengal	720 (20.6)	4078 (10.5)	41895 (5.1)	5502 (806)	665	935	834	40.6	(-)10.8
Orissa	35 (1.0)	615 (1.6)	14905 (1.8)	4265 (248)	26	122	180	369.2	47.5
Assam	87 (2.5)	652 (1.7)	7513 (0.9)	2972 (368)	68	132	155	94.1	17.4
Madhya P.	78 (2.2)	1673 (4.3)	44227 (5.4)	5819 (347)	86	297	467	245.3	57.2
Uttar P.	252 (7.2)	2680 (6.9)	71837 (8.7)	4470 (265)	231	685	774	196.5	13.0
Andhra P.	111 (3.2)	1983 (5.1)	56752 (6.9)	7715 (400)	143	589	1209	311.9	105.3
Kerala	73 (2.1)	1177 (3.0)	19957 (2.4)	6344 (489)	132	282	360	113.6	27.7
Maharashtra	777 (22.2)	9334 (24.0)	173299 (21.0)	19633 (1605)	626	1243	1476	98.6	18.7
All-India	3504 (100.0)	38860 (100.0)	825423 (100.0)	8641 (616)	2904	7093	10001	144.2	41.0

(Contd.)

Output per Employee (Rs '000) 1960	1977-8	1997-8	A	B	Fixed Capital per Employee (Rs '000) 1960	1977-8	1997-8	A	B	Fixed Capital to Output ratio 1960	1977-8	1997-8
15	57	1052	280	1746	12	61	521	411	754	0.81	1.06	0.50
12	55	502	358	813	4	15	314	263	1993	0.37	0.34	0.63
13	50	828	285	1556	13	43	847	219	1870	0.99	0.85	1.02
13	49	485	277	890	4	23	275	432	1096	0.34	0.47	0.57
9	56	947	522	1591	5	40	459	742	1047	0.53	0.72	0.48
11	39	928	255	2279	4	33	573	819	1636	0.33	0.85	0.62
8	34	469	325	1279	4	17	262	386	1441	0.46	0.52	0.56
6	42	554	600	1219	2	21	230	895	995	0.38	0.50	0.42
12	75	1174	525	1465	4	24	517	448	2054	0.36	0.32	0.44
12	55	825	358	1400	4	27	421	523	1459	0.37	0.50	0.51

Net Value Added to Output ratio 1960	1977-8	1997-8	Total emolum. per employee (1997-8) (Rs. '000)	Av. value of output per factory (Rs lakh) 1977-8	1997-8	Per capita value Added (Rs) 1977-78	1997-98	growth (Multiple)
0.25	0.19	0.32	74 (7.2)[a]	50	878	61.44	929.60	15.13
0.27	0.23	0.23	51 (7.2)	68	607	186.32	1289.00	6.92
0.24	0.27	0.25	61 (5.9)	40	907	65.84	1065.70	16.19
0.29	0.29	0.17	34 (3.0)	39	404	104.78	487.80	4.66
0.27	0.21	0.19	57 (6.5)	47	1045	72.92	1149.60	15.77
0.28	0.20	0.20	55 (4.5)	40	679	51.28	898.80	17.53
0.21	0.20	0.20	30 (3.4)	22	303	80.09	1573.80	19.65
0.29	0.20	0.16	41 (4.1)	41	408	98.14	1019.70	10.39
0.31	0.22	0.19	75 (7.8)	71	844	349.08	3869.00	11.08
0.27	0.21	0.19	52 (5.9)	46	609	128.82	1636.00	12.70

Notes: a: relate to 1977-78; A: percentage increase between 1960 and 1977-8; B: percentage increase between 1977-78 and 1997-98.
Source: GOI 1962, 1980, 2000d.

The next important industry is transport equipment, and after a fall, it showed a good recovery in recent years. In 1993-94, the industry's share in total output declined to 6.0 per cent from 10.4 in 1989-90. The share in employment, however, increased from 9.7 per cent to 11.3 per cent. The output per employee had an absolute fall in this period. However, over the period of nine years, 1989-97, it increased by 152 per cent, with fixed capital per employee rising by 98 per cent. The NVA to output ratio had a continuous fall, from 0.40 in 1989-90 to 0.15 in 1996-97.

The fastest growth in output was in electricity. Over the five-year period of 1989-94, it had risen by 377 per cent, and in the total for factory sector the industry's share rose to 24.3 per cent from 8.8 per cent. Over the entire period of nine years, the output per employee here increased 486 per cent, with the fixed capital rising by 221 per cent. The employment in the industry, however, registered an absolute fall—from 48.5 thousand in 1989-90 to 33.7 thousand in 1996-97. The NVA to output ration had a sharp fall in recent years, to 0.36 in the latest year from 0.68 in 1993-94.

Among other industries, machinery and equipment, basic chemicals etc, food products and non-metallic mineral products were important, contributing 3-5 per cent of the total output from the factory sector. But excepting basic chemicals, all others showed a fall in the share, and the output per employee increased at a lower rate than the fixed capital per employee. Some of the very minor industries have shown a relatively good performance. Paper and paper products raised the output per employee by 203 per cent between 1989-90 and 1996-97, with fixed capital rising by only 92 per cent. The industry's share in total output increased from 0.33 per cent in 1989-90 to 0.60 per cent in 1993-94. A few of the industries showed sharp swings also, mainly due to the time required to adjust to the new situation.

The factory sector industries of Bihar were heavily concentrated in the Jharkhand region. In 1977, in the total number of workers at 3.49 lakh, Singhbhum, Dhanbad, Hazaribag and Ranchi together accounted for 59.0 per cent. Another quarter was in Monghyr, Patna, Shahabad, Champaran and Darbhanga combined. Thus, these nine districts, out of the total of 17 in existence then, had accounted for 84 per cent of the total employees (GOB 1984). In the years since then no significant dispersal of industries came. Consequently, after the creation of the Jharkhand state in November 2000, the present Bihar is having very few industries.

Small-Scale Industries

Data on the SSI sector are not available on a comprehensive basis from any single source, and there is considerable overlapping among the sources. Even the ASI data include part of the SSI sector, and till early seventies it was the only source on modern small-scale industries, that is, the units registered with the Small Industries Development Organisation (SIDO). In 1972, for the first time, a census of SSI units was undertaken, covering only the SIDO units.

The units covered were those with capital of Rs 7.5lakh or less in original value of plant and machinery and Rs 10 lakh or less in case of ancillary units. There were as many as 22 types of units—including handlooms and power looms and khadi and village industries—not covered by the census. A similar second census was carried out in 1990 for the units registered up to 31st March 1988. Below we give a brief look on the findings of these two studies on Bihar.

Modern SSI Sector

Bihar presented a very gloomy picture here also. Between 1972-73 and 1987-88, the value of production in the sector increased only 12.2 times as against 16.5 times in all–India. Consequently, the relative share in the latter, which was already very low, declined further to 2.0 per cent from 2.8 per cent. West Bengal, a much smaller state, on the other hand, accounted for three times as much in the latest year. The growth in employment was, however, relatively high and Bihar's share in all-India total rose to 5.0 per cent from 3.7 per cent. The value of fixed assets in the sector also had a noticeable growth. Over the 16-year period, it increased by 949 per cent as against 781 per cent at the national level. However, the proportion of plant and machinery in fixed assets was very low here. In 1987-88 it constituted 48.0 per cent as against 59.6 per cent at the national level.

The productivity of the employees had a very low growth. It increased by only 313 per cent over the period which was less than half the rate at the national level. The value of output per employee in Bihar was a mere 41 per cent of the national average in the latest year, declining from 74 per cent earlier. This was largely due to the fact that fixed assets per employee were very low here; in the latest year, it stood at 72 per cent of the national average. The high growth in total fixed assets was neutralised by the rise in number employed. The capital-output ratio continued to be much higher than the national average, despite a significant fall. The net value added to production ratio also had a sharp fall over the years (Table 6.2).

The SSI units in Bihar suffered from many deficiencies. The number of units in the sector increased at a high rate but their capacity utilisation did not get the needed attention. In 1987-88, the capacity utilisation here was only 37.5 per cent as against 50.6 at the national level. The units in general were weak, with the proportion consuming energy at much below the national average. The low productivity of the employees was also partly due to the low wages. Per employee it averaged Rs 5 in 1987-88 compared with Rs 6 at the national level. In rural areas—where 44 per cent of the units were located—it was only Rs 4. The proportion of casual / contract employees was relatively high here—being 45.3 per cent against 32.2 in all-India.

A notable aspect of the SSI sector in Bihar is its considerable diversification over the years. In 1972-73, five industries—metal products, mineral products, basic metal and alloy, chemicals and wood products—together accounted for 70.3 per cent of total output; in 1987-88, it was down to 50.5 per cent. The share of metal products declined from 18.7 per cent to 8.9 per cent, of mineral products from 16.3 to 12.4, basic metal and alloy from 15.0 to 9.8 and chemicals from 12.3 to 11.9. Among the industries that raised their share, the important ones were rubber, plastic etc, transport equipment and machinery and parts. The share of first one rose to 5.5 per cent from 2.9.

As regards the position in recent years, detailed data are not available; we may give a brief look into only some of the aspects. In 1998-99, total number of SSI units in Bihar stood at 291.17 thousand, constituting 9.34 per cent of all-India total. This is a notable rise over 1987-88, but the units are now very small. Employment per unit declined to only 1.63 from 5.22 earlier. The total employment in the sector now became only 2.98 per cent of all-India total as against 4.96 per cent earlier. The investment per unit averaged only Rs 27.84 thousand in 1998-99, which was a mere 12.3 per cent of all-India average (SIDBI 2002).

Unorganised Manufacturing Sector

The unorganised manufacturing and repairing enterprises are a vast number scattered throughout the rural and urban areas. The first integrated survey of this sector was carried out only in 1994-95 by the NSSO. The survey covered all the enterprises that were not included in the ASI of the C.S.O. Below we give a brief look into the findings on Bihar.

The performance in this sector was very poor. Even the number of enterprises operating was relatively low. In 1994-95, there were 13.4 lakh enterprises, constituting 9.3 per cent of all-India total, which was less than in two of the eastern states. Moreover, the enterprises were of relatively small size. The own account manufacturing and repairing enterprises (OAMES)—defined as those running without any hired worker on a regular basis—constituted as much as 93.3 per cent as against the national average of 84.5 per cent. The larger enterprises, directory and non-directory manufacturing enterprises—defined as those employing less than six workers and six or more workers (including household members), respectively—constituted a very small proportion. The latter was a mere 0.9 per cent of total as against 4.5 per cent at the national level.

As the enterprises were of small size, naturally Bihar's share in all-India total of employment and in gross value added (GVA) were lower than in number of enterprises. In total employment it was 7.6 per cent, and in GVA only 5.2 per cent; both were around half the level in West Bengal (Table 6.3).

A favourable aspect of Bihar's unorganised sector is that, a larger proportion of enterprises were located in rural areas. It was found to be 85.6 per cent in 1994-95 compared with 72.4 per cent at the national level. However, probably because of this, the proportion of smaller enterprises was higher here. Among the rural areas also, Bihar had higher proportion of smaller units; 96.0 per cent of the units were OAMES here as against 90.8 per cent in rural India.

Table 6.2: Trend in Growth of the SSI Sector: Bihar Visa-a-Vis other States

States	*No. of Units*		*Production (Rs crore)*		*Employment ('000 no.)*		
	1972-3	*1987-8*	*1972-3*	*1987-8*	*1972-3*	*1987-8*	*% rise*
Bihar	6368 (4.0)	34822 (6.0)	72.0 (2.8)	877.8 (2.0)	61.5	181.8	195.6
W. Bengal	16904 (10.6)	45954 (7.9)	270.2 (10.4)	2530.0 (5.9)	176.2	311.8	77.0
Orissa	2163 (1.4)	8287 (1.4)	22.3 (0.9)	657.3 (1.5)	18.6	69.3	272.6
Assam	1739 (1.1)	4430 (0.8)	22.6 (0.9)	302.3 (0.7)	19.7	34.5	75.1
Madhya P.	8727 (5.5)	73892 (12.7)	70.0 (2.7)	1967.4 (4.6)	59.6	158.8	166.4
Uttar P.	13939 (8.7)	53282 (9.1)	222.7 (8.6)	3727.0 (8.7)	160.0	348.9	118.1
Andhra P.	8999 (5.6)	39210 (6.7)	85.9 (3.3)	3694.0 (8.6)	78.7	276.1	250.8
Kerala	6902 (4.3)	25717 (4.4)	115.6 (4.4)	1136.9 (2.6)	126.5	169.3	33.8
Maharashtra	17338 (10.9)	29586 (5.1)	529.5 (20.3)	7511.8 (17.5)	239.8	355.9	48.4
All-India	159321 (100.0)	582368 (100.0)	2602.7 (100.0)	4297.2 (100.0)	1653.2	3665.8	121.7

Net Value added as % to production		*Capital–output ratio*		*Fixed assets per employee (Rs.)*			*Output per employee (Rs.)*		
1972-3	*1987-8*	*1972-3*	*1987-8*	*1972-3*	*1987-8*	*% rise*	*1972-3*	*1987-8*	*% rise*
37.7	27	0.44	0.38	5172	18337	254.5	11.7	48.3	312.8
32.8	20	0.34	0.17	5216	13765	163.9	15.3	81.1	430.1
41.0	27	0.39	0.24	4720	22576	378.3	12.0	94.8	690.0
40.3	17	0.49	0.31	5643	27176	381.6	11.5	87.7	662.6
29.8	35	0.43	0.13	5105	16381	220.9	11.7	123.9	959.0
30.5	15	0.34	0.26	5707	28115	392.6	13.9	106.8	668.3
34.2	24	0.53	0.17	5830	22663	288.7	10.9	133.8	1127.5
31.3	20	0.38	0.34	3484	22888	556.9	9.1	67.1	637.4
36.1	33	0.43	0.17	9453	35410	275.3	22.1	211.1	855.2
32.3	24	0.40	0.22	6380	25359	297.5	15.7	117.2	646.5

Source: GOI 1976b, 1991.

In employment and GVA also the rural area's share was much higher. In employment, it was 83.8 per cent of total as against 66.6 per cent at the national level. Among the selected states, only two had better position. In GVA, the rural area accounted for 67.9 per cent here compared with 41.0 per cent in all-India.

The GVA per enterprise was very low in rural Bihar. For OAMEs, constituting the overwhelming proportion, it stood at only Rs 8,857, lower than the national average and a mere 43 per cent of that in the state's urban areas. The rural-urban difference was wider here than at the national level. The GVA per worker in rural OAMEs was also very low, although it was higher than at the national level (Table 6.3).

Exactly comparable data for earlier years are not available; but probably the relative position was better then. The 45th round of NSSO, covering the period July 1989-june 1990, on OAMEs and NDMEs had found the output per enterprise in Bihar significantly higher than at the national level. For OAMEs and NDMEs combined, in rural areas it was respectively Rs 13,643 and 11,425, and in urban areas Rs 40,859 and Rs 36,083. The GVA per worker in rural OAMEs of Bihar was found to be Rs 4,644 as against Rs 2,861 at the national level. And all these were achieved with a relatively lower level of fixed assets. The fixed assets per enterprise in rural areas were Rs 3,540 for OAME and NDME combined as against Rs 4,988 in rural India (excluding land). In urban areas, it was respectively Rs 7,021 and Rs 14,207 (NSSO 1995)

The worsening of position is further confirmed if we look at the trend in khadi and village industries[1]. The production of KVI in Bihar increased only 151.4 per cent between 1982-83 and 1993-94, from Rs 55.1 crore to Rs 138.5 crore, as against 320.7 per cent at the national level; the state's relative share in the latter declined from 7.2 per cent to 4.3 per cent. In employment, Bihar had a growth of only 19.8 per cent in this period compared with 55.2 per cent for all-India; the relative share in total declining from 8.39 per cent to 6.47 per cent. The value of output per employee stood at only Rs 4,014 in 1993-94 as against the national average of Rs 6,014, that is, the former 66.7 per cent of the latter. Earlier, in 1982-83, at Rs 724, it was 85.4 per cent of all-India average (KVIC 1983, 1994).

All these implied very low earnings by the units in the KVI sector. The total earnings of KVIs in Bihar came to Rs 12.77 crore in 1982-83, constituting 5.8 per cent of all-India total, that is, significantly below its share in output. Over the years, the position deteriorated further. In 1993-94, it was down to 3.1 per cent, with a growth of only 180.9 per cent compared with 419.4 per cent for all-India.

Causal Factors

Behind this poor performance of the industrial sector, many factors have worked. The industrial growth of a state depends on a variety of factors like availability manpower, infrastructure, institutional finance, location of the state,

Table 6.3: The Status of Unorganised Manufacturing: Bihar Vis-à-Vis Other States

States	Estimated Number of Enterprises (in '00) Rural areas Total	% of OAME	% of OAME in urban areas	All areas Total no.	% of OAME	Employment (in '00) Total no.	% in rural areas
Bihar	11493 (85.6)[a]	96.0	76.9	13420 (9.3)	93.3	25374 (7.6)	83.8
W. Bengal	15312 (80.2)	93.0	63.3	19090 (13.2)	87.2	43792 (13.2)	76.9
Orissa	13217 (95.1)	97.8	80.6	13897 (9.6)	96.9	30940 (9.3)	95.4
Assam	2749 (89.5)	89.0	56.3	3072 (2.1)	85.5	6228 (1.9)	87.4
Madhya P.	4516 (69.3)	94.6	73.0	6517 (4.5)	88.0	13317 (4.0)	63.2
Uttar P.	18359 (73.0)	90.0	72.4	25148 (17.3)	85.2	59327 (17.9)	70.0
Andhra P.	9646 (77.6)	85.6	75.7	12424 (8.6)	83.4	25503 (7.7)	73.8
Kerala	2353 (79.9)	76.9	69.1	2946 (2.0)	75.4	6820 (2.1)	78.9
Maharashtra	4371 (50.5)	89.1	52.7	8647 (6.0)	71.1	24282 (7.3)	38.9
All-India	104971 (72.4)	90.8	67.8	145041 (100.0)	84.5	332028 (100.0)	66.6

Gross Value Added Rural area (Rs. crore)	Total all areas (Rs. crore)	Per enterprise[b] (Rs.) Rural	Urban	Per worker[b] (Rs.) Rural	Urban
1134.5 (67.9)[a]	1671.7 (5.17)	8857	20359	5116	11933
1736.6 (57.2)	3034.1 (9.40)	8777	15689	4322	8991
692.0 (82.2)	842.2 (2.61)	4553	13832	2071	8399
278.2 (68.5)	405.9 (1.26)	8188	21139	4345	13528
480.7 (32.6)	1472.5 (4.56)	9561	19352	5369	10496
2689.9 (54.2)	4962.7 (15.38)	9860	19464	5022	9742
923.1 (56.2)	1642.1 (5.09)	7068	16326	3732	8644
466.0 (72.1)	646.6 (2.00)	8930	9432	5788	6645
710.6 (16.1)	4401.0 (13.64)	11559	23469	6627	12965
13243.6 (41.0)	32275.3 (100.00)	8860	19648	4734	11073

Notes: a: percentage share in all-areas' total; b: relate to OAMEs only.
Source: NSSO 1998d.

its work culture, labour situation, quality of entrepreneurship available, natural resources, and above all the attitude and policies of the government. While the broad policies are set by the Central government and the legislations affecting industrial growth also largely come from there, there is much that depends on the state government. We give a brief look into the situation on some of them in Bihar.

Infrastructure

The infrastructure for industrial growth includes a variety of items, some of which are directly related to it while others have only an indirect bearing. Particularly important are the availability of power at reasonable tariff and the transport and communication system. The situation of the latter has been note in the preceding Chapter, here we look into only the power situation in Bihar.

The power situation in the state continued to be very depressing. Over the last four decades, the installed capacity of electricity increased at less than half the rate at the national level; and the relative share in the latter's total was down to 2.2 per cent from 6.3 per cent. The growth in power generation was still worse. Over the same period, it had increased only 249 per cent compared with 3598 per cent at the national level. The state's share in the latter's total was down to a negligible 0.87 per cent from 9.24 per cent. The utilisation of capacity was extremely low (Table 6.4).

The industrial consumption of power in the state had grown at a faster rate than at the national level, but the per capita level remained very low. Between 1957-8 and 1997-8, the growth here was 19.7 times—from 983 mkwh to 7529 mkwh—as against 17.0 times at the national level, from 6229 mkwh to 10600. The per capita consumption, however, stood at only 79.1 kWh in 1998-9, much below the all-India average. This was the situation despite the tariff being lower than the national average (Table 6.4). The household industries could not expand due to non-availability of electricity. In 1992-93, 83.4 per cent of the households were without electricity compared with 49.1per cent at the national level (IIPS1995).

The government's attention to developing the rural infrastructure was, however, negligible. The state failed to spend the money available from the Rural Infrastructure Development Fund (RIDF).Till March 2004, Rs 462.34 crore was sanctioned but only Rs 103.81 crore–that is, 22.4 percent–could be utilised. The situation in Jharkhand was worse; only Rs 2.48 crore, out of Rs 263.40 sanctioned, could be used (RBI 2004).

Institutional Finance

On the provision of working capital, scheduled commercial banks (SCBs) are the most important institution, and for long-term capital, the development banks. We give a brief look into the role these institutions played in Bihar.

From the pace of industrial growth noted earlier, it is almost a foregone conclusion that none of the institutions provided any significant amount of finance to the industries of Bihar. However, the problem of getting the required

Table 6.4: Trend in Installed Capacity, Generation, Utilisation, etc of Electricity[a]: Bihar Vis-a-Vis other States

States	*Installed Capacity (MW)* 1957-58	1980-1	1997-8	Growth[c]	*Energy Generated (MU)* 1957-8	1980-1	1997-8	Growth[c]
Bihar	203.1 (6.3)	941	1988.4 (2.2)	9.79	1051 (9.2)	2281	3666 (0.87)	3.49
W. Bengal	563.1 (17.5)	1726	2904.0 (3.3)	5.16	1697 (14.9)	5563	14530 (3.5)	8.56
Orissa	95.3 (3.0)	923	1693.0 (1.9)	17.76	93 (0.82)	3137	5729 (1.4)	1.60
Assam	15.0 (0.47)	228	616.7 (0.69)	41.11	18 (0.16)	465	1074 (0.26)	9.67
Madhya P.	92.0 (2.9)	1631	3875.9 (4.4)	42.13	187 (1.6)	5952	20125 (4.8)	107.62
Uttar P.	354.9 (11.0)	3612	6168.8 (6.9)	17.38	872 (7.7)	10190	23690 (5.6)	27.17
Andhra P.	205.8 (6.4)	2240	5764.2 (6.5)	28.01	345 (3.0)	7319	29548 (7.0)	85.64
Kerala	113.8 (3.5)	1012	1775.8 (2.0)	15.60	441 (3.9)	5242	5189 (1.2)	11.77
Maharashtra	844.1[b] (26.2)	3992	8289.8 (9.3)	9.82	3386[b] (29.8)	17664	53915 (12.8)	15.92
All-India	3223.1 (100.0)	30214	89090.0 (100.0)	27.64	11369 (100.0)	110844	420405 (100.0)	36.98

Utilisation Rate (%) 1970-1	1980-1	1997-8	*Load Factor* 1991-2	1997-8	*Industrial Consump. (% share)* 1957-8	1970-1	1998-9	*Average Tariff 1997-8 (Paise / unit)* Industrial	Average (All uses)
31.39	27.67	21.05	21.3	16.1	84.01	74.71	53.88 (79.1)[e]	275.9	210.7
38.20	36.79	57.12	30.8	40.0	72.62	80.32	27.03 (75.4)	246.7	194.0
35.74	38.80	38.63	30.0	65.3	70.58	88.18	56.89 (98.8)	256.2	218.0
23.40	23.28	19.88	24.6	21.3	16.64	55.97	28.32 (32.8)	209.4	216.6
43.24	41.66	59.27	49.2	66.0	60.04	78.12	27.07 (97.6)	401.8	176.2
48.37	32.20	43.84	44.3	48.8	46.55	64.01	22.66 (38.3)	335.5	171.5
55.14	37.30	58.52	62.1	82.0	51.93	50.69	33.67 (91.5)	330.3	188.5
44.41	59.16	33.36	73.6	66.3[d]	82.64	65.93	32.59 (80.6)	160.8	124.6
49.21	50.51	74.24	61.3	68.3	70.17	69.44	36.62 (203.7)	345.3	213.8
43.33	41.88	53.87	55.3	64.7	66.06	61.56	33.65 (111.0)	284.8	184.5

Notes: a: public utilities only; b: relate to Bombay; c: growth in multiples over the entire period; d: relates to 1996-7 ; e : industrial consumption per capita in Kwh.
Source: GOI 1959, 2000d, 1997; Kannan 2001.

finance is more with the SSI units and, therefore, we focus the analysis particularly on their situation. For working capital, they meet their requirement generally from the SCBs, RRBs and to some extent from the cooperative credit institutions. We are looking here only into the role of the first one, normally providing finance more to the larger of the SSI units.

Table 6.5 presents the relative position of Bihar among the states on the finance provided by the SCBs. The growth in outstanding advances over the years was high, but as the base was low the relative share in all-India total remained extremely low. Between 1968 and 1983, there was an 87-fold rise here compared with only 28 times at the national level; the relative share rising to 2.6 per cent from 0.84 per cent. In the following years, even the rate of growth was low. Between 1983 and 1995, it was only 5.3 times, slightly below the national level. The growth dropped further in the following years, and the relative share in all-India total advances outstanding declined to 1.9 per cent in 2001from 2.5 per cent in 1995 (RBI 2002).

On the number of units assisted the growth was faster. Between 1983 and 1995 it was by 283 per cent compared with 138 per cent for all-India. Bihar's share in all-India total number rose to 7.7 per cent from 4.8 per cent. In the last few years, the growth rate was relatively low, and the proportion in 2001stood at 7.0 per cent. The amount outstanding per unit was very low here. In 2001, it was only Rs. 77 thousand, constituting a mere 26.4 per cent of all-India average; the situation for earlier years may be seen from the Table. This low level of assistance is not a surprise. Not only the units in Bihar were of small size, their capacity utilisation was also very low, as noted earlier.

As regards the provision of term finance, Table 6.6 presents the relative position of Bihar among the states. The situation is worse here than in case of commercial banks. In the aggregate of assistance provided by all institutions till March 2001, Bihar's share was only 1.25 per cent, declining from 2.51 in the cumulative till March 1989. All the neighbouring states received a much larger amount. In per capita term, in the latest year it came to only Rs. 552, a mere 11.4 per cent of all-India average.

In the provision of assistance, naturally the all-India institutions played the dominant role. The Bihar SFC had provided a per cpita cumulative total of only Rs 38.6 till March 2001, a mere 13.5 per cent of the average from all SFCs, being Rs.285.3. The role of SIDC was still inferior. The Bihar SIDC provided the lowest amount of Rs 15.30 per capita as against the all SIDCs' average of Rs. 171.8, the former constituting only 8.9 per cent of the latter (IDBI 2002).

The growth in assistance from Bihar SFC makes a sad reading. The annual average of assistance during 1970-73 was only Rs 1.33 crore, 3.41 per cent of that from all SFCs. After more than two-and-half decades, during 1996-99, these were respectively 6.83 crore and 0.31 per cent. The growth over the period thus came to only.5.1 times compared with 55.7 times for all SFCs. The cumulative total till March 2001 was Rs.423 crore, constituting 1.44 per cent of all SFCs.

Table 6.5 : Trend in SCBs Outstanding Advances to Small-Scale Industries : Bihar Vis-à-Vis other States

States	*Outstanding Advances (Rs crore)*				*No. of Units (in '000)*			*Credit per - unit (Rs '000)*	
	June-end 1968	*Dec-end 1983*	*March-end 1995*	*Growth (in multiples)*	*Dec. '83*	*Mar. '95*	*% rise*	*1983*	*1995*
Bihar	1.61 (0.84)	139.8 (2.6)	736.5 (2.5)	457.5	59.6	228.4	283.2	23	32
W. Bengal	15.52 (8.10)	398.0 (7.4)	1984.0 (6.8)	127.8	102.3	616.5	502.6	39	32
Orissa	0.85 (0.44)	64.1 (1.2)	395.5 (1.4)	465.3	55.3	154.2	178.8	12	26
Assam	1.08 (0.56)	33.8 (0.6)	224.9 (0.8)	208.2	19.4	67.5	247.9	17	33
Madhya P.	4.73 (2.47)	161.6 (3.0)	953.7 (3.3)	201.6	73.3	132.8	81.2	22	72
Uttar P.	15.55 (8.12)	478.9 (8.9)	2467.8 (8.5)	158.7	146.7	342.2	133.3	33	72
Andhra P.	13.33 (6.96)	348.9 (6.5)	1703.7 (5.8)	127.8	105.3	164.2	55.9	33	104
Kerala	18.81 (9.82)	217.8 (4.0)	1149.4 (3.9)	61.1	58.5	218.7	273.8	37	53
Maharashtra	44.96 (23.47)	984.9 (18.3)	5610.1 (19.2)	124.8	93.7	160.9	71.7	105	349
All-India	191.60 (100.0)	5389.4 (100.0)	29174.5 (100.0)	152.3	1243.8	2963.5	138.3	43	98

Source: Deb 1988: Table VIII. 2; RBI 1998a.

On the provision of finance to SSIs, Bihar's position was very poor. The Small Industries Development Bank of India (SIDBI), which commenced operation in April 1990, provided a cumulative per capita assistance of Rs. 52.5 till March 2001, constituting 16.0 per cent of the national average. The performance of Bihar's SFC was also low. The cumulative total assistance to SSIs till March 2001was only Rs. 482.8 crore, constituting 1.89 per cent of all SFCs' total. In the Bihar SFC's grand total of assistance, the SSIs' share came to only 61.6 per cent as against 71.3 per cent in case of all SFCs.

Another glaring deficiency in the flow of fund to industries is the neglect of backward areas. In the aggregate of assistance to Bihar till March 1994 from all FIs, the backward areas' share came to only 19.7 per cent, declining from 27.7 per cent in that provided till March 1989. The national average of proportion to backward areas in these two time points was respectively, 32.4 per cent and 40.5 per cent. Among the neighbouring states, Bihar's was the lowest proportion (Table 6.6)

For the low provision of finance, however, the FIs cannot be fully blamed. If proposals do not come from the industrial units, the FIs cannot do much about it. In fact, the number of business enterprises operating in Bihar itself was low. Neither the Central government nor the state government took any special initiative towards setting up of new units here, as will be evident from the analysis below.

The Licensing System

From the start of economic planning in the country, an industrial licensing system was introduced under the Industries (Development and Regulation) Act, 1951, with the objective of bringing the required pattern of industrialisation. One of the important objectives was to bring a balanced regional development. Registration with the Central government was made compulsory for a large number of industries included in the first schedule to the Act. Even after considerable relaxation over the years, around mid-eighties there were still 38 heads with about 200 items listed in the schedule. The licensing system was, however, manipulated in such a way that instead of bringing a balanced regional development it did the opposite of it. The backward areas received very little attention (Deb 1987: chap. 5).

Bihar had a negligible share of the licences issued over the years. To look at the situation in some selected years, between 1974 and 1978, total number of letter of intents (LOI) and industrial licences (IL) issued for Bihar was only 177, constituting 2.42 per cent of all-India total as against 1698 to Maharashtra, 613 to Tamil Nadu, 839 to Gujarat and 579 to West Bengal. Thus the more industrialised states continued to receive a disproportionately large share of the licences. In the following years, the situation worsened further. During 1984-88, the state received a total of 163, constituting 1.80 per cent of the national total. Maharashtra, on the other hand, received 1451 licences and LOIs (16.0 per cent), Tamil Nadu 930 and Gujarat 834. For no-industry districts,

Table 6.6: Trend in Provision of Assistance from the Financial Institutions : Bihar Vis-à-Vis other States

States	Cumulative Total Assistance from AFI[a] (Rs crore)		Per capita Assistance Disbursed: cum till March 1999 (Rs)					Till March 2001	
	Till March'89	Till March '99	AFI[a]	AIFI[b]	SFC	SIDC	SIDBI	AFI	SFC
Bihar	1129 (2.51)	4711 (1.38)	462.8	450.2	41.3	15.5	41.5	552	38.6
W. Bengal	2614 (5.80)	13993 (4.11)	1830.9	1767.9	84.3	74.4	137.7	2797	95.8
Orissa	1395 (3.10)	5788 (1.70)	1621.8	1461.6	272.7	69.4	121.9	2213	318.3
Assam	317 (0.70)	1355 (0.40)	511.9	509.3	39.4	21.6	34.0	706	41.6
Madhya P.	2213 (4.92)	14989 (4.40)	1984.2	1950.6	102.9	44.2	148.1	2187	113.6
Uttar P.	4510 (10.02)	23730 (6.97)	1457.3	1313.4	167.3	120.6	117.0	1692	163.1
Andhra P.	3667 (8.14)	22439 (6.59)	3013.2	2908.1	262.3	57.1	200.9	4083	322.3
Kerala	1114 (2.47)	5556 (1.63)	1721.9	1495.4	408.0	145.3	438.0	2644	531.8
Maharashtra	8017 (17.81)	76378 (22.44)	8619.9	8388.3	294.3	231.2	472.0	12224	279.0
All-India	45027 (100.0)	340395 (100.0)	3516.5	3369.5	256.9	133.3	275.1	4829	285.3

(Table 6.6 Contd.)

1970-73 (a.a.)	1996-99 (a.a.)	Growth (in multiple)	Assistance from SFCs (Total) (Rs crore) cum till March '72	Assistance from SFCs (Total) (Rs crore) cum till March '99	% share of SSI in cum till March'99	Assistance to Backward areas (Rs crore) cum till March '89	Assistance to Backward areas (Rs crore) cum till March '94
1.33	6.83	5.1	5.0	783.1	60.9	313.1 (27.7)[c]	519.6 (19.7)[c]
0.70	61.33	87.6	7.1	765.1	68.9	944.1 (36.1)	1849.5 (31.0)
0.58	90.83	156.6	3.4	1079.6	47.9	510.7 (36.6)	1155.2 (36.9)
0.29	2.70	9.3	4.6	113.2	73.8	316.9 (100.0)	772.5 (100.0)
0.85	60.77	71.5	6.8	875.3	64.3	1289.2 (58.3)	3805.9 (59.7)
3.60	274.13	76.1	9.9	2868.4	59.7	2292.9 (50.8)	4915.6 (48.7)
2.75	136.33	49.6	11.4	2279.2	64.4	1787.7 (48.8)	3782.7 (40.4)
1.95	193.03	99.0	7.6	1662.4	55.3	449.8 (40.4)	975.3 (36.3)
7.06	175.83	24.9	25.3	3533.7	51.1	1602.2 (20.0)	5029.8 (17.6)
39.00	2173.20	55.7	152.5	30374.5	63.0	18247.2 (40.5)	43108.6 (32.4)

Notes : a : AFI stands for all financial institutions, and include six all-India development banks, three specialised financial institutions, three investment institutions and the State Financial Corporations (SFCs) and the State Industrial Development Corporations (SIDCs); b : AIFI stands for all-India financial institutions and covers 12 FIs; c : percentage share of total.

Source : IDBI 1989, 1999, 2002; GOI 1973.

Bihar received a total of 28 LOI and IL during 1982-88, constituting 3.32 per cent of all-India total (843) (GOI 1990). Most of the districts of North and Central Bihar continued to be devoid of any industry worth the name. Development of backward areas received only a lip-service.

In recent years, when the licensing system was virtually abolished, also Bihar received very little investment. Between August 1991 and October 1999, only 42 LOIs, involving a total investment of Rs 1806 crore, were issued. In the all-India total, these constituted respectively 1.26 per cent and 1.73 per cent. All the neighbouring states received much higher investment, and Gujarat the highest of 19.2 per cent of total (GOR 2000a). Number of corporate private sector enterprises operating in Bihar stood at only 7687 in February 1998, with total paid-up capital at Rs 3468.6 crore; these were respectively 1.60 per cent and 1.73 per Cent of all-India total. This is deterioration over the situation prevailing one decade earlier; in 1988, the relative shares were respectively 1.43 and 3.87 per cent (GOI 1990, 1998).

The central government's investment in Bihar also had a very low growth. The investment in gross block of non-departmental undertakings had increased only 332 per cent between 1980-81 and 1993-94 as against 839 per cent for all-India. Bihar's share in the latter's total declined from 16.7 per cent to 7.7 per cent. The most industrialised state Maharashtra, on the other hand, raised its share from 8.6 per cent to 19.8 per cent, with a growth of 2052 per cent over the same period. It is difficult to believe that the Centre had any policy of bringing balanced regional development.

Apart from the above-mentioned factors, the general industrial climate in the state was also not good. The man-days lost due to industrial disputes were sometimes very high. In 1985-87, for example, 12.14 lakh man-days were lost annually, constituting 10.5 per cent of all-India total. Given the size of the industrial sector, this was too high a proportion. The law and order situation, as noted in chapter 2, was also not favourable for industrial growth.

Overall, it is the attitude and policies of the state government that is largely to be blamed for the depressing industrial situation. For the low growth of large and medium sector industries, the Central government might have been partly responsible, but for the small-scale industries the growth was primarily in the hands of the state government. If the government had the required determination, and took active interest in the development of SSIs, the situation would not have been so disappointing. The performance of District Industries Centres and the interest taken on the development of Industrial Estates were far from satisfactory.

Note

1. The industries included here are those located in a rural area whose population does not exceed 10 thousand and in which fixed capital investment per head of an artisan or a worker does not exceed Rs 15,000.

7

Towards Poverty Alleviation

Poverty is a relative term, relative to the average standard of living of the society in which one lives. But for survival over a reasonably long period there are certain minimum requirements. There is need for a minimum amount of well-balanced food, clothing and shelter. And then, for realizing this package in the best possible way, there is need for a minimum level of education. All these are for the vast majority of Indians still only a dream, and will remain so for a long time to come, given the quality of leadership the nation is saddled with.

The focus here is, however, limited to the absolute minimum requirement—ignoring the long-term implications—that is, the problem of getting the minimum calorie intake. In chapter two, we have noted the extent of poverty in Bihar on this basis. The proportion of population below the poverty-line continued to be much more than the national average, and the extent of disparity widened rather than narrowed.

Behind the distressing situation, an important reason is the low growth of agricultural production. It is well-known that there is a strong inverse relationship between agricultural productivity and the incidence of poverty (Mahendra Dev, S. 2000). While agricultural growth was negligible, as noted in chapter 5, the direct poverty alleviation measures also did not get the required attention. Here we look into the magnitude and manner of implementation of some of the direct measures. The focus is on the wage employment and self-employment programmes, and the public distribution system.

Wage Employment Programmes

Until the early seventies, there was virtually no efforts from the government for increasing wage employment opportunities, although the unemployment rate in Bihar was one of the highest. In 1972-73, in the rural areas it stood at 8.5 for males and 14.2 for females compared with 6.4 and 10.5, respectively, in all-India. The wage rate in Bihar for rural farm labourers this year was Rs 1.98 for males and Rs 1.41 for females as against Rs 2.31 and Rs 1.42 in all-India (Sinha 1978).

The first wage employment scheme was launched in 1971 with the Crash Scheme for Rural Employment (CSRE). Then came the Food for Work Programme in 1977, the National Rural Employment Programme (NREP) in 1980, the Rural Landless Employment Guarantee Programme (RLEGP) in 1983, the Jawahar Rozgar Yojana in 1989 and the Employment Assurance Scheme in 1993. We give a brief look first into the earlier programmes, followed by a more detailed analysis of the currently running ones.

Earlier Programmes

The CSRE was entirely financed by the Central government and it aimed to generate 2.5 lakh mandays (lmd) a year in each district. Through the work, durable assets were to be created in accordance with the local development plans. The scheme continued for three years, 1971-74, and created a total employment of 302.70 lmd in Bihar by spending Rs1245.86 lakh. Bihar accounted for 9.6 per cent of the total employment generated in the country, which was lower than in two of the neighbouring states. The average expenditure per man-day came to Rs 4.05 here compared with Rs 3.98 at the national level (GOI 1979).

As regards the nature of assets created, almost the entire expenditure in Bihar was on roads as against the average of 71.3 per cent for 16 major states. The exclusive reliance on road construction took place despite the guidelines' suggestion to give it the least importance, because of the possibility of being washed away by the very first rain itself. Moreover, even by spending almost the entire amount, the length of roads constructed was only 2678 km in the three-year period, which was much less than in many other states with a lower level of expenditure. Orissa had constructed 8,460 km even after spending money on minor irrigation, drainage, etc.

After the CSRE, there was no national programme in operation for three years. In 1977, the Food for Work Programme was launched and it continued till September 1980, when the NREP replaced it. The utilisation of the FWP was very low in Bihar. The value of food grains utilised stood at only Rs 81.20 lakh in 1977-78 as against six times as much by West Bengal. Moreover, there were reports of misuse and malpractices in the utilisation of food grains (GOI 1980a).

The implementation of NREP was also poor, as may be seen from Table 7.1. During 1985-89, a total of Rs 403 crore was spent on it, constituting 13.7 per cent of all-India total. The utilisation of food grains was substantially below the quantum released. The mandays created constituted 11.4 per cent of all-India total. The cost per manday was significantly higher here; in fact, the highest among the neighbouring states.

The effectiveness of the programme was not much. An evaluation study in the backward district of Purnea showed that the rate of out-migration of rural labour did not decrease after its introduction. This was largely because in most cases the labourers did not get the prescribed wages and often outside labourers

Table 7.1: The Implementation of NREP and RLEGP: Bihar Vis-à-Vis other States (during 1985-89)

States	*NREP*				*RLEGP (contd.)*	
	Expenditure (Rs lakh)	*Food grains utilised ('000 tonnes)*	*Mandays created ('000)*	*Cost per manday (Rs)*	*Expenditure (Rs lakh)*	*Food grains utilised ('000 tonnes)*
Bihar	40287 (98.3)[a]	4303 (84.5)[a]	168659 (119.6)[b]	23.89	35055 (94.1)[a]	3309 (86.2)[a]
W. Bengal	15625 (86.9)	1533 (88.4)	66216 (89.0)	23.60	13618 (83.5)	1377 (90.4)
Orissa	11729 (107.8)	1562 (104.7)	73585 (110.4)	15.94	11265 (87.0)	1207 (106.1)
Assam	4550 (76.2)	195 (45.6)	15641 (89.1)	29.09	3563 (78.5)	144 (36.2)
Madhya P.	26652 (95.0)	4047 (93.2)	149645 (126.5)	17.81	17636 (80.4)	2158 (112.8)
Uttar P.	53340 (95.3)	6343 (85.3)	233359 (116.4)	22.86	47328 (94.2)	5047 (71.9)
Andhra P.	26237 (94.5)	2583 (105.0)	110723 (100.4)	23.70	24732 (96.7)	2298 (101.0)
Kerala	11328 (95.3)	1170 (95.3)	43787 (120.9)	25.87	9928 (96.4)	1222 (88.5)
Rajasthan	19311 (97.6)	5142 (117.9)	189409 (398.8)	10.20	9593 (89.9)	1312 (102.9)
All-India	293987 (94.7)	35289 (91.1)	1477536 (124.9)	19.90	241199 (100.0)	24170 (87.4)

RLEGP Mandays created ('000)	*cost per manday (Rs.)*
129869 (114.8)[b]	26.99
60400 (101.5)	22.55
67504 (116.8)	16.69
12371 (66.6)	28.80
101485 (83.3)	17.38
212413 (126.2)	22.28
108277 (116.2)	22.84
35077 (124.7)	28.30
54299 (155.3)	17.67
1154382 (119.2)	20.89

Notes: a: percentage to amount released; b: percentage to target.
Source: GOI 1990a.

were hired so as to pay lower wages. The assets created were found to be not only of low quality but universally unproductive (Verma et al 1987).

The employment guarantee programme, RLEGP, was also implemented in a similar way. The cost per manday came to be very high. At the average of Rs 27 during 1985-89, it was not only much above the national average but also the highest among the neighbouring states. Naturally, the number of mandays created was relatively low. It constituted 11.2 per cent of all-India total with the share in expenditure at 14.5 per cent. The achievement in relation to target was 115 per cent in employment creation, with that in utilisation of fund at 94 per cent (Table 7.1). Thus the programme formulation itself was deficient.

The employment situation continued to deteriorate. The average earning strength of agricultural labour households declined from 1.82 in 1983 to 1.71 in 1987-88, and the disparity with the national average widened. The average daily earning for man stood at only Rs 9.02 in 1987-88 as against the national average of Rs 9.46 (Table 7.3). The government was compelled to increase its level of expenditure on employment creation, and the Jawahar Rozgar Yojana was launched in 1989 with some significant changes in policies and procedures. Below we look into the nature of implementation of this scheme in Bihar.

Jawahar Rozgar Yojana

First a brief look at the modalities of the programme. The Centre's share of the fund for the programme was raised to 80 per cent, from 50 per cent in the earlier programmes, and the allocation among the states was to be done on the basis of the ratio of the state's poor population to the total rural poor in the country. The distribution from the state to districts was to be done on the basis of an index of backwardness. Within the district, the fund was to be distributed among the three tiers of panchayat in the ratio of 15: 15:70.

The JRY initially had two sub-schemes: the Million Well Scheme (MWS) and the Indira Awas Yojana (IAY). Subsequently, in 1993-94, two more streams were introduced: the Intensified JRY and Special and Innovative Projects. The former was, however, delinked from it in January 1996 and added to the EAS. The JRY was to be implemented through the Gram Panchayat (GP) and all plans of development discussed at the village level.

In April 1999, the programme was restructured and named Jawahar Gram Samridhi Yojana.The primary objective now became creation of demand driven village infrastructure, not employment. The wage-material ratio of 60:40 laid down earlier was made flexible. Further, 22.5 per cent of the fund is to be earmarked for individual beneficiary schemes for SCs/STs.

The JRY created a much larger number of mandays in Bihar than the earlier programmes. Over the period of first six years, 1989-95, an annual average of 997 lmds were created, which was 34 per cent higher than that by the NREP and the RLEGP together in the preceding four years. The cost per manday continued to be very high. And consequently, Bihar's share in all-India total expenditure was higher than its share in mandays created, being respectively 14.5 per cent and 11.9 per cent.

Table 7.2: Trend in Operation of the JRY/JGSY and the EAS: Bihar Vis-à-Vis other States

States			*JRY /JGSY*					
	Expenditure (Rs million)			*Mandays created (lakh)*				
	1989-95	*1997-00*	*1989-95*	*%share of*		*1997-00*	*%share of*	
				SC/ST	*landless*		*SC/ST*	*landless*
Bihar	25145 (14.5)	11343 (16.2)	5983 (11.9)	63.3	64.3	1543 (14.8)	59.7	60.1
W.Bengal	12656 (7.3)	3785 (5.4)	3078 (6.1)	49.9	60.0	403 (3.9)	52.8	57.5
Orissa	8871 (5.1)	4404 (6.3)	2458 (4.9)	67.8	19.7	808 (7.8)	66.0	21.1
Assam	3778 (2.2)	2431 (3.5)	1024 (2.0)	46.4	41.1	440 (4.2)	50.9	35.9
Madhya P.	17331 (10.0)	6818 (9.7)	4982 (9.9)	65.7	35.2	932 (9.0)	63.9	36.0
Uttar P.	33531 (19.3)	13943 (19.9)	9301 (18.5)	56.5	34.1	1729 (16.6)	52.3	23.6
Andhra P.	13360 (7.7)	4341 (6.2)	4439 (8.8)	46.3	69.1	670 (6.4)	43.7	64.4
Kerala	4253 (2.4)	1140 (1.6)	946 (1.9)	38.2	16.5	119 (1.1)	34.9	12.7
Rajasthan	8139 (4.7)	2826 (4.0)	2466 (4.9)	65.5	16.6	449 (4.3)	63.5	14.1
All-India	173695 (100.0)	69973 (100.0)	50280 (100.0)	55.6	45.5	10403 (100.0)	54.5	40.4

JRY/JGSY Cost per manday (Rs.)		EAS (1993-00)				
1989-95	1997-00	Expenditure (Rs million)	Mandays created (lakh)	% share of SC/ST[b]	% share of Landless[c] (Rs)	cost per manday
42.03	73.52	13504 (59.3)[a]	2010 (9.0)	60.6	61.1	67
41.12	93.85	6782 (65.2)	915 (4.1)	56.9	58.5	74
36.09	54.48	9608 (72.0)	2001 (9.0)	68.4	24.6	48
36.89	55.20	5417 (63.5)	975 (4.4)	48.5	41.7	56
34.79	73.19	15695 (73.4)	2348 (10.5)	66.2	32.2	67
36.05	80.63	18645 (61.6)	2582 (11.6)	33.5	14.1	72
30.10	64.83	12340 (84.8)	2064 (9.2)	57.2	36.0[d]	60
44.96	96.12	2086 (64.9)	237 (1.1)	38.3	9.9	88
33.00	62.88	7625 (63.7)	1375 (6.2)	61.7	13.3	55
34.55	67.26	132051 (67.9)	22337 (100.0)	55.8	39.0	59

Notes: a: percentage to available fund; b: relate to 1994-5 to 1999-00; c: relate to 1995-00; d : average for 1996-00.
Source: GOI 1991a, 1996a, 1998a, 1999b, 2000, 2000f.

As regards the distribution of mandays among the beneficiaries, the weaker groups appear to have been better represented here. The share of SCs/STs in the total stood at 63.3 per cent in this period compared with the national average of 54.5 per cent. The proportion for the landless was also high, respectively 60.1 and 40.4 per cent.

In recent years, the importance of JRY has declined considerably. The annual average of expenditure in the last three years, 1997-00, came to only Rs 378.1 crore as against Rs 419.1 crore during 1989-95. There was a sharp fall in the number of mandays created, being the annual average of 514.3 and 997.2 lmd in the two periods respectively. In the all-India total number, however, Bihar's share increased substantially (Table 7.2).

The utilisation of available fund was generally poor. For example, in 1994-95, it stood at only 68.3 per cent under the first stream, and in the following year still lower-being 62.1 per cent; at the national level, it was respectively 82.3 per cent and 76.7 per cent. The programme formulation continued to be deficient. Sometimes the achievements were ridiculously unrelated to the target. For example, in 1995-96, the fund utilisation under the second stream was to the extent of only 71.5 per cent but on employment generation the achievement came to 235.1 per cent of the target (GOI 2000).

As regards the nature of physical assets created, Bihar gave a high emphasis on construction of wells and houses. Between 1988-89 and 1994-95, 23,991 wells were constructed under the MWS, constituting 28.0 per cent of all-India total; the relative share in expenditure was only 15.6 per cent. The average cost per well came to Rs 19,263, 56 per cent of that at the national level. In recent years, however, the picture changed noticeably. During 1996-99 the cost per well rose to Rs 33,643, 73 per cent of that at the national level. Bihar's share in all-India total number constructed declined to 19.2 per cent. As regards the IAY, during 1988-95, a total of 309,282 houses were constructed, constituting 15.4 per cent of all-India total. The cost per house averaged Rs 12,372, marginally higher than the all-India average. In recent years also the trend was similar.

The implementation of JRY suffered from many deficiencies, apart from those mentioned above. The violation of the JRY guidelines was very common. Some of them, as brought out by the concurrent evaluation in 1992, are noted below (Neelakantan 1994).

As per the guidelines, the wage component was expected to be at least 60 per cent of the resources available, but in Bihar it was found to be only 45.68 per cent; this was much below the all-India average also, being 53.64 per cent. If the guidelines were followed, a much larger number of mandays would have been created. The level of employment provided was very low. For the JRY worker himself it was 3.45 person-days in a month as against the all-India average of 3.81. To other members of the family, it was respectively 1.13, 1.34 person-days. The wage rates paid were also low, lower than the minimum prescribed, and men and women were not paid the same rate as required by the guideline.

Table 7.3: Trend in Earning Strength and Earnings of Agricultural Labour Households: Bihar Vis-à-Vis other States

States	*Average Earning Strength*						*Average Daily Earnings (Rs.)*			
	All classes of HHS.			*Scheduled Castes*			*Men*		*Women*	
	1983	1987-8	1993-4	1983	1987-8	1993-4	1987-8	1993-4	1987-8	1993-4
Bihar	1.82	1.71	1.73	1.88 (2.20)	1.81 (1.96)	1.75 (2.21)	9.02	10.93	8.03	14.78
W.Bengal	1.67	1.60	1.56	1.71 (2.10)	1.59 (2.00)	1.65 (1.71)	11.85	24.20	10.71	19.92
Orissa	2.01	1.88	1.96	1.84 (2.14)	1.79 (2.09)	1.97 (2.23)	7.89	16.30	6.01	12.09
Assam	1.50	1.58	1.64	1.45 (1.35)	1.59 (1.23)	1.40 (1.27)	12.40	26.19	11.71	23.18
Andhra P.	2.35	2.24	2.27	2.43 (2.57)	2.12 (2.48)	2.29 (2.45)	8.87	19.12	6.12	13.61
Madhya P.	2.37	2.30	2.20	2.41 (2.37)	2.26 (2.29)	2.20 (2.22)	7.67	17.04	6.74	14.29
Uttar P.	1.72	1.79	1.67	1.79 (1.77)	1.84 (1.76)	1.76 (1.94)	9.07	21.59	6.99	16.57
Kerala	1.76	1.79	1.67	2.02 (2.26)	1.89 (2.04)	1.94 (2.67)	18.29	43.18	13.52	29.88
Rajasthan	2.01	1.96	1.80	2.00 (2.40)	2.06 (2.34)	1.82 (2.23)	9.69	27.66	9.14	22.56
All-India	2.07	2.00	1.99	2.05 (2.33)	1.95 (2.22)	1.97 (2.22)	9.46	21.52	7.05	15.33

Note: figures in brackets relate to scheduled tribes.
Source: GOI 2000.

Further, among the beneficiaries, a large proportion was found to be belonging to ineligible categories, that is, non-poor. Out of 1,878 households surveyed, only 16.19 per cent belonged to those with income below Rs 4,801 whereas the proportion with income above Rs 6,400 was 51.01 per cent. The maintenance of master rolls—an important document for proper recording of employment creation—was very poor. It was not even available in 32.8 per cent of the cases in Bihar as against the national average of 15.8 per cent. The stipulation of discussing the Action Plan in gram sabha meetings was also violated in many cases. This was a serious deficiency as the JRY manual had envisaged comprehensive measures for ensuring the villagers association at each and every stage of the execution of JRY. As regards the quality of assets created, it was found to be unsatisfactory to a large extent. Only 59.0 per cent of the assets were good / satisfactory compared with 73.8 per cent at the national level.

Employment Assurance Scheme

The EAS is a demand-based programme and it aims at providing 100 days of unskilled manual work to each rural job-seekers. A maximum of two adults per family could be employed and it was to be provided during the lean agricultural season. A new project could be started by the block-level officer when about 10 workers, later raised to 20, demanded work. Through the provision of employment, the programme was to create economic infrastructure and community assets. The works were to be selected on the basis of laid-down priorities. Initially the scheme was started in a selected number of blocks, that having the revamped PDS in operation, but presently it operates in all the blocks in the country.

Recently some significant changes were made in the mode of providing fund and also in the method of work selection. Presently funds are provided on the basis of an index of backwardness, calculated by taking the proportion of SCs/STs population in the district and the inverse of agricultural production per agricultural worker. Of the funds allocated to a district, 70 per cent has to go to the blocks, and the remaining kept by the district for use in the areas of distress.

The operation of the EAS was very poor in Bihar. The fund available for the scheme remained unutilised to a very large extent. During 1993-00, the total amount utilised constituted only 59.3 per cent of that available; at the national level, it was 67.9 per cent. The annual utilisation varied between the lowest of 27.3 per cent in the first year and the highest at 85.6 per cent in 1997-98. The aggregate of expenditure over the seven-year period constituted 10.2 per cent of all-India total but in employment created it was 9.0 per cent. The cost per manday was very high here, as may be seen from Table 7.2.

A good feature of the scheme's operation in Bihar is that, as in case of the JRY, the SCs/STs were benefited to a larger extent. In the total employment provided over the entire period, their share came to 60.6 per cent compared

Table 7.4: Trend in operation of the IRDP: Bihar vis-à-vis other States

States	*Fund utilisation (Rs. million)*		*Credit mobilised (Rs million)*		*No. of Families assisted ('000)*	
	1992-95	1997-00	1992-95	1996-99	1992-95	1997-00
Bihar	2662 (10.0)	3382 (10.7)	3665 (9.4)	6665 (10.9)	824.9 (12.1)	479.5 (11.6)
West Bengal	1446 (5.4)	1458 (4.6)	2042 (5.2)	2251 (3.7)	405.2 (5.9)	248.9 (5.8)
Orissa	1567 (5.9)	2086 (6.6)	1661 (4.3)	3286 (5.4)	393.1 (5.8)	244.6 (5.7)
Assam	722 (2.7)	973 (3.1)	813 (2.1)	974 (1.6)	166.7 (2.4)	104.8 (2.4)
Madhya p.	2761 (10.4)	3356 (10.6)	3687 (9.5)	5999 (9.8)	637.4 (9.3)	372.5 (8.7)
Uttar P.	5393 (20.3)	5278 (16.7)	10904 (28.0)	14768 (24.1)	1203.1 (17.6)	803.6 (18.7)
Andhra P.	2551 (9.6)	3045 (9.6)	2800 (7.2)	4610 (7.5)	598.6 (8.8)	468.2 (10.9)
Maharashtra	2024 (7.6)	2995 (9.5)	3338 (8.6)	5785 (9.4)	592.0 (8.7)	381.3 (8.9)
All-India	26580 (100.0)	31606 (100.0)	38958 (100.0)	61345 (100.0)	6822.5 (100.0)	4294.9 (100.0)

Per capita subsidy (Rs.)		*Per capita Credit (Rs.)*	
1992-95	1997-00	1992-95	1996-99
3227	7055 (118.6)[a]	4443	10788 (142.8)[a]
3570	5859 (64.1)	5038	8242 (63.6)
3987	8527 (113.9)	4227	12048 (185.0)
4346	9285 (113.6)	4893	7794 (59.3)
4332	9008 (107.9)	5785	14000 (142.0)
4482	6568 (46.5)	9063	13334 (47.1)
4262	6504 (52.6)	4678	9109 (94.7)
3419	7855 (129.7)	5639	12734 (125.8)
3896	7359 (88.9)	5710	11600 (103.2)

Note: a: percentage increase over the period.
Source: GOI 2000, 2000f.

with 55.8 per cent at the national level. For landless workers, the relative position was still better, the proportion being respectively 61.1 and 39.0 per cent. This is quite natural, because landlessness is much more widespread in Bihar than at the national level.

Overall, the situation was very gloomy. A recent study on the programme found that about 85 to 95 per cent of the poor in Bihar are not even aware of the EAS. In one of the study villages not a single labourer benefited for even a day. The derailment of the programme is attributed to lack of trust in the motives of the lower rung bureaucracy. The district officers feared that if more earth work-oriented projects were taken up, bureaucracy at the lower levels would have indulged in corruption and loot of the resources. It was also found that the government staff sometimes connived with powerful people at the local level to allow them to manage the gram sabha on paper or simply not organise the meetings which would create awareness among the poor (Statesman 2000j).

Consequent on the implementation of the employment schemes, there was very little improvement in the employment situation. As may be seen from Table 7.3, the average earning strength of agricultural labour households had fallen over the years, and always remained below the national average. Number of households participating in rural public works stood at only 56 per thousand in 1993-94 as against 59 at the national level; earlier, in 1987-88, it was respectively 43 and 64. In recent years, there has been a sharp fall in the participation rate, being at only 42 in 1999-00 (NSSO 1998d, 2001). The average daily earnings of agricultural labour households had a sharp fall in relative position. For men, in 1993-94 it was half of that at the national level (Table 7.3).

Seeing the depressing employment situation for the rural poor, the parliament has recently, in August 2005, passed the Rural Employment Guarantee bill, which is to provide 100 days of wage employment to every rural househld in a year. The minimum wage assured is Rs. 60, and there is provision for unemployment allowance if the job cannot be provided. Given the manipulative power of the panchayats, the scheme is however, bound to get diluted in the process of implementation.

Self-Employment Programmes

The first self-employment programme to be launched in the country for the BPL population was the Integrated Rural Development Programme (IRDP) in 1977. Initially it was on a limited scale, only in 1980-81the scheme extended to the entire country. The Small Farmers' Development Agency, introduced in the Fourth Plan for assisting the potentially viable small farmers, was merged into it. The objective of the IRDP was to help the poor cross the poverty line. The eligible groups were to be from agricultural labourers, artisans and marginal farmers with an annual household income of under Rs 3,500. A third of the beneficiaries were expected to be from the secondary and tertiary sectors. The beneficiaries were to acquire income-earning asset through government subsidy and credit from the banks, in the ratio of 1:2. There were specific limits on the extent of subsidies to different categories. The name of the scheme was recently changed to Swarnjayanti Gram Swarojgar Yojana (SGSY).

The IRDP had two sub-schemes: one for the training of rural youth for self-employment (TRYSEM), introduced in 1979, and the other for development of women and children in rural areas (DWCRA), launched in 1982. Under the TRYSEM, after the training—normally for six months—a free toolkit costing not more than Rs. 800 was given to the trainee. During the training period, each trainee received stipend varying between Rs. 200 and Rs. 500 per month. The DWCRA is also primarily for skill formation. Under it women members formed groups of 10 to 15 for taking up economic activities suited to their skill and aptitude. In recent years, some significant changes have been made on both the schemes. In the nineties, two more sub-schemes were added to the IRDP. In July 1992, the scheme for supply of improved toolkits to rural artisans (SITRA) was introduced, and in February 1997 the Ganga Kalyan Yojana. Under the former, the average cost of a toolkit was to be Rs 2,000 and in case of power-driven tools Rs 4,500. Ninety per cent of the cost was to be provided as subsidy by the Government of India and the remaining contributed by the beneficiary. Below we give a brief look into how the schemes were operated in Bihar.

IRDP/SGSY

The IRDP was introduced in Bihar in 1978-79 in 310 blocks out of the total of 587. In the second year it was extended to 15 more and in 1980-81 to all the blocks in the state. In the first three years, there was very little progress. The utilisation of available fund was a bare 19.1 per cent in 1978-79 and increased to 35.3 in 1980-81. In the following years the situation improved considerably in response to some significant changes in the development administration.

However, still there was no consistent growth in expenditure. The amount spent increased from Rs. 10.3 crore in 1980-81 to Rs 52.2 crore in the last year of the Sixth Plan. In the Seventh Plan, there were wide fluctuations in both allocation and utilisation. The expenditure rose to Rs. 101.2 crore in 1987-88, from Rs 49.5 crore in 1985-86, but in the following two years it came to a total of Rs 76.7 crore. The utilisation as percentage to allocation averaged 108.6 per cent in the first three years but in the following two it was only 46.0 per cent. For the entire plan period, the expenditure totalled Rs 306.2 crore, rising from Rs. 166.8 crore in the preceding plan, that is, a growth of 83.6 per cent. The pattern of operation of the IRDP in the nineties may be seen from Table 7.4.

The growth of expenditure in the last eight years, 1992-00, was very low. It increased from the annual average of Rs 88.7 crore during 1992-95 to Rs 112.7 crore in 1997-00, that is by only 27 per cent. Even this was, however, higher than the national average, being 19 per cent. Bihar's share in all-India total expenditure stood at 10.7 per cent in the latter period, and it was the second highest among the states.

The number of families assisted registered a sharp fall. During 1997-00 the annual average came to only 1.60 lakh as against 2.75 lakh in 1992-95. In the all-India total number assisted, Bihar's share declined from 12.1 per cent to 11.6 per cent. The main reason behind the fall was a faster growth in per capita subsidy. It had risen by 119 per cent here as against 89 per cent at the national level. Even after the higher growth, the amount of subsidy, however, remained below the national average. The provision of credit also moved in a similar way. The per capita credit had risen by 143 per cent between 1992-95 and 1996-99 as against 103 per cent in all-India. But the amount of credit remained below the latter's level. The credit-subsidy ratio stood at 1.53 in the latest period as against 1.58 at the national level (Table 7.4).

The implementation of IRDP in Bihar suffered from many deficiencies. A few of the findings of a study conducted in early nineties may be noted here. First, despite the pointed instruction to select the beneficiaries through the gram sabha, nearly all the selections were made by the officials. This probably resulted in ineligible persons getting selected. Second, the quality of assets provided was unsatisfactory to a majority of the beneficiaries; the proportion satisfied was only 46.7 per cent here compared with 80.0 per cent at the national level. This might have been only partly due to the low level of investment, noted earlier; inefficiency and/or dishonesty of officials might have contributed greatly to it. The proportion of beneficiaries with asset intact was also low, being 67.4 per cent here as against 71.0 at the national level. Even the distribution of Vikas Patra was negligible here, being only 3.8 per cent of the beneficiaries compared with 38.5 per cent in all-India (Sharma 1995).

Another survey sponsored by the state government found that the programme suffered heavily due to inadequate assistance in terms of supply of raw materials, marketing support, technical advice, training etc. It also found that the development functionaries in general had the impression that their role was restricted to disbursement of credit and subsidy; the crucial role of post-disbursement activities was ignored. There was emphasis on fulfilling the target at any cost, and consequently in many cases the beneficiaries crossed the poverty-line only temporarily at the time of acquiring the assets, later on slipping back to the previous level (ibid).

TRYSEM and DWCRA

The performance of the TRYSEM—as a supportive service to IRDP—was very poor in Bihar. In 1990-91, for example, the number trained declined to 16,529 from 21,691 in the preceding year. The proportion that could get placement also dropped to 43.3 per cent from 51.9 per cent; the self-employed in them constituted respectively, 35.2 and 48.9 per cent. The guidelines' stipulation that at least 50 per cent of the trainee should be from SC/ST was often violated.

After the scheme became independent, the situation worsened further. Particularly depressing was the placement of the youths. During 1992-96, the proportion employed annually averaged only 25.5 per cent as against 45.2 per cent at the national level. Thus, an overwhelming proportion remained unemployed. In the following years, the policy changed again—only those already settled, either in self-employment or wage-employment, were to be trained. The proportion of SC/ST and women trained continued to be below the norm. During 1992-96, the former constituted only 44.4 per cent. The total number trained itself was relatively low. During 1994-99, a total of 78.4 thousand were trained, constituting 8.0 per cent of all-India total; neighbouring Madhya Pradesh, a smaller state, accounted for 14.3 per cent (GOI 2000).

The cost of training was relatively high here. Per trainee it came to Rs 4,265 during 1994-99, which was higher than the national average. The expenditure on the programme varied widely from year to year, and there was no clear relationship between the expenditure and the number of trained. In 1997-98, with the highest amount of expenditure, only 12,080 could be trained whereas in the preceding year with a lower amount the number trained was more than double.

On the DWCRA also the performance was not good. During 1994-99, a total of 13,200 groups were formed, constituting 6.7 per cent of all-India total; a smaller state, Andhra Pradesh alone accounted for 35.8 per cent. The expenditure per group was relatively low here; being an average of Rs 15,034 as against Rs 17,584 at the national level. The size of the groups was also generally small. The annual expenditure on the programme varied widely from year to year, as in case of the TRYSEM (ibid.).

On the SITRA, Bihar's performance was the worst. We look at the situation in only two of the recent years. In 1997-98, Rs 871 lakh was available for use under the scheme, but only Rs 68.6 lakh, that is, 7.87 per cent, could be utilised. The target on number of beneficiaries was 56,993 but a mere 84 were assisted. The amount per beneficiary came to Rs 81,631 as against the all-India average of Rs 2,067; probably, there was misappropriation of the fund. The next year, 1998-99, also the performance was not much better. The number benefited was 2,045, with the total expenditure at Rs 29.39 lakh; the amount per beneficiary comes to Rs 1,437 as against Rs 2,110 at the national level. The level of fund utilisation this year was 3.22 per cent, and the physical achievement at 7.46 per cent of the target (GOI 1998a, 1999b).

Public Distribution System

Distribution of essential commodities to the poor at a very low price could be an important instrument for alleviating absolute poverty. But the PDS in the country did not have any such objective; the system was utilised for the people in general. Only in recent years, some price differences have been introduced to give the BPL population an advantage over the non-poor. Below we give a brief look into how the PDS was operated in Bihar.

As the poor people live overwhelmingly in the rural areas, first we look at the rural area's share in total purchases of some of the commodities. Due to lack of data, we look at the situation in only one of the years in late eighties, but it roughly reflects the normal situation. The dependence was relatively high only in case of rice and kerosene. In 1986-87, the rural sector's share in total

PDS purchase of rice was 87.97 per cent here as against 71.01 per cent at the national level. For kerosene, the difference was wider-being 81.84 per cent and 54.58 per cent, respectively. In wheat, edible oil and sugar, the share was significantly below the national average. In wheat it was 49.12 per cent in Bihar as against 56.19 per cent for all-India, and in edible oil 54.97 and 58.71 per cent respectively (NSSO 1990).

As regards the reliance on PDS purchases in relation to total purchase of a commodity, Bihar's proportion was much below the national average in every item. In 1986-87, only 0.42 per cent of total purchase of the rice in rural areas came from the PDS compared with 16.76 per cent in all-India. In wheat, the proportions were respectively 1.51 and 12.64 per cent, in edible oil 0.15 and 11.04 and in sugar 26.81 and 61.20. Only in case of kerosene the rural Bihar's proportion was higher than the national average, being respectively 38.16 and 25.86 per cent. In all the other eastern states the reliance on PDS was much higher (ibid).

A look at PDS purchases per market dependent presents the worst picture for rural Bihar. The purchases were far less than the all-India average in almost all the items. In 1986-87, rice purchased averaged only 0.032 kg, a mere 2.9 per cent of all-India average; in wheat it was 11.4 per cent, in edible oil virtually nil, in coal 2.8 per cent, sugar 27.2 per cent and in standard cloth 22.1 per cent.

As regards the situation of the poor as a whole, it may be seen from Table 7.5 that here also the state's position was very depressing. The per capita PDS food grains for poor persons in Bihar varied between 12 and 20 kg per annum in the six time points considered. Among the selected states, Bihar's position was the worst. In two of the years, the quantum purchased was the lowest, and in the remaining ones better than in one or two states.

All the above data relate to the pre-nineties situation. In recent years, after the introduction of the revamped PDS in 1992 and the targeted PDS from June 1997, there has been considerable improvement in the position of the poor. Under the Targeted PDS, the BPL families were provided 25 kg of grains per family per month, which was later reduced to 10 kg. The price charged for it was half the economic cost to the FCI.The government of India also launched a scheme for supplying food grains to them at concessional rates to the extent of 25 per cent of the population.

But all these had little impact on the situation in Bihar. The proportion of PDS purchases of rice and wheat in their total consumption by the poor increased from 0.58 per cent in 1993-94 to 1.69 per cent in 1999-00 as against from 6.79 to 8.77 per cent at the national level. For non-poor, the rise was from 0.88 to 2.14 per cent here, and in all-India from 8.61 to 9.18 per cent (Mahendra Dev 2004). Thus, the PDS in Bihar continued to be of little importance to the BPL population.

It needs to be noted here that whatever the government's proclaimed policy on the PDS, in the process of implementation it had been always greatly diluted. The administration of PDS in Bihar is thoroughly riddled with corruption. We give a brief look into how it operated.

Quality of Administration

The department of Food and Civil Supplies, as in other states, has its presence all over the state. The lowest officials of the department are the supply inspectors, and they have to check 40-60 PDS dealers each by visiting every month. Above them, in urban areas, there are the marketing inspectors, who are supposed to visit 50 per cent of the shops every month. Then there are assistant district supply officers and district supply officers. In four urban zones, there are special officers rationing. At the block level, there are mainly two officials: the block supply officer and the supply inspector. All these people derive some extra earnings from the PDS. There are set amounts that PDS dealers have to pay to the supply inspectors, and this money is redistributed with higher-level officers. These higher level officers themselves may also be involved in money collection and/or blackmarketing (Mooij 2001).

There is also the involvement of what is called 'mafia' in the transportation of the PDS food grains. They divert a part of the food grains, and in this process are generally assisted by FCI people and/or assistant general managers of the Food and Civil Supplies Corporation. For a long time, transportation of PDS commodities was not a lucrative work. But since the introduction of targeting, the price difference between BPL food grains and open market food grains is huge. Diversion of one truck (10 tonnes) can give an illegal earning of about Rs. 60,000.

At the local level, there are many petty criminals, the so-called 'rangdars'. Many of them benefit from protection by local MLAs, and in turn, they play a role at election in booth capturing or threatening people when they cast their votes. The rangdars can force the PDS dealers to give them some money or food grains. For instance, when there are political rallies.

The transfer system in Bihar also contributes to the corruption in PDS. Sometimes money transfers are involved for influencing the transfer, and the transferee earns this money back in the course of 1-3 years. At the higher level of the bureaucracy, the transfers obstruct a longer-term commitment with the PDS. A critical attitude is never rewarded positively. Between 1997 and 1999, there were three secretaries/commissioners in the department of Food and Civil Supplies. The two that were transferred in this period were because they refused to cooperate with the food minister in his way of money collection and his decisions about transfers of the departmental staff (ibid.).

The Bihar state Food and Civil Supplies Corporation (FCSC) is the only wholesale agent for PDS food grains. There are several major problems with it. There is inadequate infrastructure of warehouses, vans etc to distribute the food grains properly. The corporation is in an extremely poor financial shape. There is no working capital to purchase the PDS commodities from the FCI; the PDS dealers have to advance the money every month. In recent years, the

Table 7.5: Per capita PDS for Poor Population for Select Years (Food grains): Bihar Vis-à-Vis other States

(Kg per annum)

States	1973	1974	1977	1983	1987	1988
Bihar	12	12	13	19	20	16
West Bengal	66	56	63	92	55	59
Orissa	15	20	15	26	23	18
Assam	31	29	48	65	83	68
Madhya Pradesh	13	9	10	15	28	22
Uttar Pradesh	13	15	10	17	16	18
Andhra Pradesh	16	15	15	65	74	47
Kerala	71	75	107	124	149	149
All-India	73	41	68	86	93	31

Source: Bulletin on Food statistics, quoted in Geetha et al 1993.

corporation often failed to pay the salaries of depot managers and other staff members. There are districts in which the arrears of salary go to the extent of 12-24 months (Jharwal 1999:46). In this situation, it is probably not surprising that illegal sales of the commodities and misappropriation of money occur regularly.

The distribution of ration-cards itself is riddled with corruption. As per the official guidelines, gram panchayat and gram sabha are to be involved in the initial identification of the eligible families. But in Bihar panchayat did not exist for more than two decades-elections were held only in May-June 2001, after 1978. In the absence of panchayat, the red cards (for BPL population) were sent to the district magistrates, who arranged for distribution through officials at different levels. In many places the cards were given to the PDS dealers themselves for distribution; and they, instead of distributing all the cards, kept a considerable part for themselves. Field surveys have found many eligible poor people are without the card (ibid.)

Part of the reason for illegal practices by dealers is their low legal income. The official income of a dealer–based on commission payable on the quantum sold—came to around Rs 500 per month in 1997, on the basis of full offtake of the commodities. However, the work of a fair price shop dealer normally takes no more than a few days in a month.

Despite the low income, people are willing to pay large amounts of money to become a ration dealer. In 1999, there were 59,000 dealers. The licences were given mainly to followers of the ruling party. The demand for dealership is because of the scope for fraudulent earnings from the sale of commodities to non-card-holders. The officials of the food and civil supply department take no action to stop the malpractices, so long as they get their share from the dealers. Many dealers are also local level politicians and their malpractices are overlooked.

Since 1997, as per the GOI guidelines, vigilance committees have been introduced at various levels: district, sub-division, and panchayat or ward and shop level. Membership of the first type is almost completely politicised and it is mainly local level politicians who are appointed. At the shop level, the members are usually selected by the PDS dealers themselves and they are often not aware of the task involved. Seeing the extent of corruption in the PDS, recently, in 2001, the Essential Commodities Act was invoked to improve the situation. But it is unlikely that there will be any noticeable improvement; those who are to implement the order are themselves thoroughly corrupted.

PART–III
THE ECONOMY OF WEST BENGAL

8

Resource Mobilisation and Deployment

West Bengal is a Leftist-dominated state, the Communist Party of India (Marxist) (CPM) being in power for more than a quarter century, since 1977. The communists are expected to be better at resource mobilisation because of the nature of their ideology and organising ability. Although the state is operating under the constraints of the Indian Constitution, its performance should be better than in most other states; there is enough scope in the Constitution for a state government to use its own initiatives. But it was totally belied, as will be evident from the analysis below.

BUDGETARY RESOURCES

The budgetary trend of West Bengal government has been very depressing. The gross fiscal deficit of the state had risen rapidly over the years. On the basis of three-yearly average, it stood at Rs 11,096 crore in 2000-03, rising from Rs 5,340 crore in 1996-99, Rs 1,380 crore in 1988-91, Rs 2143 crore in 1975-78 and Rs 514 crore in 1965-68; that is, a 21.6-fold rise over the 35-year period. As percentage to GSDP, it touched 5.23 in 1996-99, rising from 2.59 in 1987-90. In no other middle income state the situation was so bad. The high growth in fiscal deficit was due to the failure to manage the revenue account properly. The revenue deficit rose to the annual average of Rs 8358 crore in 2000-03, from Rs 544 crore in 1988-91. As percentage to GSDP, it touched 3.33 per cent in 1996-99, from 0.84 in 1987-90 (as cited in chapter 3).

The gravity of the situation may be realized from the fact that in recent years the state had been continuously drawing ways and means advances and overdrafts, and had turned to the fund meant for infrastructure development when neither was available (Statesman 2001 l). This was a product of negligible efforts at larger resource mobilisation, while continuing with lavish unproductive expenditure, as will be evident from the analysis below.

Resource Mobilisation

The growth in resource mobilisation was extremely low. The aggregate of receipts had grown only 16.9 times between 1975-78 and 1996-99 compared with 19.4 times at the level of all-states; the relative share in the latter declining to 6.37 per cent from 7.32. The per capita total receipt was always below the all-states average; in 2000-03, it was respectively Rs 3,481 and Rs 3,861.

In the aggregate again, the proportion of revenue receipt had a noticeable fall. It was down to only 52.0 per cent in 2000-03 from 60.7 in 1996-99 and 72.3 in 1975-78; at the level of all-states, the proportion in the latest period was 65.7 per cent. The growth of revenue receipts in West Bengal was noticeably below the all-States average, and among the selected states it was the second lowest. The per capita receipt was always much below the all-states average; in 2000-03, it was respectively Rs 1,811 and Rs 2,533.

In this situation, naturally the state had to rely more and more on capital receipts. The per capita capital receipt came to Rs 1,670 in 2000-03 as against Rs 1328 for all-states (Table 3.1 and CMIE 2004a). The higher level would not be a matter of concern provided it was used for investment purposes. But here, as will be seen later, a very large portion went to meet the revenue deficit. Below we give a brief look into the composition of revenue and capital receipts in West Bengal.

Revenue Receipts

In the revenue receipts, the proportion of tax revenue was always high, and showed a rising tendency until recently. In 1996-99, it accounted for 81.4 per cent of total as against below 75 per cent in the seventies and earlier; in 2000-03, however, it declined to 74.8 per cent. For all-states, the proportion was always much lower, as may be seen from Table 3.2. The growth in tax revenue was, however, relatively low in West Bengal. Over the entire period of three-and-half decades, between 1965-68 and 1996-99, it increased only 55 times as against 93.0 times for all-states. Consequently, the relative share in the latter's total declined from 10.1 per cent to 6.0 per cent. Among the selected states, West Bengal had the lowest growth in tax revenue.

In non-tax revenue the situation was worse. It had risen only 29.5 times between 1965-68 and 1995-98 as against 57.7 times for all-states. The state's share in all-states total declined form 5.9 per cent to 3.0 per cent. However, in 2000-03, with the annual average amount rising to Rs 3659 crore, the relative share improved to 4.9 per cent. It may be noted here that between 1965-68 and 1975-78, West Bengal had recorded a noticeably high growth in NTR collection, and the relative share rose to as much as 11.0 per cent. Thus, it was in the CPM's period that the growth decelerated.

Composition of Tax Revenue

In the tax revenue again, the relative share of own collection showed a noticeable fall over the years. In 1965-68, the OTR contributed as much as 75.5

per cent of the total but in 1975-78 it was down to 68.9 per cent and further to 63.4 per cent in 1995-98. The downward movement is continuing; in 2000-03, with the annual average amount collected at Rs 6510 crore, it was 59.9 percent. The growth in OTR was far below the all-states' average, as may be seen from Table 3.2.

The state's reliance on tax transfer from the Centre increased greatly over the years. Its contribution in the TTR rose to 36.6 per cent in 1995-98, from 31.1 in 1975-78 and 24.5 in 1965-68. However, the growth in tax transfer was relatively low. For all-states, it was 109.2 times over the entire period as against 84.4 times for West Bengal.

Thus, in both the categories of tax revenue West Bengal had a lower growth than in most other states. While the tax transfer depended on a number of criteria laid down by the Finance Commission (noted in chapter 3), the OTR collection was under the control of the state government. In order to find out the scope for raising the OTR, we give a brief look into its composition and the pattern of growth.

Table 8.1 presents the growth in different taxes over the last two-and-half decades. It is evident that there has not been much diversification in the sources of OTR over the years. In 1975-78, sales tax alone contributed 57.4 per cent of total OTR, rising from 43.6 per cent in 1965-68. In recent years, it rose further to 64.0 per cent during 1996-99. However, in per capita term the collection remained small. It averaged only Rs. 379 in the latest period as against Rs 517 for all-states.

The remaining portion of OTR came mainly from state excise, stamps and registration fee, taxes on goods and passengers, land revenue and vehicle tax. Their combined share stood at 27.9 per cent in 1996-99, declining from 36.0 per cent in 1988-91. Among them, the share of land revenue rose to 13.5 per cent in 1988-91, from only 3.4 per cent in 1975-78, but fell again to 9.1 per cent in 1996-99. In the last four years, there was a continuous fall in collection. Taxes on goods and passengers, which contributed 7.2 per cent in 1975-78, have become negligible now. Of the remaining three, only stamps and registration fee showed a significant growth in the last few years.

Among other items, entertainment tax and tax on electricity duty which together contributed 9.6 per cent of total in 1975-78, had a sharp fall over the years and stood at only 3.5 per cent in 1996-99. The sharpest fall was in entertainment tax, from 4.9 per cent to 1.0 per cent. The contribution from agricultural income-tax has also declined. The only new source that has shown a growth in collection is the tax on profession, etc (Table 8.1).

There was hardly any attempt to raise the tax collection. The tax-GSDP ratio of West Bengal averaged only 5.39 per cent during 1994-97, which was the lowest among the middle-income states. The other Left-dominated state, Kerala, had a ratio of 8.33 per cent in this period (GOI 2000b). The per capita tax collection here was only 78.4 per cent of the all-states' average during 1995-98, a fall from 98.4 per cent in 1975-78 (Table 3.2).

Table 8.1: Trend in composition of West Bengal's Own Tax Revenue (Rs. million)

Items	1975-78	1988-91	1994-5	1995-6	1996-7	1997-8	1998-9	1996-99
	(a.a.)	(a.a.)						(a.a.)
Agrl. Income-tax	40.8 (1.3)	168 (0.9)	82	nil	22	67	159	83 (0.2)
Tax on profession, trade, etc	—	—	999	1075	1155	1235	1400	1263 (2.8)
Land revenue	106.2 (3.4)	2617 (13.5)	5931	7553	4683	4395	3254	4111 (9.1)
Stamps & regist. fees	205.8 (6.6)	1220 (6.3)	2820	3040	3098	3358	3722	3393 (7.5)
Sales tax	1798.7 (57.4)	10845 (56.0)	20912	24472	27042	28443	31180	28888 (64.0)
State excise	282.8 (9.0)	1423 (7.4)	2330	2668	3268	3588	4000	3619 (8.0)
Taxes on vehicles	122.7 (3.9)	577 (3.0)	1134	1191	1343	1479	1581	1468 (3.3)
Taxes on goods & passgs.	227.0 (7.2)	1129 (5.8)	2163	78	1	neg.	——	neg.
Taxes on elect. duty	146.7 (4.7)	301 (1.6)	228	516	883	1369	1174	1142 (2.5)
Entertainment tax	153.1 (4.9)	346 (1.8)	460	——	450	434	418	434 (1.0)
Urban immov. property	2.2 (neg.)	11 (neg.)	17	19	23	21	31	25 (neg.)
OTR Total	3132.7 (100.0)	19357 (100.0)	37303	41329	42589	45168	47745	45167 (100.0)

Source: As in Table 3.3.

Composition of Non-Tax Revenue

In non-tax revenue also the state's own collection was poor. It had risen only 14.9 times over the period of nearly three-and-half decades, between 1965-68 and 1995-98, as against nearly four times as much at the level of all-states. Consequently, in the all-states' collection, West Bengal's share declined from 6.5 per cent in 1965-68 to 4.3 in 1975-78 and then to 1.7 in 1995-98. In the last few years, however, there has been some significant improvement. During 2000-03, with the amount annually averaging Rs 881.7 crore, the share rose to 2.66 per cent. This is, however, the result of a sudden jump in collection to as much as Rs 1214.5 crore in 2000-01; in the following two years it became around half (CMIE 2004a).

The state's dependence on grants from the Centre increased greatly over the years. In the total NTR, its share rose to 79 per cent in 1975-78, from 43.9 in 1965-68, and then declined to 71.8 per cent in 1995-98; during 2000-03, however, it rose again to 75.9 per cent, with the amount annually averaging Rs 2777 crore. All these were much higher than the all-states' average (Table 3.2). In the aggregate of grants to all-states, however, West Bengal's share declined from 6.40 per cent in 1975-78 to 5.17 in 1996-99 and 3.71 per cent in 2000-03.

There was ample scope for raising the ONTR, as evident from Table 8.2 below. To look at the group-wise collection first: Economic services had a sharp fall over the years; the relative share declining from as much as 52.8 per cent in 1975-78 to 34.8 in 2000-03 with a growth in collection of only 7.7 times. This fall is at least partly due to the recent reform measures. The highest growth was in general services, and its share was doubled over the period, contributing 30.9 per cent in 1996-99. Interest receipts also recorded a good growth in collection. The most distressing performance was in social services and dividend and profit. The former had recorded a growth of only 6.20 times over the 28-year period, and the relative share was down to 10.3 per cent in 2000-03. The dividend and profits from state enterprises continued to be negligible. During 2000-03 it contributed an average of Rs 28 million, a mere 0.32 per cent of the ONTR (Table 8.2 and ibid.).

As regards the details of collection under some of the groups, in economic services, the crop husbandry which contributed a fifth of the total in 1975-78, provided only 2.5 per cent in 1996-99. Forestry and wildlife became the most important item in recent years; the relative share rising to 23.5 per cent from 18.9, with a four-fold rise in collection. This of course, did not mean that there was no scope for larger collection. Timber smuggling continued despite legislative measures. There are a number of items with high potential, but these remained largely unexploited. The collection from fisheries continued to be very small, and so also from tourism. Irrigation projects also could have made a much larger contribution, provided proper steps were taken at the right time.

In social services, medical and public health was the most important item, contributing 60.0 per cent of total in 1996-99, followed at a great distance by education etc with 9.1 per cent. Both the items have ample potential for larger collection. Only recently some attempts have been made to raise it; but this was opposed by the vested interests. The health facilities in the state have deteriorated to an alarming extent and people have lost faith in it; they are ready to pay ten times as much to a private medical service but not to government hospital. What is required is raising the fees simultaneously with a demonstration of improved services. In educational institutions, fees have not been raised at least for four decades. But the quality of services has also deteriorated greatly. It has to be seen to be believed what the teachers, at least in general education, do. Instead of taking the classes sincerely, they are more interested in expanding the business of private tuition. There is need for dealing the educational institutions with a strong hand, and raising the fees for services by at least ten times.

As regards dividend and profits, the state enterprises are in such a poor state that it is a misnomer to call them enterprises. There are 82 PSUs in the state, including 71 government companies and 11 statutory corporations, with total investment at Rs 10,633 crore in 1999. On the equity amounting to Rs 3,227 crore, the dividend paid this year was a meagre Rs 92 lakh, a 0.02 per cent return. The state budgetary support for companies increased from Rs 800 crore in 1996-97 to over Rs 2000 crore in 1998-99 (BI 2000). The accumulate losses of public sector units increased from Rs. 45,527 crore in 1999-00 to Rs 60,996 crore in 2001-02.

An idea about how the companies are managed may be obtained from the CAG report for the year ending March 1999. It has raised many objections related to serious irregularities like theft, defalcations, non-recovery of dues and loss of revenue to the extent of about Rs 840 crore. And such irregularities were committed even by persons at the very top. For example, senior state officials in six state companies, including the WBIDC chairman (present Speaker in the Parliament), spent over $ 112,000 during tours in violation of government rules. In most cases, the officers did not even submit vouchers (Statesman 2001 k).

Central Transfers

The transfers from Union government under the revenue account have shown a relative decline over the years, as evident from Table 3.5. In 1996-99, West Bengal accounted for only 6.4 per cent of the aggregate of transfer to all-states, declining from 7.4 per cent in 1975-78. The per capita transfer stood at Rs 518.35 in 1996-99, which was 78.6 per cent of the all-states' average, and among the selected states it was the lowest but one; earlier, the relative position was better. It needs to be noted however that, in the state's total revenue, the central transfer constituted a higher proportion than at the level of all-states.

In the total transfer to West Bengal, the proportion of tax transfer was significantly higher than the average for all-states. It increased from 59.2 per

Table 8.2: Trend in Composition of ONTR in West Bengal (Rs million)

Items	1975-78	1988-91[a]	1994-5	1995-6	1996-7	1997-8	1998-9	1996-99
	(a.a.)	(a.a.)						(a.a.)
Interest receipts	95.1 (12.5)	467.0	890	509	1127	1049	486	887 (21.3)
Dividend & profit	1.5 (0.20)	77.7	10	4	5	18	4	9 (0.22)
General services	114.7 (15.1)	390.1	679	877	1105	1435	1331	1290 (30.9)
Social services	147.3 (19.4)	385.1	489	476	424	606	690	573 (13.7)
Education, etc	-	-	60	138	38	61	57	52 (1.2)
Medical etc	-	-	335	226	287	390	355	344 (8.2)
Economic services	400.6 (52.8)	821.3	1352	1408	1513	1386	1333	1411 (33.8)
Crop husbandry	81.3 (10.7)	29.7	29	33	35	35	34	35 (0.84)
Animal husbandry	7.8 (1.0)	13.4	29	25	28	44	40	37 (0.89)
Fishery	2.3 (0.30)	7.2	14	8	6	22	25	18 (0.43)
Forestry & wildlife	75.8 (10.0)	217.2	446	443	470	332	192	331 (7.9)
Cooperation	2.9 (0.38)	12.8	26	23	25	27	38	30 (0.72)
Major & med. irrig.	7.5 (0.99)	15.2	30	28	28	24	29	27 (0.65)
Minor irrigation	-	40.5	53	51	58	54	65	59 (1.4)
Industries	41.8 (5.5)	132.8	205	206	259	154	150	188 (4.5)
Tourism	-	8.6	4	14	17	18	17	17 (0.41)
ONTR Total	759.0 (100.)	2075.3	3420	3275	4174	4495	3845	4171 (100.0)

Note: a: data under this column refer to 1988-90 in respect of all the sub-items under economic services.
Source: As in Table 3.3.

cent in 1975-78 to 68.9 per cent in 1996-99 as against from 52.7 to 61.7 per cent in the latter. Thus, the share of grants was relatively low in West Bengal. In the tax transfers, the major portion came from the union excise duties, but the proportion was below that for all-states (Table 3.5).

In grants, the composition has, changed substantially over the years. During 1975-78, the state plan schemes constituted only 22.4 per cent but in 1996-99 it was as much as 50.0 per cent. The share of centrally sponsored schemes also increased, from 11.7 per cent to 26.5 per cent over the period. The proportion for non-plan grants, on the other hand, had a sharp fall; it was down to 19.7 per cent in 1996-99 from 61.2 in 1975-78. In non-plan grants, the statutory grants declined noticeably, from 84.4 per cent to 59.3 per cent. These changes were more or less in keeping with the general pattern, and on the whole for the better as it increased the state's flexibility in planning and development.

The criteria on which Central transfers are made have been noted in Chapter 3. In the context of West Bengal—a state with very high disparity in development among the regions—one point needs to be emphasised. Kolkata is a mega city and there is a natural tendency to concentrate everything within or around it. The state government also did not make any serious effort to undo it. It is probably necessary to separate Kolkata from West Bengal, for then the state's per capita income will be much lower and this will enable the backward regions to get more funds from the Centre. Until this is done, there should be separate calculation of transfers for North and South Bengal by taking into account their respective per capita income and backwardness. There should also be an arrangement for the funds to come directly to these regions, so that Kolkata does not deduct its 'commission' and actually transfers a lower amount.

Capital Receipts

In the rapid growth of capital receipts noted earlier, the most important source was loans and advances from the Centre. Between 1975-78 and 1996-99, it had grown 28.9-fold as against 23.9 times for capital receipts as a whole. Consequently, its share in the total rose to 66.6 per cent from 55.1. West Bengal's dependence on Central loans was much higher than in most other states. The central loans per capita stood at Rs 503.41 here in 1996-99 as against the average of Rs. 336.43 for all-states.

In the central loans, the proportion for non-plan purposes was very high and showed a sharp rise over the years. During 1996-99 it stood at 71.6 per cent, rising from 49.5 in 1975-78. This, however, came almost entirely from small savings in recent years. The loans for state plan, on the other hand, had a noticeable fall, from 33.2 per cent in 1975-78 to 28.3 per cent in 1996-99. The two other heads, central plan schemes and centrally sponsored schemes, always had a very low share and in recent years it was negligible. This pattern is different from the general trend. For all-states, the share of non-plan loans was lower, averaging 50.2 per cent in 1996-99, and for state plan scheme higher, at 44.2 per cent.

The next important item in capital receipts was internal debt, and its share had risen significantly over the years. With a growth of 33.9 times between 1975-78 and 1996-99, its relative share rose to 12.3 per cent from 8.7. This is however, still a relatively low dependence on internal debt; at the level of all-states, it contributed 18.5 per cent in 1996-99. In internal debt, market loans accounted for as much as 83.5 per cent here during 1996-99 as against 75.8 per cent for all-states.

Of the remaining two items, small savings, etc and recovery of loans, collection from the former had a rapid growth; there was a 43-fold rise over the 14-year period. However, the relative share was still only 6.8 per cent of total in 1996-99 as against the average of 12.5 per cent for all-states. On the recovery of loans also the state did not perform well. It contributed only 6.3 per cent in the latest period as against 7.7 per cent at the level of all-states.

This pattern of raising capital resources made West Bengal a heavily indebted state. At the end of March 2002, the total debt of the state stood at Rs 58275 crore; giving a per capital debt of Rs 7,264 as against Rs 5806 for all-states. In relation to the GSDP, it increased from 26.19 per cent in 2000 to 43.4 per cent in 2003 compared with 23.0 and 28.7 per cent respectively for all-states (Table 3.6; CMIE 2004a; Telegraph 2005b). In 2004-05, the states debt teached Rs. 99,200 crore, and on per capita basis Rs. 12,366 (using the population of 2001). The state is indebted to the centre to the extent of Rs. 15,674 crore, the third highest among the states (Statesman 2005e).

Trend in Expenditure

As the resource mobilisation was poor, the growth in expenditure could not be high. Between 1975-78 and 1995-98, West Bengal's aggregate of budgetary expenditure had risen only 14.4 times compared with 17.2 times for all-states. The state's share in the latter was down to 6.1 per cent from 7.3. The per capita expenditure was always much below the all-states' average. In 2000-03, it was respectively Rs 3,429 and Rs 3,768.

In the aggregate of expenditure, the proportion of revenue expenditure had a sharp rise. The average for 1996-99 came to 82.1 per cent compared with 71.6 per cent in 1975-78. This was, however, a general trend; at the level of all-states also it was from 67.3 per cent to 82.6 per cent in this period. As the revenue expenditure increased fast, naturally the capital expenditure declined. Below we give a brief look into the trend in composition of revenue and capital expenditure.

Revenue Expenditure

In the revenue expenditure, the developmental had a low growth, and consequently, its relative share declined to 58.1 per cent in 1996-99 from 67.2 per cent in 1975-78. West Bengal's proportion was always below the all-states average, as evident from Table 3.7. Among the selected states also it was lower than in most of them. Thus, while the development expenditure got neglected, the non-developmental multiplied rapidly. The latter had a 26-fold rise in this period.

In the development expenditure, social services accounted for the lion's share. During 1996-99, it stood at 67.5 per cent as against 59.9 per cent for all-states. However, the per capita level remained below the latter's; during 2000-03, it was respectively Rs 1010 and Rs 1062. In social services, education received the highest priority; the relative share rose to 56.6 per cent in 1996-99 from 49.4 in 1975-78. Although the latest proportion is higher than the all-states' average, the per capita expenditure on education was very low here. The average for 1996-99 came to Rs 349 as against Rs 411 for all-states. Most of the other items had a low growth, as evident from Table 8.3. The expenditure on medical, health and family welfare increased only 14.2 times, and its relative share declined from 28.0 per cent to 23.0. However, the per capita expenditure was relatively high in recent years; during 2000-03 it came to Rs 146.22 compared with Rs 132.38 for all-states.

In economic services, until recently rural development accounted for the largest proportion. Its share rose to 30.1 per cent in 1996-99, from 28.4 in 1985-88; but in 2000-03 it was down to only 22.8 per cent. Agriculture and allied services, which accounted for the highest proportion earlier, had a sharp fall in this period declining from 61.1 per cent in 1975-78 to only 25.6 in 1996-99 and 24.8 in 2000-03. In agriculture, crop husbandry had the lowest growth, and its relative share declined to 18.8 per cent in 1996-99 from 29.8 in 1975-78. The highest growth was registered by fisheries, followed by forestry and wildlife, soil and water conservation and animal husbandry. However, even with a 24-fold rise in expenditure, the share of fisheries stood at only 6.2 per cent in 1996-99. Forestry and wildlife recorded a 21-fold rise and the relative share rose to 17.8 per cent from 5.8. Among other items, in economic series, irrigation and flood control, transport and communication, and special area programmes were important in recent years. However, the share of Irrigation and flood control declined to 14.9 per cent in 1996-99, from around 20 per cent in 1975-78.

As regards non-development expenditure, its relative share in the total rose to 41.9 per cent in 1996-99 form 32.8 per cent in 1975-78. This was a very high proportion in relation to the all-states' average; the latter being 37.4 per cent in the latest period. In non-development expenditure, the most burdensome was interest payment, accounting for half of the total in 1996-99 as against 34.4 per cent in 1975-78. As percentage to total revenue receipts of the state, it was 26.52 in 1995-99, rising from 18.57 in 1990-95; during 2000-03, it shot up to 44.3 per cent, with the annual amount averaging Rs 6430 crore; for all-states, it was only 23.6 per cent.

The next important item was expenditure on administrative services, with a share of 23.6 per cent in 1996-99 as against 40.4 per cent in 1975-78. Within

Table 8.3: Trend in Composition of Revenue Expenditure in West Bengal (Rs. million)

Items	1975-78 (a.a.)	1988-91 (a.a.)	1994-95	1995-96	1996-7	1997-8	1998-9	1996-99 (a.a.)	growth*
Revenue Expenditure	6141.1	41913	76307	86263	103623	113219	142429	119757	19.50
I Development expenditure	4123.5	—	47122	51956	62698	64454	81639	69597	16.88
1. Social Services	2728.2	18658	30448	33725	40678	43913	56399	46997	17.23
Education, etc	1348.0[a]	10618	17794	19569	24201	25303	30235	26580	19.72
Medical, etc	763.9[b]	3525	5262	6175	7081	7635	11327	8681	11.36
Water supply & sanit.	—	643	1446	1299	1479	2186	2789	2151	—
Welfare of SC, ST & OBC	—	627	883	993	1218	1041	1561	1273	—
Social security & welfare	234.0	757	1119	1557	1687	1880	2723	2097	8.96
Nutrition	61.4[c]	21	58	85	104	104	143	117	1.91
2. Economic services	1395.2	10725	16674	18231	22019	20541	25241	22600	16.20
Agriculture & allied	852.5[d]	2777	3967	4406	5187	5221	6972	5793	6.80
Crop husbandry	254.0	682	692	763	902	992	1368	1087	4.28
Soil & water conservation	9.9	68	141	128	179	83	155	139	14.04
Animal husbandry	62.0	320	488	545	661	702	1097	820	13.23
Fisheries	15.2	135	229	269	361	224	501	632	23.82
Forestry & wildlife	49.1	439	791	876	1015	975	1112	1034	21.06
Cooperation	34.0	162	159	189	223	253	416	297	8.75
Rural development	—	2938	5533	5641	7140	5925	7334	6800	—
Special area programmes	74.7	458	1061	1052	1332	1385	1708	1475	19.75
Irrigation & flood control	298.6[e]	1733	2164	2443	2779	3230	4104	3371	11.29
Minor irrigation	136.1	—	—	1122	1302	1597	2075	1685	12.18
Energy	—	785	508	822	1575	914	588	1026	—
Industry & minerals	96.5	696	1014	1056	1060	1051	1182	1098	11.37
VSI	37.1	—	607	677	688	654	743	695	18.73
Transport & Communication	228.2	1321	2115	2506	2576	2417	2843	2612	11.45
Civil supplies	-	-21	25	30	37	54	40	—	

Contd.

(Table 8.3)

II Non-development expend.	1853.0	—	27131	32461	39140	46728	58737	48202	26.01
1. Interest payment	637.8	5352	13274	16162	19403	24100	29499	24334	38.15
2. Administrative services	749.3	—	7371	8349	9762	10615	13707	11361	15.16
District Administration	39.6	159	241	285	329	361	562	417	10.54
Police	500.4	2688	4630	5224	6070	6448	8383	6967	13.92
3. Pension	112.1[f]	1698	4013	4657	6247	7913	10118	8093	72.19
III Compensation & assignments to local bodies & PRIs	164.6	1159	2054	1845	1786	2036	2052	1958	11.90

Notes : a : includes scientific services and research ; b: includes water supply and sanitation ; c : this is food and nutrition and included under agriculture and allied services ; d : includes minor irrigation and food and nutrition but excludes cooperation; e : covers multipurpose river projects, irrigation, navigation, drainage and flood control and minor irrigation ; f : including miscellaneous general services; *: in multiples.

Source: As in Table 8.2.

administrative services, a distressing aspect is that the state spent a very low amount on district administration, the relative share declining to 3.67 per cent from 5.28 per cent over the period; for all-states, it averaged as much as 10.24 per cent in 1996-99. The expenditure on police, on the other hand, was very high; the relative share stood at 61.3 per cent in 1996-99, higher than the average for all-states. However, in per capita term it was lower than in the latter, being respectively Rs 141 and Rs 160 in 2000-03.

The highest growth in expenditure was recorded by pension payment. There was a 72-fold rise over the period, and the relative share rose to 16.8 per cent in 1996-99 from 6.0 per cent in 1975-78; the growth at the level of all-states was only 63.4 times. In recent years, this burden has risen further. During 2000-03, the annual average expenditure came to Rs 2199.7 crore, and constituted 9.61per cent of the aggregate of revenue expenditure, rising from 6.76 per cent in 1996-99. This is one of the items that needs to be drastically curtailed. There is no justification for such huge payments on an unproductive account, particularly when the salaries of government employees are no longer low. At the least, the rate of pension for all the grades should be reduced on a sliding scale—with lower rates for upper categories.

As regards the last head of expenditure, compensation and assignments to local bodies and PRIs, although the state boasts about its PRIs, on transfer of funds to them it is very niggardly. The growth in transfer over the period of nearly two-and-half decades was only 11.9 times, that is, much less than in the aggregate of revenue expenditure. Its relative share consequently declined from 2.68 per cent in 1975-78 to 1.63 per cent in 1996-99. At the level of all-states, on the other hand, the proportion increased from 1.13 per cent to 1.46 per cent, with a growth in expenditure of 31.2 times. In the aggregate of transfer by all-states, West Bengal's share declined from 18.3 per cent to 7.0 per cent over the period.

This was the situation despite the fact that the PRIs own collection was also low. During 1995-98, the own revenue of all tiers of PRIs annually averaged Rs 16.50 crore, which was less than a fifth (18.6 per cent) of what could be collected by the PRIs of Kerala and a little more than half of that by Karnataka. The total revenue of West Bengal's PRIs annually averaged Rs 517.53 crore and constituted only 3.16 per cent of all-states total. The position of urban local bodies was, however, much better. Their own revenue annually averaged Rs 564.45 crore during 1995-98 and total revenue Rs 815.86 crore; the latter constituted 7.83 per cent of all-states total (GOI 2000b: Annexure VIII. 2A).

Capital Expenditure

The growth of capital disbursements in West Bengal has been very low despite a rapid rise in capital receipts. This was because the latter was used largely for meeting the revenue deficit in recent years; during 1996-99, it was to the extent of 53.8 per cent here compared with only 35.7 per cent at the level of all-states. The growth in capital disbursement was only 19 times between 1975-78 and 2000-03, from the annual average of Rs 244 crore to Rs 4,624 crore, as against 37 times in revenue expenditure. The per capita capital disbursement here stood at Rs 576 in 2000-03 compared with Rs 683 for all-states.

In capital disbursement again, the share of development expenditure was very low. During 1996-99, it was to the extent of 34.0 per cent, rising from 28.3 in 1975-78; both were much below the all-states average. The per capita expenditure here was only 68 per cent of the latter's in 1995-98, being respectively Rs 139 and Rs 204 (Table 3.7). Moreover, the development expenditure fluctuated widely from year to year; during 1994-99, it was between Rs 1,407 crore in 1996-97 and only Rs 595 crore the next year. In the development expenditure, economic services accounted for the overwhelming proportion; during 1996-99, it was to the extent of 89.7 per cent. Within it, irrigation and flood control, energy and transport and communication generally had high shares.

The highest proportion in capital disbursement generally went for loans and advances. During 1996-99 it averaged 45.0 per cent, rising from 35.3 in 1988-91and 40.2 in 1975-78. This was almost entirely for development purposes, and within it economic services accounted for the dominant share—often above 90 per cent. Whether these loans were utilised properly is, however, a different matter. The fact that the repayments were tardy speaks of their poor utilisation. The repayment of loans to the Centre accounted for 17.0 per cent of the capital disbursements in 1996-99, declining from 34.0 in 1988-91and 27.8 in 1975-78; at the level of all-states, it was 18.6 per cent in the latest period.

With this nature of resource deployment, the development of the state naturally suffered. The proportion of development expenditure in the grand total of budgetary expenditure here stood at only 56.7 per cent in 1995-98, which was significantly below the all-states average. The per capita total development expenditure in West Bengal came to only Rs 935.51 in 1995-98, which was 71.0 per cent of the latter's; during 1975-78 it was 84.4 per cent (Table 3.7).

Plan Expenditure

The plan expenditures were also low here. Per capita plan outlay on five-yearly basis increased from Rs 48 in the Second Plan to Rs 281 in the Fifth, and then to Rs 1,435 in the Eighth plan, at current prices. All these were much below the all-states average, and the disparity increased over the years. In the Eighth Plan, West Bengal's per capita was only 68.4 per cent of all-states average, declining from 94.1 per cent in the Second plan. The cumulative total till March 1997 came to Rs 4,931 as against Rs 7,418 for all-states, that is, the former only 66.5 per cent of the latter. In recent years also the situation has not shown any improvement. The proposed outlay for Tenth Plan (2002-07) is Rs 28,641 crore, giving a per capita of Rs 3572, which is 64.3 per cent of the all-states' (different plan documents).

The sectoral pattern of outlay in some of the Five-year plans is presented in Table 8.5. It is evident that energy alone has been taking a large and increasing share of the total. In the last three plans, Seventh through Ninth, on the average it stood at 30.1 per cent, rising from 19.0 in the first three plans. In the Tenth plan also this sector is getting 27.4 per cent as against the all-states average of 16.2 per cent. No doubt, energy is a critical sector whose output is required by every other sectors; but if so large a share is going to one sector only then what is left for others.

In social services, the proportion for both education and health declined, despite the fact that there is still an utter lack of facilities, particularly in rural areas. In the last three plans, education etc received an average of 4.3 per cent as against more than four times as much in the first three plans. The expenditure on water supply and sanitation was negligible in the first three plans and in the recent plans also it was low, although much remains to be done in this critical area. For social services as a whole, the state has provided Rs 7868 crore in the Tenth Plan, constituting 27.5 per cent of the grand total; for all-states, it is 31.0 per cent. On per capita term, the outlay is respectively Rs 981 and Rs 1723; that is, the former only 56.9 per cent of the latter.

In the productive sectors, the proportion for agriculture declined sharply in the recent plans. Including irrigation and flood control, it came to 11.9 per cent in the last three plans (Seventh through Ninth), declining from 21.4 in the first three. In the Tenth Plan their share has declined further, being only 9.8 per cent; at the level of all-states, it is as much as 23.1 per cent. In per capita term, the outlays are respectively Rs 351 and Rs 1280. Another very important sector for rural areas, village and small-scale industries, was also neglected. While industry and minerals as a whole got 6 to 8 per cent in the different plans, the share of VSI in them was generally less than a fifth. Even if one considers the fact that the capital requirement is less for VSI, given the magnitude of problems the allocations were indeed very small. Thus, the sectors which were expected to play a crucial role in alleviating absolute poverty were largely neglected; and this happened in a leftist-ruled state.

The allocations are probably not so important, the more important is how the funds are spent. And here West Bengal is in a very poor state. There is an utter lack of control over expenditure, and time sense with project execution authorities. Leakage of funds to unauthorised purposes is a common experience in the state.

The CAG report for 1998-99 brought out gross mismanagement of funds, financial indiscipline, favouritism, poor supervision, monitoring and accounting in West Bengal. And recently, in the report for 2000-01, it was pointed out that 18 PSUs did not have their accounts audited since 1997-98 in spite of repeated reminders from the CAG. It also mentions many cases where accounts have not been prepared since inception, like the Sisal plantation scheme (1955-56),

Table 8.5: Trend in Sectoral Outlay in the Five-year Plans of West Bengal (Rs million)

Sectors	*Total for first 3 plans*	*Seventh Plan*	*Eight Plan*	*Ninth Plan*[a]
	(1951-66)	(1985-90)	(1992-97)	(1997-02)
Agriculture & allied actvts.	736 (14.1)	3072 (6.7)	3616 (3.7)	8722 (4.2)
Rural development	-	3392 (7.4)	6844 (7.0)	13531 (6.5)
Irrigation & flood control	380 (7.3)	4165 (9.0)	8692 (8.9)	17192 (8.3)
Energy	991[b] (19.0)	12623 (27.4)	28737 (29.4)	69080 (33.4)
Industry & minerals	333 (6.4)	3721 (8.1)	7024 (7.2)	16245 (7.8)
Transport	575 (11.0)	2860 (6.2)	5956 (6.1)	13036 (6.3)
Education, sports, etc	949 (18.2)	2298 (5.0)	3018 (3.1)	9833 (4.8)
Health & family welfare	482 (9.2)	993 (2.2)	1365 (1.4)	11987 (5.8)
Water supply, sanit., etc	17[c] (0.3)	5689 (12.3)	9509 (9.7)	5334 (2.6)
Total (including others)	5210 (100.0)	46142 (100.0)	97611 (100.0)	207000 (100.0)

Notes: a: proposed outlay; b: relates to power only; c: only water supply.
Source: GOW 1979, 1999a.

Oriental Gas Company (1960-61), government sales emporia in Calcutta and Howrah (1951-52), and the silk reeling scheme (1956-57).

The CAG has concluded thus in the report of 2001: "the lack of accountability arising out of the failure to prepare accounts by the departmentally-run units for years on end is a matter of serious concern, as large amounts of public funds are involved coupled with the possibility of serious financial irregularities remaining undetected for long periods. Since these are departmentally run commercial units, responsibility for failure to ensure accountability of public funds should be fixed on the Heads of Departments. The government should re-examine the justification of continued release of budgetary funds to units without finalized accounts and without assessing their financial performance...." (quoted in The Telegraph 2005: 17). This was written three years back but no one has been brought to book so far.

The legislature, empowered to oversee the PSUs' working and justify their continued funding, also takes little interest. There are many critical observations in the CAG reports of different years which have not been taken up for discussion by the West Bengal assembly. The report of March 1999 and 2002 reveals that several items, submitted a decade or more earlier, were not taken up for discussion at all. (ibid. and The Statesman 2002j: 1, 5).

As regards losses caused by delay in execution of projects, we may cite here only one instance. The Kona Expressway was scheduled to be completed in four years at a cost of Rs 3.90 crore. But it took 22 years and Rs 28.56 crore to complete just Phase-I of the project. The CAG report for the year 2000-01 states that the land acquired for rehabilitation for Rs 87.05 lakh had not been used for 12 years, resulting in a loss of Rs 1.04 crore in interest alone. Also, the delay had multiplied the land acquisition cost by 15 times (Statesman 2002 Z7).

Poor work culture of West Bengal, which is almost legendary, eats into the allocations substantially. It has to be seen to be believed how much money a government employee here earns by doing how much work. Often, many employees work for no more than two hours in a day. And then there are too many holidays. In this situation, it is no surprise that plan expenditures often remained much below the outlay proposed. The mid-term appraisal of the Ninth Plan found that the shortfall in expenditure in 1997-98 and 1998-99 were to the extent of 46.4 per cent in agriculture, 36.5 per cent in irrigation, 31.8 per cent in social services and 30.2 per cent in industry (GOW 1999). In contrast to the West Bengal scenario, in Kerala—the other Left-Front ruled state—the overall plan expenditure exceeded the approved outlay (Statesman 2000 i).

BANKING RESOURCE

Commercial Banks

The commercial banks are traditionally urban-oriented and the measures taken over the years did not bring any sharp break in it. The performance of the most resourceful group of banks, the scheduled commercial banks, was very poor in West Bengal. Between 1973 and 2001, the growth in deposits was only 52.7 times, around half the rate for all-India. The state's share in all-India total deposit declined from 12.8 per cent to 7.2 per cent over the period. The per capita deposit which was higher than the all-India average in 1977 became lower in recent years. In 2003, it was respectively Rs 10,772 and Rs 12,450.The performance in rural areas was extremely poor, as may be seen from Table 3.11.

On credit deployment, the situation was more depressing. The aggregate of credit outstanding in West Bengal had a growth of only 43 times between 1969 and 2001 as against 154 times for all-India. None of the selected states also had such a low growth. West Bengal's share in all-India total declined from 19.4 per cent in 1969 to 8.2 in 1987 and further to 5.4 per cent in 2001. The per capita credit in 2003 was only 70.2 per cent of the all-India average as against 141.6 per cent in 1977 (Table 3.11).

The credit deployment in rural areas was extremely low. In the total outstanding, its share was only 8.0 per cent in 2001, rising from 7.7 in 1987; the all-India average in these years were, respectively, 10.1 and 14.5 per cent. The C-D ratio was always much below the all India average; in 2003, it was respectively 48.2 and 59.4 per cent. For rural areas, it was extremely low, as may be seen from Table 3.11. The rural ratio was lower than the urban ratio here, in contrast to the situation in most other states. Thus, instead of developing the rural areas, funds collected there were diverted to urban areas.

The district-wise scenario was very depressing in West Bengal. In June 1999, the per capita deposit of Uttar Dinajpur stood at only Rs 1,099 which was around a sixth of the state's average (Rs 6,469). The situation of per capita credit was worse. Uttar Dinajpur had only one-eighth of the state average, the amount being respectively Rs 326 and Rs 2,713. In relation to 1994, this disparity is lower with regard to deposit but higher in respect of credit (GOW 2000, 1995).

The variation in C-D ratio was very high. In 1999, at the lowest it was 12.8 per cent in North 24-parganas as against the state average of 41.9 and the highest of 61.6 in Calcutta; five districts had less than 20 per cent. The rural C-D ratio this year was 59.8 per cent at the highest, in Cooch Behar, and at the lowest 14.6 in Jalpaiguri. This is a sharp worsening of situation over what existed in 1974. The highest and the lowest ratios then were respectively 93.0 per cent and 25.5 per cent. If the government had the slightest intention of developing the rural areas, such draining out of resources would not have been allowed. The deposit itself was low in rural areas, and then the meagre resources were transferred to urban areas. By legislative measure, the banks should have been compelled to maintain a C-D ratio of at least 100 per cent in rural areas.

Regional Rural Banks

The RRBs, as noted in chapter 3, were launched with some laudable objectives, to provide credit to the weaker sections. Their performance in West

Bengal, at least with regard to deposit mobilisation, was not bad. Between December 1981 and March 2002, the growth in deposit here was 197 times compared with the all-India average of 133 times. The deposit per branch had risen 67-fold in this period as against 44 times at the national level. Among the selected states, West Bengal had the highest deposit per branch in the latest year (Table 3.12).

On the provision of credit, however, the situation was very disappointing. In the all-India total of credit outstanding from RRBs in March 2002, West Bengal's share was only 6.0 per cent, rising from 3.9 in 1981. The advances per branch were always below the national average. The C-D ratio had a sharp fall over the years, declining from 94.7 per cent to only 33.2 per cent, and it was always much below the national average.

An important reason behind the low C-D ratio is the high level of overdues. Percentage of overdues to demand increased from 36.1in 1996 to 43 in 2002; at the national level, it was from 25.7 to 29. Earlier, in 1983-84, it was respectively 62.0 and 49.8 per cent. The level of NPA in West Bengal stood at 21 per cent in 2002 as against 16 per cent in all-India (NABARD 2002a).The high level of overdues was largely due to political interference in the disbursal of credit. In granting credit, economic considerations were often a casualty. Some times the repayment was not even considered a necessity due to political influence (200 20: BP, III). Of course, the banks were also responsible, at least partly. Misutilisation of fund by the beneficiary was not infrequent and this was largely due to lack of follow-up of credit and proper guidance.

Co-Operative Banks

The co-operative credit societies in West Bengal continued to be very weak despite so many measures taken over the years. The weakness is first reflected in the number of societies and their membership. The former reached the maximum of 23,712, covering all types, in 1989-90, from less than half this level in 1982, but dropped again to only 10,450 in 1998; the fall was due to closing down or merger of weak societies. The membership also fluctuated similarly. But ignoring it, the growth between 1970 and 1998 was only 96 per cent as against 209 per cent at the national level. The state accounted for only 2.94 per cent of the latter's total in the latest year (Table 3.10).

As regards the level of operation, the working capital of all the credit societies together had risen only 14.3 times over the period of nearly three decades, 1970 to 1998, as against 48.1 times for all-India; the share in the latter's total declined from 3.66 per cent to 1.09 per cent. In the working capital, deposits contributed a relatively high proportion here, being 53.7 per cent in the latest year as against the all-India average of 50.9 per cent. The proportion of deposit from individuals and others was also relatively high, being respectively 71.7 per cent and 67.6 per cent (ibid. and NABARD 2002).

In the aggregate of working capital, the share of ground level societies was very low. In 1996-97, for primary agricultural and non-agricultural societies together it stood at 22.5 per cent, declining from 43.2 per cent in 1988-89. The PACS had registered a growth of 150.3 per cent—from Rs 220.8 crore to Rs 552.7 crore—over the nine-year period, and for PNACS 15.9 per cent—from Rs 442.0 crore to Rs 512.3 crore; for all credit societies together, the growth in this period was 209 per cent (GOW 1995, 1999). The deposit mobilisation by PACS was very low. Data for recent years are not available, but in 1985, as may be seen from Table 3.10, per society it came to only Rs 4456, constituting 7.80 per cent of all-India average. The situation of PNACS was much better.

The growth in loans and advances was relatively good. For all credit societies, it had risen 253 per cent between 1988-89 and 1996-97, from Rs 574.4 crore to Rs 2,031.4 crore. The share of ground level societies in the loans outstanding, however, declined; for PACS from 18.0 per cent to 14.4 per cent, and for PNACS from 30.6 per cent to 22.1 per cent over the period, as the growth was much less. In the earlier years also the situation was not good. In 1985, loans outstanding per society came to only Rs 1.67 lakh in case of PACS, constituting around a third of all-India average (Table 3.10).

Within the state, inter-district, there was wide variation in level of operation. In case of PACS, membership per society averaged only 250 in Darjeeling at the end of March 1997 as against the highest of 779 in Burdwan. The working capital per society was at the highest Rs 11.16 lakh in Burdwan compared with the lowest of Rs 1.97 lakh in Purulia. There were four districts with less than Rs 4 lakh on this date. Agricultural backwardness does not fully explain the extent of variation (GOW 1999).

Behind thid depressing situation of the co-operative credit institutions, an important reason is the looting of co-operative funds by rural vested interests. It was reported recently that the network has been overtaken by a new bread of Sahukars—all allies of the left front—who use the co-operative funds for amassing personal fortunes and fostering private money lending business. The CAG report for 2001-02records the closure of 1443 PACS, 36 in Birbhum alone. The governments, investment of Rs. 1.90 crore in 638 "closed " co-operatives has gone down the drain. There is no information about the quantum in other societies, 5351 of which have already become bankrupt. The practice of milking co-operatives and discarding them as bankrupt is growing with the connivance of panchayats (Statesman 2003a).

Note

1. Very recently, it has been decided to raise the college tuition fee in general education from Rs 10 to Rs 110 and in Medical èducation for MBBS from Rs 12 to Rs 1,000 per months (Statesman 2001m; 2002 Z 15 :1)

9

Human Resource Development

In relation to the state's geographical area, West Bengal is having an unduly large human population, and it is also growing at an unreasonable rate, as noted in Chapter 2. To convert them into resource is a gigantic task. Huge investment will be required on a continuing basis for creating proper facilities for their development. The net result of the government's efforts so far in some of the areas has been noted in Chapter 2. With regard to educational performance, West Bengal continues to lag behind many of the states, despite having a good base. On the health and hygiene indicators also the state's performance was far from satisfactory (Table 2.4). Below we give a brief look into the extent of facilities created in these areas over the years.

EDUCATION

Right type of education, as noted in chapter 4, is the most essential prerequisite for developing a new society. It was expected that West Bengal, always with a strong Left base, would give the utmost attention to developing the educational facilities. But as will be evident from the analysis below it was all belied. First we look at the level of expenditure on education in the aggregate and for different stages.

Level of Expenditure

The plan expenditure on education had a very low growth in West Bengal, as noted in the preceding Chapter. The relative share in the aggregate of outlay declined from 18.2 per cent in the first three plans to 4.3 per cent in the last three, Seventh through Ninth. The growth in expenditure between the First and Ninth Plan was 83 times as against 306 times in the aggregate of plan outlay. A look at the total budgetary expenditure also does not bring any better picture. Between 1979-82 and 1994-97, the expenditure on education had risen at a compound annual rate of 11.4 per cent, which was nominally higher than the all-states average. In relation to the state's NSDP, the situation was very depressing. It was generally below the all-states average, and in the last two decades could never go beyond 4 per cent.

In the aggregate of expenditure on education, the share of elementary education was very low, and showed a decline over the years. It was down to 31.5 per cent in 1995-96 from 39.0 per cent in 1980-81; at the level of all-states, the proportion was generally around 50 per cent. Kerala, the other Leftist state, also had a much higher proportion than West Bengal's. It is not only relative share, in terms of per pupil expenditure also West Bengal's position was very inferior, being always much below the all-India average, as may be seen from Table 4.1. Further, even the available funds were not utilised properly. Evidences form surveys and reports suggest that funds were systematically mismanaged and there was considerable leakage (Chatterjee 1997).

The secondary education, which received the highest proportion of total expenditure in recent years, was also not in a very good position. Per pupil expenditure was lower than the all-India average in two out of the three time points considered. The position of University and higher education, on the other hand, was much better, being always higher than the national average; in 1995-96, to the extent of as much as 50.6 per cent. This pattern of expenditure speaks of the class character of the Marxist government. The university education is availed by the better off section of population, and its utility for development purpose is not as high as that of primary and secondary education.

Another aspect that needs a mention is the high concentration of educational expenditure in a few districts. In 1970-71, in the aggregate of direct expenditure at Rs 78.94 crore, the share of Calcutta alone was 23.3 per cent, followed by Midnapore 13.05 and 24-Parganas 12.5 per cent. Of the remaining 13 districts, the combined share of six—Cooch Behar, Malda, West Dinajpur, Darjeeling, Purulia and Jalpaiguri—was 13.7 per cent (GOW 1979). Data for recent years are not available, but the situation is unlikely to have improved much.

Facilities Available

With this level of expenditure, naturally the facilities created were far from satisfactory. The availability of schools itself was very low in West Bengal. Percentage of rural population having primary schools within the habitation stood at only 61.2 in 1994 as against 77.8 at the national level. For scheduled castes, the proportions were respectively 58.8 per cent and 64.3 per cent. On upper primary, the coverage was still poor. Only 14.2 per cent of the rural population had it within the habitation as against 37 per cent at the national level. Percentage of villages not having a school with primary stage was 28.9 and those without upper primary 86.3; both were higher than the national average (Table 4.2).

The growth in number of schools was very low here. Between 1956-57 and 2000-01, for primary schools it was only 107 per cent, from 25,272 to 52,385;

the relative share in all-India total declining from 8.8 per cent to 7.7 per cent. During 1991-92 to 1996-97 not a single primary school was started in West Bengal, the total number remaining static at 51,021 (GOW 1999). There was a net shortage of 9,478 primary schools in 2000. For middle schools, the situation was worse. With a negative growth of 24 per cent between 1980-81 and 2000-01, the share in all-India total declined to 1.16 per cent from 2.66 per cent (GOI 1959, 1987a, 2002c). The situation is unlikely to improve in near future. The state has a target of 65,000 primary schools by 2007 but the rate at whichit is progressing, it will take more than 500 years to reach the target; during 2001-03, only 41 schools could be started (Nandy 2003).

The pupil-teacher ratio was high here and continued to rise. At primary stage, it stood at 43.61 in 1994 compared with 40.17 at the national level. After seven years, in 2000-01, it rose to 55 and 43 respectively (Table 4.2 and GOI 2002c). The state government has laid down the norm of 40 students per teacher but there are several primary schools with one teacher for 200 students (Statesman 2002 m). At upper primary also the situation has deteriorated. Whereas in 1994 the ratio was slightly below the national average, in 2000-01 it became much higher, being respectively 46 and 38.The vacant posts are never filled up in time. Presently there are 30,000 vacancies in 10,000 schools across the state, some for more than three years (Stateman 2002 : BP).

As regards the quality of teachers, the proportion untrained is relatively high in West Bengal. In 1994, at primary level, it was 25.74 per cent compared with 14.87 per cent at the national level. At upper primary, these were respectively 14.11 and 13.10 per cent. Apart form this, the politicisation of teachers have also affected the quality of teaching. A large number of teachers are nominated for the panchayat bodies and this affect the teaching work. The practising of private tuition is another problem. Until recently, the government did not give any attention to it, and the teachers, instead of taking their teaching work sincerely were more interested in private tuition. Only in July 2001 the government initiated certain action in this regard.

The schools in West Bengal also suffer due to inadequate number of rooms for instructional purpose. In 1994, sixty-four per cent of the schools here had two rooms or less; for Kerala, it was only 11 per cent. Not only this, a large number was without any room for instruction. The condition of the school buildings is also extremely poor. Only 37.2 per cent of the schools had *pucca* buildings as against 83.7 per cent at the national level. At upper primary also the situation was similar, as may be seen from Table 4.2.

The availability of certain ancillary facilities was very poor. Drinking water was available in only 59.5 per cent of the primary schools in 1994. Urinal facility was not there with 78 per cent of the schools here as against 68 per cent at the national level. At upper primary, however, the position was much better. Eighty-three per cent of the schools had drinking water facility as against 63.5 per cent at the national level. The situation on urinal for girls was very poor in

West Bengal. Taking all levels of school together, it was available to only 15.9 per cent compared with 19.5 per cent at the national level. Presently also the situation is similar.

The position of secondary schools was also not good. In 1994, school within the habitation was there in only 9.6 per cent of the habitations compared with 18.3 per cent at the national level. A large proportion of the students had to walk more than 2 kms, as evident from Table 4.2. The growth in number of schools was very low here. Between 1956-57 and 2000-01, there was only a 97 per cent rise, from 3,500 to 6,882, as against 142 per cent at the national level; the relative share in the latter's total was down to 7.85 per cent from 9.64.

The pupil-teacher ratio in West Bengal's secondary schools was very high. In 1994, it was found to be 37.95 as against the all-India average of 30.21. Among the selected states, West Bengal's ratio was the highest. The situation of rural areas was gloomier; the ratio here stood at 39.23 compared with 29.33 for all-India. The latest position is much worse, being respectively 42 and 31. The vacancies for teachers presently exceed 30,000 at the secondary level (Sanyal 2002).

On the quality of teachers, the less said the better. The teachers are products of the state's universities, and the latter are in a despicable situation. And then, over 40 per cent of the schools presently do not have headmasters (ibid.). It may be noted that in many schools the percentage of students passing out is very low. Recently, the government had threatened 500 schools of losing their affiliation unless the pass percentage improved to at least 40 per cent by 2002 (Statesman 2000 i). The examination system is also full of loopholes. Never any action is taken against erring examiners (Statesman 2002Z 16: iv).

As regards the facility of science education, it continued to be very poor. Only 41.6 per cent of the secondary schools had it as against 59.7 per cent at the national level. For rural areas, the proportions were respectively 37.2 and 54.1 per cent. The facility again is only in name. The laboratories are in general utterly unequipped. Even the schools in Calcutta suffer in this respect. The provision of guidance service in the schools is virtually non-existent. In West Bengal it was there in only 3.60 per cent of the schools in 1994 as against 18.88 per cent at the national level.

Behind the low level of facilities, an important reason is that almost the entire budgetary expenditure on school education goes for paying the salaries of teachers. In 2004-05, out of the total expenditure of about Rs 1,700 crore, 96 per cent was spent on teachers salaries (The telegraph 2005a).

Enrolment

In the above situation, naturally the growth of enrolment in schools could not be satisfactory. As percentage to population in the age group 6-11, the enrolment increased to 87.4 in 1979-80 from 65.6 in 1960-61 but declined again to 83.1 in 1994; in the last few years again it improved, rising to 107.1 in

2000-01. Although these were higher than the national average, there were a number of states, with higher proportions (Table 4.3 and GOI 2002c)[1]. At upper primary level, the situation was much more disappointing. In 2000-01, West Bengal had an enrolment ratio of only 52.2 per cent, with girls at 44.3, as against 58.6 and 49.9 per cent at the national level. The relative position has worsened noticeably over the years, as evident from Table 4.3.

The data on proportion of children not attending school currently is not available, but in 1993-94 for children aged 5-14 it was as much as 34.8 per cent in rural West Bengal. The proportion of never-enrolled in the age-group 5-24 came to as much as 30.5 per cent in 1995-96, which was higher than in as many as eight major states (Table 4.4).

The enrolment is, however, of little importance; the more important is attendance in schools, and here West Bengal presents a very depressing picture. The age-specific attendance ratio in 1995-96 was found to be 67 per cent for the age-group 6-10 compared with 69 at the national level; nine of the major states had better position. For the age-group 14-17, it was respectively 48 and 50, and for 18-24 group 8 and 14. The net attendance ratio, as evident from table 4.4, was very disappointing in west Bengal, particularly from class VI onwards.

The drop-out rate was very high. For all stages combined, it stood at 64.7 per cent for rural areas in 1995–96 as against the national average of 58.1 per cent. Stage-wise, it was particularly high at the primary level, being respectively 41.4 per cent and 30.4 per cent. In more recent years, the situation has deteriorated further. In 2000-01, at the primary level, for rural-urban combined, the gross drop-out rate stood at 51.46 per cent as against 40.67 at the national level; for all stages combined, it was respectively 82.58 and 68.58 (Table 4.4, and GOI 2002c).

Reasons Behind

Behind the low level of enrolment and high drop-out rate the reasons are more or less the same as those noted in Chapter 4—that is, parents not interested in studies, financial constraint, child not interested in studies, education not considered useful, no tradition in the family, etc. All these problems ultimately boiled down to financial cost and return from sending a child to school, and could be greatly overcome if the government had the determination to achieve universal literacy. But this basic condition was lacking, and therefore, no effective measures were taken for attracting students to schools. We give a brief look into the magnitude and manner of operation of some of the measures.

The costliest item of expenditure for a student in West Bengal is private coaching. The NSSO survey in 1995-96 had found it to be accounting for as much as 40 per cent of the annual expenditure of a student, Rs 361 out of Rs 648. In no other state this item took such a high proportion, and the all-India average came to only 11.2 per cent, Rs 64 out of Rs. 570. This high level of expenditure on private coaching speaks of a very low quality teaching in schools. But the government does not dare to touch the teachers because the latter constitute an important vote bank of the ruling political party. It has to be seen to believe the extent of indiscipline and inefficiency among the teachers of the state.

The next important item is books, accounting for 22 per cent of the total expenditure, followed by stationery 15 per cent. There is provision for subsidised supply of books to the students and the coverage is substantial, to the extent of 57.6 per cent of all students as against 25.6 per cent at the national level. But its value is greatly reduced due to mismanagement;the CAG report for the yer 2001-02 stated that between the academic years 1997-2000, 20.31 crore books were short printed and supplied, depriving many students. Moreover, no definite distribution norm was followed and many schools did not receive the books on time. In 2000-2002, the delay was by 1-11 months from the commencement of the academic year. In four districts, 15.50 lakh books were supplied in excess of requisition (Statesman 2003c). On stationary, the coverage itself is very low—only 3.1 per cent of the students in 1995-96, much below the national average (Table 4.5). On the provision of scholarship to students also the state's position was not good. The coverage was only 4.5 per cent of the students as against the all-India average of 6.8 per cent. Only the proportion of students receiving free education was relatively high; but this was a negligible item of expenditure, constituting only 1.23 per cent of the total.

Probably the most important inducement for attracting students to school would have been the provision of a nutritious midday meal. But here West Bengal's coverage was very low. In 1995-96, only 4.4 per cent of the students could be covered as against the all-India average of 17.9 per cent (Table 4.5). Earlier, in 1986-87, it stood at 18.49 per cent against the highest of 81.5 per cent in Tamil Nadu. (NSSO 1993a). However, here it was discontinued after some time. The management of the midday meal scheme was very unsatisfactory in West Bengal. When it was re-launched in 1995, the programme failed to last for more than a year in most schools owing to lack of "infrastructure". According to rule, each student was to get 100 gm of rice each day. But erratic supplies made the schools to provide it once in a month, 3 kg per student. Even this is reported to be almost defunct in many schools.

Adult Education

Despite the low level of literacy in West Bengal, adult education remained totally neglected for at least three decades. The total literacy campaign (TLC) was launched only in 1978, and then also it did not gather momentum immediately. According to the Union education ministry, 53 per cent of the funds allocated to the state for adult literacy remained unutilised in 1983 (Statesman 1983: editorial). It took another decade for the adult education to start making any noticeable progress—that is, after the launch of the National Literacy Mission in 1988. Below we give a brief look into the progress in adult literacy since then.

The total number made literate in West Bengal till March 1998 under the various schemes of NLM was 89.72 Lakh, constituting 12.4 per cent of all-India total. This is the highest number among the selected ten states presented in Table 4.6. Most of the progress came from the TLC introduced in a modified form in 1989. Of the total number made literate, its share was 92 per cent here compared with 72 per cent at all-India level. It needs to be noted, however, that the achievements were far behind the targets set. On the literacy phase the realisation was 57.7 per cent and in post-literacy only 32.9 per cent.

District-wise, there was wide variation in performance. Under the TLC, at level III even after 18 months of sanction two districts—Malda and Uttar Dinajpur—had less than 20 per cent achievement as against above 60 per cent in nine districts. On the PLC, many districts had a very late start. Burdwan and Midnapore could launch it in 1991, and two districts were yet to start in 1997. Even for the earliest starter, Burdwan, the achievement was only 61 per cent, and for four districts there was no achievement at all. Even the number enrolled was very low in most of the districts. It was 1.16 per cent of the proposed number in Howrah, 2.86 per cent in North 24-parganas and none in Purulia. This negligible progress in PLC meant the adults with basic literacy were lapsing into illiteracy. It was due to this, the CAG report had stated that the net achievement of TLC in the state was only around 30 per cent of the target during 1990-97 (quoted in Sanyal 2001).

There were many shortcomings in the implementation of the programme. The number of illiterates required to be covered was often not estimated properly. In some of the districts the survey had to be conducted repeatedly to bridge the yawning gap between survey figures and those available through interpolation of census data. According to some critics, illiteracy figures were deliberately kept low with a view to showing maximum achievement. There were clear instances of fraud in the declaration of a district as "totally literate". The learners were required to complete three primers, graded according to difficulty, before facing the final test. But in Bankura out of 4.2 lakh learners, 1.32 lakh never got Primer II. Again, according to the NLM norm, a district becomes literate only after it achieves 80 to 90 per cent of the target. But Bankura was declared "totally literate" after it had reached only 71 per cent. In Midnapore, 1.04 lakh learners had never been evaluated still it was declared literate (ibid.).

And then, there were large-scale misappropriation of funds. The CAG report listed many cases of desperate violation of rules on the basis of "test checks" of four Zilla Saksharata Samitis. Purchases were often made without inviting tenders and there were also cases of over-spending. Desperate diversions of fund to unauthorised purposes were found in all test-checked districts (Sanyal 2001a). The looting continued even after the disclosure of the irregularities, and the director general of the NLM was compelled to write to the State Resource Centre in December 1999 that grants would remain withheld until "suitable actions" were taken to remedy the "irregularities".

Corruption is rampart in every sphere of education in West Bengal. Therefore, we conclude the section on education by citing some more instances:

(i) Manipulation of data was quite common in the state. Recently it came out in the CAG report that the number of primary schools operating in the state was overstated. The state primary education department had reported to the Union HRD department a total of 18,284 primary schools in the four districts of Midnapore, Malda, North 24-parganas and Nadia, whereas the actual number was only 15,662. The auditor found that in Midnapore names of 1,795 non-existent schools had been shown and in North 24-parganas 559 (Statesman 2000 j).

(ii) The primary schools in many districts are rarely inspected by the school inspectors. It was found during audit that in 32 schools in Malda, Midnapore and Nadia no inspection had been conducted in the past ten years. In the last five years, out of the total of 127,000 schools in Midnapore and North 24-parganas, only 3,667 were inspected (Ibid.). As regards the quality of inspection, it may be noted that almost invariably the information is passed on earlier and the necessary window dressing is done for some time.

(iii) At the university level, nepotism and corruption have undermined academic standards severely. Key university appointments—from Vice-chancellor downwards—are made on political and personal considerations. Recruitment and promotion rules are manipulated to push the party candidates. There are many teachers in universities holding the post of Professor without having the minimum qualification required.

(iv) On the quality of teaching and examination system, the less said the better. Members of the Calcutta University's board of studies not only run tutorial homes but also allow questions to leak to their "private" students for consideration. Many teachers say that the university's motto should be changed from advancement of learning to advancement of earning. Recently, it also came out that one out of ten mark sheets of the university are forged, stated by the Registrar himself (ibid. and The Telegraph 2005a: 1). If this is the position of the premier university in the state, one can easily imagine the situation in the lesser ones.

(v) The syllabi of the courses offered by different universities in the state are backdated by at least a decade, and in the process of teaching their coverage is reduced to less than half of what should be done. The quality of teaching is reflected in the minuscule number getting through the national level test conducted by the University grants commission. The extent of cheating by university teachers has to be seen to be believed.

With this nature of education provided by the educational institutions, it is no surprise that the work culture in West Bengal continues to be abysmally low, and the level of corruption so high. It is the product of these universities who seat in government offices and in schools. From the angle of developing the right quality human beings, educational expenditure in the state is largely a wastage.

HEALTH AND FAMILY PLANNING

Pattern of Expenditure

The growth of plan expenditure on health and family planning was very low in West Bengal. Between the first five-year plan and the Ninth plan, it had risen only 119 times in current prices—from Rs 14.5 crore to Rs 1732.0 crore—as against 306 times in the aggregate of expenditure. The relative share was as much as 21.4 per cent of the total in the small First Plan but when the plan size increased it dropped sharply. In the Second Plan itself the share was down to 8.5 per cent. The highest proportion reached in the following plans was 14.5 per cent in the Seventh Plan (Table 8.5).

Component-wise, water supply and sanitation became important only in the recent plans. In the third plan, for the first time, a separate allocation was made for it, with the share at 0.55 per cent of total plan outlay. The critical importance of water supply was realized by the government only in recent years. In the Seventh Plan (1985-90), it was provided 12.3 per cent of the total. However, in the following two plans again it dropped sharply (Table 8.5).

The relative position of West Bengal among the states on the expenditure on health may be seen from Table 4.7 in chapter 4. During 1995-98, the aggregate of budgetary expenditure on it had constituted only 5.9 per cent of the all-states total. The per capita expenditure came to Rs 116.69, which was much below the all-states average. In this expenditure, the emphasis was on medical and public health; receiving as much as 70.8 per cent of the total compared with the all-states average of 55.4 per cent. Family welfare, and particularly water supply, received a very low share. The proportion given to the latter in this period was only 18.7 per cent compared with 32.4 per cent at the level of all-states.

In the aggregate of expenditure, revenue expenditure constituted the overwhelming proportion. The average for 1995-98 came to 98.5 per cent, which was much above the all-states' average. The growth in revenue expenditure was relatively high. Between 1960-61 and 1998-99, that is, nearly four decades, it was 128 times here compared with 118 times for all-states. The per capita revenue expenditure was generally higher than the all-states' average.

As regards the composition, the highest proportion was naturally for hospitals and dispensaries, as was the pattern in other states also. But in contrast to a fall in the proportion at the national level, West Bengal had a sharp rise. In 1992-93 it stood at 38.9 per cent of the total, rising from 20.6 per cent in 1960-61. The per capita expenditure also moved similarly. It had increased 45 times over the period as against less than half this rate at the national level (Table 4.7). West Bengal's share in all-India total expenditure on hospitals and dispensaries increased from 4.24 per cent in 1960-61 to 10.28 per cent in 1980-81 and then decreased to 9.71 in 1992-93.

The next important item was family welfare, with its share rising from 7.4 per cent of total expenditure in 1975-76 to around 13 per cent in the following two time points, 1985-86 and 1992-93; these proportions were much below the all-India average. Thus, West Bengal gave a relatively low importance to family welfare. The per capita expenditure came to only Rs 7.96 in 1992-93 as against Rs 11.91 at the national level. In recent years also there has not been much improvement. The revenue expenditure averaged Rs 172 crore in 2000-03 and constituted 7.27 per cent of all-states total. The per capita levels were respectively Rs 21.44 and Rs23.42.

The national disease programme also received less importance here. The per capita expenditure was always much below the all-India average despite a relatively high growth in expenditure. In 1992-93, it stood at Rs 5.61 as against Rs 7.60 for all-India. The least importance was given to MCH activities in West Bengal, and the proportion declined from 0.11 per cent in 1975-76 to 0.07 in 1985-86 and then rose to 0.10 in 1992-93. All these were much below the national average; the proportion at the national level in the latest year was 1.80 per cent.

Medical education and research also received a low share. It increased from 2.1 per cent of the total expenditure in 1960-61 to 5.8 in 1980-81 and 7.4 in 1992-93; all these were below the national average. In the all-India total expenditure on medical education etc, the state's share declined from 5.87 per cent in 1980-81 to 4.66 per cent in 1992-93. The expenditure on health administration was, however, relatively high. Whereas at the national level there was a sharp fall in the proportion going to it-from 11.1 per cent to 4.5 per cent between 1960-61 and 1992-93-in West Bengal it was a nominal fall, from 6.7 per cent to 6.0 per cent. The growth in expenditure here was 43.3 times as against 23.2 times for all-India.

The capital expenditure on health was very low in West Bengal. Ignoring fluctuations, between 1975-76 and 1992-93 it had risen only 193.9 per cent, from Rs 6.31 crore to Rs 18.55 crore, as against 286.9 per cent at the national level. West Bengal's share in all-India total had declined from 9.37 per cent to 7.12 per cent over the period.

What was the effect of all these expenditures on the infrastructural situation, and on the incidence of diseases? Below we give a brief look into these aspects.

Infrastructure

This level of expenditure-leaving aside the question of leakages-naturally could not bring any significant improvement in the infrastructure for health facilities. The availability of health centres, dispensaries etc to the people remained very low, as evident from Table 4.8. Number of PHC per lakh population declined from 3.13 in 1991to 1.66 in 1999, and of sub-centres from 15.9 to 10.6; in the latest year, the national averages were 2.41 and 14.37. The position of hospitals and dispensaries was also very poor. In 1998, the former stood at 0.50, less than a third of the national average; and the latter at 0.71 and 2.45 respectively (GOI 2000i, 2000).

The availability of beds was, however, quite good, although the relative position worsened greatly. It increased from 80.1in 1991 to 86.0 in 1998; at the national level, it stood 94.0 in the latest year. The beds were, however, heavily concentrated in urban areas; number in rural areas stood at only 15.4 in 1991. District-wise also the beds were concentrated in a few of them. In 1998, Calcutta alone accounted for 26.8 per cent of the total number (69,321). Five districts—Uttar Dinajpur, Dakshin Dinajpur, Malda, Cooch Behar and Birbhum—together, on the other hand, had only 9.02 per cent (GOW 1999).

As regards personnel, on the availability of doctors, West Bengal's situation was very good. In 1991 there were 61.38 doctors per lakh population, rising from 58.02 in 1971; at the national level, it was respectively 47.19 and 27.57. The recent situation also appears to be very good. In 1995, number of doctors required by the PHCs was 1,262 but there were 1,547 in position. Number of nurses on the other hand, was very low. Per lakh population, it came to 25.26 in 1991as against 36.88 at the national level.

The word availability is, however, not very appropriate for West Bengal. Even if the doctors and nurses are physically present, their mind is generally elsewhere. Due to politicisation and absence of any accountability, the doctors and nurses here rarely provide any sincere service to the patients. The rural health centres, dispensaries etc are often without any doctor. The chief minister Buddhadev Bhattacharya himself said once: "Doctors sign in, but remain engaged in running nursing homes." (statesmen 2001 n: BP, I). And even if a doctor decides to turn up, most of the rural clinics do not have the infrastructure to treat patients. There is also a constant shortage of medicine (Statesman 2001n: BP, IV).

The medical education in West Bengal is in a shambles. Recently, the situation was described thus by Satadru Ojha: "The present is all about decadence, resting on the laurels of the past..... It is just one unending, disgraceful list of failed promises. Mortifying examples are everywhere to be seen—laboratory attendants being bribed before practicals, research work at the post-graduate level getting stalled because of non-availability of funds, backdated medicines being used on patients and so on." (Ojha 2001). Even the exams are conducted in a haphazard manner, and the university takes around three months to tabulate the results of a mere 700 odd students. The duration of the first MBBs has been reduced from one-and-half year to a year and the effective teaching time reduced to eight months. Practical training has been neglected for years.

On the quality of services available from government-run hospitals, an editorial of the Statesman noted : "That the state of government-run hospitals is dismal beyond belief has been amply demonstrated already—patients on the floor, dogs and other animals roaming the corridors and the wards, filthy surroundings, lower category staff stealing patients' food which is hardly edible anyway, dead bodies sold for cash while relatives are told that they cannot be found, new-born female children exchanged for others out of sheer negligence, the list is endless." (Statesman 2000k).

Incidence of Diseases

The poverty of the people, illiteracy, and utterly inadequate health facilities made the incidence of certain diseases quite high in West Bengal. Although the available data on it do not capture fully the magnitude of the problem we quote here some of them. In 1992-93, number per lakh persons suffering from tuberculosis was 357, on partial blindness 753, malaria 678 and on physical impairment of limbs 386; all these were much below the all-India average (CMIE 1996a). Probably these are underestimates; recently it came out that at least 80 people die in West Bengal every day due to tuberculosis and it constitutes not less than 8 per cent of all-India total (Statesman 2002n: BP). The incidence of anaemiah is very high here. Percentage of children under 3 suffering from any anaemiah was found to be 78.3 in 1998-99 compared with the national average of 74.3, and for married women 62.7 and 51.8 per cent respectively (IIPS 2000).

The level of MCH activities in West Bengal was very poor. In 1993-94, for TT (16 years) the coverage was only 29.0 per cent compared with 55.3 per cent at the national level, on TT (10 years) 40.0 and 70.3 per cent respectively, on DT immunisation for children 42.4 and 72.4 per cent, for measles vaccine 74.2 and 88.5, on polio 85.5 and 93.6 and on DPT immunisation for children 84.9 and 93.2 per cent. On prophylaxis against nutritional anaemia, children covered were only 58.1 per cent of the target as against 66.2 per cent at the national level, and on blindness 66.4 and 77.5 per cent respectively (GOI 1997a). The level of registration for post-natal care was very low here. In 1995-96, per thousand mothers it was found to be 246 as against the national average of 271 (NSSO 2000).

On an important factor influencing the health situation, availability of drinking water, the state's position is far from satisfactory. No doubt, statistically the relative position is very good. In 1991, the coverage of households was 82 per cent here as against 62 per cent at the national level; and in terms of habitations, by May 2004, there was 100 per cent full coverage (GOI 1999 and 2004). But the quality of water supplied is extremely poor. For example, in 2001, 50 water samples collected from different places were tested and two-thirds of them were found to be unfit for consumption; and these included even important hospitals of Calcutta (Statesman 2001: BP, I).

Family planning

Despite the critical importance of population control for West Bengal, the fall in fertility rate was slow, as evident from Table 4.11. Between 1961-66 and 1996, it declined by 4.1, from 6.7 to 2.6 per woman. However, the reduction came mainly from early eighties; even in mid-seventies, it was significantly higher than the national average.

The mean age at effective marriage (female) continued to be relatively low. In 1961-62 it stood at 14.72 years as against 16.02 at the national level; West Bengal's was the lowest mean age this year. After three decades, in 1991, also it was lower than the national average. It took another five years for the mean age to be equal to the latter's. For rural areas, however, it continued to be below the national average. The NFHS of 1998-99 found that 46 per cent of the women aged 20-24 were married before age 18 in West Bengal (Table 4.11).

The couple protection rate had a very low growth here. It increased from 21.4 per cent in 1980 to 35.7 in 1995 but declined again to 33.8 in 1998. West Bengal's proportion was not only below the national average, the disparity increased over the years and became lower by 11.6 points in the latest year. District-wise, out of 18 districts in the state in 1996 only two had CPR of fifty per cent and above; for five districts it was 20 to 30 per cent.

Apparently, the activities of the family planning department were very poor. Although the proportion of women using any family planning method in recent years was quite high, their effectiveness was low due to the nature of methods used. The proportion using modern permanent methods, that is, sterilisation, has been very low. In 1998-99, it stood at 33.8 per cent compared with the national average of 36.0 per cent. The cumulative total number of sterilisation per thousand population came to 109.4 in 2000 as against 118.6 for all-India (GOI 2002).

Behind the poor performance of West Bengal many factors have worked. We have noted earlier the low level of revenue expenditure on family welfare. The plan expenditure as a whole was also low here. During the Eighth Plan the per capita expenditure came to Rs 62.09, which was below the national average; Kerala, already having a low birth rate, on the other hand spent as much as Rs 75.74. It is not only the question of money spent, the quality of personnel in the department was also poor. The illiteracy among married women also contributed greatly to the poor performance. In 1998-99, 43 per cent of the ever married women aged 15-49 were illiterate. The exposure to media for them was also not very high (Table 4.11).

At the root of all the problems in the area of health and family planning is the administrative inefficiency, originating primarily from the politicisation of the employees. There is almost a total absence of accountability and discipline among the staff members, and quality and efficiency in service is rarely rewarded. Everything is guided by politics, and corruption is rampant. We end the section by quoting an editorial comment in the Statesman (2000a):

"The Marxists have practised committed bureaucracy theory to subserve their interests. The appointment of Ashok Chakravarty as the state's new health secretary has been guided by similar considerations. He has superseded at least 10 senior officers five of whom were eminently suitable to the job but were not considered, as they are not favourite of the Marxists. A department with one of the biggest budgets and which has mismanaged its affairs including the World Bank's Rs 700 crore health facility programme, deserved a senior and experienced secretary who could keep its crumbling infrastructure and morale intact. It has earned notoriety for corruption, callousness and lack of accountability. Marxists have preferred health secretaries who aid and abet their efforts at unionising departmental staff including doctor to spread their influence rather than alleviate distress. Patients have been the worst victims. Those without influence or contact are made to pay a bribe of Rs 1000 to SSKM's commissars for getting admission into the government hospital".

Note

1. The reliability of these data is, however, doubted. The enrolment data of class I in West Bengal are inflated for quite a few reasons. The class I figures are taken as the indicator for all official allotments to schools-such as infrastructural amenities, number of teachers and teaching-learning materials. Secondly, the inflated records enable the primary schools to get an excess allotment from the central grants for the mid-day meal programme.

10

Agricultural Transformation

The agricultural sector of West Bengal suffered a severe set back from the partition of the country, as noted in Chapter 1. Immediately after Independence, it was therefore incumbent on the government to take all possible measures for its development. The importance was more so because an overwhelming proportion of the population was dependent on agriculture for work and living; there was virtually no industry outside Calcutta and its neighbouring areas. In this chapter, we look into how the agricultural sector progressed over the years. The analysis follows the same pattern as in chapter 5.

AGRICULTURE

In the pre-green revolution period, the growth of agricultural production in West Bengal was very low. Between 1952-53 and 1964-65, the annual growth came to only 1.94 per cent compared with 3.01 per cent at the national level. The state's share in all-India total value of output came to only 5.75 per cent in 1962-65. The productivity also moved similarly, rising at the rate of 1.34 per cent here as against1.77 per cent in all-India. The value of output per hectare was, however, relatively high. During 1962-65 it annually averaged Rs 5,075 which was 36 per cent higher than the national average (GOI 1969).

In the post-green revolution period, in the initial years the state's position was not good. Between 1968-69 and 1981-82, the annual growth in production came to 2.46 per cent, which was lower than in a number of states. The relative share in all-India total value of output declined to 4.98 per cent in 1980-83. The growth in yield rate was only 5.86 per cent between 1970-73 and 1980-83 as against the national average of 19.57 per cent. The value of yield was now only 16.8 per cent higher than the national average—being respectively Rs 5,944 and Rs 5,090 (Bhalla and Singh 1997).

In the decade of eighties, however, the state had a noticeable performance in agricultural production. Between 1981-82 and 1990-91, the annual growth reached 6.88 per cent compared with 3.28 per cent at the national level. In the following years also it was good; being an annual rate of 6.6 per cent during 1991-97, the second highest among the states. In the all-India total value of agricultural production, West Bengal's share rose to 6.25 per cent in 1992-95. The yield rate rose to Rs 9,958 per hectare, which was 3.5 per cent higher than all-India's. Below we give a brief look into the pattern of growth in different crops over a period of three decades (ibid. and RBI 1998).

Food Grains

Food grains accounted for a very high proportion of cropped area in West Bengal. In the aggregate of GCA its share averaged 72.5 per cent in 1995-98 as against the all-India average of 65.5 per cent. The growth in production was relatively low. Over the entire period of three decades it was only 86.2 per cent, below the all-India average. The yield per hectare had a very low growth, rising by only 72.4 per cent compared with 89.1 per cent at the national level. Naturally, the relative position worsened. In this period of three decades, the growth however, came only in the last two decades; during 1968-71 to 1980-83, it was in fact negative. In the following 18 years, the yield rate had risen by 79 per cent here as against 51 per cent at the national level, and the production by 98 and 46 per cent respectively. In recent years, after remaining almost static for a few years, the production again increased noticeably. During 2000-03 it reached the average of 15,280 thousand tonnes, and constituted 11.7 per cent of all-India total as against 7.2 per cent in 1995-98. The latest yield rate is 2,343 kg/ha, 42.6 per cent higher than the all-India's. The per capita production has reached 190 kg compared with 127 kg at the national level (ibid. and CMIE 2005).

Among food grains, rice was overwhelmingly important. Its share in the total area was as much as 90.2 per cent in 1995-98, rising from 81.7 in 1968-71. The production of rice was doubled over the period; the growth, however, came only in the eighties and after. The state was generally the largest producer of rice in the country, with a share of 15.7 per cent in 1995-98. The yield rate declined in the first one-and-half decade, but in the following years made an impressive growth. However, in recent years the situation has worsened noticeably. During 2000-03, the production of rice here stood at the average of 14,025 thousand tonnes, and constituted only 8.7 per cent of all-India total. This is mainly because of a fall in the area under it; the yield rate, at 2,421 kg, was actually 25 per cent higher than the all-India average (Table 5.1; CMIE 2005).

Among other food grains, wheat had the highest acreage in West Bengal. But the growth in yield rate was very low, a negligible 11 per cent over the entire period of three decades. The area under the crop had however risen by 41 per cent in this period. The growth in production of wheat was only 51 per cent over the entire period, and the states share in all-India total declined from 2.51 per cent to 1.20 per cent (Table 5.1). The highest growth in yield rate among the food grains was in maize. Between 1968-71 and 1995-98 it was by 187.8 per cent, and the latest yield was significantly higher than the national average. The area under maize, however, had an absolute fall.

Among pulses, gram was the most important crop, but the area under it had a sharp fall. In 1995-98, it was less than a fifth of that in 1968-71. The yield rate increased only 15 per cent over the entire period. Even then, however, the latest yield was significantly higher than the national average. The pattern of growth in arhar was also similar. The area under it became a tenth of what had existed earlier, with the yield rate on the whole declining. For pulses as a whole, the production in 1995-98 was only 43.5 per cent of what it was in 1969-72, with the area under them declining to a third and the productivity rising by only 27.8 per cent (GOW 1999).

Non-food-grains

Among non-food-grains, the largest acreage in West Bengal is under jute, and there was a noticeable growth in it; between 1968-71 and 1995-98, it was by 59.6 per cent. The growth in yield rate was 80.7 per cent in this period; and the latest yield was significantly higher than the all-India average. The state accounted for 75.0 per cent of all-India total production in 1995-98, with the share in area at 69.9 per cent. In the allied crop mesta, however, the situation was not good. Despite a significant growth in yield rate, the area declined sharply (Table 10.1).

In Oilseeds, the most important was rape and mustard, and the area under it had grown noticeably over the years. However, there was considerable fluctuation from year to year. Between 1960-61 and 1976-77, it varied between the highest of 1.23 lakh hectares in 1973-74 and the lowest at 0.72 lakh in 1976-77. The growth in yield rate was substantial. The production had risen by 629 per cent between 1968-71 and 1995-98 as against 255 per cent at the national level; and the state's share in all-India total rose to 4.4 per cent from 2.1 per cent.

Among other oilseeds, sesamum, groundnut and coconut had a sharp growth in area. Sesamum was an insignificant crop till early seventies but by 1995-98 the area under it multiplied 14 times, and became the second important crop. The yield rate, however, declined considerably in recent years. Groundnut recorded an impressive growth in yield, and the area under it rose noticeably. Coconut also had a similar pattern, as may be seen from Table 10.1. Linseed was an important crop till early eighties but in the following years it declined. For oilseeds as a whole, the state's relative position was very poor. The annual average production in 1998-01 stood at only 453.2 thousand tonnes and

Table 10.1: Trend in Area, Production and yield Rate of different Non-Foodgrain Crops in West Bengal

Crops	1968-71 (a.a.)			1980-83 (a.a.)			1990-93 (a.a.)			1995-98 (a.a.)		
	A	P	Y	A	P	Y	A	P	Y	A	P	Y
Rapeseed & mustard	111	35	317	149	88	603	395	311	790	325	255	787
Sesamum	9	5	597	115	57	497	105	95	917	129	93	730
Linseed	39	10	267	63	17	270	9.3	2.2	237	14	3.7	263
Coconut[a]	7	22	3280	7	73	9877	20	271	13527	24	300	12618
Groundnut	—	—	—	1.9	1.2	743	21	26	1250	29	39	1331
Jute [b]	371	2471	1158	518	4233	1484	522	5739	1977	592	6903	2093
Mesta [b]	57	312	981	31	170	967	11	77	1223	9	76	1441
Sugarcane	32	1586	48413	23	1293	58297	15	906	61720	23	1649	73243
Tea	88	96	1095	95	134	1413	102	153	1497	102	164	1621
Tobacco	13	11	840	16	15	940	13	12	928	12	9	707
Chillies	8	7	903	24	18	733	58	41	787	60	52	855
Potato	73	735	10363	119	2092	17847	215	4735	22087	285	6893	24118
Turmeric[c]	1.2	3.3	2750	5.1	7.6	1477	10	19	1883	12	22	1781
Arecanut[d]	3.1	0.8	260	3.1	0.8	260	6.1	8.3	1367	7.6	11	1446

(Table 10.1 Contd.)

Period I			Period II		
A	P	Y	A	P	Y
34.2	151.4	90.2	118.1	189.8	30.5
1177.8	1040.0	(-) 16.8	12.2	63.2	46.9
61.5	70.0	1.1	(-)77.8	(-)78.2	(-)2.6
0	231.8	201.1	242.9	311.0	27.8
—	—	—	1426.3	3150.0	79.1
39.6	71.3	28.3	14.3	63.1	41.0
(-)45.6	(-)45.5	(-)1.4	(-)71.0	(-)55.3	49.0
(-)28.1	(-)18.5	20.4	0	27.5	25.6
8.0	39.6	29.0	7.4	22.4	14.7
23.1	36.4	11.9	(-)25.0	(-)40.0	(-)24.8
200.0	157.1	(-)18.2	150.0	188.9	16.6
63.0	184.6	72.2	139.5	229.5	35.1
325.0	130.3	(-)46.3	135.3	189.5	20.6
0	0	0	145.2	1275.0	456.2

Notes: A: area in '000 hectares; P: production in '000 tonnes; Y: yield in Kg/ha; a: production in million nuts and yield in nuts/ha; b: production in '000 bales of 180 kg each; c: data under 1980-83 here refer to 1983-86; d: data under 1968-71 here refer to 1970-73.

Period I: 1968-71 to 1980-83, Period II: 1980-83 to 1995-98; these figures are percentage increase/decrease.

Source: As in Table 5.1.

constituted 2.13 per cent of all-states total. On per capita tern, it was only 5.65 kg as against 21.0 kg in the latter (RBI 2003a).

Among other non-food-grain crops, tea had the largest acreage in West Bengal. The yield rate also increased but continued to be significantly below the national average. The state's share in all-India production declined from 23.8 per cent in 1980-83 to 21.0 per cent in 1995-98. In sugarcane, West Bengal was an insignificant producer and the area under it on the whole declined, despite a substantial growth in yield rate. The performance in tobacco was very poor. Both area and yield rate had a sharp fall. The production of arecanut, however, had an impressive growth.

In spices, chillies registered a noticeable growth in area but the yield rate on the whole declined. Over the entire period, production increased by 643 per cent and it was entirely a result of acreage increase. The yield rate, which was much above the national average earlier, now became much lower. In turmeric also there was a substantial growth in area but the yield rate declined. The production increased around seven-fold, with the area registering a ten-fold rise. In ginger, the production increased around nine times over the period, and this was primarily due to area increase; the yield rate remained low, and was only 62 per cent of the national average in 1995-98. For spices as a whole, the index of production stood at the average of 811.3 in 1995-98, with the triennium ending in 1971-72 = 100; the area index stood at 700.7 and the productivity at only 115.7.

In vegetables, the performance in potato was quite good. The production had increased by 838 per cent over the period of three decades, and this was a product of 133 per cent growth in yield and 290 per cent in area. In recent years, the yield rate declined somewhat, to 23,819 kg/ha in 2000-03, but the area under it rose further to 316 thousand ha, and constituted a quarter of all-India total. West Bengal's yield rate continues to be much higher than in the latter, being 18,435 kg in the latest period.

Other important crops in terms of area were cucurbits, brinjal, cabbage, cauliflower, ladies finger, tomato and radish. On brinjal, the acreage stood at the average of 143.7 thousand ha in 2000-03 and the production at 2,441 thousand tonnes; the yield rate averaged 17003 kg as against 16,207 kg in all-India. For vegetables, roots and tubers as whole, there has been a noticeable growth in area in recent years. Even in the three years of 1995-98, it doubled from 510 thousand ha to 1034 thousand. The production was nearly trebled, rising from 53.91 lakh tonnes to 150.16 lakh. The yield, however, increased by only 37.4 per cent, and averaged 13,844 kg/ha, which was higher than the national average (13,330 kg).

In fruits and nuts, West Bengal's position was not good. The area itself was low. During 1995-98, the annual average came to 116.4 thousand ha and constituted 3.28 per cent of all-India total. West Bengal's production in this period averaged 1230 thousand tonnes, constituting 2.95 per cent of the latter's. The yield rate stood at only 10,565 kg/ha as against 11,748 kg for all-India. Among fruits, mango had highest acreage here. During 2000-03, it average 64.8 thousand ha and produced 397.8 thousand tonnes. The yield rate averaged 6159 kg/ha as against 6,573 kg at the national level. The next important crop was banana, with an annual acreage of 17.4 thousand ha during 1997-99. The production averaged 256 thousand tonnes, that is, a yield rate of around 15,000 kg/ha, which was much below the national average (29,500 kg) (GOW 2000; CMIE 2000, 2005).

District-wise Disparity

Whatever the relative performance of West Bengal among the states, intra-state, district-wise, there was considerable variation. In the most important crop, rice, the yield rate had increased only 10 per cent in Darjeeling over a period of 16 years as against the highest of 97 per cent in Bankura. Even if Darjeeling—primarily a hill district—is excluded, the variation remains large. The highest yield in 1994-97 was 2,763 kg/ha in Burdwan as against the lowest of 1,159 kg in Jalpaiguri—that is, the former 238 per cent of the latter. In 1981-84, it was 192 per cent, in the same districts. Thus, the disparity widened rather than narrowed over the years (Table 10.2).

A look into the growth in production of all the commodities together also does not present any better picture. Over a period of around three decades, between 1969-72 and 1995-98, it was only 55 per cent in Darjeeling compared with 221 per cent in Hooghly. On yield rate, the highest was in Malda at 152 per cent and the lowest at 39 per cent in Jalpaiguri. The cropped area had registered an absolute fall in four of the districts as against the highest growth of 44.7 per cent in Hooghly (Table 10.2).

Causal Factors

Behind the low level of growth and the spatial disparities, the same factors as noted in chapter 5 have worked, only their intensities differed. Below we discuss first the extent of land availability and their use, to be followed by the pattern of land-holding, the irrigation facility, use of different inputs, provision of institutional credit and marketing facility.

Land Availability and Use

The land available for cultivation in West Bengal was relatively low. The total of cultivable land was only 57.13 lakh hectares in 1995-96, constituting 3.44 per cent of all-India total. Per capita it came to 0.078 ha as against 0.181 at the national level. Land not available for cultivation constituted as much as 18.9 per cent of the state's total area compared with 13.6 per cent for all-India.

Table 10.2 District-Wise Trend in Agricultural growth in West Bengal

Districts	Yield in Rice (Kg/ha)			All commodities Index No[a]		
	1981-84	1994-97	% rise	A	P	Y
Burdwan	1708	2763	61.8	129.2	254.7	197.2
Birbhum	1424	2276	59.8	94.6	171.4	170.6
Bankura	1216	2400	97.4	119.8	227.4	189.7
Midnapore	1093	2083	90.6	128.3	255.7	203.4
Howrah	1352	1729	27.9	126.8	195.3	153.7
Hooghly	1628	2465	51.4	144.7	320.6	216.6
24-parganas (N)	1423	2319	63.0			
				113.8	212.0	186.1
24-parganas (S)	923	1749	89.5			
Nadia	1378	2430	76.3	125.2	275.1	219.5
Murshidabad	1262	2385	89.0	110.8	230.7	208.0
W. Dinajpur	59	1803	88.0	97.4	189.4	195.2
Malda	1255	223	75.5	93.4	234.6	252.1
Jalpaiguri	889	1159	30.4	111.9	156.0	139.5
Darjeeling	1149	1267	10.3	94.8	154.7	154.1
Cooch Behar	961	1293	34.5	109.5	166.5	153.2
Purulia	996	1626	63.3	113.0	181.7	160.5
West Bengal	1212	2099	73 2	116.0	221.4	190.8

Note: a: Index numbers are average for 1995-98, based on triennium ending 1971-72; 1997-98 data here are provisional.
Source: CMIE 1996b; GOW 1999.

Three-and-half decades earlier, in 1960-61, it was slightly, less than in the latter, being respectively 14.7 and 14.9 per cent (GOI 1966). The relative position has worsened further in recent years; in 1999-00, it was 19.09 and 13.86 per cent (CMIE 2004b).

The net cropped area per thousand population declined from 155.6 ha in 1960-61 to 74.5 ha in 1995-96 and 68.2 in 1999-00; for all-India, it was from 302.2 to 137.5 ha over the period. The prospect of raising it further is also not high, the quantum of fallow land being only 2.43 lakh hectares in 1999-00, 2.74 per cent of the total reporting area. The scope for raising the GCA is also not much; the GCA /NCA being already 1.74, rising from 1.17 in 960-61 (Table 5.2 and ibid.).

As regards the district-wise situation, it differs widely from district to district. Even the geographical area varies extremely. The largest district Midnapore is around ten times the smallest. On the utilisation of land, there is considerable scope for improvement. The current fallows instead of declining increased in a number of districts. In Purulia, it stood at the highest of 81.4 thousand hectares in 1998-99, which was more than double the level in 1970-71. In Bankura also, although it has declined considerably, stood at as much as 54 thousand hectares in the latest year. The net area sown has declined in six of the districts. Even in some of the districts with low proportion of cultivable area, the amount of current fallows increased. Darjeeling has only 46 per cent of the area cultivable, but the current fallow was allowed to multiply more than four times.

The cropping intensity varied widely among the districts. In 1970-71, the percentage of area sown more than once stood at the lowest of 8.2 per cent in Bankura compared with the highest of 72 per cent in Murshidabad and the state average at 30.9 per cent. In the largest district Midnapore it stood at only 16.6 per cent. Such wide disparity is still there. In 1994-95, the GCA/NCA stood at the highest of 205 per cent in Hooghly as against the lowest of 105 per cent in Darjeeling; there were eight districts with below the state average of 160 per cent (GOW 1979, 2000). Thus, the utilisation of land was far from satisfactory in many of the districts.

Land-Holding Pattern

On the most vital step towards agricultural growth, that is, land reforms, West Bengal's performance was better than in many other states, but remained far behind what was expected from a Leftist-dominated state. In fact, the land reforms undertaken here in the last two-and-half decades have blatantly exposed the bourgeoisie character of the CPI (M). Particularly note-worthy is their neglect of the landless labouring class while promoting the interests of middle peasantry. Below we give a brief look into the nature and pace at which different measures were implemented.

Till the end of sixties, land reforms in West Bengal did not make any noticeable headway. The Land Reforms Act, 1955 was amended in 1970, following the coming into power of the Left coalition government in 1969. The amendment was preceded by violent upsurges by *bargadars* (sharecroppers). The Act, therefore, for the first time, gave attention to protecting the rights of *bargadars*. As this activity received the widest publicity, we look into its implementation first.

Protection of Sharecroppers

The main provisions of the Act on sharecroppers were:

1. In the case of death of a *bargadar*, his lawful heir should continue the cultivation; in the absence of an heir, his nominee would continue.
2. The bargadar is entitled to a receipt from the landowner on delivery of the latter's share of the produce.
3. The provision of the 1955 Act that enabled a landowner to eject a *bargadar* on ground of not properly cultivating the land was removed from the present Act. Now it was provided that so long as the *bargadar* continued to deliver the landowner's share of produce, or the price thereof, his right of cultivation could not be terminated.
4. Earlier, a landowner could have under personal cultivation a maximum of two-thirds of the total land owned by him, but now it became the absolute area of three hectares. It was further stipulated that in no case the land with the bargadar, after resumption by the landowner, should be below 0.8 hectare.

The most serious lacuna in the 1955 Act, that before seeking the protection of law the bargadar must prove that he had been cultivating the land as bargadar, however, remained, and this alone largely negated the improvement made in 1970; very few bargadars generally recorded themselves as bargadars. The exercise of recording the names of bargadars was started only in 1974—although it was provided for in the 1955 Act itself—and till 1977 the progress was very poor.

It was only after the Left Front came to power again in 1977 that things started moving faster. Immediately the government took certain important steps. First, the onus of proving that a person cultivating the land was 'not a tenant' was shifted to the landowner, and thus saved the former from the burden of legal expenses. Secondly, the landowners were required to issue a receipt in exchange for crop share received. The third and most important step was what was called the 'Operation Barga'—a massive drive to register the names of sharecroppers with active assistance from the peasant organisation. Resumption for self-cultivation was also made stringent.

The process of recording the names was, however, delayed for some time as the landowners sought the intervention of the High Court. Nevertheless, the performance was quite impressive in the initial years. Up to March 1981, 10.42 lakh bargadars were recorded against the total estimated number of 25 Lakhs. In the following years the progress slowed down. By September 1985 it reached 13.29 lakh, and in the following nearly one-and-half decade only 1.61 lakh could be added; giving a total of 14.90 lakh till September 1999. Thus, even now 40 per cent of the bargadars remain to be recorded. This is ridiculously below the target originally envisaged; the recording was to be completed within a year (GOW 1978: 1). The government's own deadline had to be extended five times even to achieve the level it reached. Effectiveness of the recording in preventing eviction was also not high. One departmental survey in Burdwan district in 1985 had found that 11.22 per cent of the recorded bargadars had been thrown out by one way or the other (Khasnabis 1994).

With regard to crop-sharing, the West Bengal Land Reforms Act, 1955 had provided for (a) the proportion of 50:50 where plough, cattle, manure and seeds were supplied by the land-owner, and (b) in the proportion of 75:25 in all other cases. This provision also could not be properly implemented by the Left Front government. In fact, the Operation Barga did not in any way attempt to enforce the cost-sharing. A study in four districts of south Bengal in early nineties found that in a sample of 157 tenant households there was not a single case of 50:50 crop sharing. In fact, five different crop-sharing ratios were found to be existing along with an arrangement for fixed amount of produce to the lessor (ibid.)

Although the 'Operation Barga' is in no way a great success, it is necessary to mention that the primary attention given to share-croppers is incongruous with the Marxists' policy. The share-croppers are not the most exploited class in rural areas; they are an intermediate class. Number of landless share-croppers is much less than those with some land. The poorest *bargadars* are mostly from the scheduled castes and tribes who *have* not been able to form an effective organisation of their own, and have generally been left out of the barga-recording programme.

It needs also to be noted that, the objective of land reform was not to perpetrate the tenancy system but to abolish it and make the tiller the owner of the land. The 'Operation Barga' was, therefore, a retrograde step; it created condition for its perpetuation. And presently the extent of tenancy in West Bengal is much larger than in many other states. In 1991-92, percentage of tenant holding in the state was 14.4, with 10.4 per cent of total land area, as against 11.0 and 8.3 respectively at all-India level (Table 5.4).

Land Ceiling and Surplus Distribution

On acquiring surplus land, the state's experience was no better than in most other states, and the amount of land taken possession increased only in the recent years. The Act of 1955, for the first time, imposed a ceiling of 25 acres on the individual holding of a *raiyat* (a class comprising *Jotedar* as well as owner cultivators). But to evade the ceiling restriction, a large-scale diffusion of ownership among members of the family took place and the land acquired remained very small. Till the time of the first United Front government (1967), only about 3.5 lakh acres were vested to the state, and in the following three years another 5 lakh acres. In the Act of 1970, therefore, the ceiling was imposed on the basis of a family rather than on an individual, and the maximum limit was reduced from 25 acres for an individual to 17.5 acres for a family.

The implementation of this land-ceiling faced many obstacles. The former land-owners worked hard to prevent either the government or the beneficiaries from taking possession of the vested land. At the end of 1978, the total area covered by injunction stood at 1.64 lakh acres and increased to 1.80 lakh in June 1983. There were 20,000 civil injunctions from the Calcutta High Court centering on land reforms, and the Land Revenue Courts had 27,000 cases. In this situation, the vesting of ceiling-surplus-land could not be anything impressive. Between 1970 and 1980 it came to 3.62 lakh acres and in the following two decades another 1.53 lakh; over the entire period till 2000, beginning from 1953[1], it totalled 13.65 lakh acres (Basu (1) 2000). Thus, of all the vested land, around 70 per cent was obtained by 1972, about 44 per cent during the tumultuous 1967-72. Even if it is assumed that all the land vested between 1972 and 1980 was vested with the state after the formation of the LF government in 1977, still it is evident that the 23 years of LF rule could not even remotely manage to touch the figures of the tumultuous five years (6.0 lakh acres).

The amount of land redistributed in West Bengal over the entire period till 2000 was 10, 15,475 acres, of which 4, 11,716 acres—that is, 39.2 per cent—were in the period since 1977. If the Left Front were really a Leftist government it could have easily done much better. By reducing the ceiling on landholding to 10 acres in 1977, the government could have made available an additional amount of land equal to 98 per cent of that redistributed in the past 23 years. And this would have adversely affected only 1.36 per cent of the rural households—the proportion owning 10 acres or more in 1981. This class owned 13.66 per cent of the total owned area in the state—that is, roughly 14.07 lakh acres of land.

In this situation of inaction, naturally the number of beneficiary households remained much below what could be achieved. Till September 1999, a total of 25, 01,533 households were benefited, of which 9, 84,032—that is, 39.3 per cent—were in the period till 1977. In the LF period, out of the total of 15, 17,501 beneficiaries, 31.1 per cent were benefited in the first six years (1977-83). In the total number of beneficiaries till September 1999, the share of scheduled castes was 37.0 per cent and of scheduled tribes 19.8 per cent (GOW 2000).

The relative position of West Bengal among the states improved only in the recent years. Till 1982, as evident from Table 5.3, West Bengal had distributed only 25.3 thousand hectares of land, constituting 3.3 per cent of the all-India total. By 1995, however, the proportion rose to 18.6 per cent. In the all-India total number of beneficiaries from land redistribution, West Bengal's share rose to 42.1 per cent from 12.9 per cent in this period. The amount of land distributed per beneficiary was, however, very low here, being the average of 0.18 ha in 1995, which was less than half the national average. As regards the latest position, at the end of September 1999, the total land distributed came to 10.343 lakh hectares—constituting 19.6 per cent of all-India total–among 25.015 lakh beneficiaries. The land per beneficiary came to 0.41acre as against 0.96 acre at the national level (GOI 2000h).

As a result of this redistribution, landlessness has not decreased much in the state. Percentage of households owning no land declined from 20.54 in 1953-54 to 9.78 in 1971-72 but in 1982 again it rose to 17.21 (Sharma 1994); the subsequent surplus distribution, however, reduced it considerably, to 11.0 per cent in 1991-92. In relation to the all-India average, the state's position was nominally better in the latest year as against much worse in the earlier two time points. The percentage of semi-landless households, however, continued to be very high. In 1991-92 it stood at 53.4 compared with 42.4 at the national level (NSSO 1997b).

Operational Holdings

The land reform measures have brought some significant changes in the size of operational holdings and the nature of its fragmentation. The proportion of marginal holdings (one ha or less) in West Bengal increased from 61.2 per cent in 1970-71 to 80.7 per cent in 1991-92 as against from 45.8 per cent to 62.8 per cent at the national level. Within marginal holdings again, 62.6 per cent were 0.50 ha or less in 1991-92 and 40.4 per cent with 0.20 ha or less. The area under marginal holdings increased from 24.80 per cent to 39.98 per cent over the period (Table 5.5). In recent years, the proportion in total number of holdings has declined somewhat but in area it has increased further; in 1995-96, it was respectively 76.4 per cent and 42.9 per cent CMIE 2004b).

Such a high proportion of sub-marginal and marginal holdings naturally raised the question of their proper utilisation. But there was absolutely no effort from the government in this direction. Co-operativisation was negligible here. Latest data are not available; but in June 1978, net sown area under joint forming stood at 2,381 hectares and under collective farming 295 hectares. In the all-India total area under co-operative farming, these together came to only 0.756 per cent; even in neighbouring Assam it was as much as 2.42 per cent. Total membership of societies in West Bengal was 11,951, constituting 3.41 per cent of all-India total (NABARD 1980: 217-21).

As marginal holdings constituted the overwhelming proportion, naturally other categories had a small share. Large holdings are negligible in the state; and even medium holdings constituted only 0.88 per cent of the total in 1991-92 as against the national average of 6.10 per cent. The proportion of area under medium holdings was 7.27 per cent here compared with 26.37 per cent in the latter. But the proportion of small holdings is relatively large in the state, as may be seen from Table 5.5.

As regards fragmentation of holding, West Bengal's situation was very depressing. In 1991-92, number of parcels per holding averaged 3.0 (taking all sizes) here compared with 2.2 at the national level. Even for holdings of the size of 0.21-0.40 ha it was 2.8 and for 0.51-1.00 ha at 4.1; for all-India, average number of parcels for these categories were respectively 2.0 and 2.5 (NSSO 1997a). There has been no consolidation work in West Bengal although the required legislation exists. At the national level, by October 1983, 35.6 per cent of the net cultivated area had been consolidated (Haque and Sirohi 1986: 102).

Landless Labourers

The most exploited class in rural West Bengal, and with the largest number, are landless labourers. But their plight hardly received any attention from the LF government. Adequate provision of wage employment and proper wage rates would have been a matter of highest priority for any government interested in poverty alleviation. While the question of providing wage employment has been looked into in chapter 12, here we may give a brief look at the attitude of the government on wage rate for agricultural workers.

The state government has always taken care to compensate its employees for price rises by dearness allowance and frequent pay revisions, but very little was done to protect the purchasing power of the agricultural labourers. Till 1983, neither was the statutory minimum wage revised upward nor was the minimum (based on 1975 prices) sought to be implemented strictly. The wage rate in West Bengal was Rs 7.25 per day till 1983. The index of real wage rate for male agricultural labourers here averaged 87.20 during 1982-85, taking 1956-57 = 100; in neighbouring Bihar, on the other hand, it was 137.59 and in Orissa 113.40 (Jose 1988: A 55).

In recent years also the relative position has not improved. In 1993, the wage rate here stood at Rs 26.95 per day, which was much below that in Assam or Orissa-being respectively Rs 32.60 and Rs 35.00 (Basu 2001). In the following years, when government employees got a sharp hike in their salaries, there was no noticeable improvement for agricultural labourers. In 1997-98, the average wage rate for agricultural field labourers in West Bengal was only Rs 42.54 a day, and it varied between Rs 51.84 in 24-parganas (South) and Rs 32.69 in Purulia (GOW 1999:25). This is really a starvation wage prevalent in a communist-ruled state; taking an average family size of even four, per person it comes to Rs 10.63.

For the CPI (M), keeping agricultural wages down has been one of the main instruments of containing class conflict in rural area. Since a substantial portion of the agricultural workers are hired by the middle peasantry, any reasonable increase in wages would be opposed by them. Even after two-and-half decades of LF rule in the state, effective regulation of the terms and conditions of agricultural employment are lacking. To keep the agricultural workers weaker, there is no separate organisation to protect their interests. The krisak Sabha (the state unit of the All India Kisan Sabha), the CPI (M) affiliated peasant union, has actively discouraged the formation of separate organisation for them (Basu 2001).

Irrigation Facility

West Bengal gets a relatively plenty amount of rainfall, but it is neither spatially distributed equitably nor over time. The Sub-Himalayan region gets one of the highest rainfalls in the country whereas the Gangetic region receives around half of it. During 1995-97, the annual average rainfall in the former came to 2592.8 millimeter and in the latter 1602.9 mm. This rainfall, moreover, is concentrated in the four months of June to September. The need for a proper irrigation facility is, therefore, beyond question. We give a brief look below on the nature of progress made over the years in providing this facility.

The aggregate of irrigated area in West Bengal increased from 1135.6 thousand hectares in 1956-57 to 1488.7 thousand in 1967-68, that is, a growth of only 31.1 per cent over the 12-year period. In the following years also the progress was not satisfactory. In 1996-97, it reached 2558 thousand hectares—that is, less than doubled over the period of three decades. However, there was a substantial addition by 1998-99 and it reached 3787.6 thousand ha (GOW 1966, 1979, 2000). As percentage to the NCA, the irrigated area remained very small, and the relative position worsened over the years. During 1996-99, the annual average came to 35.0 per cent here as against 39.1 at the national level (CMIE 2002a). Earlier, the state's position was better than in the latter (Table 5.6).

Crop-wise, naturally the coverage could not be high. For cereals, which accounted for the overwhelming proportion of cropped area, it was almost stagnant in the last two-and-half decades—percentage of irrigated area rising from 28.3 in 1973-74 to 29.9 in 1995-96; at the national level, it was from 28.3 to 47.1 per cent. On the most important crop rice, the proportion of irrigated area in 1999-00 stood at only 24.9 per cent as against 51.9 per cent for all-India. Among non-food grains, only in oilseeds West Bengal's position was good; the coverage reached 98.4 per cent in 1997-98 (Table 5.8 and CMIE 2004b).

As regards the source of irrigation, some significant changes have come over the years. The proportion of irrigated area irrigated by canals registered a sharp decline, whereas wells made a rapid progress. In 1995-96, the former accounted for only 37.5 per cent as against 64.5 per cent in 1973-74. This was due to a sharp fall in the area irrigated by private canals; for government canals, there was a five-fold rise between 1956-57 and 1997-98—from 240.4 thousand hectares to 1216.1 thousand. The proportion of area irrigated by tanks also declined, and stood at only 13.8 per cent in 1999-00; even this is, however, nearly three times the national average. Wells became important only in the last one-and-half decade, and accounted for 37.3 per cent of the total in 1999-00; even this is, however, much below the national average, being 58.8 per cent in the latest year (ibid.).

District wise, the irrigation facility was heavily concentrated in a few of them. In 1967-68, whereas Birbhum had 74.4 per cent of the net area irrigated, followed by Burdwan 68.6 per cent, for Nadia it was only 4.1 per cent, Cooch Behar 4.2 per cent and Malda 5.8 per cent (GOW 1974). Wide disparities persist even now. In 1997-98, in the total of area irrigated by government canals, four districts—Burdwan, Bankura, Birbhum and Midnapore—together accounted for 74.7 per cent of the total; out of the remaining 13 districts, three had no area irrigated by government canals. In 1980-81, the above-mentioned four districts had 81.9 per cent of the total.

The minor irrigation facility is also not equitably distributed. At the end of March 1998, out of 3,635 high capacity deep tubewell projects in the state, 1,712—that is, 47.1 per cent—were in the three districts of Nadia, Murshidabad and Burdwan. Another three districts—Hooghly, Midnapore and 24-parganas (N)—accounted for 30.2 per cent. The low capacity projects were heavily concentrated in Midnapore and Hooghly, their combined share this year being 55.2 per cent; another 22 per cent were in Nadia and Burdwan. The shallow tubewells were mainly in the six districts of Nadia, Murshidabad, Malda, Uttar Dinajpur, Cooch Behar and Jalpaiguri—their combined share being 80 per cent in 1998, with the first three accounting for 45.6 per cent (GOW 1999).

The ultimate irrigation potential in West Bengal is not high, as may be seen from Table 5.6; but the utilisation of even this potential remained low. On major and medium irrigation, the potential created in relation to ultimate potential stood at 62.8 per cent at the end of March 1997, and on minor irrigation at 58.3 per cent in 1991. The development of groundwater in particular was very low, being at 24.2 per cent in 1997 as against 31.9 per cent at the national level. The created potential also could not be utilised properly, particularly in case of major and medium irrigation. In 1998-99, officially it was placed at 84.5 percent[2]. The actual under utilisation was, however, much more due to factors like inadequate number of field channels and ignorance about the right cropping pattern. Even in minor irrigation the utilisation is far behind expectation. In

1998-99, it totalled 2700 thousand hectares against the created potential of 3264 thousand.

The creation of potential is hampered by a variety of factors. Delays in completion of projects come not only because of inefficiencies and poor work culture but also due to lack of funds. So far as inefficiency and mismanagement is concerned, Teesta Barrage project is a patent example. It was given technical clearance by the Centre in 1988 and the project was to be commissioned in 2003. But due to lack of fund it will take at least 10 years more to complete the project. The original cost was estimated at Rs 216 crore but now it has escalated to about Rs 600 crore (Statesman 2001p: BP, I).

Provision of Other Inputs

Although on the critical input of water the state's position was not good, with regard to use of fertilisers, HYV seeds etc on the whole the situation was better. We give a brief look into the pattern of growth in use of different inputs and some of the related problems.

Fertilisers

The consumption of chemical fertilisers has risen substantially over the years. From the annual average of 4.72 kg/ha in 1962-65 it rose to 48.02 kg in 1980-83 and then to 122.8 kg in 2001-03—a 26-fold rise over the entire period as against 20 times at the national level. West Bengal's consumption was always higher than the national average, as may be seen from Tables 5.7.

On the use of organic manures the state's position was not good, except for compost. During 1994-97, the annual average consumption of rural and urban compost came to 275.160 lakh tonnes (estimated), and constituted 13.8 per cent of all-India total, the second highest. The area under green manure, however, averaged only 0.367 lakh ha in this period, constituting a negligible 1.19 per cent of all-India total. Number of biofertiliser plants in the state was also only 5 in 1999 as against 24 in Maharashtra (FAI 2003).

District-wise, growth in consumption of fertilisers varied widely. Between 1972-75 and 1995-98, while Cooch Behar had recorded a 35-fold rise in annual consumption of chemical fertilisers, for Bankura it was only 4.6 times. However, even after the highest growth, the per hectare consumption in the former stood at only 172 kg as against the highest of 599 kg in Howrah (with the lowest cropped area). The lowest consumption was in Purulia, at 106 kg, with a growth in total consumption of 19 times over the period. The largest district Midnapore had 144 kg and 10.6 times, respectively; the state's per hectare consumption in 1995-98 came to 166 kg (GOW 1979, 1999, 2000). In more recent years also there was wide variation in consumption. In 2001-02, while three districts had above 150 kg/ha (one with above 200 kg), for three it was 75-100 kg and one with 50-75 kg (FAI 2003).

If the associated factors are not favourable, naturally the consumption cannot be high. Purulia had irrigation through government canals in only 8.6 per cent of the net sown area in 1997-98, and in minor irrigation it relied almost exclusively on open dug well. West Dinajpur with the second lowest consumption had a negligible 1.35 per cent of NSA with canal irrigation.

As regards other factors, we can look at only the state-wide situation. On the availability of extension worker, the state's position was the worst. It had only 45 agricultural extension workers per million rural population in 1993, less than half the proportion at the national level. The system of quality control for fertilisers is also far from satisfactory. There were only three laboratories for this purpose at the end of March 2003, with the annual analyzing capacity of 3500 samples, a mere 2.8 per cent of all-India total. The soil testing facility too is very inadequate, and the use of fertiliser is often not based on it. In 2001, the state had a total of 20 laboratories, including 4 mobile, with the total capacity of analyzing 218 thousand numbers, constituting 2.72 per cent of all-India total. Even this could be utilised to the extent of only 23.6 per cent in 2000-01 (FAI 2003).

HYV Seeds, Insecticides, etc.

The use of high-yielding seeds in West Bengal had a noticeable growth over the years, but most of it came only in the last one decade. The proportion of rice area under HYV increased from 14.0 per cent in 1971-72 to 29.6 per cent in 1980-81, 56.3 in 1990-91 and 84.2 in 1998-99. In the aggregate of area under rice and wheat, the share of HYV increased from 33.2 per cent in 1980-81 to 58.0 in 1990-91 and 83.0 in 1997-98. For five major cereals, the area under HYV had risen by 326 per cent between 1971-74 and 1994-97 as against 231 per cent at the national level. In the latest period, the state had 50.7 per cent of the GCA under HYV compared with 39.2 per cent in all-India (Table 5.7).

The yield from HYV seeds was, however, relatively low here. In 1990-91, for example, in wheat the state had an yield rate of only 1,771 kg/ha as against the all-India average of 1,967 kg and the highest of 3,877 kg in Maharashtra. Although from one year's data no firm conclusion is possible, there is no doubt that the potential remains largely unexploited. India's yield potential in wheat is placed at as much as 6,000-6,800 kg/ha and in rice 4,000-5,810 kg (CMIE 1996b).

The spread of HYV is limited to a few crops, and even in rice there is much yet to be done. The coverage of kharif rice area is presently only around 70 per cent. The extension is hampered by non-availability of location specific varieties for the problem areas—which is around 36 lakh hectares—and certain other reasons. The seed replacement rate is very low due to non-availability of seeds. There are about 200 agricultural farms engaged in production and multiplication of seeds but these are in a very poor state.

The non-availability is not only because of low level of production but also due to lack of proper marketing arrangement. Delayed delivery of seed is a big problem. Recently the government decided to deduct a part of the salary of those government officers who did not send seed to the farmers on time. Some workers in the seed farms were demanding holidays on Saturdays and Sundays like employees in other state government offices (Statesman 2001q: 3).

The seed certification agency of the state is also utterly ill-equipped for certifying different classes of seeds. There is need not only of more certification units but also of strengthening the existing ones. In 1997, there were only four seed certification units in the state. For popularisation of improved varieties, during the entire Eighth Plan only 30.94 lakh mini kits of different crop varieties could be distributed. There are also reports of poor quality seeds being supplied (GOW 1998: 21; Telegraph 2004b: 15).

As regards plant protection measures, the use of pesticides varied considerably from year to year, depending on the magnitude of pest attacks. However, normally there is a substantial use in the state. During 1985-88, the annual average consumption came to 5000 tonnes and declined to 3950 tonnes in 1996-99, constituting respectively 7.4 and 7.5 per cent of all-India total (GOI 2003c). Because of the danger involved in too much use of pesticides, a need-based use has been emphasised in recent years. But the result so far is insignificant and prophylactic treatment continues to be substantial. On the use of herbicides and mechanical devices no reliable data are available but probably it is negligible.

Use of Implements

Given the fact that 90 per cent of the holdings are 2 ha or less and that too highly fragmented, use of agricultural implements and machinery in West Bengal could not be high. But even the uses of animal-and hand-operated implements were very low. In 1992, there were only 44.9 ploughs per 100 households as against the all-India average of 57.0. Number of iron ploughs was only a quarter of that in the latter. The use of seed drill was only 0.56. However, harrows were used to a relatively large extent, and so also the animal drawn cart. The number of the former was as much as 32 per 100 households this year as against the national average of 24. Among hand-operated implements, only sprayer and thresher had a relatively large use. The number of the former was more than double that at the national level (Table 5.8).

Among machineries, while the use of tractor was extremely low, power tillers were used to a large extent. In 1992, there were only 37 tractors per 10,000 hectares as against the all-India average of 109. In power tiller, on the other hand, it was respectively 86 and 41. An important equipment, pumpset, had a very low use in West Bengal. The number rose to 37.36 per thousand ha in

1980-83 from 0.80 in 1962-65 but during 1994-97 again it was down to only 11.27; the latest is less than a fifth of that at the national level.

A general indicator of the extent of mechanisation in agriculture is consumption of electricity, and here West Bengal stands in a very poor position. In 1996-97, it stood at only 1372 million kWh and constituted 1.63 per cent of all-India total. In the state's total consumption of electricity, the share of agriculture was 15.7 per cent in 1998-99 compared with 30.0 per cent at the national level. In 970-71, these were respectively 0.51 per cent and 9.90 per cent (CEA 2000, 1995). One obstacle in the way of higher consumption is probably the high tariff rate. In 1997-98, the average tariff on agricultural use was 29.7 paise/unit here as against the all-India average of 27.7 paise (Kannan 2001).

Institutional Credit

West Bengal's position among the states on the provision of credit to agriculture was very poor. In 1996-97, the aggregate from all agencies constituted only 2.78 per cent of the all-India total. Per hectare of GCA it came to Rs 817, which was around half the all-India average. One decade earlier, in 1986, the relative position was better, as may be seen from Table 5.9. Among the institutions providing credit, the most important was scheduled commercial banks, providing 59 per cent of the total in the latest year, followed by the co-operative credit structure. We give a brief look into the pattern of growth in credit from both the institutions.

Commercial Banks

The SCBs provided both direct and indirect advances to agriculture. As the share of the former was much higher, we focus primarily on it. In 1971, the advances outstanding to agriculture in West Bengal stood at Rs 8.68 crore and constituted 3.30 per cent of all-India total. This was below the level in a number of states with smaller rural population. Andhra Pradesh, for example, received four times as much. After nearly a decade, in March 1980, the state's share rose to 4.8 per cent but in recent years again it declined, to 3.9 per cent in June 1997 and 2.93 per cent in 2002. In the number of accounts, however, the share was much larger, being 4.26 per cent in the latest year. Per hectare of GCA, loans outstanding came to only Rs 927 in 1998-99 as against the all-India average of Rs 1762 (Table 5.9; CMIE 2003a).

The indirect finance to agriculture had grown at a faster rate in recent years. Between March 1996 and 2002, the amount outstanding had risen by 159 per cent as against only 93 per cent in direct finance. The share of the former in the aggregate of credit rose to 26.0 per cent from 20.8 per cent over the six-year period. The aggregate of credit to the state had grown by 106.8 per cent over the period as against 122.2 per cent for all-India.

In the credit to agriculture, short-term generally accounted for the major portion. As at June-end 1997, it accounted for 51 per cent of the total as against

43 per cent at the national level. Seventeen years back, in 1980, it was respectively 44.5 and 43.6 per cent. In the all-India total of short-term credit, the state's share in the latest year was 4.68 per cent. In terms of cropped area, the amount outstanding was very low here; per hectare of GCA it came to only Rs 458 in 1997 as against the national average of Rs 470 (Table 5.9).

In the provision of credit, even in this communist-ruled state the small farmers were largely neglected. In the amount outstanding at the end of June 1997 their share was only 33.14 per cent, and in the related number of accounts 64.8 per cent; in the state's total number of holdings they accounted for more than 80 per cent. The above-5 acre holdings—with a share in total number of holdings at less than 6 per cent—on the other hand, accounted for 16.4 per cent in the total number of accounts and in the amount outstanding at 50.6 per cent (RBI 1998).

The performance of Regional Rural Banks was much worse. Loans outstanding per hectare of GCA stood at only Rs 134 in 1996 as against Rs 187 at the national level. Even in the eastern region, the state's position was the worst. The RRBs here gave less attention to agriculture. In the aggregate of advances outstanding this year, its share was only 24.9 per cent as against 46.2 per cent at the national level. A decade earlier, in 1986, also the state's position was very poor, as evident from Table 5.9.

Co-operative credit

The role of the co-operative credit system in providing credit was very poor in West Bengal. In 1996-97, in the aggregate of short-term credit flow to the ground level from all the agencies, the share of SCB/CCBs was only 31.6 per cent compared with the national average of 38.7 per cent; including the LDBs, it was respectively 36.0 per cent and 45.2 per cent. A decade earlier, in June 1986, in the total outstanding from all agencies, the co-operative credit provided only 34.0 per cent here as against 45.9 per cent in all-India (Table 5.9).

In the provision of credit to agriculture, the PACS are the most important institution, but the growth in credit from them was low. Between 1965-66 and 1985-86, it had increased only around nine times—from Rs 8.38 crore to Rs 73.36 crore—as against 10 times at the national level; the state's share in all-India total declined to 2.34 per cent from 2.67 per cent. In the nineties, the situation worsened noticeably. In 1991-92, they had provided credit totalling Rs 103.48 crore to 9.64 lakh borrowers, constituting respectively 1.66 per cent and 3.96 per cent of all-India total. The loans outstanding were Rs 214 crore this year, constituting 2.09 per cent of all-India total. The amount per hectare of GCA came to Rs 250 compared with Rs 552 at the national level. The data for recent years are not available, but the situation appears to have deteriorated further. In 1994-95, the total credit outstanding stood at only Rs 115.3 crore (NABARD 2002).

An important reason behind the low provision of credit was the high level of overdue with the PACS. Overdue as percentage to outstanding increased from 43 in 1960 to 56 in 1970 and 66 in 1985; at the national level, it was respectively 21, 38 and 42 per cent. In the nineties, the latest data, for 1994-95, gives the percentage of overdue at 52.6. The operation of the PACS here is very inefficient. The transaction cost per Rs 100 of loan averaged Rs 20.60 during 1993-97 as against Rs 18.90 for all-India. The performance of LDBs was also poor. The annual average of loans provided came to only Rs 46.04 crore during 1993-97, and constituted 2.77 per cent of all-India total; the share of Kerala in this period was as much as 8.43 per cent. Earlier, the situation was better. At the end of June 1986, loans outstanding with the PLBDs stood at Rs 45.73 crore and constituted 3.4 per cent of all-India total (Table 5.9; Deb 1988:161).

Agricultural Marketing

Marketing of the produce at remunerative prices is a big problem, particularly for small farmers and in remote areas. The problem becomes more severe at the time of a good harvest. Because of the lack of storage facility farmers are often compelled to sell their produce at throwaway prices. Proper market places are also generally not within easy reach. The price support system is there for only a few commodities, and that too is not implemented effectively. The co-operative marketing is also virtually non-existent. We give a brief look below on the situation of each of them.

The storage capacity in the state continued to be very low. As percentage to total food grain production it stood at only 14.5 in 1993 as against the all-India average of 21.4. In the co-operative sector, the marketing societies and the PACS had created a storage capacity of 510.8 thousand tonnes till 1995-96. The progress by the state Warehousing Corporation was negligible. During 1996-98 (three years) it provided an average of 258.0 thousand tonnes, rising from 186.6 thousand in 1980-82. As regards the latest position, at the end of March 2003, the co-operative sector had a total capacity of only 483.2 thousand tonnes, constituting 3.46 per cent of all-India total, and the Food Corporation of India 1036 thousand tonnes and 3.90 per cent respectively. The rural godowns scheme, meant for small and marginal farmers, made a very small contribution. At the end of December 1992, the total capacity created stood at only 20,100 tonnes, constituting 0.97 per cent of all-India total; the target was to have 38,500 tonnes (Bhatia 1999; Deb 1988 and FAI 2003).

The cold storage facility was utterly inadequate, and it hampered the growth in production of perishable commodities. There was large-scale wastage of fruits and vegetables. Recently it was disclosed by the government that the state produces 100 lakh tonnes of vegetables every year but 30 per cent of it is wasted due to lack of multi-chambered cold-storage. Whatever cold storage facility is there is used mainly for storing potatoes (Statesman 2002: BP, III).

Several thousand crore of rupees are thus lost every year due to lack of proper storage facility.

As regards market places, an overwhelming proportion of the farmers had to rely solely on unregulated weekly *haats*. Number of regulated markets was very few. At the end of October 1998, there were 46 principal market yards and 496 sub-market yards. Per 100 sq km of area, West Bengal had only 2.4 markets in 1993, which was just equal to the national average; not to speak of Punjab, even Kerala had 8.9 markets. A decade back, in 1982, there were 293 principal and sub-market yards, constituting 0.77 per cent of the state's total number of villages; for all-India it was 0.83 per cent.

The district-wise distribution of regulated markets has no relation with the cropped area or the quantum of agricultural produce produced. In October 1998, Midnapore with the largest acreage had only 27 sub-market yards whereas Cooch Behar, with less than a third of the acreage, had the highest number of 108. Even Burdwan, an agriculturally developed district, had only 40 market yards (GOW 1999). Of course, it was determined also by the quantum of disposable produce and the location of the district.

On the transportation facility in the interior areas, the less said the better. Percentage of villages connected with all-weather roads stood at 47 in 1996 as against the all-India average of 48. District-wise, the road availability is not closely related to the area of the district. At the end of March 1999, the proportion of road length was less than the district's share in area in case of seven of the districts—Purulia, Midnapore, Bankura, 24-parganas, Malda, Darjeeling and West Dinajpur. Purulia had 7.17 per cent of area but only 4.65 per cent of the road length and Midnapore 15.2 and 12.0 respectively. (GOW 2000)

As regards co-operative marketing, the situation appears to have worsened over the years. In 1995-96, there were only 269 primary agricultural co-operative marketing societies in the state with the value of agricultural produce marketed at Rs. 31.35 crore—that is, an average of Rs 12 lakh per society. Their main activity now is distribution of fertilisers (GOW 1998:49). Earlier, in 1977-78, there were 316 PAMS with the average value of produce marketed per society at Rs 2.06 lakh, which was 18.0 per cent of all-India average (Deb 1986: 116).

The price support system was generally discriminatory and not managed properly. Between 1988-89 and 1992-93, the procurement price of paddy (common) increased by only 68.7 per cent as against 80.3 per cent in wheat. Over the long period between 1982-83 and 2000-0, it was respectively 318 per cent and 308 per cent; but the base price for the latter was 16.4 per cent higher. For rapeseed and mustard, the increase in the first period was 65.2 per cent compared with 77.8 per cent in sunflower (GOI 1993a, 2003a). The price increases were based not only on the intrinsic factors like cost, productively, etc but also had an implicit element of bargaining power of the farmers concerned.

The support operations were often not carried out properly. The jute producers were frequently a victim of inefficiencies and corruption in the Jute Corporation of India. The plight of jute growers was brought out vividly by the eighteenth report (1978) of the committee on Public Undertakings. The committee pointed out that not only was the MSP fixed too low, the FCI's pattern of operation was hardly of any help to growers. The jute growers were forced to resort to distress sales at prices "much below the MSP and considerably below their cost of production". (Quoted in Deb 1997: 133). Things have not improved much over the years. Even in recent years the farmers had to face such situation (Statesman 1997).

ALLIED ACTIVITIES

Animal Husbandry

As noted in chapter 5, animal husbandry is an important activity closely related to crop farming. Its growth is, however, dependent on a variety of factors like availability of feed and fodder, status of crop farming, people's food habit, veterinary facility, etc. Overall, West Bengal's position does not appear bad. In 1992, the state had 351 lakh livestock, constituting 7.45 per cent of all-India total. This is a considerable improvement over the earlier situation. In 1956, at 170 lakh, the state's share was 5.55 per cent (GOI 2000d, 1959). In poultry, the relative position was much better. In the all-India total number, the state's share increased from 10.9 per cent to 12.2 per cent in this period. Below we give a brief look into the nature of progress in the important types of livestock, to be followed by an analysis of the situation in poultry.

Cattle and Buffalo

The cattle and buffalo are the most important among the livestock because of their multifarious uses. The primary use of male cattle is in agriculture and of females in milk production. Buffaloes are kept mainly for their higher milk yield. Number of cattle in West Bengal had a noticeable growth over the years. Between 1972 and 1992, it was by 108 per cent as against only 60 per cent at the national level. The state's share in the latter's total rose to 8.5 per cent from 6.6 per cent. In recent years the relative position has improved further. In 1997, the total number rose to 17832 and constituted 9.0 per cent of all-India total. Although the increase over 1992 is by only 2.17 per cent, in the latter it was negative 2.8 per cent (GOI 2004a)

From the angle of economic importance, however, this growth in number is not as important as its composition. The proportion of female cattle in the total had a noticeable rise over the years, being from 43.5 per cent in 1972 to 55.7 per cent in 1992, with a 167 per cent growth in number. The proportion of milch cattle in them was, however, very low. In 1992, it stood at only 36.2 per cent against the national average of 56.1. Among the selected states, West Bengal's was the lowest proportion. The proportion in milk was again the highest here (Table 5.10.).

Among the cattle, the cross-bred, with high milk yield, constituted a very small proportion. In 1992 it stood at only 5.5 per cent against the national average of 7.4 per cent; in Punjab and Kerala the proportions were respectively 56.0 per cent and 49.9 per cent. In recent years, the relative position has worsened further. In 1997, with the total number at 936 thousand, the share in total cattle came to only 5.25 per cent as against 10.1 for all-India. The proportion of females in the cross-bred was, however, relatively high—being 77.1 per cent in 1992, against the all-India average of 69.4. In the all-India total number of cross-bred females, West Bengal's share was 7.0 per cent this year.

In this situation, the milk output from cattle could not be high. The management of cattle population was indeed very poor here. The pressure of cattle on land increased enormously over the years but there was no screening from the angle of milk yield. In 1992, there were 3.27 cattle per hectare in West Bengal as against the all-India average of 1.44. A rapidly growing number was used for less productive purposes.

The management of buffalo population appears to be better, although the growth in total number was very low. Between 1972 and 1992, the buffalo population of West Bengal had increased by only 42.3 per cent as against 129.6 per cent at the national level. The state's share in all-India total declined to 1.20 per cent from 1.94. The growth in number of females was much faster, being 77 per cent, but still it was below the national average (Table 5.10). Among the females, the proportion of milch buffaloes was relatively high—being 64 per cent in 1992 as against 60 per cent at the national level. However, in the all-India total number, the state's share was only 0.53 per cent, lower than in all the neighboring states.

For cattle and buffalo together, number of females in West Bengal stood at 100.58 lakh in 1992 and constituted 5.92 per cent of all-India total. In the total number again, the share of buffaloes was only 3.33 per cent compared with 39.36 per cent in all-India. Thus, there was hardly any attention to milk production in West Bengal. The proportion of milch cattle and buffalo was also not good. In the total number of females in the state it was only 37.1 per cent as against 57.7 per cent in all-India.

An important reason behind the low proportion of females is the keeping of a large number of cattle and buffalo for work. In 1992, 27.6 per cent of the cattle in West Bengal were kept only for work, and for buffalo as much as 57.2 per cent; at the national level, it was respectively 26.9 per cent and 6.0 per cent. Thus, the priorities for use of cattle and buffalo, particularly the latter, appear to be largely different here from that in many other states.

This unfavorable composition was reflected in the output of milk. In 1995-96, West Bengal produced only 33.4 lakh tonnes of milk, constituting 5.0 per cent of all-India total. The per capita annual production came to 45.6 kg as against the national average of 72.3 kg. This was despite a very high growth in production. Between 1971-72 and 1995-96, it was by 582 per cent, three times the rate at the national level. In the last few years, however, the growth decelerated. The production stood at 40.79 lakh tonnes in 2001-02, and the relative share declined to 4.8 per cent. In the total production, buffaloes contributed only 8.6 per cent here in 1995-96 compared with 53.8 per cent at the national level (Table 5.11; GOI 2004b).

District-wise, there were wide variations in production of milk. In 1998-99, five districts—Burdwan, Nadia, 24-parganas (N), Midnapore and Hooghly—together accounted for 59 per cent of the total. On the other hand, six districts—Purulia, Birbhum, Cooch Behar, Jalpaiguri, Malda and Dinajpur—had contributed only 16.3 per cent. Each of these six districts had a lower growth in production than the state average. The per capita milk production in the latest year varied between the highest of 105 kg in Darjeeling and the lowest at 18 kg in Purulia (excluding Calcutta).

The low level of milk production in the state is partly due to its low priority in the food habit of the state's population. Inadequate availability of feed and fodder is another important reason. And this again is largely due to the extremely small size of land holding and poverty of the people. The cost of maintaining a cross-bred or a buffalo is much higher than that of an indigenous cattle.

Other Livestock

Among other livestock, the most important in West Bengal are goats, sheep and pigs. Goats are maintained mainly for provision of meat but they provide some milk also. The cost of maintaining a goat is very low, and it constitutes an important source of supplementary income to the poor. The goat population in the state had a rapid growth over the years. Between 1972 and 1992, it was by 172 per cent, from 52.11 lakh to 141.70 lakh, and the state's share in all-India total rose to 13.3 per cent from only 7.7 per cent. West Bengal's was the largest share in the latest year.

As regards the output from goat, no data on meat production separately for goat are available. But it can be safely assumed that in the total meat production at 427 thousand tonnes in 1997-98, an overwhelming proportion came from goat. Milk production is negligible. It stood at only 10 thousand tonnes in 1992, and constituted 0.36 per cent of all-India total.

On sheep farming, so far as the growth in number is concerned, the state's performance was quite good. Between 1972 and 1992, it had risen by 87.6 per cent—from 7.93 lakh to 14.88 lakh—as against only 27 per cent at the national level[3]. West Bengal's share in all-India total increased from 1.98 per cent to 2.93 per cent over the period.

Sheep are kept primarily for wool production, but the state's performance was very poor. In 2001-02, the production stood at a negligible 0.64 tonnes, declining from one thousand tonnes in 1995-96; the relative share in all-India total declined to 1.27 per cent from 2.41 per cent. One reason behind the low production is that the proportion of cross-bred sheep is low here. In 1992, it constituted only 1.95 per cent as against the national average of 4.75 per cent. Moreover, a relatively large proportion of cross-bred was too young here for production of wool.

As regards pig farming, generally practised by certain communities only, the state has made a substantial progress over the years. In 1987, there were 9.55 lakh pigs, constituting 7.47 per cent of all-India total. In the following years, the growth was insignificant, the number in 1998 being only 10.98 lakh. In recent years, however, the government has taken a number of steps for developing the piggery as there is a good prospect of selling pigs to the neighbouring states.

Poultry Development

In poultry development West Bengal's performance has been quite impressive. Number of poultry in the state increased by 198 per cent between 1972 and 1998, and the share in all-India total rose to 12.2 per cent, next only to Andhra Pradesh. None of the eastern states could reach even half this level. In the composition of poultry, ducks have a relatively large share here. In 1992 it constituted as much as 15 per cent of total, around four times that at the national level. In the all-India total number of ducks, West Bengal alone contributed 53.0 per cent. Fowls constituted 73.4 per cent of total as against 92.5 per cent in all-India. The higher proportion of ducks here is probably due to their low maintenance cost. A serious draw back in poultry management here is, however, that the improved variety constituted a very low proportion. In fowls, it was only 20.2 per cent as against 34.8 per cent at the national level. In ducks, the position was still inferior—being 3.06 per cent and 6.73 per cent, respectively (Table 5.12).

It is probably because of this inferior composition, in egg production the state's performance was relatively poor. Over a period of one-and-half decade, between 1987-88 and 2001-02, it had risen by only 41.9 per cent—from 2155 million to 3057 million. West Bengal's share in all-India total declined to 9.0 per cent from 12.1 per cent over the period. The per capita egg production here was less than a third of that in Punjab (Table 5.12; GOI 2004b). The demand-production gap is enormous. The present daily consumption in West Bengal is 75 lakh eggs as against the production of a mere four lakh (Statesman 2002Z 17: 1).

District-wise, the egg production has been heavily concentrated in a few of them. In 1998-99, six districts—24 Parganas (S), Midnapore, Murshidabad, 24-Parganas (N), Burdwan and Hooghly—together contributed 59.2 per cent of the total; in 1990-91, their share stood at 62.3 per cent. On the other hand, another six districts—Darjeeling, Purulia, Jalpaiguri, Cooch Behar, Howrah and Bankura—had a combined share of only 19.0 per cent; the proportion remaining almost unchanged over the years. The growth in production has been very low in some of the districts, some even registering an absolute fall. Over the nine-year period, Burdwan had recorded a growth of 108 per cent, and its relative share increased from 5.2 per cent to 9.3 per cent. Three districts—Jalpaiguri, Midnapore and Howrah—on the other hand, had absolute fall. The per capita egg production in 1998-99 (based on 1991 population) varied between the highest of 61 in South 24-parganas and the lowest at 28 in Jalpaiguri (excluding Calcutta and Howrah), with the state average at 39.

Reasons Behind

The low growth of the animal husbandry sector is largely because it is predominantly a poor man's area and is practised mainly as a backyard venture. At the end of Eighth Plan, the state had 157.48 lakh backyard livestock units managed by 80 lakh farming families; commercial livestock units numbered only 86,200 (GOW 1999a: 8). These units required not only financial help but also constant guidance through proper extension service and adequate infrastructural facilities, including proper marketing arrangements.

The government's attention to the sector's problems was, however, utterly inadequate. The fund allocation itself was very low. The total expenditure in the first three five-year plans came to only Rs 4.05 crore and constituted 0.78 per cent of the aggregate. When the plan size increased in the recent plans, the relative share, however, declined. The Seventh plan had provided for Rs 24.64 crore and the Eight Rs 53.26 crore, constituting respectively 0.53 and 0.55 per cent of the total. The quality of implementation of the programmes can be gauged from the fact that in the Eighth plan only Rs 24.22 crore—that is, 45.5 per cent of the allotted amount—could be spent.

To look at the level of certain facilities available: There are presently 67 Livestock Farms in the state for breed upgradation and also for demonstration and training. Of them, 21 are poultry/broiler farms, 11 duck farms, 11 cattle farms, 8 sheep and goat farms, 9 rabbit farms and 7 pig farms. The levels of activitics in most of them are very low. The facility for artificial insemination was utterly inadequate until recent years. For the interior areas, some arrangement was made only from the Eighth plan. The annual number of artificial insemination registered in the recent years was a little more than 6 lakh through 2,878 artificial insemination centres (GOW 1999).

The feed and fodder situation continues to be very difficult in many parts of the state. Availability of balanced livestock feed is extremely inadequate. It has been given some attention only in recent years. There are presently three plants for this purpose. The fodder development activities also received attention only in recent years. Two research stations have been established with assistance from the World Bank. There are 17 fodder farms in the state which produce around 13,000 tonnes of fodder and 22 quintals of fodder seed annually (ibid.).

The control of animal diseases did not receive sufficient attention and the farmers were discouraged from going for costly animals. Preventive vaccination programmes were extremely rare until recently. Organisation of health camps in the villages were few and far between. Number of veterinary hospitals, dispensaries, etc is very few in the state. At the end of March 1998, there were only 110 veterinary hospitals/polyclinics and 612 veterinary dispensaries. In the all-India total number, these constituted respectively 1.42 per cent and 3.93 per cent. Only veterinary aid centers were available in relatively large number. There were 3,245 centres in 1998, constituting 11.78 per cent of all-India total (GOI 2000e). The quality of service provided is, however, far from satisfactory. The extent of improvement over the years may be gauged from the fact that in 1962 there were 41 hospitals and 250 dispensaries in the state (GOW 1966).

Fishery Development

West Bengal is the largest fish consuming state in the country, and naturally therefore, the development of fishery received much attention. The fishery resources are also large. Apart from the marine resource, inland water resources are also substantial, as evident from Table 5.13. Particularly important are tanks and ponds. The state accounted for 13.1 per cent of all-India total in 1998. There is also a large area of brackish water—to the extent of 2.1 lakh ha. For marine fishery, the state has 27,720 sq km within the continental shelf, along with a stretch of 150 km coastal length excluding 'Hooghly-Matla Estuary' (GOW 1998: 38).

The production of fish increased rapidly over the years. During 1967-69 (three years), the state had an annual average production of 222 thousand tonnes, constituting 14.8 per cent of all-India total—the second largest. By mid-eighties, West Bengal became the largest producer and it is continuing in this position. In 2000-01, with the total production at 10.60 lakh, the state accounted for 18.74 per cent of all-India total (Table 5.13 and GOI 2004a). It is necessary to note, however, that the growth in fish production was much faster in a number of states, albeit from a low base. Over the entire period, West Bengal had registered a growth of only 332 per cent as against three times as much in neighbouring Orissa.

In the total production of fish, inland fish accounted for the overwhelming proportion. Till the end of eighties, its share was 90 per cent or more. In the nineties, however, the relative share declined due to a faster growth in marine catches. Between 1980-81and 2000-01, marine production had recorded a six-fold rise–from 30 thousand tonnes to 181 thousand as against 2.6 times in inland production–from 3.40 lakh tonnes to 8.79 lakh.The annual average production of the former during 1996-99 came to 1.69 lakh tonnes and constituted 17.6 per cent of the total (GOW 1995, 2000).

Despite the large share of West Bengal in all-India production, the potential remains far from being exhausted. The brackish water area brought under culture so far is no more than 10 per cent of the total. The Brackish-water Fisheries Development Agencies were set up in the *coastal* districts only in the Eight Plan, and the coverage so far is around 1.5 thousand ha. The ox-bow lakes *(beels*), with an area of 41,000 ha, have also remained grossly underutilised. A programme for their reclamation has been taken up only recently. The potential of reservoirs also remains largely unexploited. The fish culture practised in large areas of the state is still not even of semi-intensive type. The production of fish seed increased considerably over the years, from 2300 million numbers in 1980-81 to 8610 million in 1998-99, but instead of using them within the state a significant proportion was sent to other states.

As regards the rivers and canals, their productivity has fallen due to a number of reasons. Construction of dams and other human interferences in the flow of rivers and canals have not only reduced the volume of water but have also polluted them. The run-off from agricultural fields and discharge of pollutants by industries has endangered the survival of a variety of fishes. A recent status paper has brought out that a variety of fishes are now almost extinct in the rivers of North Bengal due to indiscriminate use of pesticides and other chemicals in the tea gardens (Statesman 2001 r).

While emphasising increased production of fish, probably we can no longer ignore the question of sustainable exploitation of "wild fish population". The pollution of river water and unscientific ways of fishing need to be controlled rigorously. There should be a limit to destruction of natural habitat of fishes. But given the spectre of uncontrolled human greed, it is futile to think that much success can be achieved. The only way to save the rapidly vanishing species is probably to go for captive breeding.

The marine fishery did not get any attention until recent years, and this is primarily because it has a very low priority in the local consumption. Production for export is not given much attention and it is confined largely to prawns. Another reason for low exploitation is that going beyond the narrow coastal belt requires much larger investment in mechanisation of fishing fleet and in berthing, landing and other facilities. Marine fishing is presently confined to the inshore area of up to 50 metres depth with a fleet comprised of 2,584 mechanised and 3,494 traditional craft.

That the state did not give any serious attention to development of fishery is evident from the amount allocated to it under different five-year plans, and the manner in which the funds were spent. The Second Plan had provided for Rs 75.74 lakh but only Rs 26.79 lakh-that is, 35.4 per cent-could be spent. In the Third plan, the expenditure came to Rs 135.32 lakh out of Rs 204.83 lakh provided. In the recent plans, however, the allocation to fishery had increased greatly. The Seventh plan had provided Rs 38.00 crore, constituting 43.8 per cent of the aggregate for agricultural programmes, and in the Eighth plan Rs 79.17 crore and 29.0 per cent respectively. Thus, it took a long time for the state to realize the importance of developing the fishery sector.

Forestry

West Bengal is having a very small proportion of forest area, but even this could not be maintained properly. In 1952-53 the state had a forest area of 14.83 lakh hectares, constituting 1.83 per cent of all-India total. But by 1970-71 it declined to 11.88 lakh. Over the following three decades, there was a nominal rise, to 11.92 lakh hectares in 1999-00, constituting 1.73 per cent of the national total. In relation to the state's total area, forest constitutes only 13.76 per cent as against the national average of 22.57 per cent. The per capita forest area came to only 0.015 ha in 1999-00 compared with 0.067 at the national level. Even if the village orchards are included, the state remains far behind the norm of one-third of the geographical area as laid down by the National forest policy (CMIE 2004b; GOW 1999).

The quality of West Bengal's forest area is also very poor. The actual forest cover in 1997 was only 70.3 per cent of the forest area compared with the national average of 82.8 per cent. The proportion of dense forest is also low. It is not only much below the national average but also the lowest among the selected states. And this is the position despite 91 per cent of the area being either reserved or protected (Table 5.14).

Although this depressing situation is basically due to the population pressure and greed of the people, there is no escaping the fact that the blame for it falls squarely on the government administration. The government collected substantial revenue from the forest but there was hardly any attempt to protect the forest until recently. The revenue receipts from the forest increased continuously from Rs 47.03 lakh in 1952-53 to Rs 211.47 lakh in 1965-66. And then, after some fluctuation for a few years it reached Rs 1576 lakh in 1980-81, Rs 3394 lakh in 1990-91 and Rs 7479 lakh in 1996-97. The fall in collection came for the first time, after 1970-71, only in 1997-98 (GOW 2000).

The expenditure on forest, however, remained very low until recent years. With fluctuations, it increased from Rs 55.46 lakh in 1952-53 to Rs 260 lakh in 1970-71 and Rs 9129 lakh in 1995-96. The relative position of West Bengal among the states in recent years, however, has not been bad. In 1995-96, the expenditure per hectare of forest area came to Rs 763 as against the all-India average of Rs 290. The plan expenditure on forest also moved similarly. In the first three five-year plans, the aggregate of expenditure came to Rs 3.15 crore, constituting 6.84 per cent of the total for agriculture and allied sectors. In the last three five-year plans, the seventh through ninth, it was respectively Rs 369.71 crore (outlay) and 25.0 per cent.

The forests were looted ruthlessly, openly as well as clandestinely. The outturn of forest produce (timber and firewood) annually averaged 1035.8 thousand cm during 1952-53 to 1961-62. Sharp reduction came only in recent years, to 176.3 thousand cm in 1997-98 from 664.8 thousand in 1985-86; the average for last five years came to 248.6 thousand cm. The proportion of timber in them, however, increased from 16.5 per cent during 1952-62 to 34.8 per cent during 1993-98 (GOW 1996, 1999). The smuggling of timber and firewood from the forest in collusion with the departmental officials was also not negligible. Even head-loads of firewood constitute a large drain on forest resource. It may be noted here that even in 1999-00, 78.5 per cent of the rural households and 12.1 per cent of the urban households were depending on firewood and chips as the primary source of energy for cooking (NSSO 2001).

The measures taken to compensate for this ruthless exploitation were negligible. The poor people living near the forest and surviving on it, did not take any measure for protection primarily because they were uncertain about the possibility of drawing on the forest in future. The government also did not take any worthwhile measure. The apparent expenditure itself was low, as noted earlier, and then it was further reduced due to corruption. The government began to take some important steps only in the recent years. We give a brief look into some of them.

The West Bengal Forest Development Corporation was set up in 1974, with some laudable objectives like i) conserving the fragile eco-system of the Darjeeling Himalayas, ii) promotion of joint forest management with people's participation in South-West Bengal, iii) offer forest produce and value-added products at reasonable prices, and iv) develop awareness for conservation of nature through eco-tourism. The corporation did virtually nothing for conservation of the forest. It was leased out 440 sq km in the Kalimpong division and every year afforestation of degraded areas was taken up for 200 to 250 hectares. The corporation's main activity gradually became harvesting and marketing of timber and other forest produce as an agency of the forest directorate. Only recently the afforestation activity went beyond the degraded areas of Kalimpong.

The overall achievement of the state in plantation was very poor. Over a period of nearly five decades, 1951 to 1999, the cumulative total of plantation area came to 11.58 lakh hectares, constituting 3.71 per cent of all-India total. In the total, the share of block plantation was 52.8 per cent and the balance from seedlings distributed. The former, at 6.11 lakh ha, constituted only 2.92 per cent of all-India total. Most of these plantations came only in recent years. During the eight years of 1990-98 alone 5.12 lakh hectares were added and another 2.95 lakh had come in the preceding five years. Thus more than 70 per cent came in the last one-and-half decade (GOI 2003c; GOW 1995, 1999).

The joint forest management began only recently, with the formation of Forest Protection Committees (FPC) in 1993. Till March 1999, 3,431 FPCs have been formed covering an area of nearly 4.91 lakh hectares, with the involvement of 4, 03,160 households in the forest fringe areas (GOW 1999a). In order to encourage the active participation of people in the FPCs the government allows them a share of usufructs from the forest. In case of *sal* forests, for example, 25 per cent of the revenue generated through resuscitation is shared among the members of the committee.

To ameliorate the poor men's problems, the government has also recently started an area-oriented fuel and fodder project for producing fuelwood and fodder in the degraded forest fringes and vested wastelands. The people are directly involved in the implementation of this project. The scheme is operating in the fuel deficit districts of Bankura, Midnapore, 24-Parganas, Burdwan and Birbhum. The progress is, however, very slow. In 1997-98, only 3,442 hectares of plantations were raised under it.

There is no doubt some substantial progress have come about in recent years. But unauthorised felling of trees and pilfering of fuelwood have not stopped despite promulgation of stringent regulations. It was reported recently that there are more than 100 illegal saw-mills in Cooch Behar forest division alone. Timber illegally felled from the nearby forests are supplied to these saw mills. Timber smuggling is quite common in Jalpaiguri also, and forest staff has been found to be involved in it (Statesman 2001s: BP, IV; 2001t: BP, II). Even seized produce worth lakhs of rupees are stolen from beat depots in different ranges of North Bengal (Statesman 2002 Z8).

The FPCs are also not functioning well in many places; there are reports of members being involved in unauthorised activities. The income to members has shown a continuous decline. The total of usufruct distributed by the FPCs was down to Rs 160.42 lakh in 1999-2000 from Rs 246.50 lakh in 1997-98 (GOW 2001: 157).

The encroachment on forest land is another big problem yet to be solved. The principal chief conservator of forest had in a circular issued in September 1990 observed that eviction of forest encroachers be given top priority. But so far nothing has materialised. The Public Accounts Committee, in its latest report, estimated the revenue loss from encroachment of forest land at Rs 20.28 crore, based on the out-turn of pulpwood in the traditional 10-year rotation cycle (Statesman 2002 Z 9).

Notes

1. In the Estate Acquisition Act, 1953, there was no ceiling on the holding of a raiyat provided he had not leased out land in excess of 33 acres.
2. There is some discrepancy in the data. The state government shows the created potential in major and medium irrigation at 1394.60 thousand hectares up to March 1999, whereas the government of India shows it at higher level even in 1997.
3. In the following years, however, there was no growth in number of sheep. In 1998, it stood at only 14.62 lakh. Goat population, on the other hand, rose to 156.48 lakh this year.

11

Pattern of Industrial Growth

The industrial growth in West Bengal since Independence is a matter of great interest, because it started the new era with some unique position. It was the most industrialised state in the country, as noted in chapter 1, accounting for 27.2 per cent of the country's total gross industrial output in 1951. Another uniqueness, a negative aspect which needed to be corrected, was that the industries were heavily concentrated in and around Calcutta; no other state in the country had so much of concentration. The objective of this chapter is to look into how the industrial structure changed over the years, and how the growth here compares with that in other states. The pattern of analysis follows that in chapter 6.

Factory Sector

The factories registered under the Factories Act 1948 are the most important contributor to industrial output in the state. But the performance of the sector over the years had been very disappointing. The value of output had registered a growth of only 5.7 times between 1960 and 1977-78 and another 10.3 times by 1997-98; at the national level, it was respectively 11.1 and 21.2 times in these periods. West Bengal's share in all-India total output declined from 20.6 per cent—second only to Maharashtra—in 1960 to 10.5 in 1977-78 and 5.1 in 1997-98. The per capita industrial output here was only 63.7 per cent of the national average in the latest year as against 130.8 per cent in 1977-78 (Table 6.1). The position worsened further in the following two years. In 1999-00, the state accounted for only 3.88 per cent of all-India total output, and the per capita output was halved–being respectively Rs 4,345 and Rs 8,743 (based on 2001 population; GOI 2002).

The employment scenario was extremely gloomy, and so also the productivity of employees. In the first period, 1960 to 1977-78, number of employees had increased by 40.6 per cent, and in the second it was negative to the extent of 10.8 per cent; the growth at the national level was respectively

144.2 per cent and 41.0 per cent. The state's share in all-India total employment by the sector was down to 8.3 per cent in 1997-98 and 7.4 per cent in 1999-00, from 22.9 per cent in 1960.

The productivity of employees had a very low growth. The output per employee increased only 358 per cent in the first period and 813 in the second; the latter was much below the national average. Per employee, the value of output came to only Rs 5.02 lakh in 1997-98, which was 60.8 per cent of the national average. The position deteriorated further in 1999-00, being only 52.7 per cent, Rs 7.53 lakh and Rs 14.30 lakh respectively. The fixed capital per employee also remained low despite a notable growth. In 1999-00, it was around half the national average, being respectively Rs 3.76 lakh and Rs 6.40 lakh. Total emolument per employee is, however, relatively high. In 1999-00, it was Rs 81,635 here as against Rs 76,176 for all-India; in relation to output per employee, it was respectively 10.8 per cent and 5.3 per cent (Table 6.1; GOI 2002).

The inefficient use of capital is reflected also in the capital-output ratio. It rose to as much as 0.63 in 1997-98, from 0.34 in 1977-78; the latest was much above the national average as against lower earlier. The position in 1999-00 is also not good; the ratio being respectively 0.50 and 0.45. The ratio of net value added to output has also worsened. In 1999-00, it was 0.16 here as against 0.17 for all-India; earlier, the situation was reverse. The per capita value added came to Rs 715 and Rs 1,509 respectively (ibid.).

Structural Change

The industrial structure of West Bengal has changed noticeably over the years. The important industries, in terms of value of output, are presently metal and alloys, electricity, machinery and equipment, chemicals and chemical products, jute textile, food products and rubber, plastic etc, in this order. Their combined share in 1993-94 was 73.9 per cent, declining from 77.1 per cent in 1989-90. Excepting the first two, all others had shown a relatively low growth and consequently their share in the aggregate output declined. Over this five-year period, the share of metal and alloy rose to 16.0 per cent from 14.8 and of electricity from 11.2 to 13.7. Their share must have increased further in the following years as the growth rate was faster than in other industries. Between 1989-90 and 1996-97, the highest growth was in electricity, at 298 per cent, followed by metal and alloy 208 per cent.

Of the remaining five industries, the share of machinery and equipment was down to 9.8 per cent in 1993-94 from 10.7 in 1989-90 but recovered again in the following years, becoming the third important industry in 1996-97 from fifth earlier. The chemical industry also had a similar pattern, and by 1996-97 it became the fourth important industry, overtaking food products and rubber and plastic. The sharpest fall was in rubber, plastic etc as it had the lowest growth of 64.7 per cent between 1989-90 and 1996-97; its position was now down to seventh from third earlier. The food products also had a similar situation.

In 1989-90, it was the second largest industry with a share of 11.4 per cent in total output, but in 1996-97 it was down to sixth position, with a growth of only 66.2 per cent. Jute textile's position also declined in this period.

To look at the situtation of some of the technical coefficients: Among the major industries, the output per employee had the highest growth in electricity. Between 1989-90 and 1996-97 it was by 284 per cent, and stood at Rs 11.02 lakh in the latest year as against the all-India average of Rs 8.09 lakh. This was achieved with a relatively low growth in fixed capital per employee—being 230 per cent. The fixed capital per employee here was, however, much higher than the national average, being respectively Rs 21.94 lakh and Rs 12.55 lakh in 1996-97. The capital-output ratio turned out to be as much as 1.99 as against 1.55 for all-India. This low efficiency is a matter of serious concern because electricity accounted for nearly half of the total value of fixed capital in the factory sector. In metal and alloy, the situation was still worse. Fixed capital per employee had risen by 392 per cent between 1989-90 and 1996-97 but the output per employee increased by only 192 per cent. In the latest year, the output per employee was only around half of the national average, being respectively Rs. 6.42 lakh and 12.15 lakh, as against Rs 7.24 lakh and Rs 8.37 lakh in fixed capital. The capital-output ratio stood at as much as 1.13 as against 0.69 for all-India. These two industries together accounted for 78 per cent of the total fixed capital in the sector in 1993-94, and their inefficiencies had a big impact on the sector as a whole.

In most of the other industries also the output per employee increased at a lower rate than that in fixed capital per employee. The highest growth in fixed capital per employee was in leather and fur products, at 782 per cent in this 8-year period, but the growth in output was only 291 per cent. Non-metallic mineral products also had 650 per cent and 235 per cent, respectively; for rubber, plastic etc 304 per cent and 81 per cent; and for paper and its products 379 and 135 per cent.

The net value added to output declined noticeably in some of the industries. Particularly noticeable was the fall in rubber, plastic etc, down to 0.08 in 1996-97 from 0.16 in 1989-90; at the national level, it stood at 0.18 in the latest year. Similar was the situation of food products—declining from 0.11 to 0.07; at the national level, the latest proportion was 0.10. In beverages and tobacco, West Bengal had only 0.20 in 1996-97 as against 0.33 in all-India; in metal products and parts it was 0.15 and 0.22 and in machinery and equipment 0.21 and 0.27, respectively (CMIE 1997; GOI 2000g).

Small Scale Industries

The small-scale industries, which are of critical importance for decentralised industrialisation, also did not perform well in the state. First we look into the pattern of growth in the larger of the SSI units, which are generally called the modern sector, and then into the unorganised sector.

The Modern Sector

On every parameter, the modern sector of SSI in West Bengal showed a poor performance. The value of production had increased only 9.36 times over a period of 16 years, between 1972-73 and 1987-88, as against 16.5 times for all-India. Consequently, the state's share in the latter declined to only 5.9 per cent form 10.4 per cent. Not only the growth in production was low, the ratio of net value added to output had a sharp fall over the years. In 1987-88, it stood at only 0.20, declining from 0.33 in 1972-73. The latest was much below the national average as against marginally higher earlier (Table 6.2).

The units in West Bengal were of relatively small size. The average value of production per unit came to only Rs 5.51 lakh in 1987-88 as against Rs 7.38 lakh at the national level. It was because of this the state's share in number of units was higher than that in production, as may be seen from the Table. Thus, the units here were in general very weak.

The growth in employment was low, and so also in productivity of the employees. Over the 16-year period, employment had increased by only 77 per cent here compared with 122 per cent in all-India. The state's share in all-India total employment by the sector declined to 8.5 per cent from 10.7 per cent. The productivity of the employees also increased by only 430 per cent compared with 646 per cent at the national level. In the latest year, the output per employee was only 69.2 per cent of the latter's (Table 6.2).

This low productivity was largely due to low level of fixed capital per employee. Fixed assets per employee here increased by only 164 per cent over the 16-year period as against 297 per cent at the national level. In 1987-88, West Bengal had only Rs 13,765, which was around half the national average and lowest among the selected states. The level of mechanisation was relatively low. Percentage of units consuming energy stood at 74.4 in the latest year, which was lower than in all but two of the states.

The capacity utilisation was also very low. In 1987-88 it stood at 36 per cent compared with 51 per cent at the national level. The consumption of energy per unit came to only Rs 23,000 as against the all-India average of Rs 24,000. One reason behind this situation might be that a larger proportion of the units was located in rural areas with poor infrastructural situation. In 1987-88, 37.7 per cent of the units were in rural areas, which was significantly higher than the national average. In rural West Bengal, even the electrification progressed very slowly, not to talk of the frequent load shedding. The depressing situation is reflected in the high proportion of closed units in the state. In 1987-88, 36,607 units were closed, constituting 44.3 per cent of the total number. In the all-India total number closed, West Bengal's share was 12.1 per cent.

As regards the industrial composition of the modern sector, there has been a significant change over the years. In 1987-88, four industries-basic metal and alloy, food products, rubber, plastic etc and metal products and paints—together accounted for 52.0 per cent of the total output. Another 29.4

per cent came from textile products, machinery and equipment, basic chemicals and products and wood and wood products combined. Thus, these eight groups together contributed 81.4 per cent of the total output. Earlier, in 1972-73, also their share was the same, with the first four accounting for 49 per cent of the total. But among them considerable changes took place now. The share of metal products was almost halved over the years, declining from 20.2 per cent to 10.6 per cent, and of basic metal and alloys from 19.3 to 13.9 per cent. The share of food products on the other hand, was nearly quadrupled, rising from 3.7 per cent to 13.9 per cent, and of rubber, plastic etc from 5.8 to 13.6 per cent. In the second group, the share of basic chemicals was down to 5.3 per cent from 11.0 and of machinery and equipment from 13.2 to 11.5. On the other hand, textile products raised its share from 5.1 per cent to 8.5 and of wood products from 3.3 to 6.8.

As the above data are very old, we may give a brief look into the position in recent years. In 1999-00, the state had an estimated 140.54 thousand units in the sector, constituting 4.51 per cent of all-India total, which is less than half the proportion in 1987-88; the growth in number of units was only 8.3 times here as against 19.6 times for all-India. The state's share in employment also had a sharp fall over the period; with the total employment at 5.85 lakh, it was down to 3.68 per cent, less than half the earlier level. The average employment per unit came to only 4.16 in 1999-00 as against the all-India average of 5.09 (SIDBI 2002). Thus, the SSI sector has fallen further over the last decade.

The Unorganised Sector

In the unorganised manufacturing sector the state's performance was somewhat better. According to the NSSO survey, in 1994-95 the gross value added of the sector stood at Rs 3034.06 crore and constituted 9.4 per cent of all-India total. This was higher than in most of the states. The size of the units was, however, relatively small here, and therefore, the share in all-India total number of units was as much as 13.2 per cent (Table 6.3).

These enterprises were located overwhelmingly in rural areas—to the extent of 80.2 per cent in West Bengal compared with 72.4 per cent at the national level. The rural enterprises are generally of smaller size than in urban areas everywhere, but here it was smaller than at the national level also. The OAMEs—that is, those working without any hired worker—constituted as much as 93.0 per cent of the total in rural West Bengal as against 90.8 per cent at the national level. In urban areas, on the other hand, the OAMEs constituted only 63.3 per cent and 67.8 per cent, respectively.

Due to the smaller size, the rural areas' share of total GVA was found to be only 57.2 per cent; but even this proportion was much higher than at the national level. The GVA per OAME was lower here both in rural and urban areas than at the national level. The NDMEs—which constituted only 7.0 per cent in rural areas and 36.7 per cent in urban areas—were also relatively weak in West Bengal, particularly in urban areas. The GVA per rural NDME was nominally higher than the all-India average, but in urban areas it was much lower, as may be seen from Table 6.3.

On the provision of employment, the sector's performance was much better. In the all-India total number, the state's share was 13.2 per cent this year, next only to Uttar Pradesh. The rural area's share was 76.9 per cent here compared with the national average of 66.6 per cent. The productivity of the workers was, however, very low. The GVA per worker in rural OAMEs was only Rs 4,322 in West Bengal compared with Rs 4,734 at the national level. In Urban areas it was respectively Rs 8,991 and Rs 11,073. The rural NDMEs had Rs 9,949 here as against Rs 10,683 at the national level; and in urban areas, it was respectively Rs 14,347 and Rs 18,662.

Over time, West Bengal's position appears to have deteriorated. In the all-India total of GVA for rural enterprises, West Bengal's share declined from 20.90 per cent in 1989-90 to 13.11 per cent in 1994-95, and in case of urban areas from 8.10 per cent to 6.82 per cent. The GVA per OAME in rural areas was higher than the national average in 1989-90, respectively Rs 5,319 and Rs 4,953, but now it is lower. As regards GVA per worker, the disparity has widened now; in 1989-90, it was respectively Rs 2,768 and Rs 2,861.

An important reason behind the low productivity of West Bengal's enterprises is their low level of fixed assets. In 1989-90, in the rural areas, per OAME it was estimated at Rs 1,998 for all fixed assets excluding land as against the all-India average of Rs 3,947. For OAME and NDME combined, it was respectively Rs 2,344 and Rs 6,338. For urban areas, the disparity was considerably less. For OAME and NDME combined, it stood at Rs 8,262 here as against Rs 14,027 at the national level. All these refer to owned assets. The not-owned assets were very low in rural areas—excluding land it was Rs 89 per enterprise as against Rs 483 at the national level. For urban enterprises, it was respectively Rs 5,596 and Rs 9,549 (NSSO 1995).

Khadi and Village Industries

The above data are estimates based on sample surveys, for a more authentic idea we give a brief look into the position of khadi and village industries in the state. In 1982-83, the value of production from the KVIs totalled Rs 20.20 crore and constituted only 2.66 per cent of all-India total. There were as many as eight major states, with smaller population, having a larger share of total output. In employment, however, the relative position was not so bad. At 1.39 lakh, the state's share in all-India total stood at 4.05 per cent. This, however, meant a very low level of productivity of the employees. The output per employee came to Rs 1,453 here as against the national average of Rs 2,215 (CMIE 1996[c]).

In the nineties, however, the situation improved considerably. With a growth of 551 per cent in 1993-94, over 1982-83, the value of output rose to Rs 131.48 crore and constituted 4.07 per cent of all-India total. There were, however, still four smaller states—Karnataka, Rajasthan, Tamil Nadu and Andhra-with larger share in the total. The employment in KVIs rose to 3.02 lakh persons this year and constituted 5.67 per cent of all-India total. The output per employee was still much below the national average—being respectively Rs 4,354 and Rs 6,070 (KVIC 1994).

As regards the composition of KVIs' output, five items—silk, palmgur, cottage leather, processing of cereals and pulses and bamboo and cane products—together accounted for 59.8 per cent of the total in 1993-94. Silk under khadi alone had 17.8 per cent, followed by palmgur 12.0 per cent; the shares of the remaining three were nearly equal. Another seven items—cottage pottery, lime manufacturing, fibre, carpentry and blacksmithy, ghani oil, muslin under Khadi and bio-gas—together contributed 32.3 per cent of the total.

To look into the relative position of West Bengal on some of the important items: In silk khadi, the state is the second largest producer in the country, after Tamil Nadu, with a share of 34.1 per cent in 1993-94. The productivity of the employees here is, however, very low; the output per employee came to only Rs 6,686 as against Rs 54,309 in Tamil Nadu. The employment in the industry this year was 35,000, seven times that of Tamil Nadu. There is need for qualitative improvement both in the fibre and in the system of processing. In palmgur also the state is the second largest producer. But it is a very poor second; the state's share in all-India production in 1993-94 being only 11.0 per cent compared with Tamil Nadu's 76.8 per cent. The output per employee here came to Rs 1,787 as against Rs 1,991 in Tamil Nadu. In bamboo and cane also West Bengal is the second largest producer, with a share of 10.7 per cent this year. But the output per employee was only Rs 4,476 as against Rs 6,571 in Maharashtra—the largest producer with a share of 27.4 per cent. The low productivity of employees is a big problem in a number of other industries like cottage leather, cottage pottery and muslin.

District-Wise Disparity

The state's industrial position was extremely depressing not only inter-state but also intra-state, among the districts. The industries were heavily concentrated in a few of them. In the absence of data on output, the situation of employment has been looked into.

In the most important segment, factory sector, in 1956 three districts—24-parganas, Howrah and Calcutta—together accounted for 74.2 per cent of the daily employment; the share of first one alone was 50.5 per cent. On the other hand, five districts—Malda, Cooch Behar, Nadia, Murshidabad and West Dinajpur—together contributed a measly 0.68 per cent. After around two-and-half decades, in 1980, the share of the three dominating districts declined to 68.8 per cent; for the most important one, 24-parganas, there was a nominal fall. The share of the five deprived districts rose to 1.50 per cent. Among them, however, the maximum gain was to the district nearest to Calcutta—that is, Nadia. There were two backward districts, Bankura and Birbhum, registering absolute fall in employment in this period.

In the following years also there was virtually no reduction in the imbalance. In 1996, seven districts—Cooch Behar, Malda West Dinajpur, Bankura, Murshidabad, Birbhum and Purulia—together had a share of only 2.38 per cent of total daily employment. On the other hand, four districts nearest to Calcutta—24-parganas, Howrah, Burdwan and Hooghly—together contributed 87.8 per cent. If Calcutta and Nadia are included, the share of central districts rises to 91.4 per cent. The factory sector employment per thousand population was only 0.39 in Malda in 1996 as against the highest of 42 in Howrah. For four districts—Cooch Behar, Murshidabad and West Dinajpur, apart from Malda—it was less than One and for ten districts less than five (based on 1991 population; GOW 1996). The growth in number employed over the period of four decades, 1956-96, was 8.6 per cent in Jalpaiguri, 17.6 in Birbhum, 29.4 in Bankura, 37.8 in Cooch Behar, 39.4 in Darjeeling, 50.6 in W. Dinajpur and 56.3 in Midnapore as against the highest of 1466 per cent in Nadia (GOW 1966, 1995, 1999). There was thus no decentralisation of industries in the last four decades, so far as the factory sector is concerned.

The SSI sector also did not play any compensatory role. In fact, the modern sector as a whole showed a negative growth in employment in the last decade, 1985-86 to 1995-96. There were only two districts—Murshidabad and Burdwan—showing a positive growth. The negative growth was highest in Malda, at 80 per cent, followed by Darjeeling 69 per cent. The employment per thousand population stood at the highest of 2.42 in Howrah in 1995-96 and at the lowest 0.29 in Cooch Behar; seven districts, out of 16, had below one (GOW 1995, 1996).

Causal Factors

There are many reasons behind this depressing industrial scenario. But the most decisive one is the character and quality of government the state has been burdened with. The party in power for two-and-half decades has encouraged indiscipline and inefficiency at every level throughout the state; there is a total absence of accountability. The government has no interest in a decentralised industrial growth of the state; its only concern is somehow to remain in power. In the absence of a viable alternative, the CPI (M) continued to be reelected. Below we give a brief look into the state's position on some of the factors that directly affect industrial growth.

Industrial Relations

The industrial relations scenario in West Bengal has always been poor. Mandays lost due to strikes and lockouts were almost always much higher than in most other states. During 1967-70 (calendar year), it annually averaged 70.39 lakh mandays and constituted 39.5 per cent of all-India total. In 1973-75, it reached 99.91 lakh, constituting 36.2 per cent. The share of strikes in the total in these two periods was respectively 58.4 per cent and 69.0 as against 69.5 and 77.6 per cent at the national level. Over the decade of 1967 to 1976, the mandays lost reached the maximum of 135.81 lakh in 1975 and the minimum at 36.16 lakh in 1992 (Mallick 1993: 200).

In the period of Left-Front rule, the mandays lost increased greatly, but strangely it was mainly due to lock-out, not strikes. Between 1977 and 1997, the total of mandays lost varied between the highest of 317.70 lakh in 1988 and the lowest at 61.80 lakh in 1980. The average for 1977-79 came to 131.07 lakh and increased to 231.13 lakh in 1985-87; in the last three years, 1995-97, it stood at 89.7 lakh. But the main contributor to loss of mandays in each of the years since 1976, except 1979, was lockout. The share of lock-out in the total rose to 86.8 per cent in 1995-97 from 77.9 in 1985-87 and 44.7 per cent in 1977-79 (ibid; GOW 1995, 1999).

The increased number of lockouts is a reflection of the management's stronger position, and this was largely due to the changed position of the CPI (M). The CPM's return to power with an unassailable majority put their trade union movement in a dominant but awkward position. The communists now emphasised the use of the state government's collective bargaining machinery; strikes were to be resorted to only in cases of extreme provocation (Ghosh 1981: 2).

Consequent on the weakening of trade union movement the wage increases were generally less in West Bengal. For the manufacturing workers earning less than Rs 1,000, the index of money wages stood at 142.1 (with base 1976 = 100) here in 1981 compare with 154.2 in Maharashtra and 155.3 in Gujarat (GOI 1985: 434). Number of persons laid off increased greatly over the years. In 1980 it stood at as much as 11,966, and in the following years although declined still averaged 1,365 during 1991-93 and 4,046 in 1996-98 (GOW 1999). Thus, the worsening of industrial relation was primarily due to the employers. Of course, they did not do it for nothing. The employers faced a variety of problems, and the overall environment in certain other states was better.

Infrastructural Situation

The overall infrastructural situation of the state deteriorated sharply over the years. An index prepared by using 13 items gave West Bengal only 94.2 (taking all-India = 100) in 1992-94, a fall from 132 in 1979-82 and 152 in 1966-67. Below we give a brief look into the position of the most critical item, the power supply.

On the provision of power the state performed very badly. First, the growth of installed capacity itself was low due to lack of proper advance planning and/or slow implementation. The state's share in all-India total of installed capacity declined from 17.5 per cent in 1957-58 to only 5.7 per cent in 1980-81 and 3.3 per cent in 1997-98. The utilisation of capacity was also very low, as evident from Table 6.4. The energy generation had a growth of only 3.58 times between 1970-71 and 1997-98 compared with 7.53 times at the national level. The load factor was always much below the national average.

The under-utilisation of capacity was primarily due to the low quality of personnel employed in the state electricity board. Appointments were often made on political considerations and overstaffing made the SEB inefficient. And this was there in the Congress period also. It was reported in 1982 that, of the 32,000 employees in the Board, 10,000 were completely redundant congress supporters whose only function was to obstruct the work of the new Left Front government (Statesman 1982). Number of employees per MU of energy sold was as much as 6.7 in WBSEB in 1992-93 compared with the national average of 4.5.

The overstaffing and inefficiency resulted in a very high cost of the electricity sold. In 1997-98, West Bengal had 254.67 paise/unit as against the all-India average of 227.89 paise. In this situation, the average tariff was relatively high, being at 194 paise per unit this year compared with 184.5 at the national level. But then also the tariff / cost ratio stood at only 71.4 per cent as against 81.0 at the national level. The SEB is presently suffering an average monthly loss of Rs 65 crore (Statesman 2002r: BP, III). A significant part of it is, however, due to theft of power. Only recently, in 2002, the government started taking some stringent measures against it (Statesman 2002 Z3: BP).

The industrial production in the state had been seriously affected by the power shortage. The rural electrification progressed at a very slow pace, and the power supply became highly erratic, particularly in the rural areas. In this situation, naturally the development of small and cottage industries suffered. The share of industry in total consumption of power declined everywhere but it was the sharpest in West Bengal, from 80.3 per cent in 1970-71 to 27.0 per cent in 1998-99; at the national level, it was from 61.56 per cent to 33.65 per cent (Table 6.4).

Another aspect that needs a mention is the political string attached to electric connections in villages. If the villages are to get electricity, they must vote for the Left Front. There are many villages without electricity because they are supporters of the Congress or the Trinamul. Recently it came out that a string of villages in Birbhum district did not get electricity even ten years after putting the application because of their not voting for the Left. (Statesman 2002Z 10:1).

The government's lack of interest in developing the rural infrastructure is evident also from the slow utilisation of the fund available for the purpose. The RIDF had sanctioned Rs 2486.69 crore till March 2004, but only Rs 1446.64 crore—that is, 58.1 per cent—out of it could be spent (RBI 2004).

INSTITUTIONAL FINANCE

Commercial Banks

For the provision of working capital to industries, the SCBs are the most important institution. But they did not play any noticeable role here. We give a brief look first to the position of large-scale industries. In the aggregate of industrial advances outstanding from the SCBs, the share of West Bengal declined to 10.6 per cent on June-end 1981from 15.7 per cent at December-end 1973. Maharashtra, the most industrialised state, on the other hand raised its share in this period from 26.8 per cent to 27.8 per cent (Deb 1988: 246). In recent years, the state's share has fallen further. The credit outstanding in March 2002 stood at Rs 18,021 crore, and constituted only 6.63 per cent of all-India total; six years back, in 1996, it was 7.82 per cent. The share in number of accounts was, however, much higher, declining from 22.0 per cent to 18.2 per cent over the period. The average amount of credit outstanding per unit was very low here; in the latest year, it stood at Rs 2.34 lakh as against Rs 6.42 lakh at the national level (CMIE 2003a). This fall is more or less in keeping with the state's share in all-India total output from the sector, and the health of the units operating here.

As regards advances to the SSIs, the situation is worse. It is evident from Table 6.5 that there was a continuous fall in the relative share of West Bengal among the states. In the aggregate of advances outstanding from the SCBs to the SSI units, the state's share was down to 6.8 per cent in 1995, from 8.1 per cent in 1968. The growth in advances over the period was 128 times here compared with 152 times at the national level. Maharashtra's share also declined but it was still around three times that of West Bengal.

The number of units getting the credit was, however, relatively high, and consequently, the amount outstanding per unit was very low. In the all-India total number of units, West Bengal's share increased from 8.2 per cent in 1983 to 20.8 in 1995. The growth in number of units was 503 per cent here compared with 138 per cent at the national level. This rapid growth led to an absolute fall in the credit per unit as against a rise in case of every other state. In the latest year, the credit per unit here was only Rs 32 thousand, a third of the national average.

Development Banks

The provision of long-term finance from the development banks, numbering 12, was also not appreciable. The cumulative total of assistance from all the institutions till March 1999 stood at Rs 13,993 crore and constituted 4.11 per cent of all-India total; Maharashtra, on the other hand, received as much as 22.4 per cent. One decade earlier, West Bengal's share was 5.80 per cent and of Maharashtra 17.8 per cent. On per capita basis, the cumulative till March 1999 came to Rs 1,831 which was only 52.1 per cent of the national average. There has been slight improvement in 2001; the state's share in all-India cumulative total rose to 4.52 per cent, and the per capita level reached Rs 2,797, constituting 57.9 per cent of the latter's (Table 6.6; IDBI 2002).

In the provision of finance, the state-level institutions played an insignificant role. In the per capita total till March 1999, the SFC and the SIDC together provided only 3.4 per cent. The SFC which is the older and larger institution, provided a per capita cumulative total of Rs 84.3 as against the all SFCs average of Rs 256.9—that is, the former a third of the latter. The SFC's role was still worse in the earlier years; during 1970-73, it had provided an annual average of only Rs 0.70 crore, constituting 1.79 per cent of the aggregate from all SFCs. The SIDC was also not in a much better position. The cumulative per capita assistance till March 1999 came to Rs 74.4 which was a little more than half the national average.

The development banks were concerned overwhelmingly with the large-scale sector of industry. For the SSIs, there were only two institution, the SIDBI and the SFC. The former commenced operation only in 1990, after taking over the IDBI's operation in the sector. West Bengal's position here also is not good. Till March 1999, the per capita cumulative assistance received by the SSIs stood at Rs 173.70, which was only half the national average. In the following two years, there was a sharp fall in assistance, and it declined to Rs 167.0 for the period till March 2001.

The provision by the SFC has, however, improved considerably in recent years. In the cumulative total till March 1999, the share of SSI was 68.9 per cent as against 63.0 per cent for all-states, and it improved further to 69.5 and 62.0 per cent respectively in 2001; earlier, the state's proportion was below the latter's. However, in the all-states cumulative total of assistance to SSIs, West Bengal's share is very low; with the total at Rs 654.0 crore till March 2001, it was only 2.94 per cent (ibid.).

It needs to be noted, however, that the smaller of the SSI units generally did not get the deserving treatment from the WBFC. To cite a recent instance : The state government had last year stipulated under its *Banglar Swanirbhar Karma Sangsthan Prakalpa* (a self-employment programme) that loans within Rs 5 lakh should not require any collateral security. But violating this rule, the WBFC continued to demand collateral security from the borrowers (Statesman 2001 u: 4). It also did not give adequate attention to the industrially backward districts. Till March 1999, the percentage of sanctions and disbursements to industrially backward districts, numbering 13, ranged between 19 and 32 per cent (Statesman 2002p).

For the low level of assistance from the commercial and development banks, probably these institutions cannot be blamed much. If due to infrastructural and other constraints the industrial units do not expand their operation much, or new units are not set up, the commercial banks cannot provide larger working capital. Similar is the position with regard to term-lending institutions. The state government has to create the right environment for larger investment. The pace at which work in government offices proceeds, and the frequency at which *bandhs* are called—often supported by the government itself, directly or indirectly—do not encourage investment in this state. We may cite here a few instances of inaction and inordinately slow action from the government:

1. The Behala Industrial Estate (IE), inaugurated in 1986, is now struggling for survival, largely because of the government's apathy to provide it with even basic infrastructure like water supply and

sewerage. The drains are clogged and during monsoons the whole estate is submerged. Thirty five out of a total 140 units have been closed; and of the remaining, 50 are in bad shape (Statesman 2001 v). And this is happening to an IE located within the capital city area of the state.

2. The condition of the IEs in and around Siliguri is probably worse. Faced with a skeletal infrastructure and official apathy all of them are on the brink of survival. Entrepreneurs suffer not only because of poor communication and erratic power supply but also due to the fact that for every small thing they have to run from pillar to post, not to speak of major clearances like land allotment and factory and building plans. The promises made on infrastructure for the IEs remain largely unfulfilled. The Dabgram IE was to be supplied with 3,000 liters of water per day to each unit, but at the most 500 liters are supplied (Statesman 2000 O).
3. The Supreme Court had ordered relocation of tanneries from Calcutta by 28th February, 2002. But the state leather complex at Bantala—where the units were to be shifted—was far from being complete even in December 2001, and many of the units were planning to move to Maharashtra.The company that was given the contract to provide 19 infrastructure facilities, could complete only two by the stipulated date (Statesman 2001w: BP, IV).
4. In September 2001, a special 'task force' was constituted by the entrepreneur development institute, a wing of small-scale industries department, for locating entrepreneurs to start SSI units. But by the end of February 2002—that is, after five months—only 24 could be found out, and that too all in one district (Burdwan) near Calcutta; it was to be from five densely populated districts (Statesman 2002 q).
5. The central Howrah Expressway project was taken up 15 years ago for constructing the six-km four-lane expressway but it is still a distant dream. The Howrah Improvement Trust, the implementing agency, was yet to complete the process of acquiring land for the project at the end of 2001 (Statesman 200 IX).

Hundreds of such instances can be cited. Things move in such a way that often it becomes difficult to believe that there is a government in the state.

In this situation, number of private corporate sector companies operating in West Bengal had a very low growth. Between 1988 and 1998, it increased by only 178.7 per cent here—from 23,786 to 66,299—as against 212.0 per cent in all-India. The relative share of the state in the latter's total declined from 15.40 per cent to 13.76 per cent. The fall was sharper in paid-up capital, from 15.3 per cent to 11.4 per cent, with a growth of 13.2 times—from Rs 1,727 crore to Rs 22,836 crore—as against 17.8 times at the national level. (GOI 1990, 1998).

The Central government investment also had a slow growth here. Between 1980-81 and 1993-94 it increased by 746 per cent—from Rs 1,736 crore to Rs 14,680 crore—as against 839 per cent in all-India. The relative share of West Bengal declined from 8.2 per cent to 7.4 per cent whereas for Maharashtra it was more than doubled—rising from 8.6 per cent to 19.8 per cent (CMIE 1996c).

The licensing policy of the Central government, which was launched with some laudable objectives, was not helpful in promoting industrialisation of backward districts. The state's share in total number of licences issued was not very high, and those issued were generally for Calcutta and its surrounding areas. In the all-India total number issued between 1974 and 1988, West Bengal's share was 7.1 per cent, 697 out of 9,817, as against 20.9 per cent for Maharashtra (GOI 1990). The implementation of the policy rarely gave attention to removal of regional imbalance, inter-state or inter-district within a state.

The Center's policy of freight equalisation, followed since mid-1950s to 1994, also had an adverse impact on the industrial growth of the state. This policy denied West Bengal of the comparative advantage it enjoyed because of proximity to coal and iron deposits and the location of steel factories. The distant states using coal from this region began enjoying some cost advantage in relation to West Bengal and the neighbouring states.

12

Towards Poverty Alleviation

It has been noted in chapter 2 that the poverty situation of West Bengal continued to be very depressing even in recent years. In 1999-00, the state had 27.0 per cent of the population living below the poverty-line, which was higher than in as many as eleven of the major states and also above the national average. In the fifties, the state's relative position was much better. At 50.3 per cent during 1957-58 to 1959-60, it was below that in nine of the major states, including Kerala, Tamil Nadu, Andhra and Maharashtra (Mahendra Dev et al 1999).

Any sustainable and significant poverty reduction require a radical redistribution of land and other productive assets. As stated by Mahbub Ul Haq: "I am afraid that the evidence is unmistakable and the conclusion is inescapable: divorce between production and distribution policies is false and dangerous. The distribution policies must be built into the very pattern and organisation of production" (Haq 1978: 34). But even in this Marxist state, nothing of the kind came up in the last two-and-half decades; rather reverse policies were followed to make the rich richer. We have noted in chapter 10 the nature of land reforms undertaken and how the agricultural labourers were neglected. Here we look into only how some of the direct poverty alleviating measures were implemented.

Wage Employment Programmes

The importance of wage employment programmes in West Bengal may be gauged from the fact that the labour force participation rate in the state in 1961 stood at only 33.25 per cent as against 45.24 for all-India. Among the major 15 states none had such a low level of participation (census data). After more than a decade, in 1972-73, on the basis of NSS data, the LFPR was found to be 33 here compared with 44 at the national level (Sinha 1978: 296). There was, however, no effort until early seventies, to improve the situation.

Earlier Programmes

The first scheme for rural employment came only in 1971 and that too on a negligible scale. Under the crash scheme for rural employment, during 1971-72 to 1973-74 a total of 197.43 lakh mandays (lmd) were created in West Bengal, constituting 6.25 per cent of all-India total. In the following three years there was no special programme. The food-for-work programme came in 1977 but under it also the state's position was not good. Number of person-days created per family (employed) stood at only 320.8 in 1977-78 and 342.1 the next year, both were much below the average number in the other states (GOI 1980a).

The National Rural Employment programme substituted the FWP in December 1980, and it was operated on a larger scale. During the Sixth Plan, a total of 1182.40 lmd, that is, an annual average of 236.48, were created with an expenditure of Rs 110.40 crore. In the Seventh Plan, however, there was a sharp drop in employment creation. During 1985-89, 662.16 lmd were created, that is, an annual average of 165.54 lmd. In the all-India total, this constituted only 4.48 per cent. The cost per manday was relatively high here, being the average of Rs 23.60 in this period as against Rs 19.90 at the national level (Table 7.1).

Under the RLEGP, launched in 1983, also the state's performance was not good. In the first year, the centre had released Rs 7.70 crore but nothing could be spent due to administrative problem. In the second year, 1984-85, also the progress was very unsatisfactory. The Centre had released Rs 23.08 crore but only Rs 9.45 crore could be spent. The Sixth Plan had a target of creating 301.02 lmd in the state but only 72.84 lmd, that is, 24.2 per cent, could be created. In the Seventh plan, however, the performance improved noticeably. During 1985-89, 604 lmd were created, constituting 5.23 per cent of all-India total. Even this was far from satisfactory; the utilisation of available fund was much below the national average (Table 7.1).

The relative position of West Bengal among the states on employment creation remained very poor. In 1987-88, covering all public works, per thousand number of households participating in any public work came to only 55 here as against the national average of 64 and the highest of 178 in Gujarat (NSSO 1998e). In 1989, the JRY—a bigger employment programme—was launched. We give a brief look below on the magnitude and manner of its operation.

Jawahar Rozgar Yojana

The JRY made some significant changes in the policies on employment creation, as has been noted in chapter 7. However, West Bengal's performance here also was dismal. During 1989-90 to 1994-95, a total of only 3078 lmd—that is, an annual average of 513—were created, constituting 6.1 per cent of all-India total. The cost per manday created was high here. The average for 1989-95 came to Rs 41.12 as against the all-India average of Rs 34.55 (Table 7.2). The high cost is probably due to inefficiency and corruption in the panchayats, and not because of higher wage rate.

As regards the distribution of employment among different groups, the SCs/STs were benefited to a smaller extent here. Their share in total employment in this period stood at only 49.9 per cent as against 55.6 per cent at the national level; in the state's population they constituted 29.21 per cent in 1991 as against 24.56 per cent in all-India. Bihar with a much smaller proportion of SC/ST provided 63 per cent of the total employment to them. This happened probably because the SC/ST were not supporters of the CPM party in large numbers. The proportion of landless beneficiary was, however, relatively high.

In recent years, the importance of JRY has declined in most of the states, but the fall is sharper here. During 1997-00, the annual average of expenditure came to only Rs 126.17 crore as against Rs 421.88 crore during 1989-95. The total employment created in the three-year period was 403.3 lmd, constituting 3.9 per cent of all-India total. The cost per manday averaged as much as Rs 93.85, 40 per cent higher than the national average. The representation of SC/ST continued to be relatively low.

Another serious drawback is that the available fund often remained unutilised to a large extent. In 1995-96, for example, under the first stream only 76.1 per cent could be utilised; earlier, in 1992-93, it was to the extent of 71.4 per cent. In the second stream, the performance was still poor. In 1994-95, West Bengal could utilise only 58.7 per cent of that available compared with 67.9 per cent at the national level. On employment generation also naturally a wide gap between target and achievement appeared. Under the second stream, in 1994-95 for example, the achievement was only 79.9 per cent of the target compared with 110.5 per cent for all-India, and in the following year 150.5 per cent and 229.2 per cent respectively.

As regard the nature of assets created, it was always of several types, including social forestry, minor irrigation and flood control, soil conservation, construction of village tanks, drinking water wells and ponds, rural roads, school building, houses, etc. The proportion of expenditure for a particular item varied considerably from year to year, but on the whole a very large proportion went to construction of rural roads.

With regard to the sub-schemes also the state's performance was not good. Particularly depressing was the situation of the MWS. The resource utilisation on it totalled Rs 323.71 crore during 1992-93 to 1998-99 and constituted 8.35 per cent of all-India total. But the number of wells constructed in this period totalled only 23,641 and formed 2.52 per cent of all-India total. The cost per well was very high here; the average came to Rs 136,926 as against only Rs 41,375 at the national level. On the IAY also the situation was not good. The expenditure in this seven-year period totalled Rs 307.03 crore and the number of houses constructed at 191,392; in the all-India total, these were respectively 4.29 per cent and 4.52 per cent. The average cost per house came to Rs 16,042, slightly below the national average.

In the implementation of the JRY, the violation of the guidelines was quite common. We note here some of the findings of the concurrent evaluation carried out in 1992 (Neelakantan 1994). The proportion of total expenditure going for wage payment was found to be only 48.99 per cent as against the requirement of at least 60 per cent. This norm was violated in most other states also, but it was not on such a scale. The wage rate paid was below the minimum fixed, and it was not the same for both male and female as required by the guideline.

The employment created under the scheme was found to be very low here. For the JRY worker himself it was 2.65 person-days as against 3.81 at the national level, and for other members of the family 1.08 and 1.34 respectively. Further, among the beneficiaries, a large proportion was found to be belonging to non-eligible categories. Those with annual income above Rs 6,400 constituted as much as 54.25 per cent of the total.

A good aspect of the implementation here is that the record keeping was relatively better. The muster roll was not available in only 1.27 per cent of the cases as against the national average of 15.85 per cent. The quality of assets created was also found to be better. The good/satisfactory assets constituted 97.86 per cent here compared with 73.80 per cent at all-India level. The discussion of Action Plan at Gram Sabha meeting was practised to a larger extent here. In only 13.9 per cent of cases it was not followed as against 39.3 per cent at the national level.

Employment Assurance Scheme

The EAS was launched only in 1993 and in the last few years it has undergone a number of changes, as noted in chapter 7. The operation of the scheme in West Bengal has not been significant. As evident from Table 7.2, between 1993-94 and 1999-00, the total expenditure on it came to Rs 678.20 crore and constituted 5.14 per cent of all-India total. The growth in annual expenditure varied considerably from year to year and there were absolute declines during 1997-99. The utilisation of available fund was very low in the state. The total amount utilised over the entire period constituted only 65.2 per cent of that available as against the all-India average of 67.9 per cent, and the highest of 84.8 per cent in Andhra Pradesh.

The employment created in this seven-year period totalled only 915 lmd and constituted 4.1 per cent of all-India total; among the selected states, it was the second lowest. The cost per manday was very high, averaging Rs 74 as against Rs 59 at the national level. Partly because of this high cost, the state failed to provide employment to a large number of registered persons. In the provision of employment, the share of SC/ST was relatively low; at 56.9 per cent for the entire period, it was marginally higher than the all-India average. For landless labourers, however, it was relatively good, as may be seen from Table 7.2.

Consequent on the implementation of different employment programmes the rural employment situation has not shown any consistent improvement. According to the NSS, per thousand number of households participating in public works rose to 66 in 1993-94 from 55 in 1987-88, but declined again to only 25 in 1999-00; at the national level, it was respectively 59, 64 and 29. The rural unemployment rate on current daily status basis stood at 17.00 per cent in 1999-00 as against 7.20 for all-India (NSSO 2001; GOI 2002a: I). The earning strength of agricultural labour households declined, and it continued to be below the national average. The relative position on average daily earnings of men and women has also worsened (Table 7.3).

This depressing situation for the poorest group of people in the so-called Marxist state of West Bengal is to a considerable extent due to misuse of funds meant for them. We quote here some of the unauthorised activities and misuse of funds as reported in the Statesman (Chatterjee 1998; Statesman 2001Z):

(i) Rarely were people living below the poverty line selected as beneficiaries of the IAY. An internal survey report stated: "selection of IAY beneficiaries are not done as per our guidelines".

(ii) In Murshidabad district IAY houses were constructed with mud walls and tin sheets for roofing but in other districts, with the same expenditure, these were built of brick walls. In Malda, the misappropriation of fund was so rampant that the Zilla Parishad decided not to release more funds of the IAY until papers of utilisation, annual action plan and a proper list of beneficiaries were submitted.

(iii) Contractors were hired and moneylenders' help taken to build roads and houses, flouting the JRY and EAS rules. The contractors were mostly selected by panchayat leaders, and the building materials supplied by local businessmen.

(iv) The CAG report of 1993-94 stated that the JRY work was not monitored properly. "Reports received were not scrutinised and analysed by any officer to verify the authenticity of physical and financial progress recorded therein".

The constitution of beneficiary committees—expected to select the beneficiaries and also oversee the spending under the employment schemes—itself was not done properly. The guidelines say the committees should be formed with labourers and local people "who have interest in social work" to bring "maximum transparency" to rural development. But a PRD internal survey report stated: "Beneficiary committees whenever formed are not constituted as per guidelines". "No labourer or local people who are not members of panchayats but have interest in social work are included in the beneficiary committee".

Self-Employment Programmes

As in case of wage employment schemes, the self-employment programmes also became important only from the beginning of 1980s. The IRDP, launched in 1978-79, in 169 blocks of the state, covered the entire rural area by 1980. Under the programme, as noted in chapter 7, assets were provided to the selected families below the poverty-line through a mix of government subsidies and institutional credit. Below we give a brief look into the performance of the programme in West Bengal, including the sub-schemes-the TRYSEM, DWCRA and the SITRA.

The Integrated Rural Development Programme

Initially the progress of IRDP was very slow in West Bengal due to some procedural wrangling with the centre. In 1980-81, only 14.17 per cent of the target beneficiaries were covered. In the following two years also it was far below expectation, being only 26.92 per cent and 48.07 per cent. West Bengal's performance was the lowest of all the states (Mallick 1993: 145-46). The government failed to utilise the central release during 1978-80—only Rs 10 million out of the admissible Rs 90 million could be spent—and, therefore, the centre decided not to make any allocation for 1980-82. By 1983-84, however, the situation changed, and in terms of number of beneficiaries the target was over fulfilled to the extent of 17.5 per cent; for the entire Sixth Plan the over-fulfillment came to 68.73 per cent. Total number of beneficiaries assisted in this period stood at 690,769 with an expenditure of Rs 53.55 crore. The per capita investment (subsidy plus credit), however, averaged only Rs 2,012 as against Rs 2,876 at the national level (GOW 1987:19).

The scheme's effectiveness in enabling the poor to cross the poverty line was, however, negligible. The concurrent evaluation of 1985-86 had found only 8 per cent of the beneficiaries crossing the poverty line. Inclusion of ineligible beneficiaries in the programme was found to be the extent of 3 per cent. The coverage of SC/ST was very low; during 1980-83, it averaged 34.5 per cent.

The performance in the Seventh Plan was better. It had a target of assisting 12.50 lakh families, but was over-fulfilled to the extent of 27.9 per cent, with the expenditure exceeded by 5.7 per cent. The proportion of SC/ST beneficiaries was, however, only 37.26 per cent, and of women 24.35 per cent. The trend in recent years is presented in Table 7.4. There has been a sharp fall in number of families assisted. The number assisted in 1997-00 was only 61 per cent of that in 1992-95.

The utilisation of fund was very poor. During 1992-95, in relation to that available it came to 62.6 per cent and declined further to 48.4 per cent in 1997-00. In fact, after 1992-93 the utilisation was always around 50 per cent or less. The per capita subsidy in the latest period was only 79.6 per cent of the national average. The mobilisation of credit was also very low. In the all-India total credit mobilised, West Bengal's share declined from 5.2 per cent in 1992-95 to 3.7 per cent in 1996-99. The per capita credit in 1996-99 stood at only 71 per cent of that at the national level.

The implementation of IRDP suffered from many deficiencies even in the nineties. We may quote here some of the findings of the concurrent evaluation carried out in 1995-96 (CSSS 1997):

(i) Time taken in sanction and disbursement of bank loan to the beneficiary was often too long. It was found to be more than six months in 22.2 per cent of all new cases, with Darjeeling districts at 55.0 per cent, Burdwan 47.4 per cent and Nadia 45.0 per cent. After sanction again the disbursement was found to be delayed by more than a month in 69.0 per cent of all cases.

(ii) Loss in wage employment for follow-up with block/bank staff for IRDP assistance was found to be significant in a large number of cases. Loss of two weeks was reported in 32.1 per cent of all cases and three weeks in 12.4 per cent of cases. The beneficiary also incurred expenses by way of consideration to government/bank staff. It was found to be present in 8.4 per cent of all cases, with 24-Parganas reporting 32.5 per cent and Purulia 28.7 per cent.

(iii) Assistance (subsidy plus loan) for purchase of assets was very inadequate in many districts. Up to Rs 5,000 was received by as many as 51.8 per cent of all beneficiaries; above Rs. 10,000 constituted only 2.7 per cent. Inadequacy of assistance was reported in 24 per cent of all cases.

(iv) In many cases the asset was not in productive use. The average for all districts came to 19 per cent of cases, with Midnapore, Dakshin Dinajpur and Purulia reporting 40-44 per cent. The asset was reported as being sold off by 6.56 per cent of all new beneficiaries and 22.4 per cent of old beneficiaries.

(v) Distribution of Vikas Patrika (Pass-book)—a way of keeping track of IRDP loans and their use—was very rare. In case of new beneficiaries, only 8.6 per cent received it; there was no distribution at all in five districts.

(vi) The net income received from the asset was very low in many districts. While the average for all old beneficiaries in the state came to Rs 2,075, in 24-Parganas it was only Rs 774 and in Purulia, Jalpaiguri and Burdwan around Rs 900. The proportion of beneficiary crossing the poverty-line was therefore very low. Only a little more than a sixth of the target groups managed to cross the poverty-line in 1991.

(vii) There was a clear bias against the weaker of the target groups in the selection of beneficiaries. Agricultural labourers constituted only 30.0 per cent of the total and marginal farmers 4.76 per cent, while small farmers formed as much as 21.9 per cent. Women-headed households and SC/ST families were also systematically worse off and received lower level of benefits.

(viii) The after care service was very poor. A majority of 61.2 per cent of old beneficiaries reported requiring additional finance for working capital, 30.3 per cent reported needing input supply and 30.8 per cent training for acquiring or upgrading the skill. These needs were met to the extent of only 36.1 per cent, 5.6 per cent and 9.1 per cent, respectively.

On the situation in recent years, we may quote the findings of the CAG report for the year 2001-02. The CAG found that the state government was deprived of central assistance to the tune of Rs. 81.69 crore due to poor utilisation of funds while Rs. 3.27 crore was spent in five districts flouting the government of India norms. It is also stated that in 1999-2000, out of a total 8.85 lakh targeted families, only 1.26 lakh were covered under the scheme. The key activities were selected without market survey (Statesman 2003C : 6).

TRYSEM

The scheme of training of rural youth for self employment as a supportive service to the IRDP did not perform well here. Not only the number trained fluctuated widely from year to year, their placement was also very poor. To look at the situation in some of the years: In 1985-86, the total number trained stood at 8,092 but in the following year it dropped to only 4,943. After five years, in 1989-90, the number rose to 12,689, to fall again to only 9,415 in the following year against the target of 25,378. Even the highest number trained in 1989-90 constituted only 5.97 per cent of all-India total. The proportion of SC/ST trained was always low.

As regards placement, although the basic objective was self-employment, a large number was absorbed in wage employment. The number remaining unemployed was also high. In 1985-87, for example, the proportion getting self-employed averaged 38.9 per cent and another 21.8 per cent got wage employment; the balance of 39.3 per cent remained unemployed.

After the programme became independent in 1991-92, the situation improved considerably. The number trained annually averaged 14,234 during

1994-99, which was higher than the highest reached in the entire eighties. In the all-India total number, the state's share rose to 7.31 per cent. This was, however, inferior to the performance by some of the smaller states like Madhya Pradesh and Andhra Pradesh; the former's share was as much as 14.3 per cent in this period (GOI 2000).

The quality of training provided was probably inferior here. The expenditure per trainee came to the average of Rs 2,711 in this five-year period, which was only 65 per cent of the national average. Another aspect is that the representation of SC/ST continued to be very poor. They constituted only 34.8 per cent of the total trained during 1992-96 as against the all-India average of 45.2 per cent.

With regard to placement, on the whole, West Bengal's situation improved significantly. During 1992-96, 57.8 per cent of the trained youth were settled as against the national average of 49.0 per cent. There was, however, extreme of variation from year to year. The proportion self-employed in this period stood at 72.8 per cent compared with 68.3 at the national level.

DWCRA

The scheme for development of women and children in rural areas was also primarily for skill upgradation. However, the coverage of the scheme in West Bengal remained very limited for many years. A third district, Jalpaiguri, was added only in 1986-87; earlier, it was operating only in Purulia and Bankura. Till 1986-87, 373 women's groups, with 3,072 members, were formed by spending Rs 15.80 lakh.

In recent years also the state's position was not good. During 1994-95 to 1998-99, a total of only 6,293 groups were formed, constituting 3.5 per cent of all-India total. The relative share in expenditure was still lower, only 1.62 per cent. None of the major states had such a poor performance. The expenditure per group came to only Rs 8,177, less than half the all-India average (GOI 2000). The leading ruling party, CPI (M), being interested in 'purchasing' more supporters, spread the amount thinly. The low level of expenditure must have resulted in low level of income for the beneficiaries.

The low expenditure was not due to nonavailability of fund. During 1993-96, the state could spend only half the fund available, Rs 93.82 lakh out of Rs 184.32 lakh released by the Centre; at the national level, the utilisation averaged 64.7 per cent in this period. In the following three years, however, there was a noticeable improvement; being 161.3 per cent of the amount released. But even this was less than the national average, being 170.8 per cent.

On the scheme for rural artisans, launched in July 1992, also the state's performance appears to be poor. To look at the situation in two of the recent years: In 1997-98, the utilisation of available fund in West Bengal was only to the extent of 32.3 per cent and in the next year 62.5 per cent; at the national level, it was respectively 54.4 and 42.9 per cent. The assistance provided per beneficiary was always low here. In 1997-98, it came to only Rs 1,090 as against the national average of Rs 2,110, and the next year at Rs 1,975 and Rs 2,067 respectively. The state's share in all-India total expenditure in these two years were 4.6 per cent and 6.7 per cent, respectively; and in number of beneficiaries 8.9 per cent and 7.1 per cent (GOI 1998a, 1999b).

Although the CPI (M) takes pride in the operation of its panchayat system, for the malaise in implementation of the programmes the panchayats are largely to be blamed. It is necessary to know the character of the panchayats. Studies have shown that the panchayats are controlled by the village middle and elite classes (Mallick 1993: 137-141). Now the interests of this class of people are by no means synonymous with those of the poorer sections in the villages. The programmes were, therefore, not implemented with any amount of sincerity; rather, taking advantage of illiteracy and ignorance, they lined their own pockets. It may be noted here that in the last four years (1997-01) alone the state government had failed to utilise more than 1200 crore of Central funds meant for various rural development programmes. These funds had reverted back to the centre (Statesman 2002 Z 11: BP).

Public Distribution System

The PDS in West Bengal has the following major components:

(i) A statutory system of rationing mainly in urban areas of greater Calcutta, the neighbouring districts of Howrah, Hooghly and North 24-Parganas, and the highly industrialised areas of Asansol and Durgapur; (ii) A modified system of rationing for the other, predominantly rural, areas of the state; (iii) A revamped distribution area since 1992, for the tribal, drought-prone and designated hill areas (Darjeeling); (iv) Special allocation for the tea garden areas.

Apart from rice, wheat, sugar, kerosene and edible oils, the PDS has been supplying a number of other commodities like biscuit, turmeric powder, exercise book, match box, laundry soap and iodised salt. Presently, as in other states, there are two types of PDS, one for the people above the poverty line and the other for those below the poverty line. In 1998-99, the latter was getting 500 gms of rice/wheat per head per week at the rate of Rs 4 per kg for rice and Rs 3 for wheat. Presently, the prices are, respectively, Rs 6.15 and Rs 5; for others, it is Rs 7 and Rs 5. Total number of ration shops in the state increased from 17,660 in 1980 to 20,497 in 1998. The proportion of statutory ration shops declined from 15.2 per cent to 12.6 per cent over the period. There are presently nearly 7.8 crore ration card holders (GOW 1999: SA).

The distribution of food grains through ration shops has on the whole declined in recent years. In 1997, the total quantum distributed stood at 1433.6 thousand tonnes as against 1693.8 thousand in 1991 and 2065.2 thousand in

1987. The proportion of rice in them stood at 38.2 per cent in the latest year. The distribution of edible oils had a sharper fall. In the last three years, 1995-97, it averaged only 9.3 thousand tonnes compared with 102.2 thousand in 1987-89. For sugar, on the whole the off-take increased, rising from the annual average of 304.7 thousand tonnes to 327.9 thousand over the period (GOW 1991, 1992, 1995, 1999).

For the small size of PDS, the state government generally blames the Centre. But the fault lies primarily with the state. Apart from its failure in procurement, the central supply is often delayed, or even not available, because of its inefficiency and corruption. We may have a brief look at the sources of supply of food grains and the fluctuation from year to year.

During the last six year, 1991-97, the internal procurement or rice by the FCI-which generally constituted no more than a sixth of the total supply-stood at the highest of 170.6 thousand tonnes in 1992-93 and at the lowest 79.8 thousand in the preceding year. The target of procurement always remained unachieved, and for this the state government is squarely to be blamed. Procurement of rice as percentage to production reached the highest of 1.49 per cent in 1992-93. Recently, in 2001-02, the rice procurement programme collapsed as the government failed to clear its debt to the RBI on the food credit account; only about 40,000 tonnes could be procured as against the target of 600,000 tonnes (Statesman 2002s).

The receipt of rice from the Centre—depending on the quantum internally procured–varied between the highest of 640.9 thousand tonnes in 1991-92 and the lowest at 487.0 thousand the following year, during 1991-97. The supply of wheat varied between 889.8 thousand tonnes in 1995-96 and 715.2 thousand in 1992-93. The central supply to the state was always much less than the demand. During 1987-91 (five years), in each of the years the state demanded 18 lakh tonnes of rice but the supply varied between 5.85 lakh tonnes in 1989 and 8.81 lakh in 1988. In wheat, the demands were 15.60 lakh tonnes each year and supply varied between 10.99 lakh tonnes in 1988 and 8.95 lakh in the preceding year. The supplies were always less than the allotment also. The requirement of a state was worked out on the basis of 453.6 gms per head per day.

The pattern of PDS food grains distribution has changed considerably in recent years. The share of statutory rationing area in the total was down to 31.0 per cent in 1995-97 from 40.2 per cent in 1991-93. Similarly, the share of other categories—that is, tea gardens, relief camps, etc—was nearly halved in this period, declining from 8.6 per cent to 4.8 per cent. For modified rationing area, on the other hand, it increased from 51.2 per cent to 64.2 per cent (GOW 1995, 1999).

On the comparative position of West Bengal among the states, first we look at the data for seventies and eighties. As a large majority of the poor live in rural areas, we focus on the overall rural situation first. In the distribution of food grains, the rural sector's share of total PDS purchases in the state was quite low. In 1986-87, in both rice and wheat it was much less than the national average. In rice, which is more important, the proportions were respectively 50.01 and 71.01 per cent. In fact, it was the lowest among the neighbouring states. This was a really gloomy situation because the state had the largest proportion of landless and sub-marginal land-holding households. In edible oil and sugar also the situation was bad. In the former, the deprivation was particularly glaring, the rural areas' share being only half of that at the national level. With regard to kerosene, however, the rural West Bengal's share was very high. It was as much as 69.7 per cent as against 54.6 per cent in all-India (NSSO 1990). How much of it actually reached the poor is, however, doubtful, because a large portion went to the black market. In fact, to prevent it the government was compelled to change the colour of PDS kerosene.

In this situation, the PDS purchase per market dependent could not be high. In rice, in the same year, it stood at 0.726 kg compared with the national average of 1.107 kg; Kerala, the other communist-dominated state, provided as much as 4.256 kg. In sugar also it was very low, being 0.297 kg as against 0.613 kg at the national level. The situation of the poor did not show any improvement until recent years; rather there was deterioration. In the six time points considered, the availability of PDS food grains per poor person reached the maximum of 92 kg per annum in 1983; in the following two time points there were sharp declines (Table 7.5).

The government subsidy on PDS was very low in West Bengal. Per capita monthly subsidy in 1986-87—taking all goods into consideration—came to Rs 2.19 for rural areas of the state as against the national average of Rs 2.54. There were as many as six major states providing a higher subsidy—with Andhra at Rs 9.43 and Kerala Rs 7.67. The subsidy for the urban areas, where a very small proportion of the poor live, was however much higher, at Rs 5.04. This was much above the all-India average, being Rs 3.23. The rural/urban ratio of subsidy here came to 0.43 this year compared with 0.79 for all-India. Thus the state is patently anti-poor.

In recent years, after the introduction of targeted PDS, the situation of the poor vis-à-vis the non-poor has improved considerably. In 1999-00, the proportion of PDS purchases of rice and wheat in their total consumption by the poor increased to 9.50 per cent from 1.96 in 1993-94; at the national level, it was respectively 8.77 and 6.79 per cent. For non-poor, the rise was from 1.75 to 1.83 per cent here as against from 8.61 to 9.18 per cent for all-India. Overall, the role of PDS in West Bengal remains small. For poor and non-poor together, the proportion of purchases here increased from 1.83 per cent to 3.85 per cent as against from 8.02 to 9.08 for all-India (Mahendra Dev 2004).

The corruption and inefficiency in the running of the PDS here continues to be one of the highest in the country. We give below a few examples:

(i) Hundreds of tonnes of rice meant for the BPL population were recently found to have been smuggled out into Bangladesh. The state food commissioner has found that an "unscrupulous alliance between some rice millers and modified rationing distributors" had let to rice being diverted to Bangladesh and the open market. To prevent further diversion, the government stopped the procurement of rice and this hit the supplies to PDS.

(ii) There have been always a large number of fake ration cards in every district which are used for taking out the PDS commodities to the black market. During 1991 a total of 4, 79,558 ration cards were seized. In 2000, by June, 37,500 ration cards were cancelled in the three hill sub-divisions of Darjeeling, and the total number of fake cards there is estimated at about 3 lakh (Statesman 2001).

(iii) The submission of accounts relating to rice procurement is often unduly delayed, resulting in non-release of dues from the Centre. Recently, the Centre told the food department that it 'won't release a single penny till accounts relating to rice procurement in the past three years are submitted'. The amount due to the state government is a staggering Rs 70 crore (Statesman 2000m).

(iv) In April 2002, despite a central directive, the state government did not reduce the price of wheat and rice supplied through the PDS. It was also unable to procure new stock from the FCI due to a funds crunch. Most of the ration shops were empty and the owners went on a strike in protest (Statesman 2002t: BP).

We concluded the chapter by citing an example of how the poor tribals were being cheated by the so-called Marxist government. The situation of the Kheria-Saban tribals in Purulia became so intolerable that their *Kalyan Samity* had to file a petition to the Calcutta High Court about it. On direction from the Court, the district Judge conducted a thorough inquiry into the matter, which brought out the destitution of the tribals and the misappropriation of welfare funds. The report states: "At Amjharna village in Purulia, almost all the naked male members fled from the village during my visit. They had nothing to wear even after 50 years of Independence. Even a couple who had something to cover their bodies could not stand up". The distribution of surplus land was a mockery. At many places, *pattas* had been given to them but not the land; other villagers were cultivating the land. As regards construction of houses under the IAY, at Balakdih, Bansketya and Chirugorah many houses were built over the years but all of them collapsed within a short period. The bills for construction of these houses were passed without checking. An equally sordid affair was the disbursement of loans granted to tribals. In most cases, the amount a Sabar got was much less than half of what was granted (Statesman 2000 n).

The Marxists' anti-poor attitude is apparent also from a recent action of the government. The Planning Commission had fixed the poverty-line income at Rs 409.22 monthly for urban areas for 1999-00 but the state government set it at Rs 313.12. Not only this, the state government also instructed the officials to limit the percentage of the urban BPL population. The Darjeeling DM was instructed that the proportion should be between 14 and 16 per cent, and not more than 22 per cent in any case (Statesman 2002 Z 18:1).'Such actions are probably not surprising for a government that spends 111.5 per cent of its revenue on salaries, pension and other fixed expenses (Telegraph 2005b).

In this patently anti-poor situation, it is no surprise that starvation deaths are reported from West Bengal even after nearly three decades of the CPM's rule. The continuation of such a political party in power for so long a period is a reflection on the character of the Bengalis as a whole.